Encyclopaedia of ISLAMIC LAW

Volume 2

FOUNDATIONS OF ISLAMIC LAW

Editors

Dr. Arif Ali Khan

Tauqir Mohammad Khan, *et. al.*

PENTAGON PRESS

ENCYCLOPAEDIA OF ISLAMIC LAW
Vol. 2: Foundations of Islamic Law

First Published: 2007
Reprinted: 2009

© Reserved

ISBN - 81-8274-221-8

All rights reserved. No part of this publication may be reproduced, stored in a retrieval system or transmitted in any form or by any means, electronic, mechanical, photocopying, recording, or otherwise, except for the inclusion of brief quotations in a review, without prior permission in writing from the publishers.

Published by
PENTAGON PRESS
206, Peacock Lane, Shahpur Jat
New Delhi-110049
Phones: 011-64706243, 26491568
Telefax: 011-26490600
email: rajan@pentagon-press.com
Website: www.pentagon-press.com

Printed at New Elegant Printers, New Delhi.

CONTENTS

Preface　　　　　　　　　　　　　　　　　　　　　　　ix

1. **Legal Dimensions**　　　　　　　　　　　　　　　　　1
   Knowing Law • Two Sources • Responsibility of Law • Importance of Rights • The Governance • Religion and Secularity • Constitution and Law • Rulings for Law • Concepts of Law • Bottlenecks

2. **The Fundamentals**　　　　　　　　　　　　　　　　　35
   Law at Work • Provisions of Law • Positive Aspects • Juristic Method • The Problems • Components of Unity

3. **Quran, the Original Source**　　　　　　　　　　　　　75
   Non-material Aspect • Different Names of Quran • Signs of Punctuation • Theories of Quran • Concept of Free Will • Reality of a Muslim • Objectives of Islam • Noble Examples • Perfect Life

4. **Lessons from Quran**　　　　　　　　　　　　　　　　95
   The Functioning • Philosophy of Islam • Reality of Islam • Global Fraternity • Quranic Wisdom • Islamic Code • Practical Life • Sainthood Nowhere • Power of Bearing

5. **Legal Principles**　　　　　　　　　　　　　　　　　109
   The Judges • The Provisions • Rights of Mankind • Assessment of Rights • Traits of Duties • Role of the Subjects • Strength of Law • Total Strength • Bonded Slaves

6. **Various Aspects of Law** — 139
Various Traits • Role of the Caliphate • Law in Practice • Law for Minorities • Law for Insanity • Law for Idiocy • Law for Forgetfulness • Law for Death-illness • Law for Intoxication • Law for Jest • Law for Indiscretion • Law for Coercion/Duress • Aims and Objectives • Definition of *Maslaha* • Other Aims

7. **Various Categories of Law** — 181
Constitution at Work • Role of Revenues • Role of Imam • Handling Justice • Posting of Judges • Importance of the Judge • Muslims vs Non-Muslims • Imposing War • Two Important Concepts • Rights in Islam • Types of Obligation • Types of Common Rights • Kinds of Rights • Nature of Rights • Private Rights • Personal Rights • Alternate Rights • Importance of Preparatory Cause • Various Crimes • Issue of Security • Various Torts • Loss of Property • Theory of Responsibility • Various Crimes

8. **Security and Safety** — 219
Protective Laws • Almighty Supreme • Equality under Law • Effect of Other Laws

9. **Guidelines for Rulers** — 279
Art of Governance • Just System • Motives and Aims • Fundamental Guarantees • Wings for Governance • Setup and Structure

10. **Status of Believers** — 299
Special Status • Basic Regulations • Laws in Force • Man at the Helm

11. **Non-Muslims Protection** — 309
Rights at Par • Equal Protection • No Discrimination

12. **Criminal Law** — 321
Laws in Force • Setup of Government • Kinds of Punishment • Particular Rules • Origin of Specific Laws • Suggestive Measures

Contents   vii

13. **Judicial System**   **357**
    Theory of Justice • No Difference • Reality of Democracy • Role
    of the Prophet • A Perfect Life • Peace Everywhere

14. **International Law**   **389**
    Global Law and Islam • Global Law in Older Times • Prominent
    Jurists of Islam • Understanding Global Law

    Bibliography   401

    Index   409

PREFACE

The foundation stones of Islamic law have been chiefly laid by the Holy Quran and the Tradition on the sayings of Prophet Muhammad (Pbuh). The Quranic commands and the exemplary lessons and teachings of the Holy Prophet, perceived by any scholar of Islam are in fact the commandments of Allah, the Almighty. Besides, there are other divine books, sayings of the prophets, consensus in opinion and speculation or analogy, which constitute the basic principles of Islamic law. The basic ethos or tenets are common and equally applicable to all factions, castes and communities, within the fold of Islam, around the world. Different schools of thought, such as Hanafi School, Shafii School, Hanbli School, Maliki School and Jafri School express consensus over the basic tenets or ethos of Islamic religion or law.

Islamic laws are oriented at ensuring social solidarity, peace and harmony and a just social system. Islam has strongly supported the notion of social justice, which mainly means equality and positivity in one's deeds and needs. The democratic and secular institutions have also been given due weightage in the formation of Islamic laws. Due consideration has also been made about the social, economic and political socialisation of different sections, castes, classes and communities, within Islam. The women, children and old persons have been properly secured by the Islamic law and day to day code of conduct. For instance, the Islamic law of inheritance provides a proper economic and social safety-valve for women and children. The laws of revenue, crime and punishment, war, judgement, economic activities, marriage and divorce etc. and above all religious and sacred acts are well equipped with rationality and are also progressive and practical. All discriminations on any ground such as sex, caste, age, religion etc. have been made illegal. The preventive and curative ideas have been codified for the rehabilitation and punishment of the deviants and criminals. In Islamic society, the minority communities have been given adequate protection and due privileges.

To make pace with the prevalent laws of the changing world and the modern global order, Islamic scholars have, to some extent, made efforts to adjust with the current situation by making new interpretations of the age-old laws and regulations. However, they cannot and do not make alterations in the basic structure and there is no question of accepting anything against the spirit of Holy Quran or Traditions. It implies that the Islamic law or ethos of law are not rigid and easily fit in the changing circumstances.

Present book 'Foundations of Islamic Law', covers all legal dimensions, Quranic ethos, lessons, basic principles, various facets of law, guidelines for rulers, status of believers, criminal laws and the entire judicial system under Islam. We hope, it is equally useful and indispensable for lawyers and scholars. All wise comments and suggestive ideas from the esteemed circles are welcome.

Arif Ali Khan

Foundations of Islamic Law

1

LEGAL DIMENSIONS

KNOWING LAW

Here, we describe in a general way the nature and scope of *Usulul-Fiqh*[1], also called *Ilmul-Usul*, which, is the Islamic science of jurisprudence, and of Ilmul-Furu, also called Fiqh, which is the science of the material law of the Muhammadans. It is, however, necessary that we should try to follow the definitions of these sciences as given by the Arab jurists themselves.

Definition of Usulul-Fiqh : Usulul-Fiqh, which literally means the roots or principles of Fiqh, is described as the 'knowledge or science of those rules which directly or proximately lead to the science of Fiqh; and hence it discusses the nature of the sources or authorities (*i.e.*, of law) and what appertains thereto, and of the nature of what is established by those sources or authorities, namely, law and what appertains thereto.' As included in the last part of the definition the discussion relates to the lawgiver (*hakim*) the law (*hukm*) the objectives of law (*mahkum bihi*) *i.e.*, acts, rights, and obligations, and the subjects of law, that is those to whom the law applies (*mahkum alaihi*) or persons.

Definition of Fiqh : The nature of the science of Fiqh is thus discussed by the Arab writers. Fiqh (literally, understanding or knowledge) according to Abu Hanifa[2], is 'the knowledge of what is for a man's self, and what is against a man's self. Sadrush-Shariat in discussing this definition says that it may mean that the science in question, in so far as it is concerned with man's acts, deals with their consequences in the sense of being spiritually profitable to or injurious to him, or in other words, that the object of Fiqh is the knowledge of spiritual rewards the punishments. If that be the meaning, the definition, the commentator goes on to observe, is apparently based on the well known verse of the Quran, 'for every soul there will be (that is, on the day of judgement) whatever it has earned and against it whatever it has earned.' Sadrush-Shariat then urges that taking it in that sense the definition would be defective, as it would fail to cover acts which are spiritually indifferent, such as contracts to sell, lease and the like.

But this difficulty, he goes on to suggest, would be obviated if Abu Hanifah, be taken to have meant by 'profitable' what does not entail punishment, and by injurious' what entails punishment. The definition in the above sense would also be complete, if by 'profitable' be understood what brings spiritual reward, and by injurious' what does not bring spiritual reward. There is another possible interpretation, the commentator observes, namely, that Fiqh is the knowledge of what is permissible for a man to do, and what he is under an obligation to do.

But this again, he urges, would leave out from its purview the doing of acts which have been forbidden, and the omission of what has been made obligatory. The definition, he adds, is capable of a third meaning, namely, that Fiqh is the knowledge of things which are permissible for a man to do and of things that are forbidden to him, including both acts of commission and omission. In this sense it is a science which points out the extent and limits of a man's liberty, in other words, it is the science of rights and obligations.

The above discussion proceeds upon that aspect of Abu Hanifa's, definition which relates to man's acts. The language of the definition, however, shows that in Abu Hanifa's conception of the science, which he called Fiqhul-Akbar, or the great science of Fiqh, it would comprehend within its scope pure questions of faith which, strictly speaking, are the subject of the science of divinity, and also abstract questions of ethics. It would indeed appear that the object of Fiqh in the first era of Islam was to attain a knowledge of the affairs of the next world, and of the subtle dangers and trials which beset the human soul in this world. But as pointed out by Ghazzali[3] Fiqh in its current acceptation is confined to the science of the rules of law.

The author of the 'Taudi' gives the definition of Fiqh as the knowledge of the laws (*ahkam*) of the Shariah which are intended to be acted upon, and have been divulged to us by revelation or determined by concurrent decisions of the learned, such knowledge being derived from the sources of the laws with the power of making correct deductions there from. The Shafii[4] jurists define Fiqh as 'the knowledge of the laws of the Shariah[5], relating to men's acts and derived from specific sources', and the Maliki jurists call it 'the science of the commands of the Shariah in particular matters deduced by the application of a process of reasoning.' Whatever be the wording of the different definitions the conception of this science is the same in all the four Sunni schools. Let us now analyse the leading ideas in these definitions.

In the Shafii definition, the restrictive words 'derived from specific sources' are intended to exclude from the science such knowledge of the sacred laws as the Prophet possessed, and which he derived from inspiration.

By the use of the word Shariah it is intended to exclude mere concepts of the reason or of the senses, such as our knowledge that the world is liable to changes and that fire burns. Shariah, which may be translated as the Islamic code, means 'matters which would not have been known but for the communications made to us by the lawgiver.'

Definition of Law and its Postulates; Iman or Faith : Law, (hukum), according to Islamic jurists, is 'that which is established by a communication (khitab) from God with reference to men's acts, expressive either of demand or indifference on His part, or being merely declaratory.' The first postulate, therefore, of Islamic Law is Iman or faith, the essential constituent of which is belief in God and *acknowledgment* (tasdiq) of His authority over our actions.

Faith Founded on Human Reason; Human Reason the Ultimate basis of and Justification for Law : Belief in God is assumed to be inherent in man, arising from the promptings of his heart or conscience (tanbihul-qalb), and *acknowledgment* of God's authority is classified by the jurists as a mental act (filul-qalb), as contra-distinguished from iqrar or declaration of faith, which is a physical act. Knowledge of the existence of God, which is the basis of faith, is classed as necessary (daruri) and manifest or intuitional (badihi) knowledge. But maturity of reason is the condition for accession of such knowledge; for it is when reason illuminates a man's faculties, to use an imagery employed by the author of 'Taudi, that he can perceive in sufficient clearness the proofs which are discernible in the Universe of the existence of One Supreme Intelligence, Creator and Ruler of life and things.

Given, however, maturity of reason, knowledge of God is irresistibly and inevitably brought home to man. The generality of Islamic jurists, therefore, hold that faith is founded on reason, and is not the creation of, although enjoined by, revealed religions. In fact, the contrary view would, according to them, lead to arguing in a circle, for the truth of all revealed religions necessarily depends on belief in God for its acceptance. Hence in Islamic Jurisprudence the ultimate basis of and justification for law must be sought in human reason.

The attitude of the atheist, who does not believe in God and would not acknowledge. His authority, is defined as that of a person who, to use the words of the Quran, has belied his own self; and those who believe in a multiplicity of Gods or impute to the Creator attributes implying imperfection, are described as men who have allowed themselves to be deluded by passions and desires (ahlul-hawa) instead of being guided by the true voice of reason.

Origin of Law, a Covenant between Man and God; According to some Jurists the Covenant is Merely an Allegory : *Acknowledgment* of God's authority follows upon and is inseparable from belief in His existence; in other words, recognition of His authority to issue commands to us is also embedded in our constitutions. It is further urged that, granted a Supreme Being of perfect knowledge, and wisdom and of infinite power, who has created mankind and, for their use and benefit, the world and all that it contains, it would be ingratitude (the literal meaning of the word kafir is ungrateful), as well as folly on their part, not to obey His commands.

In fact, the theory of some jurists is that the origin of law, as creative of obligations and rights, is to be found in a primordial covenant (*mithaqi-azali*) entered into between man and God at the beginning of creation, when the spirits of future humanity are supposed to have vowed allegiance to God, and God to have promised to create the world for their use and enjoyment.

Other jurists regard the alleged covenant to be merely an allegory, apparently understanding it to mean that men's recognition of God's authority over their actions is coeval with the life of the human species, and that it is in the design of the creation itself that life should have dominion over physical objects and the higher life over lower life. This theory, whether understood literally, or only as having a metaphysical significance, serves to explain some of the ideas of Islamic Jurisprudence. For instance, the doctrine that fitness or capacity for rights and obligations (ahliatul-wujub) exists in man, even before birth, manifesting itself first when the embryo quickens into life in the womb of its mother.

Sources of Law. God the only Lawgiver; Promulgation of Laws through Prophets; Belief in the Truth of Muhammad's Mission : The authority to enact laws primarily belongs to God, and He alone has supreme legislative power in the Islamic system. And ever since the days of Adam, God has promulgated His laws on this earth from time to time through His messengers (*rasul*) and prophets (*ambiya*). This succession of revelation was partly necessitated by changes in the needs and affairs of men, a concomitant of all created things, calling for the repeal or modification of previous laws.

For instance, in the days of Adam and his immediate progeny, the closest relationship by blood was no bar to intermarriage, but when the female population sufficiently increased, marriage was prohibited within certain degrees of relationship.

The main principle of law, namely, submission to the wishes of the One, Divine, Superior Power and Wisdom has, however, never been lost. But it often happened that men either tampered with the revealed laws or forgot them, and that furnished an additional reason for a fresh revelation. Before the birth of the Prophet of Arabia, the laws previously revealed had, according to the Islamic religion, been considerably corrupted; even the very basis of such laws, namely, submission to the will of One God, had been obscured. It was because of this, that Muhammad was charged with the mission of reviving the eternal principle of all laws, namely, submission to the Perfect Will, by preaching Islam. Hence belief in the truth of Muhammad's mission is another constituent element of Iman.

Two Sources

Quran is the name of the book containing direct revelation from God to Muhammad, and Hadith or Traditions are the inspired precepts of Muhammad in matters of law and religion.

Ijma or Consensus of Opinion : But as laws are needed for the benefit of the community, the Divine Legislator has delegated to it power to lay down laws by the resolution of those men in the community who are competent in that behalf, that is, the Mujtahids or jurists.

The laws so laid down are presumed to be what God intended, and are thus covered by the definition of law as a communication from God. This source of laws is called Ijma⁶ or consensus of opinion. But though in strict theory the jurists acting in a body only expound the laws, the laws which they so lay down have most of the attributes of legislative enactments. Their validity cannot be disputed, and is not affected by the reasons with which it may be supported. The presumption that such laws are in accord with the principles of the Quran and the Hadith is conclusive, and they cannot therefore, be treated as invalid on the ground of repugnancy to the revealed laws.

Further a law resolved on by the Mujtahids can be repealed by a subsequent resolution of a similar body of men. Thus it would be substantially correct to say that the Islamic Jurisprudence concedes legislative powers to the jurists acting in a body. Such powers, though derived from the Divine Legislator, are practically unlimited, and since the Muhammadan religion does not admit the possibility of further revelation after the death of the Prophet, the principle of Ijma' may be regarded as the only authority for legislation now available in the Islamic system.

Judges on Decrease : The bulk of the Islamic corpus juris, however, has been built up by the individual deductions of jurists as distinguished from their collective resolutions. But a jurist deducing a law by using the process of analogy, or otherwise, properly speaking, only expounds the law and does not establish it (*la muthbatun*). The validity of such a rule of law rests on its consonance with the principles established by the laws based on revelation or on Ijma.' It is, therefore, merely an application or extension of the law established by a binding authority to a particular case, and not a new rule of law.

And so the definition of law as the speech of God also holds good in the case of such deductions, as in the case of laws founded on consensus of opinion. With this important difference, the presumption that a rule of juristic deduction is in consonance with the principles of revealed law is not conclusive, as it is in the case of laws laid down by consensus of opinion.

The essential characteristic of a rule of juristic law is that its authority is 'merely presumptive' (zanni), and it is open to a judge or a jurist not to follow a particular ruling of this category if, in the exercise of his judgement, he holds it to be based on incorrect deduction. It must not be acted upon; if it be found to be in conflict with the text of a revealed law or with Ijma.' In other words, the juristic laws of the Muhammadans occupy much the same place in their system as what are commonly called judge-made laws in the English system.

Customs and Usages as Sources of Laws; The Juristic basis of Such Laws: The Islamic system also recognises the force of customs and usages in establishing rules of law. The validity of such laws rests on principles somewhat similar to those of Ijma.' In the case of those customs and practices which prevailed in the time of the Prophet when revelation, the recognised primary source of laws, was still active, and which were not abrogated by any text of the Quran or Hadith, the silence of the Divine Legislator is regarded as amounting to a recognition of their legal validity.

And as to customs, which have sprung up since the Prophet's death, their validity is justified on the authority of the text, which lays down that whatever the people generally consider to be good for themselves is good in the eye of God.

Thus the conception of law as an emanation from God is said to hold good in the case of customary laws as well. Custom as a source of laws resembles analogical deduction in one important respect, it has no legal force if it be repugnant to the revealed law, or to the law founded on Ijma.' It resembles Ijma' to this extent that the legal character of a custom has no relation to juristic reasoning, just as the authority of a law passed in Ijma' is not affected in any way by the reasons which influenced the learned. But customary law is of inferior authority compared to Ijma', in as much as it is based on the practice of the people generally, while Ijma' implies deliberation on the part of men well versed in the principles of law. It is, however, of superior authority to a rule based merely on analogy.

RESPONSIBILITY OF LAW

The function of law, as is to be gathered from its definition, is to control and guide men's conscious actions by creating restraint on their freedom. This presupposes ability in man to choose to do or not to do an act, namely, the existence in him of will-power (*ikhtiar*). It is by this characteristic that laws, which are the subject of jurisprudence, are distinguished from physical laws, by which the involuntary movements of men and of the physical world generally are regulated.

The Scope and End of Law : The scope of law, which is determined by the end it has in view, covers the entire field of man's actions. The end of law is to promote the welfare of men both individually and socially and not the glorification of the lawgiver, for God *ex-hypothesi* is above all wants and weaknesses. The welfare of men as individuals which the law seeks to promote is not in respect merely of life on this earth, but also of the future life, so that imperishability of human life is another postulate underlying the Islamic conception of law.

Indicated by our Instincts : There are four main principles of action implanted in our natures, namely, the instincts of self-preservation, of self-multiplication and of self-development and the social instincts. These, in the language of Islamic religion, are signs (*ayat*), as it were in the pathway (*Shara*) of life laid down by the Creator for our guidance.

The instincts of self-preservation and self-multiplication mainly indicate the range of our freedom, and the social instincts and the instinct of self-development indicate chiefly the character and amount of control to which that freedom is subject. The control implied by the social instincts is the expression of the relation of the individual to the communal life, and the control necessitated by the instinct of self-development represents that side of our nature which impels us to strive after progress.

With regard to man's spiritual welfare, the purpose of law is the discipline of human life, so that it may attain qurbat or nearness to the Perfect Being. So far as the regulating of man's actions in their bearing on earthly existence is concerned, the aim of law is the preservation of the human species and the support and well-being of individual and social life.

IMPORTANCE OF RIGHTS

The media through which the law exercises its function are rights (*haq*) and obligations (*wujub*). The two are generally speaking correlative terms. Right means the authority recognised by the law to control in a particular way the action of the person against whom it exists, the latter being obliged or under an obligation to act as required. Rights are primarily the privilege of God, but in as much as men in their communal life are dependent on each other for their wants, God, having regard to such necessities, have authorised men individually to control each other's actions, though within limitations.

That is to say, law permits one man to acquire rights against another, and thus to control the freedom of the latter to a certain extent. In so far, however, as there is no legal restraint on a man's actions by virtue of a right existing either in another individual or in God, his innate freedom of action remains unaffected, and hence according to many jurists ibahat or permissibility, is the original principle of human action.

The Term Law not Confined to Mandatory Commands, or to Commands Enforceable by the Courts : It will have been noticed from the definition of law that the application of the term is not limited in the Muhammadan system to mandatory commands, for less to commands enforceable by the courts. It comprehends all expressions of the lawgiver's will and wisdom, whether laying down what a man must do or must not do, what he may do and what he ought to do or ought not to do, or merely making a declaration.

What constitutes law of the former class is what the lawgiver has said with reference to men's actions, whether his words be expressive of a desire that hose to whom they are addressed should act in a particular way in certain matters, or that they should be left to act as they like in certain other matters. When the lawgiver expresses a desire of either kind, there is then the further but distinct question, whether the desire should be enforced or not, and this is provided for by another and additional expression of the lawgiver's will to that effect, though it is not necessary that such expression should be by a separate speech. For instance, the law says: 'every man is entitled to possess and enjoy as he pleases what he has acquired by his own labour', or putting it in the imperative form, 'possess and enjoy as you please what you have acquired by your own labour.' This pronouncement is law, and the lawgiver if he so chose might stop there.

But if he further wished that the magistrate should protect the acquire of property in the possession and enjoyment of it, he would say to the magistrate: 'whoever deprives a person of possession of his property, inflict on the delinquent such and such penalty, or compel him to restore the property or something

Legal Dimensions

equivalent thereto.' Take another illustration. Suppose the lawgiver says: 'educate your children', and instead of providing a penalty for failure to educate, he directs the magistrate to give a certain sum of money to the parents who may educate their children.

The wishes expressed respectively to the parents and to the magistrate are both distinct commands, whether they happen to be expressed in one speech or more. Or suppose the legislator says: 'Do not tell a lie, but tell the truth', but prescribes no penalty for lying.

The injunction, according to Islamic jurists, would nevertheless create a legal obligation, as it is an obligation imposed by the lawgiver, and none the less so because no penalty awardable by the magistrate is attached to its violation. Similarly, when the lawgiver declares that a contract is concluded when the person to whom a proposal is addressed accepts the proposal, the declaration is law, though it is merely an affirmative proposition and not a mandatory command.

Enforce ability by a distinct human tribunal is not, therefore, and essential attribute of law in Islamic Jurisprudence. Injunctions which are capable of being enforced are of a limited class. The question of the enforce ability of laws forms the subject of the administrative branch of the law, while it is the function of law in its substantive side to define the character of men's acts, or to assign to such acts their legal effect and relation.

Sanctions : The means by which compliance with the laws is secured are also of a wider character in the Muhammadan system than the sanctions of modern European laws. Since Islamic Law has twofold objects, spiritual benefit and social good, its policy is to encourage obedience by offer of reward, and to discourage disobedience by imposition of penalty. Penalty may be awardable in this world (*iqab*) or in the next (*adhab*), or in both, but reward (*thawab*) is awardable only in the future life.

Application of Law to Muhammadans Personal; To Non-muslims, Territorial: In Islamic Jurisprudence law is personal in its application to the Muhammadans, that is to say, it is not affected by the constitution of a particular political society. This is because the authority of law, according to the Islamic theory, is primarily based on men's conscience and not on political force. Thus, if a Muhammadan goes from one State to another, he is bound by the same laws and, if he does not live within the jurisdiction of a Muslim State, the Islamic law still applies to his conscience. Having regard to the theory of Islamic law, law is inherently inapplicable to those who do not believe in the one and only God. Not acknowledging the authority of the Lawgiver, such men are neither bound by the law, nor can they claim its protection and privileges.

But it is nevertheless his pleasure that they should be allowed to live their own lives on this earth as they please, provided they are not hostile (harabi) to the law, and are willing to submit to its authority in so far as it is necessary for its upholding.

If, therefore, a non-Muslim lives under the protection of a Muslim State, the secular portion of the legal code would apply to him, that is, generally speaking, so much of it is in substance common to all nations, and not such rules as are specially identified with the tenets of Islam. For instance, a non-Muslim drinking alcohol is not subjected to punishment and his transactions in wine and pigs are valid. The application of Islamic law to non-Muslims is entirely territorial, and hence it does not apply to those among them who do not live within the jurisdiction of the Imam.

THE GOVERNANCE

The right to administer the laws, as well as the affairs generally of the community, belongs to the community itself which may exercise the right through its chosen representatives. The administration of the State in the olden days was entrusted to Imams or Caliphs.

The Imam or the Caliph was the executive head or chief of the Muslim State. He was not vested with any legislative powers and was bound by the laws like any other person. He was subject to the ordinary jurisdiction of the courts though it may be that, as he was the chief of the executive and had thus the control of the administrative machinery, it practically depended upon his pleasure whether he would submit to the decrees and sentences of the courts or not. The Islamic law does not concede to any individual any of those powers and prerogatives which are ordinarily the essential attributes of sovereignty.

Sovereignty : In the Islamic system sovereignty primarily belongs to God, but as he has delegated to the people powers of legislation and of absolute control over the administration, it must be held that next to God the sovereign power resides in the people. It would also appear that the Islamic law does not admit of the sovereign power being dissociated from the people, however, they might choose to exercise it.

The State : The law seems to contemplate, that there should be a single Muslim State, and that the Caliph, as its chief representative, should administer the executive affairs of the community living within such State through his delegates and governors. But when there is no *de jure* Imam or Caliph, there seems to be nothing in the law which precludes the recognition of politically independent Muslim States. In fact since the extinction of the Abbaside Caliphate, different

Muslim States have existed as entirely independent political units, without acknowledging a common over-chief as Imam or Caliph.

Classification of Laws; Defining and Declaratory Laws : Let us now see how laws are classified. That part of the definition of law which relates to the objectives of law or human acts, indicates one primary division of the laws into what I shall call 'defining' and 'declaratory.' When the communication from the Lawgiver assumes the form of a demand it may be absolute or not absolute. If the former, the demand may consist in requiring men to do something in which case the act demanded is regarded as obligatory (*fard*), or it may require him to forbear or abstain from doing something, in which case the act to be forborne or abstained from is said to be forbidden (*haram*), or in other words, such a speech imposes duties of commission or of omission. When the demand is not of an absolute character, the act to which it refers, if it be one of commission, is called commendable (*mandub*), and if it be one to be forborne or abstained from it is called condemned, or abominable or improper (*makruh*).

An act with reference to the doing or omission of which there is no demand or, in other words, with respect to which the lawgiver is indifferent, is regarded as permissible (*mubah*). All acts which are neither obligatory, nor forbidden, nor commended, nor condemned fall within the last category. Laws which thus define the characteristics of a man's acts, namely, whether they are obligatory, forbidden, condemned or permissible or indicate the legal effects of acts, for instance, that the rights of ownership arise from an act of purchase, the obligation to pay rent, from possession of another's land and the like are called in Arabic taklifi (lit. controlling), which I have translated as 'defining', since they define or indicate the extent of a man's liberty of action and the restraint imposed upon it, or in other words, his rights and obligations.

The other class of laws indicated by the words of the definition are called in Arabic wadai, which I have translated 'declaratory', as proximately conveying its meaning. Laws of this class indicate the component elements of a defining law, namely, whether certain facts or events are the cause, condition or constituents of a command. The function of a declaratory law is interpretive in relative to a defining law. For instance, it is by means of a declaratory law that we know that proposal and acceptance, in a transaction of sale, are the cause originating proprietary rights in the thing sold in the buyer, and extinguishing those of the vendor; that the pronouncement of the formula of divorce is the cause of extinction of the marital rights and obligations of the husband and the wife; that the death of a person is the cause of the rights of the heirs to the inheritance; and that usurpation of a man's property is the cause of obligation on the part of the usurper to restore the property to its owner or to pay its value. Similarly a declaratory law tells us that maturity of understanding is the condition of a voluntary disposition such as by hiba[7], will or waqf.

Laws Perfect and Imperfect Obligation : Laws having regard to the question of their enforce ability are broadly divisible into three classes:

(1) Those which concern men in their social and individual existence in this world, their object being to regulate men's relations to and dealings among one another. Since observance of laws of this class is necessary to the preservation of humanity, their enforcement has been delegated to and is made incumbent on the community.

(2) Laws which solely concern the spiritual aspect of individual life, though some of them may relate to worldly transactions; there are enforced by God alone by means of spiritual rewards and punishments.

(3) Laws which mainly concern the spiritual aspect of individual life, but also affect the Islamic communal life in its religious aspect; the enforcement of these is not incumbent on the State, but is left to its discretion. Belonging to the first class are laws relating to contracts, transfer of property, succession, domestic relations, wrongs, crimes, and the like. As an instance of the second class may be mentioned laws enjoining commendable acts, such as alms, supererogatory prayers, and fasting, or prohibiting condemned acts, such as sale during call to prayers, and laws imposing the duty of making atonement. To the third class belong laws enjoining the duties of saying the five daily prayers, of paying the poor-rate, and of fasting during the Ramadan[8]: these duties the State may enforce by means of disciplinary measures.

RELIGION AND SECULARITY

The jurist broadly divide laws having regard to their purpose into religious and secular. In summing up his discussion of the scope of Fiqh, Taftazani[9] says" it (*i.e.*, Fiqh) is the knowledge of such laws of the Shariah as are intended to be acted upon, as already stated. These laws relate to matters appertaining to the next world, namely, acts of worship (*ibadat*) or to matters appertaining to this world. Of laws of the latter class, some have in view the continued existence of men as individuals, and are called laws relating to muamalat[10] that is, dealings among men, while the others, namely, laws relating to domestic relations (*munakahat*) and to punishments ('uqubat), have in view the continued existence to men as a species, having regard respectively to their natural place in the scheme of life and as members of organised society.

Revealed and Unrevealed Laws : Having regard to the sources of our knowledge of the laws, some laws are revealed and others are unrevealed. Laws, which are to be found in Quranic or an authentic traditionary text are revealed, and those determined by agreement of the learned, or deduced by individual jurists, are unrevealed.

Certain and Presumptive or Discretionary Laws : In this connection there is another classification of laws of greater practical significance, based on the nature of the proof as to their divine source, namely, that into certain (yaqini) and presumptive or discretionary (zanni). The theory being that all laws are of divine origin, unrevealed laws are laws by presumption, being based on revealed laws which are the original authorities or sources of the knowledge of law. In the case of a conclusion arrived at by the learned as a body, the presumption is conclusive that it is what God intended, while in the case of a deductions made by individual jurists, the presumption is not conclusive, but of sufficient force to justify a Muhammadan to act upon such rules. A deduction of the latter class may be correct or incorrect and, therefore, does not compel certainty of belief, while revealed laws and laws founded on Ijma' must be correct and compel certainty of belief. Hence, a Muhammadan acting upon a rule of law juristically deduced, incurs no spiritual liability if it happens to be wrong.

A jurist or a Qadi is free to make his own deductions in matters of juristic law, while so far as laws based on a text, or on Ijma, are concerned, he is absolutely bound to follow them. If a Qadi or judge goes wrong on a question covered by an express text or by Ijma', his decree must be set aside either by himself when he discovers his error, or by the succeeding Qadi. But his decision in a matter of analogical law may not be reversed, because with respect to it, it cannot be said with certainty that his view is wrong. As for proof of the divine origin of Quranic and traditionary texts, the Quranic texts are accepted as proved, beyond a possibility of doubt, to be of divine origin: they are in the very words of God, which were preserved with so much care that all chances of mistake or error are excluded.

The precepts of the Prophet on questions of law are also revelations from God, but expressed in the Prophet's own language. With respect, however, to a few only of the precepts can it be said that they are proved for certain to be what the Prophet enunciated. Those that are so proved rank as high as a Quranic text, and demand implicit faith and obedience. There are a few more, the proof of the genuineness of which is regarded as of a high order though not absolutely conclusive. The authority of laws based on such traditions is held by some to be as absolute as of the other class. As regards the rest of the precepts, that is, those which are proved by isolated testimony, a jurist must satisfy himself as to their genuineness. If he is so satisfied, he is bound to accept the law as laid down by it but not otherwise. Laws based on traditions of this class cannot, therefore, be said to be certain, for it is open to a jurist to contest their genuineness. In that sense, laws based on isolated traditions may be said to be discretionary like laws based on juristic reasoning.

Strict and Modified Laws : Another fundamental division of the Islamic laws is into strict azimat and modified (rukhsat). The two are relative terms. The former class consists of laws in their original theoretical rigour and of rules in strict adherence to the letter of the texts, and the latter class consists of rules with their rigour modified and relaxed in the application of the principles to particular circumstances so as to obviate hardships and inconveniences.

This division runs through the entire range of the Islamic laws, whether based on texts or on analogy, and bears resemblance to the common law and equity law of the English system. Sometimes one text relaxes a rule previously enunciated in another text, and sometimes a rule, strictly deducible by the application of analogy, is relaxed by the exercise of what is called juristic equity, or preference, having regard to the needs habits and usages of men.

For example, according to the strict law a sale is valid only of an article which is in existence at the time of the contract, and of which it is in the power of the vendor to give possession to the buyer. But the rule is relaxed in the case of salam sale, which is a contract for sale of goods of a specific description, which are not in existence at the time of the contract, but which the vendor has promised to deliver at a future date, in consideration of the price paid to him in advance.

This modification of the rigour of the law in its original form is perceptible in all the departments, and has both a spiritual and a secular aspect. From a spiritual standpoint it is considered more meritorious for a man to conform to all the strict conditions of the law, and in its secular aspect an act does not cease to be valid and operative, because it does not conform to such conditions.

Interpretive Laws : I have already adverted to the division of laws into defining and declaratory, and I have said that the function of the latter is in one sense interpretive. But declaratory laws must be distinguished from interpretive laws properly so called. It is doubtful whether in Islamic Jurisprudence rules of interpretation which have been devised by human reason, for the purpose of understanding the texts by applying our knowledge of the language and grammar to their words, can be called laws properly so called.

Interpretation by means of such rules is, however, to be distinguished from authentic interpretation, that is, interpretation of a Quanic, or traditionary text by another such text. The object of an interpretive text may either be to explain the

Legal Dimensions

meaning, or to indicate the limit and the extent of the application of another text. What is laid down by such interpretive texts is undoubtedly law.

Repealing and Amending Laws : There are some texts of the Quran, and the Traditions which have either been totally repealed, or their application limited or modified by subsequent texts. Many jurists hold that repealing and amending laws belong to the category of interpretive laws. They argue that when certain laws have been promulgated, and the time within which they are to have operation has not been specified, and the Lawgiver afterwards repeals them, he must be taken to mean thereby that the laws previously enacted were intended to have force until the time when the repealing laws were passed and not thereafter. Similarly, when one text is modified by a subsequent text what is meant is that, when the amending text comes into operation, the original text is to have a modified or limited application. Only a revealed law can be repealed, limited or modified by another law of the same class. One juristic deduction cannot be said to be repealed or modified by another, because of neither of them can it be affirmed with certainty that it is correct.

Public and Private Laws : Laws having regard to the classification of rights as made by the Muhammadan jurists, divide themselves broadly into public and private. They divide rights into rights of God and rights of men; the former corresponding to rights of the public and the latter to private rights. Rights of the former class reside in God, but since they exist for the benefit of the community, they are described as rights of the community or public rights; private rights reside in individuals.

For instance, the right to levy revenues belongs to the community, and is exercised on its behalf by the Imam, as contrasted with the right of a private owner of a house to receive rent from the tenants. The punishment of crimes is a right of the community, as distinguished from the right of an individual affected by a wrong to exact restitution or satisfaction. That is to say, there are some wrongs which the State thinks fit to punish without consulting the wishes of the person wronged, and these come within the purview of public law; other wrongs are regarded as a matter for redress, which it is for the individual wronged to seek and to enforce, and these are the subject of private law.

Law of Persons : What is called law of persons relates, according to Muhammadan jurists, to the question of the application of law, having regard to the fitness (ahliyat) of men for the inherence and the exercise of rights and the discharge of obligations. Under this head they discuss the legal capacity of infants, lunatics, infidels, slaves, sick persons and the like.

Law of Things not a Separate Division : The Islamic jurists do not recognise laws of things as forming a separate and independent juristic division. Laws, according to them, are concerned with the acts of men through the juridical medium of rights and obligations. Often such acts have reference to physical objects but not always; and the law does not deal with such objects except as 'property', that is, things over which men exercise acts of possession and enjoyment.

Laws of Evidence; Law of Procedure : The law of evidence in the Muhammadan system falls partly within the scope of substantive law and partly of adjective law. The right to give shahadat or oral testimony, is a question of capacity of the witness to create liability. On the other hand the object of evidence generally (bayyanat)[11], including oral testimony, is to enable the court to ascertain the truth with a view to enforce rights and obligations. The Law of Procedure is dealt with in Islamic Jurisprudence as law appertaining to adabul-Qadi or the duties of the magistrate.

CONSTITUTION AND LAW

Constitutional law of the Muhammadans, which is generally dealt with in the textbooks in the chapter on Siyar[12], defines the duties and rights of the executive head of the community.

International Law : What approaches nearest to international law in this system is the law defining the relations of the Muslim State and of the Muslims towards non-Muslim States and the non-Muslims. But the rules under this department of law bind only the Muslim State and the Muslims, and are not based on any international arrangement or comity. This branch of the law is also discussed in most legal treatise chiefly under the heading of As-Siyar.

RULINGS FOR LAW

Conception of a Family : The central idea in the family law of the Muhammadans is the institution of nikah or marriage. It is through marriage that the paternity of children is established and relationship and affinity are traced. The Muhammadan family is based on the patriarchal principle and there are also indications in this department of Islamic Law to show that the family as a social unit was evolved among the Arabs out of the large unit of tribes.

It has been seen that, among the pre-Islamic Arabs, a woman's legal status was of too precarious a nature to have been an important factor in the conception of family life. Their social system was dominated by the tribal idea and families were regarded as so many sub-divisions of tribes. It was by the strict enforcement by Islam of the institution of marriage in social life that the tribal system was effectively changed into the family system.

Legal Dimensions

But it must be borne in mind that the Islamic Law does not allow the conception of a family life to overshadow its fundamental principle, namely, individual responsibility and liberty. Each member of the family is endowed with full legal capacity and the law does not sanction any joint family system of holding property as is prevalent among the Hindus. Whatever authority the law vests in the head of the family is based either on contract or on necessity for the protection of those members of the family who are unable to take care of themselves. Apart from certain conjugal rights of the husband and the wife, the idea of commensality or residence in a common house does not from any part of the Islamic legal conception of a family; the family relations are founded on consanguinity and affinity.

Concepts of Law

The Islamic Law has ordained the institution of marriage sanctioning thereby sexual relations between two members of the opposite sexes with a view to the preservation of the human species, the fixing of descent, restraining men from debauchery, the encouragement of chastity and the promotion of love and union between the husband and the wife and of mutual help in earning livelihood. The Islamic jurists, therefore, regard the institution of marriage as partaking both of the nature of ibadat or devotional acts and muamalat or dealings among men. It is founded on contract for which the consent of both the parties is essential. The relations between two members of the opposite sexes which marriage legalises are, however, so subtle and delicate and require such constant adjustment involving the fate and well-being of the future generations that in their regulation the law considers it expedient to allow the voice of one partner more or less predominance over that of the other.

This which is regarded as involving the practical subordination of one of the partners to the other is spoken of as the alienation of conjugal society (muta) by the subordinate partner to the predominant partner with the effect of pacing the marital freedom of the one at the disposal of the other. As regards the next question, that is, which of the two partners should have the right to predominance, the law decides in favour of the husband, because generally speaking he is mentally and physically superior of the two; and some theorists would treat the dower payable to the wife as consideration for the alienation of her marital freedom. The husband does not, therefore, lose his marital freedom merely by a contract of marriage. The lawgiver has, however, deemed it expedient to place certain limitations on such freedom having regard to the necessities of social life from time to time.

The Islamic Law undoubtedly contemplates monogamy as the ideal to be aimed at, but concedes to a man the right to have more than one wife, not exceeding four, at one and the same time, provided he is able to deal with them on a footing of equality and justice. This is in accord with the scheme of Islamic legislation which sets up certain moral ideals to be gradually realised by the community positively forbidding only such acts as must clearly be injurious to social and individual life at all times. As for the other prevalent practices and institutions of the people which did not come up to the ideal of Islam, the positive law places such restrictions, limitations and conditions on them as are calculated to remove the existing abuses.

That this is so would seem to be especially clear from a comparison of the provisions of the Islamic Law relating to family life and also those relating to torts and crimes with the customs which in such matters prevailed in Arabia and most other parts of the world at the time of the promulgation of Islam.

It also follows from the above theory regarding marriage that the husband has a right to dissolve the marriage as by such dissolution he only gives up his own right. But as marriage is founded on contract and the above rights of the husband arise by implication of such contract, it is open to a woman at the time of marriage or subsequently thereto to stipulate for their curtailment or to get some of them transferred to herself, such as the right to dissolve the marriage.

It is of the nature of the contract of marriage that it cannot be made contingent on a future event. Nor can marriage be expressly limited for a time. The reason is that, if marriage were allowed for a limited period of time, it would fail to fulfil most of its essentials purposes.

How Marriage is Contracted ? : A marriage like any other contract is constituted by proposal and acceptance and does not depend for its validity upon the observance of any religious rite or ceremony. But, according to the Hanafis, the proposal and acceptance must, in a contract of marriage, be witnessed by two properly qualified witnesses; otherwise the marriage would be invalid. According to the Malikis the presence of witnesses is required only for the sake of publicity.

The law imposes certain restrictions on the right of person belonging to one sex to enter into marital relations with a person of the opposite sex.

Persons Between Whom Marriage is Forbidden : Such prohibition is in some cases of a perpetual nature as when it is based on the ground of consanguinity, affinity or fosterage. Persons so prohibited from intermarrying are called muharim.

By reason of consanguinity a man cannot marry any female ascendant or descendant of his or the daughter of any ascendant how high soever or of any descendant how low soever, or the daughter of his brother or sister or the daughter of a brother's or sister's daughter, and so on. On the ground of affinity he is debarred from marrying a woman who has been the wife of any ascendant of his, any ascendant or descendant of the wife if marriage has been consummated, or of any woman with whom he has had unlawful connection and any woman who has been the wife of his son or grandson. Generally speaking fosterage induces the same limits of relationship prohibitive of marriage as consanguinity.

There are again obstacles to intermarriage of a temporary character. For instance, radical difference in religion, such as between Islam which is a monotheistic religion and polytheism is a complete bar to intermarriage, but when both the man and the woman are followers of some revealed religion, the disability is only partial. Hence a Muslim cannot marry a polytheistic woman but a Muhammadan man can marry a Christian woman or a Jewess, though a Christian or a Jew cannot marry a Muslim woman.

This distinction is drawn between the case of a Muslim man and a Muslim woman because if a Muslim woman were allowed to marry a Christian or a Jew, there would be a likelihood of her being converted to the faith of her husband, while there could be little apprehension of a husband adopting the faith of his Christian or Jewish wife.

This bar, as I have said, is a temporary one, for it can be got rid of by the woman embracing Islam. There is a further obstacle to intermarriage of a temporary nature but exclusively affecting a man who desires to have more than one wife at the same time. This is expressed in the rule which prevents a man from having at the same time more than four wives or two wives so closely related to each other that if one of them had been a man, there could have been no intermarriage between them on account of such relationship. For instance, a man cannot marry the aunt or niece of his wife and the prohibition against a man combining in marriage two sisters seems to be covered by the rule. Again a woman who is observing iddat is forbidden to marry until such period of probation has come to an end.

Void and Vitiated Marriage : Marriage between persons who are permanently prohibited from intermarrying is Batul or void, such as with a man's own sister, niece or the like and marriage between persons whose disability to intermarry is for a temporary cause, such as marriage of a woman during her iddat or marriage in violation of the condition requiring the presence of two witnesses, is fasid or vitiated. The author of 'Raddul-Muhtar' regards the marriage of two sisters at one and the same time as an instance of a fasid marriage, but it was to be void in the case of *Aizunnissa Khatoon* v. *Karimunnissa Khatoon* (23 Cal., 130).

A Batul marriage will be treated as if it was never contracted and thus no legal effects would flow from it. A fasid marriage, although it may be annulled by the Court when the fact is brought to its notice, is treated as capable of giving rise to certain legal effects, for instance, the parentage of the child born of such marriage will be established from the husband, he will be liable for proper dower if consummation has taken place and the wife will have to observe iddat on separation.

Capacity to Enter into Marriage Contract : According to the Hanafis, every person who is not a minor whether male or female, maiden or thayyiba (that is, a girl who has had sexual intercourse), is competent to contract marriage and cannot be given in marriage without his or her consent whether by the father or any relative. The Shafiis and Malikis[13] agree with the Hanafis so far as boys and thayyibas who have attained majority are concerned; the former, however, hold that a minor thayyiba is competent to contract marriage and a maiden even if she has attained majority cannot marry without the consent of the guardian, while the Hanafis in each of these two cases hold the contrary view.

Thus, with the Hanafis, so far as the females are concerned, minority is the test whether the intervention of a guardian is necessary or not and with the Shafiis the test is whether a girl is a maiden or thayyiba[14]. The difference between the two schools on this point though not perhaps of much practical significance, involves a question of principle. The Hanafis allege that the Shafiis refusal to acknowledge the right of a maiden of full age to contract marriage of her own will amounts to a breach of a cardinal principal of Islamic Law, namely, that the legal status of a grown-up female is as complete as that of a male.

Guardianship for Purposes of Marriage : Guardianship for purpose of marriage is allowed because of necessity, for a proper and suitable match may not always be available. It is extended by the Hanafis to the father and grandfather and other relatives; among the latter the order of priority is the same as that in respect of their right to inherit. But when a minor is given in marriage by a guardian other than the father or the grandfather, he or she can, in the exercise of what is called the option of puberty (Khayarul-bulug)[15], refuse to be bound by the marriage and ask the Court to pass a decree annulling the marriage. This absolute option does not exist in the case of a marriage contracted by the father or the grandfather in whose favour the law rises a presumption that they must have acted in the best interests of the minor.

The Malikis would confine the right of matrimonial guardianship to the father, whose right is expressly recognised by a tradition and the Shafiis would also recognise the right of the grandfather by giving an extended application to the words of that text. The Hanafis in recognizing the right of matrimonial guardianship in other relatives as well base it on what in their opinion, is the policy of the law.

In the absence of the father or the grandfather among the Shafiis and the Malikis and of the other relatives as well, among the Hanafis, the guardianship for the purposes of marriage vests in the Sultan or the Qadi. Even in the case of a marriage contracted by the father or grandfather as guardian, the presumption that it is for the benefit of the minor is not conclusive and such a marriage is liable to be set aside in certain cases, where it is plainly undesirable and injurious to the minor.

For instance, according to the Shafiis, if a minor girl is married by the father to a person who is not her equal it will be invalid according to some jurists and according to other Shafii jurists she will have the option to get rid of the marriage on attaining majority. There is a difference of opinion among the Hanafis as to the circumstances under which a marriage contracted by the father can be set aside. The accepted view seems to be that if the father was not a man of proper judgement and was of reckless character, and married his minor daughter to a man of immoral habits it is liable to be set aside. According to Abu Yusuf[16] and Muhammad, an evidently unequal and undesirable marriage or a marriage for less than the proper dower of a minor female, or marriage for an excessive dower of a minor male if the deficiency or excess be gross, is not Sahih or valid but Abu Hanifah holds a contrary view.

Unequal Marriage : Apart from the question of guardianship the law confers on certain relatives of a female of the age of majority to object to a marriage contracted by her with a man who is not her equal. The law recognises this power of intervention in order to save the family from social disgrace.

Equality is generally had in regard with reference to the following matters: (1) lineage, (2) character, (3) property, (4) profession, (5) status, such as of a freeman, a freedom or a slave and perhaps (6) education. The condition of equality is insisted on only with respect to the husband and not the wife.

Husband's Responsibility : Marriage confers important rights both on the husband and the wife against each other, subject to any especial stipulations which the parties might have entered into at the time of marriage or afterwards.

The husband has the right to insist that the wife should live in his house and afford him access, abstain from undue familiarity with strangers, obey him in all reasonable matters and be faithful to him. He can control her freedom of movement within certain limits and correct her for unseemly behaviour. This restriction upon her liberty is, however, measured by the necessities of his own right. He cannot, therefore, refuse to afford her opportunity to see her relatives. The exercise of most of his rights by the husband will be suspended if he does not satisfy the corresponding rights of the wife. Similarly, if he treats her with such cruelty as to endanger her personal safety she will not be bound to live with him. The husband has also the right, as we have seen, to dissolve the marriage at his discretion. Under the Islamic Law the husband does not acquire any right to or control over his wife's property by the fact of marriage.

Whatever property she had at the time of marriage remains absolutely her own and at her disposal and she is under no disability to acquire property by reason of coverture. That is to say, a woman's legal capacity is no way affected by marriage, expect as regards contracting conjugal relations with others.

The husband's right to divorce or to marry another wife may be effectively though indirectly clogged by a stipulation fixing the dower at the time of marriage at a sum out of all proportions to the means of the husband as is the custom in India. It may also be lawfully stipulated in so many words, as is often done that if the husband marries another woman the latter will be divorced at the instant of such marriage. The wife may also, as already mentioned, stipulate for power to dissolve the marriage.

The wife has a right corresponding to that of the husband to demand the fulfilment of his marital duties towards her. She is also entitled to be provided with proper accommodation separate from the husband's relations and to be maintained in a way suitable to his own means and the position in life of both. If the refuses or neglects to maintain her she can pledge his credit. She has also a right if the husband has more than one wife to be treated on terms of strict equality with the others. She is further entitled to the payment of her dower. If such portion of her dower as is payable before dissolution of marriage has not been paid and she has not yet surrendered her person, she may refuse her conjugal society and according to Abu Hanifah she may do this even after surrender.

Concepts of Dower : Mahr[17] or dower as it is usually translated is either a sum of money or other form of property to which the wife becomes entitled by marriage. It is not a consideration proceeding from the husband for the contract of marriage, but it is an obligation imposed by the law on the husband as a mark of respect for the wife as is evident from the fact that the non-specification of dower at the time of marriage does not affect the validity of the marriage. She or her guardian may stipulate at the time of marriage for any sum, however, large as dower. If no sum has been specified she is entitled to her proper dower (mahrul-mithl), that is the dower which is customarily fixed for the females of her family.

The wife's right to dower becomes complete on the consummation of marriage either in fact or what the law regards as such, namely, by valid retirement or on the death either of the husband or the wife. In case of dissolution of marriage by the husband or of separation for some cause imputable to the husband before there has been consummation or valid retirement, the wife becomes entitled to half the specified dower and if no dower has been specified to a present called muta. In case the separation was due to some cause imputable to the wife herself, she will not be entitled to any dower or present if there has been no consummation of the marriage. If a marriage has been annulled on the ground of invalidity, the wife will not be entitled to more than her proper dower.

Having regard to the time when it becomes payable dower may be muajjal that is, immediately exigible or prompt, or muajjal that is, deferred. Whether a dower should be entirely or in part exigible or deferred depends on the contract of the parties and in the absence of any contract, on the custom of the country. Even during the subsistence of the marriage the wife is entitled to demand so much of her dower as is exigible, but she, is not entitled during the continuance of the marriage to demand the deferred portion of the dower.

Dissolution of Marriage : Divorce : The law as we have seen concedes to the husband the right to dissolve the marriage. He can, therefore, put an end to the marriage at his uncontrolled option and the wife may do the same if the husband has conferred such a power upon her. The dissolution of marriage by the husband's own act, that is, by his making a declaration to that effect in appropriate words is called talaq which is usually translated as repudiation, divorce. The husband cannot, however, exercise the right unless he is of mature age, and possessed of understanding.

Talaq or divorce is strongly condemned by the Muhammadan religion and it should not be resorted to unless it has become impossible for the parties to live together in peace and harmony, but once it is pronounced it is upheld as valid, although there may be no good cause for it. It is described in a precept of the Prophet as the worst of all the things which the law permits.

It is a maxim of Islamic Law that the jurisprudence cannot deprive anyone of his rights except for hostility to the authority of law. But if the exercise of a particular right is likely to lead to abuses the law would guard against such a contingency by imposing conditions and limitations. There are certain limitations imposed by the law upon the right of the husband to dissolve the marriage. The object of these rules is to ensure that the husband was not acting in haste or anger and that separation became inevitable in the interests of the husband and the wife and their children.

Talaq or repudiation is of two kinds, rajai or that which permits of the husband resuming conjugal relations and bayan or that which separates. The former is generally translated as revocable and the latter as irrevocable or absolute. A divorce which is revocable in the inception becomes absolute or irrevocable if the iddat or period of probation is allowed to elapse without the husband having revoked his act either by express words or conduct.

The most approved form of repudiation is, that the husband should pronounce the sentence once during a tuhr or period of purity of the wife and then let the divorce become absolute by expiry of the period of probation. The next best form is to pronounce one sentence of repudiation during a period of purity for three such periods so that on the third pronouncement the repudiation would become irrevocable.

In the first form there is a greater guarantee than in the second against hasty and ill-advised action. But if divorce be pronounced while the wife is not in a state of purity or if divorce is at once expressed to be irrevocable such as the husband saying I have divorced thee irrevocably' or by the pronouncement of three sentences at one and the same time, the husband saying three times I have divorced thee or saying at one and the same time I have divorced thee thrice, the result will be irrevocable divorce though the law regards a repudiation in this form with disapproval as being an innovation (*bidat*).

Even after an irrevocable divorce the law permits the parties to remarry, but in case the divorce was by pronouncement of three sentences or a triple divorce, the law adds as a condition precedent to reunion that the woman should be married to another man and such second marriage should have been lawfully terminated after consummation (*tahlil*)[18] and the period of probation on account of the second marriage should have expired. The professed object of the law in adding this condition is to discourage such divorces.

It was also evidently the object of the precept of the Prophet wherein he says that in three things, namely, marriage, 'divorce and manumission, jesting is not allowed to dissuade men from trifling with such solemn affairs of life. The interpretation put upon the tradition, however, is that a divorce pronounced even in jest holds good and the juristic principle on which the rule is sought to be based is that a divorce regarded from the point of view of the wife means her restoration to liberty, which the law always favours. Some Hanafis, as we have seen, would carry the doctrine still further by force of analogy holding that divorce under compulsion is also binding.

But on this question they are opposed by a formidable array of great jurists like Shafii, Malik, Hanbal, 'Umar ibn Abdul-Aziz, Ibn 'Umar, and Qadi Shuraih. Similarly, divorce pronounced in a state of intoxication brought about by the husband's own voluntary act is also valid according to the generality of Hanafi jurists, but not according to Malik and Tahawi and at least one version of Shafiis opinion.

I may remark that the interpretation of the law of divorce by the jurists, especially of the Hanafi School, is one flagrant instance where because of their literal adherence to mere words and a certain tendency towards subtleties they have reached a result in direct antagonism to the admitted policy of the law on the subject.

Ila, Zihar : In some cases the conduct of the husband will have the effect of a repudiation, though he did not use the word talaq or any other expression with the intention of dissolving the marriage. This is, when he swears that he will have nothing to do with his wife and in pursuance of such oath abstains from her society for four months. The legal effect of such conduct would be a single irrevocable divorce. This is called Ila. Ila must be distinguished from Zihar[19] which consists in the husband expressing his dissatisfaction by comparing his wife to the back of his mother or some other female relative within the prohibited degrees of marriage. Such imprecation has not the effect of a divorce, but only makes the husband liable to make atonement (kaffara) for his improper behaviour.

Dissolution of Marriage by the Wife : The husband, as I have said, may confer on the wife the power of pronouncing talaq, and thereby dissolving the marriage. Once he has conferred such power, he cannot afterwards revoke it and it will depend upon the wife whether to exercise the power or not. Such conferment of power is called tafwid[20] or delegation. The delegation may be in three forms:

(1) *al Ikhtiar* the husband saying 'choose thyself or 'divorce thyself,

(2) *alamru bil yade* the husband saying thy business is in thy hands', and

(3) almaShiaht the husband saying if thou wishest, divorce thyself. If the husband confers the power of dissolving the marriage on the wife in exchange for money or property, it is called khula or mubarat that is, mutual release.

Breaking Marriage : Divorce like any other juristic act may be effected by express words (*sureeh*) or by allusive words (*kinaya*), whether spoken or in writing. The word *talaq* in its different grammatical forms is regarded as express and other expressions which may be construed as meaning repudiation of the marriage by the husband, but are also capable of other meanings, are regarded as allusive.

When express words are used no question can arise as to what was meant, but allusive expressions require construction. In cases of the latter class the husband is entitled to say whether he meant divorce or not, and his word must be accepted. Another important question which arises in this connection is whether the language used has the effect of a single or triple divorce, and rules are laid down for determining such questions.

Separation : Apart from the dissolution of marriage by the husband or by the wife in exercise of the authority derived from him, the law allows of a marriage being dissolved in certain cases by a decree of the Court. It is called furqat literally separation. If a decree of separation be for a cause imputable to the husband, it has, generally speaking, the effect of a talaq. If the decree for separation be for a cause imputable to the wife, then it will have the effect of faskh or annulment of marriage. The difference between the two cases mostly consists in their effect on the liability to payment of the dower or observance of the iddat.

For instance, if the husband charges his wife with adultery, the Court after giving certain oaths to the wife and the husband will pass a decree of separation. This procedure is called Lian. If the husband is impotent or wanting in the male organ, the Court at the suit of the wife will annul the marriage. In these cases the separation will have the effect of talaq. On the other hand, if the wife in exercise of her right of puberty, or on ground of inequality gets the marriage set aside, it will be regarded as due to a cause proceeding from the wife. So also if the husband sues for annulment of the marriage on the ground of serious malformation in the wife, the decree for separation will be deemed to be for a cause proceeding from the wife. If one of the spouses apostatizes that will also be a cause for separation.

In connection with the law of divorce it should be pointed out in fairness to the jurists that the wide interpretation which they have given to the traditions bearing on the subject was evidently influenced by their anxiety to avoid the evil of the pre-Islamic customs which empowered the husband to divorce the wife as often as he chose, which had the effect of depriving the wife of her conjugal rights, without setting her free from the matrimonial ties of a man who had ceased to regard her with affection and respect.

The rules enunciated by the jurists have undoubtedly been effective in preventing the power of repudiation being used merely for purposes of oppression, but it may well be said that they have made divorce too easy. At the same time it must be remembered that the law admits of proper precautions being adopted to guard against the latter evil in as much as it is open to the wife or her friends either at the time of marriage or afterwards to stipulate against the exercise of the power of talaq. The practical result is that the realisation of the ideal aimed at by marriage in the Islamic Law as a bond of life-long union has been left to be achieved by the people in the course of their progressive social development in conformity to the surrounding conditions and circumstances. In India, for instance, it may be greatly doubted whether divorce among the Muhammadans as a body is more frequent than in Europe or America, whose law permits of divorce only by decree of the Court, while among the upper classes of Indian

Muhammadans divorce is almost unknown and I think it may be safely asserted that the cases of divorce among them are rarer than even in England. In Arabia, on the other hand divorce, I believe, is very frequent.

I may also observe here that a similar effect of leaving many of the incidents of marriage to be settled by the contract of parties is noticeable in connection with questions relating to monogamy. If we leave out of account that class of the people who, owing to abnormal conditions of society, are not, generally speaking, influenced by the ideals of law and religion or by healthy public opinion, monogamy is certainly the general rule and not the exception among the Muhammadans, while polygamy is regarded by them as a safeguard, however, undesirable in itself, against great social evils.

Iddat : Even an dissolution of the marriage tie whether brought about by an act of the husband or of the wife under his authority or by an event of nature such as death of one of the parties or by a decree of the Court, the marital relations cannot be said to cease altogether. In fact the affairs of conjugal partnership would not be completely wound up until a certain time called the period of probation or iddat has expired. Iddat literally means counting and in law it means the time during which the wife must wait after the cessation of marriage before she can marry again. Iddat has been ordained with a view to ascertain correctly the paternity of the child that may be born to the wife after the termination of the marriage. When dissolution of the marriage has been brought about by talaq, Iddat will be imposed only if there has been consummation or valid retirement. The period of probation for a woman, who has been divorced, is according to the Hanafis the period covered by three menstrual courses and according to the Shafiis and Malikis the period covered by three intervals and in the case of an old woman or of a girl of immature age it is three months. Iddat of a widow is four months and ten days, of a pregnant woman whether divorced or a widow the period of probation does not end until delivery. Until iddat is over the woman cannot marry again and she has a right to reside in her former husband's house and if she was divorced to be maintained by him.

Paternity : One important incident of the institution of marriage is that it settles the paternity of the child born in wedlock. The provisions of Islamic Law in this matter are extremely liberal. There are several reasons for this. The paternity of a child determines, in the first place, whether the child is to be treated as a Muslim or non-Muslim, a freeman or a slave. Further, if the law is not able to ascertain the father of a child, it is likely to perish for want of some person who can be made responsible for its support and maintenance. The marked leaning of Islamic Law in favour of legitimation is also partly due to the fact that the Arabs who were noted for their pride of birth and genealogy condemned a man whose parentage is unknown (*majhulun nusab*) to considerable social disgrace and is partly traceable to the custom of adoption which prevailed among the Arabs.

The parentage of a child is determined on the principle that it always follows the marital bed (*firas*). The father of a child born in wedlock is presumed to be the husband of the woman giving birth to it and a child which is born after six months of marriage and during its continuance is said to be born in wedlock. The legal effect of marriage in fixing the paternity of a child also continues according to Hanafis for two years and according to Malikis and Shafiis for four years after separation by divorce or death of the husband. These are the maximum periods of gestation according to the different schools. Any child that is born to the woman within that period is presumed to be begotten by her previous husband. But this presumption is liable to be rebutted as when the woman has married another husband and the child is born after six months of such marriage.

The minimum period of gestation is six months. A child born within six months of marriage cannot, therefore, be legitimate. The husband is entitled to claim the child born in wedlock as his and according to the Hanafis contrary to the Shafiis even if he had no access to her. If he wishes to repudiate a child so born he can only do so by the procedure of laan already mentioned. That is to say, if he swears before the Qadi that the child is illegitimate and fruit of adultery, the Court will pass a decree not only dissolving the marriage but declaring the child to be illegitimate.

Even if there has been a legal defect in the marriage making it fasid or invalid, paternity of the child would be imputed to the man who begot it on the woman with whom he believed he was legally entitled to have connection though such belief was founded on a misapprehension of the law or the facts.

Acknowledgment : Even when a man whose marriage with the mother of a child is not proved acknowledges him as his, the law will establish the paternity in him provided the child is of discretion and accepts the position and there is nothing in the circumstances to make such relationship impossible or to disprove it. For instance, if the respective ages of the man acknowledging and the person acknowledged be such that it is physically impossible that the latter could have been the child of the former or that it is shown that he is in fact the child of somebody else or well known to be so or that the person acknowledging could not have been married to the mother of the person acknowledged when the latter was born the *acknowledgment* will have no effect in law. *Acknowledgment* (*iqrar*) is regarded as sufficient proof of legitimacy.

Kids and their Care : Children have a right to maintenance primarily against their father. This right continuous in the case of a boy until he is able to earn his livelihood or if he is disabled so long as his disability lasts and in the case of a girl until she is married. If the father be poor and the mother is well-to-do, she will be ordered to maintain the child, but she will have a right of recourse to the husband when he has sufficient means. If the mother is also poor, but the father's father or father's brother is rich, he will be directed to maintain the child, but he will be entitled to recover the expense from the father when he acquires sufficient property. If a child who has been weaned is possessed of property, then the father will be entitled to discharge the expense of maintenance out of the property.

Of Poor Relatives : The poor though under some restrictions are also entitled to have recourse to their relatives for maintenance. This right is available only against men falling within the prohibited degrees of relationship and in the order of proximity of such relationship.

As regards poor and disabled parents and grand parents, the son or the grandson is bound to maintain them even if he is not well-to-do. But a person is not bound to maintain any other poor relative unless he is in easy circumstance himself and the destitute relative is helpless by reason either of infancy or infirmity or is an unmarried or widowed female.

Guardianship : Guardianship or wilayat is a right to control the movements and actions of a person who, owing to mental defects, is unable to take care of himself and to manage his own affairs, for example, an infant, an idiot, a lunatic. It extends to the custody of the person and the power to deal with the property of the ward. The rights of guardianship of person and of property may sometimes, however, centre in different individuals. Guardianship has been instituted solely for the benefit of the minor and cannot, therefore, be said to be the absolute right of anyone in the sense that the Courts will be bound to recognize it apart from the question whether in any individual case it will promote the welfare of the minor or not.

Guardianship of Person : It is primarily the right of the parents to have the custody (hizanat) of the children. The law gives the custody of a child which is too young to be independent of another's help in feeding, clothing and the like— for a boy the limit is fixed at seven years and for a girl when she attains puberty to the mother or a near female relative. The female relatives in order of precedence in this connection are the mother's mother, the father's mother, sisters, sister's daughters, and the aunts and so on.

As the right to the custody of an infant is recognised solely for the infant's benefit, an infant will not be entrusted to or permitted to remain under the guardianship of the mother or any other woman above named if, in the circumstances of her life, the law would presume that the physical or moral welfare of the child would not be safe in her care. For instance, if she has married a man who is not closely related to the minor or lives a life of open immorality or her occupation be such as to make it difficult for her to look after the child properly the law will not give her the custody.

After a boy has attained his seventh year or a girl has attained puberty, the right to his or her custody belongs to the father, subject of course to the consideration of the welfare of the child, because at that age they have to be educated and require such protection as women are not expected to give. The father is also entitled to make provision for the custody of such a child after his death by appointing a proper guardian or executor in that behalf. Failing the father or his executor the paternal grandfather has the right of custody and failing him other agnates. In the absence of any proper natural guardian the care and custody of a minor devolve on the Court.

Guardianship of Property : The right of guardianship with respect to a minor's property belongs, in the first place, to the father, and on his death it devolves on his executor if he has appointed one, and on the latter's death to his executor. In their absence the guardianship of property belongs to the grandfather and then his executor. Failing them the Court is charged with the superintendence of a minor's property. The guardian is entitled to hold the property of the ward and to manage it as people of ordinary prudence manage their own affairs. He can do all acts on behalf of the ward which are entirely beneficial to the latter, such as acceptance of a gift, and the like and he is not entitled to bind the ward by any act which is absolutely injurious to the latter's interest so that the guardian cannot make a gift, a waqf or a testamentary disposition of the ward's property, nor pronounce divorce on behalf of the ward.

As regards transactions which may be profitable or may result in loss, such as sale or purchase, the guardian can enter into them and such transactions will be binding on the minor unless they have resulted in a gross and evident loss in which case according to Abu Yusuf and Muhammad whose view on this point seems to have been accepted in preference to that of Abu Hanifah the transactions will be set aside.

Inheritance : One important branch of the family law of the Muhammadans is that relating to inheritance. The death of a person brings about a transfer of most of his rights and obligations to persons who are called his heirs and representatives. The transmissible rights include all rights to property, rights connected with property, many dependent rights, such as debts and choses in action, rights to compensation, etc., and the transmissible obligations are, generally speaking, those which are capable of being satisfied out of the deceased's estate.

Legal Dimensions

What is left after the last needs of the deceased have been satisfied, namely, after the payment of his funeral expenses and the discharge of his obligations and debts is to be distributed according to the law of inheritance.

The rules regulating inheritance in the Islamic system are based on the principle that the property which belonged to the deceased should devolve on those who by reason of consanguinity or affinity have the strongest claim to be benefited by it and in proportion to the strength of such claim. The deceased may, however, leave behind more than one person so related to or connected with him that it would be difficult to say with regard to anyone of them that this claim should altogether supersede that of the others. It is laid down in the Quran of thy parents and sons thou dost not know which of them are the nearest and of most benefit to thee.' The Islamic Law in those cases distributes the estate among the claimants in such order and proportions as are most in harmony with the natural strength of their claims. I propose here to set out the important rules of this scheme of succession, which is a most elaborate and scientific attempt to adjust the claims of the different relatives of a deceased person on an equitable basis.

BOTTLENECKS

There are certain impediments to succession:

(1) slavery, because a slave being himself the property of another as I have mentioned elsewhere, cannot hold property at all;

(2) homicide, so that a person killing another does not inherit form the latter;

(3) difference of religion;

(4) difference of territorial jurisdiction either actual or constructive, so that a subject of a non-Muslim country cannot inherit from a non-Muslim subject of the Muslim State, nor a non-Muslim sojourner in the Muslim State from a non-Muslim subject and *vice-versa*.

Variety of Heirs : Of the heirs there are some whose shares or portions have been fixed in the Quran. These are called Ashabul-faraid or 'sharers' as commonly translated. They are altogether twelve in number, four males and eight females: father, father's father how high soever, half brother by the mother, the husband, the wife, daughter, son's daughter how low soever, full sister, consanguine sister, uterine sister, mother and true grandmother, that is, grandmother in whose line of relationship to the deceased no false grandfather intervenes.

True grandfathers are those between whom and the deceased no female intervenes; other grandfathers are called false grandfathers. The shares of the 'sharers' in the inheritance are either one-half, one-fourth, one-eighth, two-thirds, one-third, or one-sixth.

The husband has one-fourth when there is a child or son's child how low soever and one-half when there is no child or son's child; the wife has one-eighth when there is a child or son's child and one-fourth when not; the daughter's share is one-half when only one and no son, and if there are two or more daughters and no son, they take two-thirds between them; the son's daughter takes one-half is only one and there is no child or son's son; if there are two or more son's daughters they take two-thirds when there is no child or son's son, and the son's daughter takes one-sixth when there is one daughter or a higher son's daughter and no son; the sister takes one-half when only one and there is no so or son's son how low soever, father, daughter, son's daughter or brother and if there are two or more sisters, they take two-thirds under the same circumstances; the consanguine sister takes one-half when only one and there is no son, consanguine brother or sister, if there are two or more consanguine sisters under the same circumstances they take two-thirds and the consanguine sister takes one-sixth when there is one full sister but no son, etc. or consanguine brother; the mother's share is one-sixth when there is a child or son's child or two or more brothers or sisters and one-third when not, but she takes one-third only of the remainder after deducting the wife's or the husband's share when there is wife or husband and the father; the true grandmother has one-sixth when she is not excluded; the father takes one-sixth; the grandfather's share is one-sixth when he is not excluded and the uterine brother or sister gets one-sixth when only one and no child or son's child, father or true grandfather, and if there are two or more of them they will get two-thirds in the same circumstances.

Under certain circumstances some of the sharers become residuaries or take both as sharers and residuaries.

Residuaries : The next class of heirs are called asba which is ordinarily translated as 'residuaries', because they take the residue after such of the sharers as are not excluded have been satisfied. The residuaries are of three kinds:

(1) residuary in his own right,

(2) residuary in another's right, and

(3) residuary with another.

To the first category belong all male relations in the chain of whose relationship to the deceased, no female enters. They are divided into four classes:

(1) parts (*juz*) of the deceased, that is, his sons and grandsons how low soever then,

(2) roots (*asl*) of the deceased, that is, his father and grandfather how high soever,

(3) parts of the father of the deceased, that is, brothers, brothers' sons how low soever, and

(4) parts of the grandfather of the deceased, that is paternal uncles and their sons how low soever.

Residuaries in another's right are those females who as sharers are entitled either to one-half or two-thirds and who become residuaries, if they coexist with their brothers. For instance, if the heirs of a deceased person are his widow, brother and sister, the widow will get one-fourth and of the remaining three-fourths, the brother will get two portions and the sister one portion as residuaries.

A residuary together with another is a female heir who becomes residuary because of her coexisting with another female heir, for instance, when there is a sister along with a daughter. Besides residuaries by consanguinity there are residuaries for especial cause, namely, patrons of freemen. If there be no residuary then the residue returns to the sharers by consanguinity in proportion to their shares.

Distant Kindred : The next class of heirs are known as (dhawil-arham) or distant kindred. They include all relations who are neither sharers nor residuaries; they inherit only if there are no sharers or residuaries. Shafiis and Malikis, however, do not include such relations in the category of heirs at all.

The distant kindred are divided into four classes:

(1) those that are descended from the deceased, for instance, children of daughters and children of sons' daughters,

(2) those from whom the deceased is descended, for instance, the excluded grandfather or grandmother,

(3) those that are descended from the parents of the deceased, namely, the sisters' children and the brothers' daughters, and

(4) those that are descended from the grand parents of the deceased, namely, paternal aunts, maternal uncles and aunts. Among heirs of this category succession is regulated in the order of the above classification.

Other Heirs : The next class of heirs in the order of succession are mawlal mawalat or successor by contract, that is, a person with whom the deceased entered into a contract that he would be his heir, such person undertaking on his part to pay any fine or compensation to which the deceased might become liable. Then a person whom the deceased had acknowledged as a relation through another. If there be no heir of any of the above classes, then the estate goes to the person or persons to whom the entirety has been left by the deceased's will, otherwise to the public treasury (baitul-Mal).

Exclusion : Then in order to regulate the number of relations who might inherit together the doctrine known as that of exclusion (hujub) is applied. There are some persons, however, who are never totally excluded; the son, the father, the husband, the daughter, the mother and the wife. Exclusion may be sometimes partial. Exclusion is based on two principles; firstly, a person who is related to the deceased through another is excluded by the presence of the latter, for instance, the father excludes the grandfather brother, and sisters and the son excludes the grandson, and this principle is extended among the residuaries so as to give preference to the proximity of degree, for example, a son excludes another son's son; secondly, the nearest in blood excludes the others, hence a relation of full blood always takes in preference to a relation by the father only, for instance, a brother excludes a consanguine brother or sister.

To the first rule there is one exception, namely, that the mother does not exclude brothers and sisters from inheritance and the second rule is subject to the exception that uterine relations are not excluded on that ground. A person who is himself excluded may exclude others. It is also a general rule that when there is a male and a female heir of the same class and degree the latter will take only half of the former.

References

1. SC of deriving laws of Islamic jurisdiction.
2. Founder of the Hanifite school of thought; also called scholar the great.
3. One of the most authentic and learned theologist-turned sufi; also called the Proof of Islam (Hujjat-ul-Islam).
4. One of the four famous Imams of Muslim Theology. Founder of the Shafii school of thought.
5. The Islamic law, derived from Holy Quran and Tradition of the Prophet (Pbuh).
6. Laws laid down by resolution by those who are well-versed in theology.
7. Voluntary disposition.
8. A sacred month of the Arabic calendar in which Muslims observe fasts.
9. A great Islamic scholar of his time.
10. Social relationship, e.g. transaction, etc.
11. Objects of guidance.
12. Biographics.
13. One of the four great scholars of Islamic Theology, Founder of Maliki throught of school.
14. A girl who has had sexual intercourse.
15. The option of Puberty.
16. One of the great powers of Am.
17. Wife's share given by husband in the first night.
18. Lawfully term in and after consummation.
19. Expressing of husband dissatisfying by comparing his life to the back of his mother or sister.
20. Conferment of Power.

2

THE FUNDAMENTALS

LAW AT WORK

The Supreme Fundamental Islamic Principles are related both to matters of Faith and Law and, in conjunction with Islamic ideas, retain the distinction of immutability. The encompassment of the characteristic vision of an Islamic society is an attribute of these fundamentals. To view these as universal "process ideals" in law, so that, statutes ought to be interpreted in accordance with their purposes and meanings, is appropriate. The capacity of transforming the law into an activity, rather than allowing it to remain an entity, is thus apparent. Implicit in human responsibility for the acts is the capability for compliance, which is inclusive of the rational aspects of the law. These considerations together necessitate the law to be based upon an explicit "ila" which is extendable upon legal situations.

The immutability of the Supreme Principles remaining established, the demand for legal change is accommodated by the "process method" of "Ijtihad"; the legal features of the Supreme Principles provide its basis and direction, and establish the limits of legal change in conjunction with the relevant law.

This, more than any other approach deserves to be designated as the foundation of an Islamic legal system, an assertion whose elucidation is provided in the subsequent portions of this discourse. Recognition is due to the fact of principles and rules being of a conceptually different order; the differentiation being that the former is not entitled to any exception.

The Supreme Principles are concerned with the interpretation and application of law, and are proximately related to the process of "law-making." In an Islamic social ethos, the conduction of administration in society and the governmental decision-making are spheres of national life, which also come within the scope of the functions of Supreme Principles, a measure that mitigates the cause for the establishment of administrative courts.

Ascertainment of *legal validity the* recognition of law as a part of the Islamic legal system-is their juristic attribute. The act of *legal adjustment,* whereby the legal harmonisation of law with the remaining laws is attained to establish uniformity in the legal system, is another legal characteristic. Eradication of stationary quality of law, to introduce legal "mobility" through "finding" laws, is the additional feature of *legal supplementation.* All these desirable legal characteristics are maintainable due to the condensation of seminal concepts as inexhaustible source of legal values and ideas which are available in the Supreme Principles.

On the analogy of seed harbouring a dormant potential, these concepts can find expression as a stupendous "tree" in the form of legal development, with the application of the Principles according to the Legal Method described in this discourse.

Without the support of the legal attributes ascribable to the Supreme Principles, the law functions as a part of simple process, without imparting full legal expression to law, for a similar form of social order, which are not in conformity with the Islamic socio-legal objectives. Because, lacking this Legal Method, the general policy of Islamic Law remains unpromulgated.

Essentially, the basis of law and, hence, of society is established by the Supreme Principles, as the laws of the political constitution are themselves derived from their universal explanations. The primary purpose of the principles is to provide Islamic conceptual frame-work for the remainder law, inclusive of the formulation of the legal rules. To visualize these as the evolutionary elements in the Islamic Law which otherwise retains a dormant tendency of development, and the "character keel" of the legal system, to describe in the Platonic phrase, is the proper assessment.

In the words of Shah Wali Ullah[1], originally meant to describe a related subject, within the confines of these "all-embracing principles" resides the solution to universal law. The terms of revealed guidelines and the exact scope of Divine "legislative will" for the law are contained in the Supreme Principles. The universal process-ideals, comprising these principles, underscore the necessity for the development of Islamic Law from the original sources, according to the Legal Method.

The Fundamentals

Provisions of Law

The Quran : The juristic provisions in the primary source of Islamic Law are not exhaustively stipulated, and the grounds for the law in the various legal schools, and ever since, have come to lie in the explicit provisions of the Quran. The cessation of revelation, in combination with the preceding factors, necessitates the availability of principles within the framework of a legal methodology for the development of law. Due to these reasons, the possibilities of interpreting the sources of law in Islam gradually diminished. Therefore, search for the intensive general principles from the Quran, which encompass the particular laws, is imperative.

For the maintenance of the universality of those principles, their preeminent meanings should not permit to be regarded as general in a secondary sense. A properly conceived formulation, resulting in the inclusion of such principles in a legal method, with the jurisprudential attributes for the demonstrable eradication of the aforenoted legal shortcomings in Islamic Law and to make it evolve into a comparable legal system, is justifiable.

The Shariah : The doctrine of the unity of Shariah law signifies the legal conformity in the interrelationship between rules. The existence of contradiction in law has the implication of the imposition of an impossible obligation. Accordingly, Shatibi also believed in the non-existence of disagreement in Shariah law. The Muslim legal theorists recommended the replacement of contradiction in the Shariah law by the supersedence of the superior statement over an earlier edict, with the inference of non-permissibility of "disagreement" in the law. On the contrary, the application of this concept upon Islamic Law means the unity of its intent, a subject whose import should not be unheeded. The prescribed Legal Method, incorporating the Supreme Principles, is operative according to present-day juristic idea of non-contradiction among the norms of law and, therefore, exercises a unifying influence upon the law's intent.

This approach places reliance upon the doctrine of "pre-established harmony," to preserve the legal unity of the system. In this respect, a similarity exists between law and empirical sciences, where the issue of the compatibility of a particular law with the hitherto accepted facts in a system recurringly arises. As a matter of fact, with the concomitant existence of Supreme Principles and the explicit rules in the Shariah law, the law remains heterogeneous unless a formulation for defining an interrelationship between the two becomes a part of Islamic jurisprudence.

Realisation is due to the fact that the Supreme Principles existed antecedently to, in actuality or in legal effect, and independently of, the other enactments of legal importance in Shariah law. As can be seen, the method for the development of the Islamic legal system establishes a relationship between revealed doctrine and practice of Shariah law.

Lacking this approach, aspirations of an ascendant legal system will prove elusive; and the Shariah may remain in quest of itself. The fact is of far-reaching significance that the contemplation of Shariah in divergence from its implementation is in contravention of the jurisprudential dictates. Additionally, not to ignore the legal truism will be rewarding that the application of law is conducive to its own future creation.

Islamic Law : The Islamic concept of law as a derived code of ordained law for obligatory behaviour, founded upon the Supreme Fundamental Islamic Principles, which, within these limits, encompasses the aspect of legal change, is adoptable without any conflict in meaning with another realistic definition. The complexities due to evolved social situation, which require adaptive legal response, are the essential substitute in Islamic legal order for the social change, often alluded in literature in the context of law. In the opinion of Coulson, the traditional Islamic jurisprudence has relegated its provisions to the category of moral injunctions, in particular, concerning the status of women. The distinction between legal and moral norms, and the concept of law intimately associated with sanctions, are relevant considerations in this respect. For the adoption of the revealed moral injunctions as a source of relevant law-making, and not the law *per se,* is a legal objective for the future, and it will foster a creative unity of purpose in society.

As a matter of belief, as a requirement of wisdom and as a demand of legal system, Islamic Law is intended to be complete. With the understanding of Islamic legal history, a legal formulation such as would result in the uncurtailing of the formative potential in Muslim jurisprudence, in reversal of the self-inimical approach in law due to imitation or "taqlid"[2] and due to the disuse of the juristic principle of "Ijtihad," is indicated. As an extension of the scope of Ijtihad, the individualisation and concretisation of law will produce enhanced instances of legal relationships and cause a reduction of the arbitrariness in law. In addition to the fulfilment of the requirements of the rule of law, this approach as a legal process imparts law the eminently wise character, an attribute which is impressively emphasised in the Quran."

Within the meanings of the wisdom of law is the issue of the legal statutes that may produce results other than intended by the legislation, which evokes the subtle but functional distinction between the fact and the effect of law. For instance, the Islamic Law of inheritance of property could not have been conceived to create the issue of the status of women in society. Hence, in relation to Islamic Law, the preservation of the intent of the Law-giver remains a vital concern.

Pertinence of these evaluations is augmented by Plowden's analogy of the letter of the law as the body, and the sense and reason of the law as the soul. Desirable becomes the function of a legal method that satisfies the demand for the sense and reason of law. The observation by Mill, that political institutions are the product of deliberate efforts by men, finds a relevant application on other allied social systems as well. The same lesson is implicit in the traditional Islamic Law, which lost its institutionalised usefulness due to inadequacies in Islamic legal philosophy and legal methodology long after the Islamic schools of law came into existence. Any juristic formulation, embodying the measures based upon the same lesson, will be of benefit in the development of Islamic legal system, suited to an ascendant social order.

According to Fuller's theory, concept of law is comprised of certain implicit principles which constitute morality, and the law is lacking to the extent these principles are violated. Notwithstanding the issue of the place of morality in legal positivism, however, the preceding assertion finds relevant application upon the Supreme Fundamental Islamic Principles, with the differentiation of religio-legal for moral principles. Any legal formulation that addresses itself to the implementation of Supreme Principles, evidently brings to completion the higher functions of Islamic Law. The legal capacity to fulfil this and other aforementioned requirements of jurisprudence, delineated in this section, is available in the Legal Method explained during this discourse.

Islamic Values : The theory of Islamic value draws a distinction between instrumental and intrinsic values in relation to their role as means and ends, respectively. Perry explored eight realms of values, including religion and law. The subject of intrinsic value evoked varied responses, including pleasure from hedonists, harmonious self-realisation from humanists and love of God from the Christians. On the other hand, Pluralists, and Perry among those, believe in the multiplicity of intrinsic values-any number of intrinsically valuable things. The correlation between desire and value identifies one or the other as of primary significance. The idea of the independent mode of manifestation of the value, which is contained within a norm, is of interest. Adam Smith's classification of values in use and in exchange, an observation which is sometimes referred to as the "paradox of value," has remained the subject of explanation by the theories of value. Generally, the term value is applied to all those objects deemed to be worthy of human pursuits on various grounds. From a pragmatic standpoint, any ideal be it religious, legal or political, which has the purport of existing, prevailing or recommending itself to others, of necessity, upholds the objectivity of value judgments.

The formulated Legal Method is an approach by which legal system will give effect to the particular scale of values that ought to obtain in the Muslim society. In accordance with it, the judicial process becomes the instrument for giving scope to the development of and adherence to built-in values, and for removing the threat to those essential values such as may arise due to the administration of legal rules, within the framework of law. In this connection, it is often ignored and frequently forgotten that the application of laws also gives rise to values. All norms, legal or moral, can be viewed as a more or less imperfect reflection of some values, and a legal method for the improvement of their value-content, in effect, has its own desirability in an Islamic society.

A consummate value as a measure of all other values in terms of implementation is the "best community" for the Islamic legal system. Assuming a value system to have a somewhat hierarchical pattern and, while maintaining an ultimate value, which in Islam is identified as success or "falah" in a transcendent sense, it should be sufficiently composite of values for the attainment of diverse objectives. Enhanced possibility for the same is dependent upon the substantive nature of the included values, which can serve as the source of multiple derivative values. These substantive or superordinate values are inherently prior to all other values, and possess the attribute of stability in the sense of specificity of interpretation. Such values are describable as preeminent Islamic conceptions of social reality.

The classification of derivative values offers a further categorisation into ordinate values, offering a certain desirable flexibility of interpretation, and subordinate values, allowing generous latitude of interpretation. The subordinate values are available for pursuance in case the other category of values prevails. With the correlation of norms and values already identified, the Supreme Fundamental Principles are recognisable as superordinate values, and the constitutional and statutory norms are describable as the derivative values-ordinate and subordinate, respectively, in the general sense.

The preceding discourse delineates the rationale for the Supreme Principles which, on the biological analogy of genetic system, retain the immanent potential of providing change through new mutants and, simultaneously, are the principal means of maintaining evolution control. Insofar as the inherent power of these Supreme Principles to influence the social order is concerned, the archetype of the Fundamental Principle of "Tauhid"[3] is citable.

The derivative or ordinate value of fidelity to principles vis-a-vis personalities is an "instrumental value" as a necessary condition for creating a preeminent value of "Nomocracy," that is, government by laws! As an irony of history, the significance and practical realisation of this particular value into meticulous socio-political expression has eluded the Muslim Civilisation, and the type and development of constitutional law in Islam is citable in evidence, wherein the law was not distinctly preponderant to the interests of statecraft.

Rule of Law : In derivation of the injunction with the message for the observation of the revealed law, as an epitome of the Scriptural text, in conjunction with the fact of law and moral tenets in the original source of Islamic law being inseparable, immoral law is excluded from the observation of law. This requirement is a provision of the Islamic rule of law. With this in view, the Supreme Fundamental Principles, which are religio-ethical ideals, are to be transformed into operative legal ideals, and the Legal Method herein described is a most suitable approach for this purpose.

Due to the fundamental nature of these principles, as these underlie the purpose and provisions of revealed law in all their different aspects and developments, their legal influence should be traceable throughout the constitutional and statutory law in its application. As a further requirement of the Islamic rule of law, Divine intention in relation to the revealed law, embodied in the Supreme Principles, is not to undergo infringement or contravention during the future enactments. This is necessitated because the divine law, being an outline for guidance, is in requirement of the supplementation of law. Additional distinguishing legal features pertaining to Islamic rule of law have been enumerated at an earlier juncture, and those provide a persuasive part of the rationale for adoption of the Legal Method which is founded upon the application of Supreme Fundamental Islamic Principles.

Legal Validity of the Supreme Principles : Adoption of the definition of the validity of law as a rule court ought to apply, removes the difficulties in the way of its discussion. However, for the legal rule to be lawfully part of the law, that is, according to the legal norms or constitutionally in conformity with an established criteria, is an essential aspect of this consideration. The rule of recognition described by Hart is typically composed of a number of criteria which aid in the recognition of the validity of other rules. The validity of this rule itself, however, is beyond reproach, so that, there is no question of its conformity with higher order rules. From among the criteria specified to assess the validity of other rules, one criterion is supreme, and the rules identified by reference to it are rules even if in conflict with other criteria, while its exact opposite is not true.

The rule of recognition is not an extra-legal juristic hypothesis, but rather a rule of positive law. And the conformity with the rule of recognition is a sufficient but not a necessary condition for the existence of a valid law. In comparison, the Supreme Principles as a vital component of the Legal Method conform the rules of adjudication to the requirements of Islamic legal validity.

The Supreme Principles are neither an extra-legal juristic hypothesis, nor a set of rules of positive law by any means. Conformity with these principles is both a sufficient and necessary condition for the validity of law. The very title of the principles settles the issue of their own legal validity. Nonetheless, moral validity of the principles resides in the rational justification, comprising the advantages in reference to the legal conceptions that accrue in conforming with, the drawbacks on similar grounds that ensue from the contravention of, and the innate legal merit that is characteristic of, the principles. And no legislative revision in the criteria of validness for the Supreme Principles is anytime obtainable, for the constitution and the political authority are reliant upon the principles. These distinguishing jurisprudential features of the Supreme Principles are understandable, as the Islamic Law, due to the ideological necessities, maintains a unity with religion. This fact itself affords the delineation of universal religious principles underlying all the legal rules.

In some systems, the ultimate criterion of legal validity explicitly incorporates the principle of justice, or substantive moral values. The Legal Method, due to its foundation upon the Supreme Principles, establishes a scrupulous conformity with absolute higher morality, including justice, in the criteria of legal validity. The Legal Method based upon Supreme Principles of absolute higher morality is verifiably then of universal validity, hence, the desirability for validation of man-made law according to this method is persuasive.

The legal validity through this way acquires the meanings of the "ought," or the appropriate nature, of law. The subject is proximately allied to the consideration of a single law to cover all categories of theft, as an instance, in contrast with individualisation of justice. In this legal context, the Legal Method appears a superior mode of justice in relation to legal validity of the relevant law. In this respect, realisation is due that legal positivists usually adopt a relativist approach to moral values. The prospects of the Supreme Principles as a higher law with the universal application, therefore, are entertainable.

The eminent Muslim jurist, Shafii, maintained that in all matters which touch the life of a Muslim, there is either a binding decision or an indication as to the right answer. Correlation of this observation with matters pertaining to law indicates the desirability of distinguishing one situation from the other, and the criteria available is the Legal Method with Supreme Principles. This approach averts the self-imposition of limitations or subjectivity in Islamic Law. As a result, a binding decision will not undergo alteration to any extent.

The underlying juristic measure is definable in terms of *"authentic interpretation,"* to mean construction of one revealed text by another. Importantly,

The Fundamentals

the Supreme Principles do not deprive the interpreted text of all its legal effects in any case, for the former is not a repealing law, a function which will be contrary to the meaning and purpose of interpretation.

It lends full credence to the proposition that interpretation is the discovery of the intention of the lawgiver with respect to the operation of a text in the significant sense. The realisation, that the manner of interpretation of law and the character of legal change are indispensable, is a juridical maxim whereupon reliance has been reposed in the Legal Method. This method of interpretation is then also applicable to other than Islamic revealed texts on their acceptance as a supplementary source of Shariah law. The legal meanings and religious significance of this observation have proven elusive during the whole course of Islamic history, and the consummation of Islam as an essentially universal religion is contingent upon its fine intellectual apprehension.

Law-Making : For an Islamic legal system suited to an ascendant social order, reinterpretation of the law from its original sources is to be effected; a view which was also supported by Abdu and Iqbal, among others. With this proposition in view, and the realisation that the legal system will be a product of sustained, purposive effort, then it is a matter of inference that, in essence, the Islamic legal system is to be established.

For this objective of "law-making," the Islamic legal history spanning the initial two centuries, till the advent of the law schools, is available as a source of emulation. The sound approach, based upon the principle of revealed ordinance and juristic appraisal, produced the legal contents to result in the partial codification of the schools of law.

In describing ways of failure to make law, Fuller mentioned the enactment of contradictory rules and failure to achieve rules, among several other causes. The same author mentioned that a total failure in anyone of these directions does not simply result in a bad system of law, but it results in something that is not properly called a legal system. In this perspective, the laying of emphasis upon the necessity for the establishment of authoritative law-making procedures in a society is due. Some of the other notable suggestions for law-making included the envisioning of law as essentially a dynamic affair, elimination of the reductionist impulse and the need for the recognition of conceptual issues in law. The deficiencies in the credible interpretation and proper implementation of law are the recognisable causes of the inadequate lawmaking. Insofar as the last cause is concerned, the motivation to bring it about is notice-worthy Inability to maintain minimal conditions of literacy which are required for compliance of law, and to enhance the respect for law in society are the additional factors in relation to the defects in law-making.

A jurisprudential reconstruction of the legal system is the solution to overcome the aforementioned hindrances in law-making. The logical positivists set for themselves the task of rational reconstruction, and the principal interest was situated in natural sciences and mathematics. On the other hand, Kelsen applied the notion of rational reconstruction in the sphere of law. The idea of reconstruction, however, had its origin in antiquity with Euclid's development of geometry with the method of rational reconstruction. Afterwards, the most notice-worthy instance of reconstruction is the Principia Mathematica of Russell and Whitehead, preceding the logical positivist attempt at it. According to Euclid's rational reconstruction, the corpus of geometrical knowledge acquired a systematic order, relevant terms were defined with precision, and with the use of less than a dozen axioms and postulates, whose verity was beyond doubt, the truth of a multitude of complex theorems was ascertained.

With the Islamic legal history as a guide, the jurisprudential reconstruction should entail a judicial process, with emphasis upon the meaningful in law, for the jurist's law bears academic connotation. The method envisaging the adjunction of Supreme Principles, such as are an assumption in every single legal instance, for the individualisation of law, engenders the transition form a law in quest of itself to a legal system for an ascendant social order. For without this adjunction, no legal norm, that prescribes sanction, can lay claim to be an Islamic legal norm due to the requirements of Islamic rule of law and lacking the legal validity of the full expression of Islamic Law. The paraphrasing of this methodological approach in the language of rational reconstruction will be the securing of guarantee about the inevident truth of the rule by deriving it from a set of fundamental principles with transcendent truth.

A systematic reformulation of law with the instrumentality of Supreme Principles as the terms of Islamic legal reconstruction, and with the contribution of the juristic responsibility, are the conceptual features of the Legal Method. This approach is accommodative of the legal implications of the maxim that law cannot be laid down a priori, nor can it reside exclusively in the rules of enacted law. This reconstruction of law, while it avoids the shortcomings of the mechanical application of law; a barren jurisprudence can be described as the result-however, it retains the advantages of perpetual creativeness in law.

The reductionist concept of legal rule, as an instrument for the settlement of specific legal disputes, is often upheld in societies with adopted systems of law. However, as a part of the function of law, and as policy-directing aspect of law, the rule is a means to the organisation of society in its original social milieu. In this perspective, the attributes of a rule underscore the significance of the methodological application of the Supreme Principles in an Islamic social

The Fundamentals

organisation. The conceptual justification of this approach furnishes a characteristic definition of the Islamic legal rule:

> As a part of the function of Islamic Law, inclusive of the dispensation of justice with equity, the legal rule is a means for the propagation of such values as are facilitative of the individual success (falah) in a social organisation, with the objective of producing an Islamic society that is recognisable for its paradigmatic attributes, on consideration from internal and external viewpoints. The basic function of the legal rule as a means of adjudication according to Islamic injunctions in a litigational instance is recognised, and the rule thus is an extension or reflection of Islamic values. For the fulfilment of these functions of rule, a conjunction of the "general" and "particular" provisions of law in a judicial process is necessitated.

The Legal Method, based upon the use of Supreme Principles in the prescribed process, satisfies the aspirations for Islamic resurgence, a demand whose expression is a constitutional requirement for conforming the Law to the injunctions of Islam. Thus, Shariah law will remain no longer in quest for itself, and the jurists, inspired by the authority of a prospective major legal system, to be established with their own striving and ability, will make their universal contribution towards the ascendant cause. With these resources of legal development, the law will endure; and with the built-in capacity for Islamic reconstruction, the legal edifice will prove durable to outlast and to overcome the challenges of time.

Mandatory Application : The Supreme Fundamental Islamic Principles are of a compound nature so that their transformation in the form of conventional law is not easily codifiable. The legal characteristic of the recalcitrance demonstrated in the comprehensive framing of statutory law is not a unique attribute identifiable with the Supreme Principles, for the same legal trait is not uncommon with the basic constitutional elements, in general.

The identity with the constitutional elements ends in the instance of the Supreme Principles on consideration of their religious origin which lays demand upon the obligatory legal application of the principles. Additionally, the social ramifications of those principles are of such a universal scope as to require each legal instance to acquire the benefit of assessment in accordance with their Islamic meanings and legal demands. These dual requirements are fulfilled by the application of the method in the form of the modified extension of Islamic injunctions upon the individual legal situation, so that, the dispensation of law is effected according to the distinct legal implications of the Supreme Principles for the full expression of Islamic Law, and the formulation of secondary rules for utilisation in future.

The mandatory nature of the Supreme Principles from the religio-ethical standpoint then alone is directly transferable for the socio-legal usefulness by the Legal Method.

Principle of Falah : The Islamic revealed law cannot but accord with norms of "higher morality" and, in this respect, it has some degree of identity with Natural Law which is synonymous with moral rules. The justification for the rules of morality in natural law was contained in certain aims of human life, which were determined by the desires of mankind, designated as "passions" by Hume, and no role was assignable to reason in this.

However, the norms of higher morality in Islamic revealed law are of transcendental nature due to their proximate affiliation with the revealed doctrine of Salvation and, although, their moral value is demonstrable by reason, yet the desires of mankind obviously have no determining role in relation to those norms.

In order to furnish a substitute for the natural law, the issue of discovering a rational standard to provide the means of judging the moral nature has proved intellectually engaging. The Kantian "categorical imperative" was the absolute rule of morality encompassed in the realm of "ought" rather than in "is." This postulation, however, proved to harbour limitations on empirical grounds, for particular problems could not assuredly find the resolution according to its dictates. With the similar purposes in view, Bentham formulated the principle of utility, which acquired acceptance and, later, it was to make the tangible conceptual contribution towards legal positivism.

The assessment of maximum stock of happiness of the largest numbers was the criterion of utility. This principle provided the measure for the evaluation of the moralness of law, and its main advantage was considered to be the distinction it offered between legal and moral obligations. In comparison, the Supreme Islamic Principle of Success or "falah" is of universal scope in the realm of morality due to its transcendent nature. As a juristic principle of reasoning, it has the conceptual profundity to furnish frame of reference for the evaluation and development of law related to the legal and social reformation.

The implications of the derivative principle of the right to equality for all human beings are of basic import concerning all the orders in a society, without exception. But, more importantly, this fundamental principle is not a metaphysical conception, for its reality can be demonstrated or proven while, at the same time, itself affording a usage as the standard of universal proof. Appropriately then, moralness of law for Hobbes resided in the law itself, to Bentham it reposed in the principle of utility, and in Islam it is identifiable with the Supreme Principle of Success or "falah." With these legal and moral attributes embedded in the

Islamic Principle of Success, to ascribe this Supreme Principle as a higher law, adoptable by humanity, is a philosophically unassailable proposition.

Modern Legal Concepts : According to Hart[4], the union of primary and secondary rules is the key to the science of jurisprudence. The foundations of a legal system are constituted by the acceptance of the secondary rules with the criteria for the identification of the primary rules of obligation, in the setting of a complex social situation. In this view, the primary rules of obligation comprise of the legislative enactments, customary practices, general declarations of specified persons and judicial precedents in particular cases. In the description of Hart, the secondary rules are classified into the rules of recognition, rules of change, and rules of adjudication.

The rules of recognition function to eradicate the "uncertainty" of the primary rules such as would not form a system. The rules of change are the remedy for the static quality of the regime of primary rules. And the rules of adjudication, intended to rectify "the inefficiency of its diffused social pressure" concerning the regime of primary rules, allow the "authoritative determinations" of the issue of violation of the primary rules.

In his appraisal of the dual distinctions drawn between the two types of rules by Hart, attention towards the ensuing features is drawn by Summers. The one type of distinction is characteristically between "duty imposing rules" and "power conferring rules." The other type of distinction is between the primary rules that impose duties and the secondary rules of recognition, change and adjudication. These distinctions, on more profound evaluation, were characterised as somewhat "hybrid" or "ambiguous" in the critique.

The essential significance of Hart's description of the two types of rules in their combination is the retrospective insight it lends into the organised legal systems. This is evident from the claim that the addition of secondary rules to a set of pre-existing primary rules marks the transition from the pre-legal into the legal world. The importance of legal obligation and of constitutional law in the context of vertical view of law-making is signified. In contradistinction, the Legal Method founded upon the Supreme Principles is of prospective nature, for it serves as a formulation for the establishment of a legal system. The subscription to the legal idea of the vertical image of law-making is ascertainable to a certain extent, however, the combination of the full expression of Islamic Law and the individual judicial responsibility are the distinguishing legal concepts functional in the Legal Method.

The formulation, therefore, places substantive reliance upon the characteristic Islamic concept of justice, which comprises of features in addition to the conventional authoritative determinations of the fact of the violation of legal rule. In this perspective, then, it is appreciable that the Supreme Principles are the rational standard which provide the means of Islamic adjudication. This approach is in obvious contrast from Austin's definition of the concept of a legal rule in terms of a notion of "command" and "habitual obedience," and is more in accordance with the legal realists view of the rule. As a matter of comparison, Islamic concept of the legal rule cannot maintain conformity with its elucidation provided by Austin, for then it is in contravention of the Islamic rule of law, wherein the legal obligation is contingent upon the consonancy of the legal rule with the Islamic injunctions.

A characteristic aspect of "Kelsenism" in law is embodied in the observation that the reason for the validity of a norm is always another norm and never a fact. The hierarchy of legal norms is thus based upon the scheme of justification and, as it constitutes the systematic character of legal system, it is considered to be an important contribution to the concept of legal system. A similar, if not the same, view is entertained about the constitutional rules in relation to their legal role in the law. In the opinion of an authority on this subject, the provisions of law issuing from various sources are situated in a hierarchy whose summit is formed by the constitutional laws. A matter of unanimous opinion, the constitutional provisions are of more substantive legal value than the ordinarily enacted laws, for being the means of controlling the constitutionality of enacted legislation.

Now, Kelsen's theory is considered not to be free from shortcomings, and not alone because it imparts a "misleading picture of legal systems. The systematic character ascribable to legal system then is not unexceptionable. The constitution that includes the basic rules of recognition for a legal system, cannot derive its authority from the system itself. In the opinion of Salmond, the constitution is "necessarily prior to the law" and it is a matter of fact and practice rather than of law in reality.

In contrast the term validity "within" the system, which is central to the theory as well as to the concept of intramural justification of the legal norms, used by Kelsen, is an important step in the Legal Method founded upon the Supreme Principles for the organisation of Islamic legal system. This particular notion of unexceptional validity is only entertainable with the use of the Legal Method, for the legal norm demonstrably valid in one system is not assumable to be valid in another system.

Another important contribution to legal theory, made by Kelsen, is the emphasis that in order to ascribe the characteristics of legal system to a set of norms, designated as secondary norms, in contrast with the genuine legal sanction-

The Fundamentals

prescribing norms, there must also exist rules of different type, which enable to identify such norms as elements of an order. The basic soundness of the contribution notwithstanding, a profound assaying of this idea imparts a systematic character to the general content, structure and operation of a legal system, which lends itself to misgivings.

Now the Legal Method based upon the Supreme Principles, in addition to "identifying" the "secondary norms," as a part of the general function of making norms to be the elements of an Islamic legal order in a systematic manner, provides in such instances the prescription of sanctions.

The imparting of the characteristics of the Islamic legal system to the "secondary norms" fulfils the function of the identification. And the legally important role of prescribing sanctions in the case of "secondary norms" is performed due to the legal authentication lent from the Quranic injunction, requiring "the wrong-doers who debar (or detract) from the way of Allah" that "such will not escape in the earth...." This measure resolves the difficulty in law due to the differentiation that exists between moral and legal norms, distinguishes the legal order from all other social orders due to the fact, that it regulates human conduct and exercises social control by means of a specific legal technique of sanctions, and also fulfils the requirements for a genuine legal norm, delineated both by Kelsen and Hart.

As its but one legal instance, the law pertaining to inheritance of property in Islam is citable. Devoid of formulation for the sanctions in the event of the violation of the relevant rules, in effect the laws of inheritance remain a matter of conscience alone, not possessing the legal means to uphold their religious sanctity and legal inviolability in the event of oftener than not breach. The prescribed Legal Method ascribes the characteristics of the Islamic legal system to the cited "secondary norm," and maintains the legal jurisdiction to transform it into a *"genuine legal norm"* by prescribing legal sanctions in the event of its violation. In distinguishing between law and jurisprudence or the science of law, Kelsen assigns the function of "representation" of the law produced by the legal authority to jurisprudence. The law, whose "description" is given as legal norms which, in their "specific connection within a legal order," are viewed as the "ought" representation of the law.

The emphasis is laid upon the distinction to be drawn between the "legal norms" the "prescriptive" elements of the law of community-designated to be the "objects of jurisprudence," and the representation by the theorist of law, designated as the "statements of jurisprudence."

Now, in accordance with the requirements of the Legal Method, and with the usage of Kelsenian descriptive terms for the purpose of legal comparison here, the "objects of jurisprudence" are the legal rules, the Supreme Principles and the legal features in an individual instance of adjudication.

The "ought" of law, as a result of the method, is the juristic form as the representation of the Islamic "rightness" of law. In other words, the Islamic legal character of the legal rule is its "ought" juristic form as determined with the utility of the Legal Method.

The determination of the Islamic law relevant to the legal rule during judicial evaluation is the fulfilment of the requirement of a Supreme Principle. In addition to the Islamic "groundnorms" of Tauhid, the consummate legal concepts of "public beneficence," "best community," and success ("falah"), are the wellspring for the elements of Islamic legal character. No less significant are the superordinate legal concepts of justice, equity and vicegerency, the components that by no means exhaust the enumeration.

With the individualisation of the process of "representation," though of a circumscribed legal scope, the Supreme Principles are to be imparted, through concretisation of a general or abstract law, a characteristic Islamic legal expression, which has the potential for influencing indeterminately large instances and aspects of the law. Consequent to the juristic conjunction between two types of laws, designated here as general and particular rules, the methodical approach for the individualisation and concretisation of a composite law imparts the legal system an "open" texture.

The U.S. Constitution incorporates by positive enactment certain value judgments or principles. This approach makes explicit the underlying main assumptions of the legal system, and it renders these into obligatory or "overriding" legal norms, capable of being enforced by the legal process. In comparison, the Supreme Principles represent the multifarious fundamentals which underlie the religious and legal structure in Islam and, hence, in general serve as the determinants of the values in religion, jurisdiction of laws and legal development in the legal system. Due to the contrasting fact of the Supreme Principles constitutionally not being upheld only in their legal breach, but their legal functions are also availed through their systematic exercise, the Legal Method constituted of those fundamentals acquires the following distinguishing functions:

(1) The administration of justice is fundamentally altered to its appropriate Islamic requirements.

(2) The role of judiciary in the structure of legal system is altered from the simplistic ascertainment of the violation of law to its feasible creative function.

The Fundamentals

(3) The effectiveness of the law is extended and enhanced to the full Islamic scope of its application.

(4) The Supreme Principles viewed as the indispensable fundamental Islamic values, in conjunction with the law through the process of adjudication, in accordance with the demands of Legal Method, transform the law into a constant medium for the propagation of those values in the society.

(5) The invaluable legal notion of the "separation of powers," with the distinct implication of the independence of judiciary, finds its logical expression in the application of the method, for the extra and vital dimension of the independence of judiciary in its comprehensive sense is manifested in the universal exercise, to an extent, within a predetermined framework of law, of the individualisation of legal judgments.

(6) The judicial latitude accrues from the fact that the Supreme Principles carry the legal validity of confirming the "norms for decision," assigning to them new authority or imparting to them equitably different effect from that which had been previously attributed to them.

The issue of any similarity of the Legal Method with the existence of "general legal principles" in the constitutions of other states as, for instance, affirmed in the preamble of the French Constitution itself, is relevant. The Spanish Civil Code enumerates among the possible sources of law the general principles deduced from the Spanish codes and legislation. The series of judicial judgments in the GFR stipulated that the constitutional law is not limited to fundamental legislating texts, but is also made-up of "certain general principles which the legislators have not rendered in the form of positive rules."

Now the consonancy of law with the fundamental principles and values of the constitution is a common legal aim in all the legal systems, at least on a theoretical basis. However, the mandatory creative objective underlying the Legal Method has distinct differentiation from the preceding feature recognised in all legal systems.

The Islamic legal system is to address itself to the substantive issues of Islamic legal concepts including the legal rules, legal positivism, and the Islamic concern for the just social order. The implications of the last issue entail the legal rules which would not be socially unjust and, by the same token, there is no divergence between law, justice and equity in accordance with Islamic requirements. The *result-orientation* of the Supreme Principles, in contrast with mere process-orientation, in their application is an Islamic legal characteristic, which is ensured through individualisation and concretisation of the legal implications of the superordinate principles, describable for clarity of apprehension as legal *constellation-concepts.* In summation, the Legal Method represents the present stage of Islamic legal theory, which does not lend itself to sufficient similarity with any other theory of law in promulgation.

The conventional elements in the constitution are also known as its understandings. And other functional designations such as the constitutional and political ethics, and constitutional morality depict the nature of constitutional conventions. In describing the salient characteristics of the understandings which make the constitutional morality. Dicey identified one common quality, that is, determinant, in general, of the mode in which discretionary powers belonging to the political sovereign ought to be exercised. Notice-worthy is the translation of the discretion into reasons for use in juristic preference by the court. In contrast with the constitutional law, the conventions of the constitution are not in reality enforced by the courts.

The legal binding force of the latter, then, is derived from the fact that their breach should necessarily reflect in the violation of law, finally. On comparative evaluation, the Supreme Principles belong to a different category as explained earlier. The realisation is due that one essential principle of the constitution is obedience to the deliberately expressed will of the lawgiver, however, the Supreme Principles are a set of religio-legal maxims, meant to secure deference for this principle in the context of the primary source of law.

The legal concepts and values that ensue from the Supreme Principles necessitate their individualisation due to the religious basis of Islamic Law. This then becomes the expression of the connection between the law and the Supreme Principles, however, no ascertainment of the nature of connection between the law of the constitution and the constitutional conventions, if at all, can be made with exactitude. The reiteration of the observation by Gibb to the effect that Islam is to be evaluated essentially in its own terms, is pertinent at this juncture. This legal nexus relating to the Supreme Principles and the law, as the former are the superordinate concepts and consummate values, is applicable by conscientious interpretation to all claims, relationships and conflicts of interest. No symmetrical analogy in legal history is available to explain the legal usage of the Supreme Principles as formulated in the Legal Method. Nevertheless, the effect of equity law on the stationary medieval English Common Law, and the Ordinance on Civil Justice of 1900 A.D. in the Sudan to provide the necessary development of law, are citable to impart some idea of the legal usefulness of the Supreme Principles.

The definition of legal system or the correlation of rules to legal system is of relevance. Kelsen considers the identification of legal system to reside in its systematic character due to the common denominator of basic norms for the rules.

The Fundamentals

These norms in the analogy of reconstruction are the initial maxims for the derivation of subsequent propositions. The law emanating from the same sovereign is also viewed as the characteristic of legal system. In Austin's opinion, "a legal system is a system of rules within rules."

In this description, a general habit of obedience was not attached significance, but the acceptance of a set of constitutional norms for the identification of the rules of the system is its characteristic. Hart considered the union of primary and secondary rules to be the criterion in addition to its conforming with the requirements of moral nature of laws as the definition of legal system. In Salmond's[5] observation, Hart and Austin, like many other legal theorists, described a working model of a standard legal system.

In this perspective, the important juristic issue of the determination of the constitution of a state by law, if at all it can be accomplished, remains. According to Rawls' description, constitutional rules are logically prior in existence to that of the institutions defined by those rules. Salmond has addressed this engaging issue in the following terms: Constitution includes basic rules of recognition of a state's legal system which cannot derive their authority from the legal system itself. Further, a poignant query is raised by the same source. Does this mean that the state and its constitution are necessarily prior to the law, and that what passes as a constitutional law is in reality not a law, but a matter of fact and practice?"

Against this background, the definition of a legal system stays in want of completion, for the constitutional rules are non-derivable basic norms in the legal system. In this respect, the Legal Method removes this legal deficiency, so that the Supreme Fundamental Islamic Principles are situated prior to the state and the constitution.

Opinions of other Islamic Jurists : The conflict was natural to arise between the antithetical viewpoints concerning legitimacy of standards for society to be set by law and the law as the outgrowth of the experience of society. The reconciliation of the differences between traditional law and the demands laid upon it by the social change were engaging the interests of Muslim jurists. The advocation for the reinterpretation of the principles embodied in the divine revelation by the great Egyptian jurist, Abdu, at the end of nineteenth century, was in response to legal reformation.

Another Islamic thinker of eminence, Iqbal, emphasised the revitalisation of Ijtihad and described it as "the principle of movement in the structure of Islam," with the same objective in view. Adopting the line of thought that the founders of the Islamic schools of law could not have envisaged finality for their legal reasonings and interpretation regarding the sources of law, the same thinker underscored the need for reinterpretation of the Islamic legal principles in consonance with the newly emerged social and empirical demands. However, the onus of this far-sighted response was both substantive and intricate, for it required a legal formulation as a framework for systematic Ijtihad.

Without such an essential basis the reality of Ijtihad would have remained a mere aspiration. Yet the irreducible minimum requirement for such a formulation was for it to stay indisputable in accordance with Islamic religious as well as modern juridical criteria. In the absence of these antecedents, the challenging task of reinterpretation of the primary sources of Muslim law, that is, independent of the traditional Muslim juristic construction of the law, has since existed unattended and incomplete.

The Muslim theologian, Shah Wali Ullah, has pointed out the prophetic aim, including all-embracing principles in the sublime teachings, with the view to satisfy the requirements of different times, peoples and places. These principles, in practical effect, are of usefulness in the construction of "Universal Shariat." An Islamic legist of incomparable vision and wisdom in his times, whose legal theories did not find assimilation into the traditional legal system of Islam, Shatibi propagated the comprehensive legal concept of "Masla." This juristic principle was deemed to find a wide applicability in law as the objective of Shariah, and as a method of legal reasoning. These legal uses of Masla, or public welfare, would have proven to be the precondition for the reintroduction of Ijtihad in the Islamic legal system.

The "habit" of adherence to the respective school doctrine among the legal scholars constituted the "science of jurisprudence" according to Ibn Khaldun, as referred to before. This obviously indicated a need for reform in this lingering approach. A similar view was formulated by Fazl-ur-Rahman, who pointed out that Islamic scholarship during the past a few centuries had been more or less mechanical and semantic rather than interpretative or scientific. And his suggestion for the re-exercising of Ijtihad as a prerequisite for ensuring an honourable place for the Muslims in the community of "progressive, dynamic and living nations of the world" is intellectually engaging.

The following observation attributed to famous Muslim jurist, Shafii, is reiterated to a similar interpretation: On all matters which touch the life of a Muslim, there is either a binding decision or an indication as to the right answer. On the basis of hierarchy of law, the juristic criteria for the evaluation and differentiation of the alternatives in law according to Shafii should also be ascertainable from the same sources. This subscription to the idea of "all-embracing" principles in the present-day legal terminology is paraphrasable as a legal formulation, representing the hierarchy of law, for the ascertainment and validation of legal rules.

Ideological Necessity : The term ideology is credited to Tracy for utilising it at the end of the eighteenth century. Viewed as a science of ideas, the power to demonstrate the relationship between ideas and experience on the one hand, and reality and well-ordered human world on the other, was ascribed to it. However, Marx become popular for using the term ideology in literature.

Another notable theorist, Mannheim, is recognised for making original contribution to the concept of ideology. It is to be realised that the term ideology has triple differential characteristics that impart distinct applicability to its each classical concept. Now, the recognition of a new concept, with its definition according to a neologistic term, and the existence of its dynamics antedating to that discovery are not extraordinary. Accordingly, the Islamic definition of the ideology is distinct and its identifying criteria of a coherent world-view, rationale of its pursuit, and the justification to establish an identifiable social order as well as to reform the world were available preceding the advent of the term ideology.

With this in view, the assumption that the adoption of ideology somehow guarantees the attainment of ideological objectives in the society is erroneous as it is not borne out by historical experience. An interrelated fact is the furnishing of directions for the achievement of ideological objectives, which is not a recognised function of ideologies.

The significance of human factor in the successful implementation of ideological theories, therefore, is worth of mentioning. On another level, the ideological objectives remaining constant, ideological theories should necessarily retain adaptability for rational reconstruction and reinterpretation in the light of new experience on the analogy of law. The proposed theory of law, founded upon the Supreme Principles, is in fulfilment of the pointed out ideological necessity which is further emphasised by the primal importance of law in the Islamic social order—an ideological fact which yet awaits its full realisation.

Throughout the course of legal history, ideas have served as legal values, as basis of legal reasoning, as criteria of interpretation and as framework of standards. Greek thought developed into and centred upon the idea of social harmony, with characteristic meanings, which would be of equal utility even today.

The Roman jurists adopted the idea of social control as a constituent of the legal theory. The Islamic legal concern focused upon "Masla" or public interest, a legal principle which was markedly elaborated by Shatibi subsequently. During the Reformation, the individual self-assertion emerged as the preeminent legal notion. In this succession of legal ideas, the engaging concepts of economic infrastructure and the end of law held ideological sway.

The competing idea of legal value, the maintenance of strength and efficiency in an organised society, was to emerge. To maintain the evolving sequence of ideas, the Islamic Civilisation for its *new legal age* is anticipated to subscribe to the concept of "best community." According to Pound, application of standards and legal interpretation are done with reference to received ideals, while ideals are described as the authoritative pictures of social order, and are viewed to be as much a part of the law as rules and principles, conceptions and techniques.

The relevance of these aspects in relation to the Supreme Principles as ideological and legal foundations for the Islamic Law is evident, and the resolution of the juristic and political dilemmas, which have historically stalled the evolution of the corresponding systems in Islam, appears conceivable. The juristic issues of the reintroduction of Ijtihad for the establishment of legal system, to sustain the desirable legal development in order to cope with the requirements of evolving social organisation and to reconcile the conflicting demands of stability and change in law, find the suitable response.

On the other hand, development of the political constitution, rule of law and matters related to the legal concept of sovereign and subject, issues with substantive political ramifications and proximately interrelated, find their appropriate resolution through Islamic system of Nomocracy. Notice-worthy is the definition of rule of law as projected by the remarkable Greek genius, Plato[6], and according to it the law is not to serve the interests of the ruler, but the reverse ought to be true. The political view of sovereign and subject expresses only one aspect of the relationship between state and individual. In that instance, the sovereign will as expressed in legislation may be arbitrary, despotic or irrational. A consideration which may not be within the ambit of its validity as law, the social and moral content of such an expressed will is not unlikely to be deficient.

The passive reception of orders is the political distinguishing mark of such a legal relationship. Now, due to the singular fact that the Supreme Principles are situated prior to the constitution which finds its validity from the principles, and not conversely, therefore, the type of constitution, its continuation in force as a legal document and development of constitutional law are reliant upon the former. A modern constitutionalist, Dicey, ascribes noticeable legal value to this sequence of constitution with the law in context, of human rights. The fundamental legal concept of Islamic rule of law as a constituent of the Supreme Principles is then immune from amendment, abridgement or abrogation due to any imaginable constitutional uncertainties.

The Fundamentals

And this rule of law, finding its diverse implications in the law and expression in the legal precedents, provides a double guarantee against its own violation in the specific Platonic context, which is relevant to the immediate purpose of present discourse. Moreover, due to the characteristic attributes of Islamic rule of law, the political distinction between sovereign and subject is legally not valid, for the contractual ground between the ruler and the populace is formed by consonance with the provisions of Islamic Law as a condition for political allegiance.

The judicial independence is a logical deduction from the Islamic rule of law as a source of impartial arbitration, for without its surety in advance, the rule of law is theoretically unsustainable and, indeed, more often than not, may prove a hollow principle. The same issue of sovereign and subject is relevant in the context of Austin's legal concept of command and obedience. However, within the meanings of the Quranic rule of law, allegiance to the political authority cannot legally be construed as subordination which is reserved for law as a common denominator, both for the ruler and the citizens.

The consideration of political authority itself, under the command of an external source as a sovereign, will be then a contradiction in terms. Hence, the Islamic legislative texts are guides rather than commands, for the latter emanate from the political sovereign, considered strictly according to the demands of Islamic rule of law. A matter of far-reaching significance, the source of essential definition and limitation of political authority in Islam is not the political constitution, but the Islamic Law, a fact that confers the valid designation of "Nomocracy" upon the Islamic political system, with the basic differentiation of real obedience in Islam being to legal principles and not to political authority. This legal relationship between the political authority and the populace in Islam is demonstrable, on theoretical grounds, to become the antecedent of the "end of law" in society, a utopian objective entertained in the communism, provided the law is deemed as man-made and society is construed at the zenith of its evolution, so that, the primary source of Islamic Law will then suffice.

POSITIVE ASPECTS

Source of Law : Any Supreme Principle is comprised of *Islamic constellation-norms,* and each can result in the deduction of a legal system. This substantive observation emphasizes the legal value of the principles as an inexhaustible source of law. Representing Islamic religio-legal fundamentals, these principles offer themselves to be systematically analysed, reconciled with maxims available in modern knowledge, and developed along rational lines consistent with legal modes of reasoning. The last designates a more intense and systematised form of ordinary human reasoning, according to Lloyd. Due to the creative religio-legal concepts in the Supreme Principles, the prodigious potential for the opening of new vistas of legal creativity is to be realised.

The judicial interpretation of law is within the legal framework of the Supreme Principles as prescribed by the Legal Method, and all of these legal factors will lend incentive to the work of legal scholarship as well. The legal importance of this last effect resides in the fact that the products of legal scholarship were the fundamental source of law in Romano-Germanic system for a prolonged period. Legal scholarship is, therefore, of fundamental value, for it creates ideas and initiating bases for the juristic output. With these legal advantages in relation to the source of law, the formulated Legal Method can be envisaged to be the *"principle of legal development"* in the Islamic legal system.

Interpretation of Law : In Kelsen's view, jurisprudence or science of law is the "representation," that is, rational reconstruction, of the law of community." According to Amos, the French utilise this term to mean interpretation, which is not essentially different from the former. This fact, no doubt, underscores the significance of the interpretation of law as a process in a legal system. A pronounced accentuation of this conclusion is observed in the instance of religious fundamental laws which possess special authority in the related communities.

These set of laws, considered as exceptional legislation, then, are in need of interpretation with the aid of methodology and principles which are different from those utilised for that purpose in "conventional" legislation. A more profound appreciation of this view is acquired by realizing that the usual legislative concerns-the provision of all the necessary regulations not feasible during the legislation, with the result that the usual outcome is the statement of principles and general rules pertaining to a relevant area-are augmented in religious law." Additionally, the interpretative approach must take into account the identification of law with a juridical objective.

The law in the Western Civilisation is identified with the safeguard of individual rights in the community, the socialist law identified itself with the omnipotence of state which, in traditional Islamic Law, is equated with religion. This last view merged substantive discipline of law into the "science" of religion, and omitted to grant it the due recognition as a distinct "science." Now the practical value of any enacted law depends upon the technique of its application, an outcome which is intricately associated with the antecedent of a process of interpretation, whose real importance has proven elusive in the traditional Muslim Law.

The identification of Islamic Law is not suited to any other objective, on the basis of knowledge of religion or legal reasoning, than with the Supreme Principles and, in particular, its more tangible-in the sense of concrete-objective of "best

The Fundamentals

community." From this discussion it can be concluded that the interpretation and application of the Supreme Principles, as a fundamental part of the religious law, are of essential juridical value.

The singular characteristic of the Supreme Principles is their interpretative inexhaustibility due to the lack of complete definability of legal relationships under various associable circumstances, and due to their prodigious explanatory powers. To reiterate, one essential principle of the constitution is obedience to the deliberately expressed will of the law-giver. From the religious viewpoint, the abiding obligation towards the essentials of religious faith and morality is derived from the same principle. However, from the legal viewpoint, the Supreme Principles are a set of maxims, meant to secure respect for this principle.

The necessity for the methodical application of the Supreme Principles is further reliant upon the justification that the violation of the principles is a proof of the particular legal norm not being identifiable with Islamic Law to the extent of its divergence from the requirements of those principles. In other words, with the application of the Supreme Principles, with the interpretative function of the measure of the essential Islamic religio-legal values, deficiency from the provisions of Islamic religious law is sightable.

The legal controversy that exists between rule and the law demands a serious attention in the instance of a religious law. The conventional interpretation of rule, under an ordinary legislation, usually results in a narrowly materialistic, in the sense of worldly, application of law, which is not justifiable in the case of a religious law. The desirable avoidance of mechanical deductions from rules with predetermined meanings, without reference to all the attendable legal relationships envisaged in a religious law, is exercisable through the systematic interpretation of law in accordance with the legal formulation described. Due to the manner of interpretation of law and character of legal development are recognised to have an indispensable linkage, the legal approach embodied in the Legal Method in relation to the former objective is denotable as the *Islamic juristic method* for the interpretation of law.

Composite nature of the objectives in a religious law is recognisable, yet the literal interpretation of the legal rules is rather routinely exercised, and due to the synonymity of the process of adjudication with the dispensation of law or administration of justice, the intention of the Law-giver is not necessarily considered. This outlined variance between the law and the legal rule concerning the religious law, in particular, is averted by the legal approach comprising of Supreme Principles. Moreover, law at times, is insufficient and incomplete, and the same approach is of assistance in that ascertainment and supplementation. Against this perspective, the law may be deemed as a well-defined *juridical framework* which the act of interpretation, with the use of the method, will complete. Additionally, in the routine application of law, the possible inconsistency of the statutes with each other, a counter to the concept of legal system according to Fuller, is remediable with the legal use of a systematic standard of superordinate principles.

Islamic Jurisprudence : The jurists consider the characteristics of legal system to be the fundamental elements through which the rules to be applied are themselves discovered, interpreted and evaluated. These elements are viewed as determinants of the social objectives to be achieved with the assistance of legal system, and the place of law itself within the social order. In the instance of German Law, the general provisions of law are allowed to neutralize the more specific provisions.

As a result, without changing the meanings of the text, the new demands upon law are fulfilled. In order for the comparison to emphasize the distinction between fundamental elements and Supreme Principles, the latter represent the law's Islamic religio-legal conceptual structure and are the embodiment of the theory of the sources of law. The Supreme Principles epitomize the idea of the universe and society that ought to permeate the law. In essence, then, the Supreme Principles reflect the specific ideological outlook the law is founded upon, comprised of religious, philosophical and socio-political dimensions.

The consideration of Islamic economic and defensive frameworks of society is the prominent aspect of the law. The scope of social objectives to be achieved with the assistance of legal system, thus, is evidently extensive, and the place of law within the social order, considering it as an indispensable part of religion, is indeed of primal importance. Insofar as the methodological approach is concerned, the fundamental elements of law, as part of the general provisions, are allowed to prevail over the special provisions for the juridical advantage of consideration to constant and more fundamental elements rather than the less stable legal rules. This primary legal function is described as subordination of law to the commands of essential legal principles, and standards of higher morality, in one constitutional system, and as the overriding influence to certain elements in law in another system.

The Legal Method relying upon the Supreme Principles basically purports to impart full effects to Islamic Law, whereby the juridical notions of "subordination" and "overriding influence" in law find a primarily contrasting substitution of conjunction and supplementation of law. The reiteration of the fact is due that Supreme Principles comprise of *constellation-concepts* and, viewed strictly in terms of law, constitute its Islamic purposes, whereas the instrumentality of the

The Fundamentals

Legal Method is the source of their implementation. And the overall purpose of Islamic Law is none other than the establishment of a social order suited to the organisation of such a society as is definable in revealed Islamic terms. The intricate and pervading concepts of individual success ("falah"), the dispensation of justice with its undissociability from equity alongwith other Islamic attributes, and the characteristic requirements of Islamic rule of law are prominent distinguishing legal features in such a society.

The valuable legal notion of sociological jurisprudence is credited to Roscoe Pound. Among its objectives are the quest for means of making legal rules effective and individualisation of legal decisions. In connection with the legal rules, the important question of terminology, whether rules of conduct or laws is settled, for the legal discrepancy between the two is resolved by the usage of the Legal Method. The Supreme Principles confirm the "norms for decision," assign new authority and impart equitable Islamic effect to them in the face of competing legal values.

The explanation resides in the fact of the Supreme Principles being both more fundamental and wider in scope than the statutes and enactments which are to be construed in conformity with those principles. The approach is essentially to be looked at as means to avoid the resignation to serviceable substitutes in law, given the Islamic desirability for the use of high juridical standards. In resultant, as the law becomes devoid of any possibility for social injustice, so the Legal Method becomes a way to a just social order. On the basis of another consideration, any legal measure that augments the principle of social interdependence, designated as solidarity ordinarily or, conversely, eradicates the potential for social friction, it can be deemed to enhance the effectiveness of legal rules. And, more importantly, the effectiveness of legal rules is inseparable from the position for the law in the social order and its general reverence.

A direct correlation apparently exists between the immediately preceding reason for the effectiveness of rules and the availability of the constitutional guarantees for the individual rights towards their enforcement. Due to the vital fact of the preeminent characterisation of Islamic society being a Nomocracy, as ascertained from the primary source of law, the essential requirement for Islamic rule of law extends the safeguard to the continuity of constitution and, simultaneously, establishes the lawful grounds for the legal enforcement of individual rights. According to the requirement of the Islamic rule of law, the abrogation or abridgement of the individual rights, granted in Islam, is not without legal infraction.

The legal attainment of individual rights is fortified by the demands of the rule of law, which make it incumbent upon the individuals to attend to the legal obligations and, as its necessary counterpart, the attentiveness to the legal rights is ever kept within social consciousness. In this background, the rationale to give the Supreme Principles a mandatory legal expression, as prescribed in the Legal Method, is obvious. And the same legal formulation is a means for the attainment of the other objective of the sociological jurisprudence.

The maintenance of political constitution and the judicial independence are among the legal consequences ensuing from legal application of the Supreme Principles in the Legal Method, which becomes the justification for the adoption of the formulation. If one is the consequence of, then the other is the only effective guarantee for, the pivotal requirement of Islamic Nomocracy—the observance of law—as epitomised in the previously referred Quranic injunction. For not finely apprehending the legal value of the Islamic juristic truism, that Islamic fundamental of the rule of law is the basis of the law of constitution and not its result, the muse of history has exacted a heavy toll from the incautious, and repeatedly.

The resolution of the rule and law controversy has its demonstrable desirability in Islamic Law, and it is attainable through the prescribed legal approach. The right of inheritance available in Muslim laws is identified with Islamic concept of social values, whereas it is a distinction which indeed is legitimately owned by the Supreme Principles. The considerations of the *ratio legis,* with the special meaning of the adaptation to wholesome experience of society, and the rare possibility of the provisions in a code may be a "dead letter," also demand a suitable legal formulation.

A matter of fundamental significance, law in Islam is a means towards a certain defined end, and not the latter *per se,* which is explicit from the illustration in political jurisprudence. As an instance of "neologism," this category of jurisprudence is more suited to Islamic Law due to its comprehensive nature than, perhaps, to any other legal system. And Islamic economic laws can afford to be included into an independent type of jurisprudence. Since law in Islam is based upon the ordained set of revealed injunctions, then jurisprudence is deemable as the science of understanding and ascertaining that law, as suggested by Coulson, however, this objective is lent specificity by enhancing its scope to defining the "ought" or rightness of Islamic Law. And the present legal formulation endeavours towards the attainment of that redefined juridical objective. In consonance with this description, the Islamic political jurisprudence is the definition and limitation of political authority within the Islamic scheme of state and society.

The basic differentiation from other constitutional forms that exists in Islam is the political identity of the society, which emanates from its *legal personality,* and not *vice versa*. The invaluable distinction denies the political authority to supersede over legal sovereignty. An instance of legal history, in the domain of Muslim public laws, political interests necessitated additional jurisdiction and, hence, the politico-legal doctrine of "siasa Shariah" was evolved, whose inimical consequences upon the Islamic legal and political systems have already been dwelt upon.

However, the legal formulation envisages to forestall the legal ramifications of the traditional doctrine in the new age of Islamic Law for an ascendant social order. On the same grounds the philosophical correspondence that exists between obligations and rights, the political jurisprudence will provide a legitimate accommodation to the latter. The Supreme Principles furnish the adequate conceptual basis for the balancing addition of individual rights; it is a legal measure whose value cannot be over-emphasised as it is overdue and consonant with the demands of Islamic rule of law.

The primary right of the ruled to opt for the political authority ensues from the mandatory provisions of Islamic rule of law, and it is inherent in the qualified right to refusal of the authority's obedience. This essentially is the legal basis for the security of political freedom in society as a universal religious requirement of "Tauhid." The belief, and not just the recognition as is provided for in the Universal Declaration of Human Rights of 1948, in the common source and hence equality of humankind, is the foundation of Islamic political freedom. This heritage of religious belief, translatable in legal terms, hence, claiming cumulative weight for implementation, is an Islamic political distinction which, as an invaluable legal concept, should not remain without full recognition or complete legislative expression. Alternatively, the denial of political freedom in Islam will convey the religious implication of the abrogation of a Supreme Principle.

The fact is to be granted that the general principle of justice finds diverse application for the idea in various legal theories. However, Islamic concept of justice is inseparably allied with the legal notion of equity. The Legal Method provides utility for the principle of equity, without the need for autonomous rules or courts of equity. Besides, it is a practical means for the desirable alternative to the traditional Islamic approach of dual court system comprising of "Qadi"[7] and "Mufti," and allows its effective unification.

And the potential for the legal formulation to furnish a substitute for administrative and constitutional courts, as are available in some legal systems, cannot be underestimated.

"Best Community": End of Law : The juridical features of the legal system in "best community" are as follows:

(1) The "ought" or rightness of law is a constant objective.

(2) The practical manifestations of law, rather than the theoretical content of the legal precepts, draw attention.

(3) Law due to the requirements of its science, is regarded as an improvable social institution as well as in constant need of improvement.

(4) Law is not merely an instrument of social control but, being of primal significance in the social order, it is the means to social ascendancy.

(5) Due to the essential differentiation that exists between law and rule, the legal rule is definable as to give full individual expression to the requirements of Islamic Law, rather than remaining the simple and artless instrument of settling the individual legal controversies.

(6) The past of Islamic Law is deemed to reveal ideas and principles in inductive, historical and empirical terms and the law is thus not only found but also developed.

(7) In accommodation of the teleological view of law, and with the attainable ends of law in sight, accessibility to an established criteria for the "adjudication" and "supplementation" of "law" is available.

(8) Law is oriented towards serving the interests of the Islamic rule of law in juxtaposition to the interests of the political authority.

An Aspect of "Jihad" and Law : The right to the ownership of firearms is cognate to the individual Islamic obligation of Jihad and, therefore, is an indispensable Islamic right. The legal issue of the correspondence between rights and obligations is involved in this instance, and the juristic consideration of capability as an antecedent of legal obligation is no less important. An appropriate analogy from the evaluation of legal history belonging to other systems of law becomes available to be drawn.

The 18th century jurist, James Wilson conceived that a moral right, due to its moral nature, is also legal. The right of the citizen to keep arms was deemed necessary against the historical perspective of the encroachment upon political liberty, and it was viewed to be a palladium of the liberties of a republic.

As another instance, a guarantee in the first bill of rights was the right to bear arms, which was secured to the king's Protestant subjects by the English Bill of Rights. This was necessitated against the background of James II, who had sought to hold down a Protestant majority by disarming them while allowing a nostile minority to bear arms. The reluctance to vividly recall the episodes in the historical experience, that led to the usurpation of Islamic political sovereignty during the 18th century in the subcontinent, has manifested in the perpetuation of those policies and enactments, in effect. An allusion in this regard is appropriate that the constitutional privilege allowing a citizen the initiative of submitting the petition for the conformity of a law in promulgation to the injunctions of Islam was availed by this author. In respect of the relevant appeal in that instance, it is suggested that the constitutional provision of empowering the court to take cognizance on its own, of any law in force which is contrary to the Islamic injunction, should have proven facilitative in the adjudication of the appeal that contained a set of comprehensive arguments.

Judicial Virtues : A not so rare mistake of equating the display of judicial virtues with legislative activity is made. In the opinion of Hart, these virtues besides including the impartiality and neutrality, in surveying the alternatives and consideration for the interests of all who will be affected, additionally consist of the concern to employ some acceptable general principles as a reasoned basis for decision. The inference that the judicial process in an advanced legal system entails creative functions of the courts is, therefore, inescapable. In the instance of Islamic Law, the judicial interpretation of the legislative enactments is indicated due to the legal value in the full expression of law, rather than the rule alone, in the individual legal decision, as a process.

It is not inexplicable, for it is recognised that each legal system has concepts through which its rules are expressed and legal decisions are made. In Islamic Law, perhaps, more than in other legal systems, the legal rules are not deemable as complete, and only as the "fragments," without conforming to the original intent of the Lawgiver, which may require their "recasting" in that direction.

Lacking the assimilation of these considerations into the legal process, the identity of Nomocracy in Islam will remain incomplete without the use of law as a source of societal reformation, and this is an objective whose achievement is inconceivable unless the court is transformed into an organ of Islamic social purposes. An exercise in abstraction in the realm of idealism, no doubt, has its definite role. However, to impart a tangible form to the preceding conclusion, a legal formulation in concrete, to serve as a framework to define the role of the jurist and to provide a desirable direction for the juristic efforts to adopt, is necessitated.

The issue of correct judicial decision in the context of judicial virtue is unavoidable. In routine understanding, simply the application of a formally valid law to the legal facts of a case is recognised as its definition. However, the controversy that exists between law and rule is more pertinent in the instance of Islamic legal system. Fulfilment of the requirements of justice according to the prescribed legal norms, and propagation of the original intentions of the Lawgiver in relation to the law, will be the constituents of such a judicial decision in Islam. Islamic legal concepts, as a characteristic of the legal system, own features which are not completely identifiable with the same concepts in other systems of law. And justice is but one such example of the legal concepts whose differentiating attributes have been outlined earlier.

In addition, importantly, judicial decisions often involve a choice between moral and other legal system-characteristic values, which is a demand upon the decisions in excess of the mere application of some single outstanding value or principle. Now, an appraisal of the Supreme Principles is demonstrative of the desirability for such an approach in a judicial decision, for the demands laid in the balancing of competing claims in respect of various principles, that is, the derivative concepts and values, are to be met in order to satisfy the integral dispensation of the Islamic Law.

The precedents for this distinctive Islamic juridical demand for the law are the fundamental Islamic Principles in a setting of the circumscribed individualisation of legal decision. As a matter of high legal import, the valuable legal doctrine of the "separation of powers," which is reflected in the judicial independence, is less than adequate in accordance with the meanings of the outlined demand. Not without establishing the "judicial balance of power," the Islamic juridical demand can be unequivocally satisfied.

Now, the understanding of a principle, viewed in the light of its opposite, is critically enhanced. The attainment of the highly valuable objective under review is not imaginable according to the dictates of the doctrine of Siasa Shariah, whereby the political authority has the power to control the jurisdiction of the courts.' In contrast, the Legal Method comprised of the Supreme Fundamental Islamic Principles has the demonstrable potential to suitably fulfil the positive Islamic demands laid upon the law.

Acceptance of the crucial proposition for the reinterpretation of law in Islam from its primary sources will rely upon the judicial vision for an auspicious denouement. The measure of such a vision will become available from the following:

(i) juristic awareness of the status of Islamic Law in the social order;

(ii) the role of law in imparting ascendancy to the social order in future;

(iii) juridical insight to read into revealed law the universal socio-legal conceptions;

(iv) the recognition of the fact that implicit in the proposition for the reinterpretation of law is the construction of an Islamic legal system *de novo;*

The Fundamentals

(v) to be inspired by the enterprising task of organizing an original legal system in the world;

(vi) a profound appreciation for the unifying role an Islamic system of law potentially has in the Muslim world;

(vii) the realisation of originality as the paradigmatic key-factor in the formation of traditional Islamic schools of law, and exemplified in the juristic endeavours of eminent Abu Hanifah; and,

(viii) an owning of the consciousness that the manner of interpretation of law and the character of legal development maintain a productive correlation.

Legal Change : In the agreeable opinion of Coulson, the attitude of detached idealism dominated Shariah Law in the past." The desirability for the purposive nature of law has already been emphasised and, in the case of Islamic Law, it is inseparably allied with the Scriptural standard of "best community," thus, setting for itself a definite social objective. In the attainment of this purpose, the law is required to cope with dual demands laid upon it.

The maintenance of balance between legal stability and social change, and the ascertainment of those "social desiderata" which are desirable as well as achievable for the law to satisfy.

In delineating the factors causative of the "rigidness" in the traditional Islamic Law, Coulson[8] mentions the ethical mould, concept of "taqlid" as blind orthodoxy in law and literal interpretation of law.

A legal formulation such as can satisfactorily incorporate the demands for the adaptability of law, obviates the causative factors underlying the stagnation of legal development, and demonstrably is founded upon principles underlying the Islamic religio-legal tenets, is suited for adoption.

The additional commendable features of this approach should include the fostering of the evolution of law through self-creative process, substantive contribution of judicial responsibility and the reorganisation of a comparable legal system suited to the Islamic genius.

The stability of the law is preserved as the new law-making is developed within a legal framework and, therefore, the process is neither uninhibited nor unguided. Obviously, then, the Islamic legal framework, essentially based upon primary Islamic sources of law and, importantly, in accord with the higher principles of modern jurisprudence, is the incontrovertible prerequisite of a contemporary legal system, and the Legal Method provides a formulation for the attainment of these ends.

The Legal Method is founded upon the doctrine of the full expression of Islamic Law in individual instances and the Supreme Principles represent the time-honoured wisdom of the Scriptures where prolific contents are conveyed in laconic form. Islamic legal history is a testimony to the vision of Shafii and the originality of Hanifah as the insubstitutable instruments of legal change, and it should become the guiding principles of any legal process that aspires to establish a contemporaneous legal system.

The prospective salient benefits ensuing from the Legal Methodology are enumerated hereunder:

(1) A systematic form is imparted to Islamic jurisprudence.

(2) Consistency, with the elimination of antinomies, in the principles of revealed law is restored.

(3) The long-standing and staunch recommendations of renowned Muslim jurists, thinkers and other legists in the reformist mould, that is, the reinterpretation of revealed Islamic Law, the reintroduction of "Ijtihad," and the reorganisation of a process of legal development find an institutionalised expression.

(4) Systematisation of the invaluable Islamic juristic principle of "Ijtihad" is an attainment, while the principle in no other way can find an exit from the mere ambit of juristic aspirations.

(5) With a demonstrable potential for the organisation of an "original" and at least comparable Islamic legal system, with evidently surpassing juridical merits, the legal methodology brings the establishment of such a legal system within the scope of realisation.

(6) Due to the interrelationship of basic significance that exists between the law and society in Islam, an original legal system, organised and developed along the parameters prescribed in the legal methodology, will exercise its causative influence upon the effecting of an ascendant social order.

JURISTIC METHOD

All modern Islamic jurists committed to legal reformation concur about the dispensing of "Taqlid," and the reintroduction of Ijtihad, described often in terms resplendent with imagery such as of door to be thrown open. This is considered necessary for the evolution of laws required for meeting new facts and situations that may emerge in the Islamic social institutions. The persistence of this appraisal over a prolonged duration, however, is not the representation of an exactly appropriate outlook.

The adoption of the legal means and the method for the utilisation of Ijtihad to its full juridical benefits in the society is the real issue. Many a time in life, the dilemmas are resolvable only by developing the correct approach which can claim the benefit of profound insight, for the definition of the attainable objective may otherwise remain an inert inference for an indefinite period. Notice-worthy, however, is the critical point that Ijtihad is not to be misconstrued as the independent exercise of juristic opinion.

The legal acumen underlying Shafii's equation of Ijtihad with "Qiyas" or analogous reasoning is comprehensible in this perspective. On the other hand, Ijtihad and Qiyas[9] are considered two essential conditions for participation in Ijma. Now, the Supreme Principles utilised in the Legal Method are viewable as the determinants of the jurisdiction for the terms of Divine Will on religio-legal aspects and, in the final analysis, are usable for the validation of the interpretation of primary sources of Islamic Law and the results of analogical reasoning.

The emphasis is to be made that the Islamic legal concept of validation, besides its reliability as the standard for the full expression of law, is a fortiori the case where the legal principles of interpretation and construction are involved. In this regard, invaluable lessons are available to be drawn from the legal precedents set in the initial period of Islamic history.

As a chronicled fact, Caliph Umar[10] and Abu Yusuf are associated with many a legal decision which, though prima facie seemed contrary to the strict letter of law, nevertheless, those were more in harmony with the underlying principles of the accessible primary source of law. With this in view, it is evident that the legal formulation, prescribed in this treatise, is a reliable expression of the juristic desire for the revitalisation of Ijtihad and, more importantly, it is adoptable as a process within the delineated framework of its application.

If this approach embodies the vital principle of optimal legal development, then, it also is decisively exclusive of any consideration of the independent expression of the juristic opinion in matters of Islamic Law. Additionally, it is also appreciable that the criterion for academic research and intellectual effort, as the suggested requisite of Ijtihad, is satisfactorily fulfilled with the implementation of the legal formulation. Appropriate definition of the various juristic principles of legal utility has been provided at other junctures during the course of this treatise. However, an abbreviated account of the fact of their incorporation in the functions of the Legal Method, founded upon the Supreme Principles, is to be furnished here. Equity is described by Aristotle in the "Ethics" as a correction of legal justice. The construction of equity as an intrinsic ethical superiority of law has also been adopted.

The fact of Islamic Law transforming the Islamic principles of beneficence, repentance and moral rectitude, through the individualisation of the dispensation of justice, in contrast from a tendency of their universalisation generally existing in law, has already been dwelt upon, and it will be an Islamic expression for the granting of formal recognition to the legal notion, already known to the latter-day social jurisprudence. Among the other juristic principles, Istihsan and Istislah are basically doctrines of equity and if the former is identified with juristic preference, then, the latter is credited to the Muslim jurist Malik for its legal applicability as benefit to the community.

This legal notion of Istislah was further markedly developed and the scope of its juristic application was extensively enlarged by Shatibi under the general designation of "Masla." And the juristic principle of "Istihsan" is in the nature of future juristic exposition and development of Islamic Law. Now due to the simple reason that the Supreme Principles are of wider and fundamental legal scope, the aforementioned juristic principles will discover evident expression through the formulated Legal Method.

The Problems

Notwithstanding the repleteness of legal literature with the usefulness of Ijma, which has been adequately dwelt upon during the earlier course of this discourse, the all-important issue of an efficient method for the utilisation of this source of law-making in the present-day is in demand of a convincing response. Ijma can be viewed as an organised form of Ijtihad; Iqbal also subscribed to this viewpoint and suggested that the only possible form Ijma can acquire in modern times is the adoption of its role by the legislative assembly. According to this suggestion, the Islamic religious doctors are considered as the "vital part" of a legislative assembly for matters related to law.

Adherence to this opinion was reflected during more contemporary times from the observation made in a legal precedent: A prerequisite for every member of a legislative assembly should be a fair amount of knowledge of law-making in Islam. The variance of academic viewpoint from reckonable socio-political realities is not the only issue that arises after a profound evaluation of the previous observations. The criteria for the merit of reason in the assignment of legal authority to Iima is another issue which is as substantive as it is of historical relevance.

The eminent Muslim jurist, Shafii, is credited with the original contribution of Ijma by extension of the principle of agreement on matters of law into a source of law-making. The most notable quotation associated with the legist's name in this respect, to reiterate, is: whatever the community of Islam has agreed upon at any time is of God!

If this juristic principle incorporates the underlying concept of consensus without the concurrent inclusion of the merit of reasons, then, an important prototypical issue, adoptable to be the augury for the consideration of far more weighty matters, whether the common political error can lay claim to Ijma, is to be seriously addressed. In the opinion of Coulson, the elected office of the Caliph as the basic article of Muslim constitutional law, is not derived from any text in the primary sources of law or analogy therefrom, but from the agreed practice of the early Muslim community.

Two points of immediate and substantive significance arise. Firstly, the issue of the source of political authority of the Caliph in Islam is to be responded. The characteristic requirements of the Islamic rule of law, the legal expression of the Quranic idea of political allegiance, and the Scriptural precept about the mutual consultation as a means to the conduct of affairs are affirmative indications concerning the consent and consensus as the requirements for the conduct of political matters.

In addition, the Quranic ideas of the vicegerency of man, collective evaluation of a nation, and the fundamental prerequisite of self-determination in the sense of individual freedom of informed choice, in matters related to religious obligations, in general, and to the participation in Islamic defensive war ("Jihad"), in particular, are no less contributory towards the legal concept of political authority in Islam.

Notice-worthy is the historic fact in this connection, the role of later Ijma in respect of the political tradition for the office of the Caliph was consonant with the political convention established during Omayyad and subsequently in Abbasid dynasties, rather than with the political prerequisite of allegiance ("baiya") for the office of Caliph, which was in practice during the early Islamic community. The inference is of significance that it was a matter of fact, and not of law in consonance with the Islamic requirements of the rule of law as alluded to before, which was sustained through the "informal" Ijma or consensus in the Islamic society. And, secondly, the much professed value of Ijma as a source of law has not resulted in its institutionalisation with the delineation of well-defined criteria for its legal authority.

The proposed Legal Method has the demonstrable advantage of compensating the shortcomings outlined in relation to Ijma. The judicial implementation of the method will equate with the satisfaction of the underlying concept of consensus or the Ijma of jurists, that is, special Ijma. However, its ratification by common Ijma will await the popularity of the Islamic legal system. But the most important requirement of the "merit of reasons" for the legal authority of Ijma is constituted by the set of Supreme Fundamental Islamic Principles as the foundations of the Legal Method. The juridical contribution of the method will repose reliance upon the approach that the conversion of a Fundamental Principle into a secondary sense will violate its universality, thereby, granting it the superseding hierarchical legal role in respect of the legal enactments.

COMPONENTS OF UNITY

The legal formulation provides the basis for the consensus concerning the definition of Islamic legal rule, and the legal conceptions in the Islamic Law. In addition, the relationship of the law to the Supreme Principles, by allowing Islamic legal scope to the individualisation of judicial decisions, will foster a community of common legal outlook. The exercise of juristic discretion will repose reliance upon the Fundamental Principles, derived from the primary sources of law, which, by establishing a framework of legal reasoning, further fortifies that outlook.

The vital judicial dimension, a constituent of the "separation of powers," in its purposeful sense, that is, the exercise of legal judgment in the arrival of individual judicial decisions, will prove facilitative. And judicial decisions, acting as legal precedents, in addition to imparting stimulus to juristic scholarship in Islamic societies, are likely to engender similar results.

The need for a formulation to furnish a wide basis for the uniformity of laws in Islamic countries has been latent since the legal "sectarianism" that surfaced consequent to the various schools of law. And the fact that the blind legal orthodoxy or "taqlid," a juristic dogma which is exclusive of "Ijtihad," stymied the legal development in Islam further, is citable as its testimony. The role of "Ijma" assignable to the Islamic legislative assemblies, as envisaged by some renowned Islamic legists and allusion to this effect has been made in the preceding sections, is also identified with a drawback in the performance of that function by the assemblies independently of each other. This had led to the justifiable apprehension that the resulting variations in Ijma will undermine the Islamic unity. In contrast, the Legal Method establishes a genuine basis due to the available criteria for the foundation of Ijma, and relocates it to the juristic realm where it essentially belongs according to its definition.

This uniformity of approach in relation to Ijma, insofar as the justifiable criteria of its application and the source of its exercise-the consensus of the learnedare concerned, can be an antecedent of unity in different Muslim societies. As an impact of the Legal Method upon the scope of law-making and adaptability of law, the influence of the legal system upon other parallel social systems and institutions will be positively enhanced. This becomes a determinant factor in allowing a primal role to the legal system in the social order.

The crucial issue of the adaptability of law finds a judicious response in the legal formulation, which allows accommodation to the vital aspects of "stability" and "change," and reconciles the dimensions of Faith and law as indispensable requirements for the reconstitution of Islamic legal system. This establishing of a set role for law in independent societies will improve Islamic unity.

The legal system will be comparable with other leading systems of law in the world. The verification of this assertion is demonstrable on theoretical grounds and it is the onus of this discourse. As a matter of fact, the envisaged Islamic legal system will consist of certain salient legal features ensuing from the concept of law, which bestow upon it a relative superior merit.

The operative ideals of a genuine Islamic society are to find legal expression towards the organisation of Islamic Nomocracy. The legal formulation entails an approach which guides towards a judicial direction, nearly in diametric opposition compared with that made available by the constitutional requirements in some Muslim countries.

In the latter instance, the mere demand of the law not to be repugnant to the Islamic injunctions results in the orientation of law to the past, in the sense of the law being incapable of facing to the future, and the reductionistic definition of law whereby it is a corpus of rules, hence, imputing to the legal system an artless form.

From the foregone, the conclusion of an insufficient legal development is available. The serious dual drawbacks of this outcome are the law not being contributory to the formation of an ascendant Islamic legal system, and the law tending to impart the characteristics of a "closed society." The latter drawback is indicative of the law resembling with a municipal setup, wherein individual interests are suppressed by the society. In contrast, the Legal Method embodies the principles of self-sustaining legal creativity, which becomes a precursor of the reconstitution of the legal system. The law no longer becomes so much a process of external imposition, as it represents the internal development from within the law *per se.*

And the individualisation of legal decisions, as a pronounced feature of the emphasis upon individual interests in the law, will serve both as a distinguishing juridical characteristic of the new era of Islamic legal system, and the vital means for the organisation of an "open society."

These and other interrelated social and legal objectives, attainable with the application of the Legal Method, represent the uniformity of attributes associated with an ascendant social order, which will acquire the new basis for Islamic unity.

In essence, the continuous social movement from being to becoming in the realm of law, caused with the application of the Legal Method, has the convincing constituents of an ascendant society, with its potential of lending vehement impetus to the concept and reality of Islamic unity.

References

1. *A great scholar and thinker.*
2. *Obedience, copy, imitation.*
3. *Oneness of Allah (there is no god share Allah)*
4. *A famous jurist.*
5. *A great thinker and philosophic.*
6. *A Greek genius and philosopher of his time.*
7. *An Islamic jurist.*
8. *A renowned thinker and philosopher of Islamic history.*
9. *Inference which is used in deriving ruling.*
10. *Second most important Caliph about whom once Prophet (Pbuh) said that if there were any Prophets after him, Umar would have been.*

3

QURAN, THE ORIGINAL SOURCE

It must be admitted on all hands that the Quran occupies a supreme position among the great religious books of the world and has exercised a remarkable influence on the thoughts and philosophy of the generations of the people. It deserves the highest adoration for its clarity of conception of the Omnipotent and Omniscient Allah in respect of the attributes of Power, Knowledge, Universal Providence, Monotheism (Tauhid) and the Transcendence of creativity.

Laura Veccia Varlieri in his book "*Apoligie de L'Islamisme*" expresses rightly: "The proof of the Divinity of the Quran is that it has been preserved intact through the ages since the time of its Revelation till the present day....Read and re-read by the Muslim world, this book does not rouse in the faithful any weariness, it rather, through repetition, is more loved every day. It gives use to a profound feeling of awe and respect in the one who reads it or listens to it.

NON-MATERIAL ASPECT

Dr. Hartwig Hiraschfold[1] comments reasonably; "We must not be surprised to find the Quran the fountainhead of the sciences. Every subject connected with heaven or earth, human life, commerce and various trades are occasionally touched upon, and this gave rise to the production of numerous monographs forming commentaries on parts of the Holy Book. In this way the Quran was responsible for great discussions, and to it was indirectly due the marvellous development of all branches of science in the Muslim World. This again not only affected the

Arabs, but also induced Jewish philosophers to treat metaphysical and religious questions after Arab Methods. Finally, the way in which Christian Scholasticism was fertilised by Arabian theosophy need not be further discussed.

> "Spiritual activity once aroused within Islamic bounds was not confined to theological speculations alone. Acquaintance with the philosophical, astronomical and medical writings of the Greeks led to the pursuance of these studies. In the descriptive revelations Muhammad (SAW) repeatedly calls attention to the movement of the heavenly bodies, as parts of the miracles of Allah forced into the service of man and therefore not to be worshipped. How successfully Muslim people of all races pursued the study of astronomy is shown by the fact that for centuries they were its principal supporters. Even now many Arabic names of stars and technical terms are in use. Medieval astronomers in Europe were pupils of the Arabs."

> "In the same manner the Quran gave an impetus to medical studies, and recommended the contemplation and study of Nature in general."

It has, therefore, now become imperative to have a complete glimpse of the collection and arrangement of the Quran as guided and directed by the Prophet of Islam. It cannot be denied that during the Four Caliphs[2] (Khulafa-e-Rashideen) no sciences grew and developed but the seeds of Islamic sciences were sown with the collection of the Quran and the preservation in memory of the Hadith (Traditions).

The Glorious Quran was not revealed as a whole but gradually and in parts. The revelation continued for 23 years, according to the demand of the conditions from the advent of Islam to the death of the Prophet Muhammad (SAW).

Some were revealed in Mecca and some in Medina. All the verses and chapters revealed from time to time during the life of Prophet were written down by the companions in the order in which the Prophet personally directed them to be inserted. The practice with the Prophet was that whenever a verse or a chapter was revealed, a double process was adopted to preserve it. There were companions always at hand who committed to writing; and also there were those who committed to memory. Now the verses (Ayat) or chapters (Surahs) were written down on the writing materials available in those days. They comprised vellum or parchment, wide thin bones, ribs, leafless palm trees, thin and white stones, woods of the saddle.

The Prophet died in 11 A.H. (632 AD) and the Glorious Quran was either collected in the book form (as mentioned above) or was preserved in the memory of the people, and those who learnt it by heart were called Qurras[3].

The Prophet recited various chapters in his daily prayers. The order and arrangement was all done under his own direction in consonance with relevance of chapters; and Allama Suyuti thinks that it is Taufiqi *i.e.*, according to the Divine Commandment.

Among those who showed great interest in the collection of the Quran in the days of the Prophet were Ali Ibn Abi Talib[4], Saad Ibn Ubaid[5], Abu Dardah[6], Maadh Ibn Jabal[7], Zaid Ibn Thabit[8], Ubay Ibn Kaab[9] and others. When Abu Bakr became Caliph (Khalifah) and the people of jaziratul Arab apostatised Islam, an expedition was sent against Musailama, the Imposter. In this war a large number of the companions were killed and specially in the battle of Yamamah where the number of martyrs was about 1200 of whom 500 were Qurra (*i.e.,* reciters) those who had learnt the Quran by heart.

This news reached the people of Medina and they were considerably perturbed, particularly 'Umar ibn al Khattab, one of the pillars of Islam. He came and advised Abu Bakr to collect the Quran, lest he should lose something great at the demise of his people. Abu Bakr paused to think and said, "how can I do a thing which has not been done by the Prophet and he has not enjoined it on us." Umar continued his discussion until Abu Bakr was convinced about its collection. He then appointed a commission under Zaid ibn Thabit who was the chief companions of the Prophet to write down the whole text in book form. He collected what was preserved with the companions. He often found the surahs written twice, thrice or more. He did not find different versions of the Surah Taubah. He found it only in one copy which was with Abu Khazumah Ansari[10].

He collected from these preservations and the memories of the people, and carefully handed it over to Abu Bakr (in the book form). Hadrat Umar was Hafiz. He in association with Zaid received all the Ayat and Surahs, and after confirming them by two witnesses accepted them. The Book was preserved with him till he died in 13 A.H. (634 AD) When Umar became Caliph he kept it with him till 'Uthman succeeded him in 24 A.H. (644 A.D.) It then was handed down to his (Umar's) daughter Hafsah, the wife of the Prophet.

Caliph Umar during his regime introduced the teaching and recitation of the Quran. He appointed teachers and Qurra with emoluments in his conquered countries. He deputed Abu Sufyan to travel in the villages and inspect the people in the reading of the Quran. Those who could not read the Quran were punished. The five Companions who were great reciters, *viz.* Maadh ibn Jabal[11], Ibadah ibn Samit[12], Ubay ibn Kaab[13], Abu Ayyub[14], Abu Darda[15], were called to teach the Quran to the people of Syria. The two were exempted on the ground of ill health and the other three: 'Ibadah ibn Samit, Maadh ibn Jabal and Abu Darda, accepted readily. First they went to Hims. When teaching was introduced 'Ibadah settled down there. Abu Darda then went to Damascus and Madah ibn Jabal to Jerusalem. Umar gave scholarships to the students of the Quran. Thousands of reciters were produced. Only under Sad ibn Waqqas there were 300 reciters (Huffaz).

In the days of 'Uthman the banner of conquest spread far and wide and the Muslims spread in Egypt, Syria, Iraq, Iran and Africa. Among them were the reciters of the Quran who possessed the text of the Book and they compiled in the particular manner. The people of Egypt relied upon those reciters who lived there. The people of Damascus and Hims learned from Miqdad ibn Aswad and the people of Kufa from Ibn Masud, the people of Basra from Abu Musa al-Ashari. The great interest exhibited by the reciters in its preservation and collection were not safe from the divergence in the style of reading some of the verses.

During this time it so happened that Hudhaifa bin Yaman who was one of those who witnessed the war of Armenia and Azerbaijan observed (during his travels) the divergence in the reading of certain verses and heard some of them saying that "My reading is better than yours." When he returned to Medina he informed Caliph 'Uthman about this and apprised him of the dangerous consequences if no action was taken.

> "You have found out the nation," said Hadrat 'Uthman, "before the occurrence of difference in the book like the Jews and the Christians." Uthman sent a man to Hafsah with this message, "Please send me the Book, we will transcribe with it, then return it to you."

She complied with his request. Hadrat Uthman then appointed a new commission under Zaid ibn Thabit, Abdullah ibn Zubayr, Said ibn al 'As and Abdur Rahman ibn Harith b. Hisham and ordered them to transcribe the copy and seek the help in its reading of the reciters. He said to them, "If you find any difference of opinion in any matter write down in the dialect of the Quraish because it was revealed in their language." They set to this work in 30 A.H. and prepared seven copies of the Book. Uthman sent them to five cities — Mecca, Yemen, Basra, Kufa and Syria. The two Books remained in Medina —one for the people (citizens) and one for his personal use. This copy was called the "Imam." He then ordered that all books previously written be collected and rolled up as tattered clothes.

Its Style : The Quran is the finest and sublime masterpiece of literature. The outstanding poets of the Jahiliya who prided themselves on the excellence of their poetry failed to produce a single Surah like the Quran's when challenged to do so. Its dynamism and perfection of harmony in thought and diction elevates it to the acme of expression beyond the reach of human mind.

John Penrice in his preface to the Dictionary and Glossary of the Quran rightly expresses: "It is not to be expected that all the transcendent excellencies and miraculous beauties discovered in the Quran should immediately unveil themselves to our cold and unsympathetic gaze; beauties there are many and great; ideas highly poetical and clothed in rich and appropriate language, which not unfrequently rises to a sublimity far beyond the reach of any translation."

The Quran is replete with the qualities of sound and eloquence, rhetoric and repetition, assonance, alliteration, onomatopoeia, rhyme, cadences and deliberateness. The rhythms are maintained throughout, changing their timbre from serious to sonorous, thundering to mellifluous according to the theme, switching from heavy prose to light wings of sublime verse. Thus the transcendental excellencies of diction and style, cadences and rhythms stand supreme and matchless. There are delicate similies and metaphors, brevity and details and forceful arguments which are beyond the bounds of human power. The opponents and rivals are silenced and spellbound. Its style varies according to the purpose and subject matter. The Mecci surahs (86 in number) are short, incisive, full of cadeness, excellent and superb parables (or similitudes) and move the heart. It comprises invitation to monotheism (Tauhid) by glad tidings and wraths, by eloquent exhortations and sermons and irrefutable arguments. The Medini surahs (numbering 28) are long with rhythmic beauty, clear in guidance, perspicuous in details, appealing to reason and mind. It consists of unambiguous laws, commands and prohibitions and resplendent ethics and codes of life.

Etymology of the Quran : The Quran is known as al-Kitab (the collection) because it contains all kinds of learning and past stories in the best possible way.

There are various opinions regarding its derivation:

(a) Al-Shafai thinks it proper noun, non-derivative peculiar to the Quran and ghair mahmuz (not marked with the sign hamza).

(b) Baihaqi thinks it unmarked with the sign hamza and not derived from Qirait.

(c) Others including al-Ashari think it is derived from Karant- al Shai-o-bil Shaie. The Quran is called so because its verses, words and letters are written together.

(d) Al-Farra' thinks its derivation from qarain because some of its verses verify others and some of them are similar in mode and order.

(e) Some are of opinion that is marked with the sign hamza but Hajjaj has refuted this view and says that hamza has dropped out for Takhfif (facility) and pronunciation).

Al-Ashri and al-Farra think that the letter *nun* of the word Quran is original and real.

There are two schools of thought who hold it mahmuz (marked with the sign hamza). One thinks it as masdar (verbal noun) on the measure of foelan like rujhan, ghufran but in the sense of ismmaful (passive participle). The others hold the view that it is adjective on the measure of foelan from al-qarra' literary al-jama'(540). They say: Quran al Mae fil Hauz, as the surahs are collected therein.

DIFFERENT NAMES OF QURAN

Al-Quran is the name of the Divine Book revealed to Muhammad (S.A.W.), and it literally signifies," a widely read book." Really it is the most widely read book in the world. The Book mentions other names for itself, for example, Al-Kitab[16] (the Book), Al-Furqan[17] (the criterion of Truth and Falsehood), Al-Hakim[18] (full of wisdom), Al-Huda[19] (the guidance), Al-Shifa[20] (the Healing), Al-Zikr[21] (the Reminder), Al-Rahmat[22] (the Mercy), Al-Khair[23] (the Benevolent), Al-Ruh[24] (the Spirit or Life), Al-Bayan[25] (Explanation), Al-Qayyim[26] (Upholding of the Truth), Al-Nur[27] (the Light), Al-Haqq[28] (the Truth), Al-Mubarak[29] (the Blessed), Al-Burhan[30] (the Argument) and Habl-ullah[31] (Covenant of Allah).

Its most popular epithets are Kitabullah (the Book of God), Al-Mubin (the Book of Clear Record), Al-Majeed (the Glorious), Al-Karim (the Bounteous) and Ummul Kitab, the Mother of the Book. It came from heaven and were taken from a well-guarded Tablet *i.e.* Lauh-e-Mahfuz[32]— Surah 85: 21-21.

The Quran was revealed with the main object of educating and guiding the mankind. Its teachings were to be disseminated to the widest circle of people. Thus a clear direction was given to the Prophet: "Recite that which hath been inspired in thee of the Scripture" so that "thou mayest explain unto them that wherein they differ, and (as) a guidance and mercy for a people who believe."

Who can deny that the Quran exalted the use of Pen as a key to the development of new knowledge: "Read: And thy Lord is the Most Bounteous, Who teacheth by the Pen. Teacheth man that which he knew not." The Pen-cum-Writing process being an important developmental stage in the intellectual history of mankind, the Quran called it to witness while underlining further guidance for man: "By the Pen and that which they write therewith."

Pen as the most effective instrument for writing and recording knowledge, had set a new stage of achievement in man's unique ability to record his thoughts and experiences, to transmit and communicate them to others far and near conveniently, and to preserve them for future from generation to generation.

Quran, the Original Source

'Book' being the manifestation of the Pen-cum-writing process, the Quran's predominant use of the term 'Book' was in consonance with the dawn of new civilisation. The word 'Book' as such was almost unknown before.

There is undoubtedly coherence in the Quran among various parts which are completely in conformity with the logic of necessity and principles of eloquence. The apportionment of the parts is consistent for the addressing and for clear understanding. Maurice Bucaille, the French scientist and scholar in his small booklet, "The Quran and Modern Science," rightly remarks:

> "The slightest alteration to the text would automatically have destroyed the remarkable coherence which is characteristic of them, and have prevented us from establishing their conformity with modern knowledge."

The Prophet has left a permanent legacy to the world wherein no havoc of time has yet been able for centuries to make the slightest conceivable alteration and which is handed down from generation to generation ad verbatim.

SIGNS OF PUNCTUATION

It is astonishing and most surprising that the punctuation marks have been followed in the Quran centuries before the Western civilisation adopted it. In classical Europe, Greek had practically no punctuation marks. Later Latin had one or two rudimentary ones. In modern Europe they developed with printing. Aldus Manutius[33] (16th century) was the firs to work out a regular system.

The most outstanding linguist and grammarian Abul Asad Duali[34] (7th century) introduced vowel signs (I'rab) of Fatha, Kasra, dhammah and jazma on the Qurani words on the advice of the fourth caliph, Hadrat Ali, or Ziyad ibn Sufyan. Another prominent scholar, Khalil ibn Ahmad (7th century AD) provided Tashdid and Hamza to the verses and Nasar bin Asim[35], a renowned scholar devoted his time to marking dots (Nuqta) on the Quranic words.

It seems necessary to give details of the vowel signs:

1. *Fatha*, a small diagonal stroke over a consonant.

2. *Kasra*, a small diagonal stroke under the consonant.

3. *Dhamma*, a small above a consonant.

4. *Jazma* or Sukun, the sign indicating the absence of a vowel is written above a consonant.

5. *Tanween Nunation:* The above mentioned vowel signs written double are called tanween.

6. *Tashdid:* When a consonant occurs twice without a vowel sound between, it is written once only and the sign Tashdid is placed over.

7. Hamza is generally written above, but sometimes under also, and independently as well.

8. *Madda* really the second alif written horizontally above, which is pronounced a *i.e.*

The division of the Surah into sections is shown in all Arabic texts. These are logical divisions according to the meaning. The word translated "Section" is in Arabic Ruku. The end of a Ruku is shown in Arabic by 'Ain.

It will not be out of place to mention the opinions of some distinguished Western scholars and thinkers about the divinity of the Quran." F.F. Arbuihnot in his "Construction of the Bible and the Quran writes:

"From the literary point of view, the Quran is regarded as a specimen of the purest Arabic, written in half poetry and half prose. It has been said that in some cases grammarians have adopted their rules to agree with certain phrases and expressions used in it, and though several attempts have been made to produce a work equal to it as far as elegant writing is concerned none has a yet succeeded."

Harry Gaylord Dorman[36] in book, "*Towards Understanding Islam*", comments:

"It (Quran) is a literal revelation of God, dictated to Muhammad by Gabriel, perfect in every letter. It is an ever-present miracle witnessing to itself and to Muhammad, the Prophet of God. Its miraculous quality resides partly in its style, so perfect and lofty that neither men nor jinn could produce a single chapter to compare with its briefest chapter, and partly in its content of teachings, prophesies about the future, and amazingly accurate information such as illiterate Muhammad could never have gathered of his own accord."

Paul Casanova Opines : "Whenever Muhammad was asked a miracle, as a proof of authenticity of mission, he quoted the composition of the Quran and its incomparable excellence as a proof of its Divine origin. And, in fact, even for those who are non-Muslims nothing is more marvellous than its language which with such apprehensible plentitude and a grasping sonority with its simple audition ravished with admiration those primitive peoples so fond of eloquence. The ampleness of its syllables with a grandios cadence and with a remarkable rhythm have been of such movement in the conversion of the most hostile and the most sceptic."

Prof. A.G. Arberry has very correctly remarked: "Bad translation is not the

Quran, the Original Source

whole story by any means. In fact the Quran has not been unlucky in its English translators; Sale and Palmer were talented writers ....No, the fault lies not so much in the manner of translation as in the manner of reading the translations. The root of the trouble is that the ordinary reader, and for that matter the extraordinary reader as well, has not been sufficiently advised how to read the Quran.

In the first place, the Western reader must get rid of the assumption that the Holy Quran is more or less like the Old Testament. The misapprehension is natural enough, when the first casual glance picks out the names of Adam, Abraham, Moses, David, Soloman, Jonah, Joseph, Jacob the Biblical style of the popular translations does not furnish exactly a corrective.

Misled by these early impressions, the reader makes the fatal mistake of trying to take it too much at once; he opens at a likely place, the beginning of a Surah, and is lulled into suspicion by the familiar layout of chapter and verse; he finishes his first Surah and goes on to several more; he is bewildered by the rapid and seemingly illogical changes of subject, and he quickly wearies of the frequent repetitions of themes and formulas, he misses the homely straightforwardness of Kings or Samuel, the sustained eloquence of the Psalms or Isaiah.

Having no clue to the Quran's own excellences he compared it unfavourably with what he has known since childhood, and is now ready to concur with Carlyle.

The Quran, like the poetry which it resembles in so many ways, is best sampled a little at a time; and that little deserves and needs meditation. He (the reader) will become gradually familiar with the Quran's claim to be a confirmation of earlier Scriptures. He will observe how the Quran assumes a knowledge of the contents of those scriptures, and only expands the individual narratives into something like connected stories. He now follows step by step the gradual unfolding of the full prophetic power; and when comes to the polemic and the legislation he is readier to receive and understand them. "He, the uninitiated inquirer, however, strenuous and sincere his purpose, will always be denied participation in the believer's joy because he is screened from it by the double veil of a printed page and a foreign idiom. Yes, a foreign idiom, for the Quran is God's revelation in Arabic, and the emotive and evocative qualities of the original disappear almost totally in the skilfullest translation.

"When appreciation rests upon these foundations, the charges of wearisome repetition and jumbled confusion become meaningless. Truth cannot be dimmed by being frequently stated, but only gains in clarity and convincingness at every repetition, and where all is true, inconsequence and incomprehensibility are not felt to arise."

THEORIES OF QURAN

It is an axiomatic truth that man is beset with innumerable riddles of life but finds it hard to extricate himself from such entanglements. It is the lack of knowledge and dormant consciousness that preclude his understanding. Sometimes when he enjoys comfort and ease suddenly and to his surprise some calamity upsets all his calculations' and his future achievements are completely demolished. It is imperative to scientifically ponder and find out the why and wherefore of such abnormal events in order to make him aware and guide him on the true path of happiness.

Science will not guide him as the scientists believe that everything in the material world runs on pre-ordained lines, events being already pre-ordained, therefore it must be the same with human affairs. If he needs a light to guide him out of the intricacies of life, it is only the Quran that will enlighten him. It shows him an open path (Minhaj) and saves him from groping in darkness. Misfortunes attack him in battalions when he is most unaware.

But the Divine Book should enable him to tackle them when they come; as man has not yet propounded any philosophy to solve such problems. There is a misunderstanding created by the Orientalists in respect of Qismat—an Arabic word to convey the idea of predestination —though its literal meaning is 'division' or 'distribution.' A good number of people are under this impression that good and evil are prearranged entities, and that they have already been allotted by Allah the Creator, Evolver and Sustainer of all the worlds, amongst the people of the world.

Therefore, nothing can be changed in their course of life by human endeavour and they are subservient to the Fate. There is no such Divine ordinance, as no Prophet ever taught a tenet so dastardly. There is, however, a similar doctrine in the Church Creed, but it is not the teachings of Jesus. It is since the days of saint Athanasius (293-373AD) that the doctrine of predestination has been laid down in all Christian Creed as an article of faith. It has taken a practical shape in every Christian home at the births of babies still born, or who die before they can be baptised.

The Quran gives us a fresh direction through which we can tide over all difficulties and mishaps The Quran ordains that man is under the governance of Law, which are unchangeable and admit of no infringement. There breach is sin which entails penalty. Respect and obedience of law is a must if we want to be immune from complexities.

The laws of causation and Requital are complementary. We must know that events occur under a course prescribed by Allah, and everything has got its cause, as a result of which it inevitably appears. Similarly no action remains without its requital under Divine Decree. God, has therefore described as the cause of all things. We create circumstances, that develop under Divine Ordinance, to produce a result. We touch the cord and the instrument begins to sound automatically in accordance with His Laws.

We often commit wrong and think we would escape the consequences. The Quran clearly says that we are under the eye of a Supervisor, Who reads all that is bidden in the innermost recesses of our hearts and knows everything that is concealed. "Hide not testimony. He who hideth it, verily his heart is sinful. Allah is Aware of what ye do." As to the consequences, we are warned that these must inevitably ensue under the working laws concerned. The Quran expresses this with clarity:

> "Allah tasketh not a soul beyond his scope. For it (is only) that which it hath earned, and against it (only) that which it hath deserved. Our Lord! condemn us not if we forget, or miss the mark! Our Lord! Lay not on us such a burden as Thou didst lay on those before us! Our Lord! Impose not on us that which we have not the strength to bear! Pardon us, absolve us and have mercy on us."

> "Whosoever goeth right, it is only for (the good of) his own soul that he goeth right, and whosoever erreth, erreth only to its hurt. No laden soul can bear another's Load. We never punish until we have sent a messenger."

God has created many things which work under different measures and in different ways to serve our purpose. But if we do not follow the fixed Divine Law, it may result in great calamity. These measures should be followed as enjoined by Divine will. In the Quranic words they are termed as "Bounds of God", and whoever transgresses them are liable to punishment. It is, therefore necessary to be fully conversant with these bounds. The Quran delineates three ways to acquire them.

1. The first way is through observation. We have been given all possible means of information; we possess various senses and we have been advised to use them. The Quran says "Thus We arranged. How excellent is Our arranging."

2. We must not behave like animals in the use of our eyes and ears, but we must make scientific and penetrating deductions and inferences from the knowledge we receive, otherwise through ignorance we shall fall into a terrible misfortune.

The Quran speaks of such people: "Already have We urged unto hell many of the jinn and humankind, having hearts wherewith they understand not, and having eyes wherewith they see not, and having ears wherewith they hear not. These are as the cattle—nay, but they are worse! These are the neglectful.

3. We should not forget that there are various things which require minute observation which is beyond the capacity of every individual, and consequence take a longer period of time. The patience in some cases is lost and thus the value of moral laws are disregarded. In such dire circumstances, the revelation from God enlightens us on these crisis as the Quran states: This is a scripture which We have revealed unto thee (Muhammad) that thereby thou mayst bring forth mankind from darkness unto light, by the permission of their Lord, unto the path of the Mighty, the Owner of Praise."

Ups and downs of life occur for our guidance and for teaching us a lesson for our future actions. The mind has to recreate and rethink on currents and crosscurrents of life and plan the life on the Divine ordinances of Commands (Amr) and Prohibitions (Nahy)[37]. The Divine Book styles Him as the "Owner of Requitals." He may award punishment to an offender or He may remit it, but He never makes an arbitrary use of His direction. The three redeeming factors which invite His forgiveness are man's forgetfulness, his mistakes and his inability to meet the requirements of the case. Every case is decided on its own merits and God deals graciously with cases which deserve His consideration. When people are immersed in sin and crime, punishment becomes inevitable and is meted out in proportion to measure of evil done.

CONCEPTS OF FREE WILL

Free will is one of the most precious gifts granted to human beings by the Almighty. No other creature in the world besides man has been blessed with freedom of action. Other creatures live and work like machines. But man is His vicegerent and endowed with reason and discretion (Furqan) to discern between good and bad, right and wrong, evil and virtue. He had been endowed with three sterling qualities and talents.

1. He had been given all necessary knowledge and information and instructed how to attain it so that it may guide mankind in the exercise of right judgement.

2. There is no interference on anybody's action. Every one is allowed to pursue the course which he chooses for himself. Equal facilities are given

to pious and evil-doer in this respect and Quran expresses thus: "Each do We supply, both these and those, from the bounty of thy Lord. And the bounty of thy Lord can ever be walled up."

Men choose whatever course they like. They achieve what they exert, whether it is right or wrong. They enjoy fully all amenities of life which make them forgetful of actual situation. They continue in their sinful actions, until the Law of Recompense moves and they are brought to ruin.

3. Chastisement is absolutely necessary as a disciplinary measure. The doer must be punished and suffer the consequences of wrong judgement and should realise the effects of wrong discretion. He becomes dumb and deaf and blind for the purpose of guidance. The words of advice fall on him as though on deaf ears. The Quran speaks about those who sin consistently over a long period: "Their likeness is as the likeness of one who kindeth fire, and when it sheddeth its light around him Allah taketh away their light and leaveth them in darkness, where they cannot see."

Dr. Shah Muhammad Sulaiman[38], an eminent lawyer and scientist of repute, expresses his opinion thus: "A clear distinction exists between natural phenomena and human actions. All Natural Laws are unchangeable and admit of no infringement. The Law of causation works inexorably. A natural event is the inevitable result of a cause, but freewill has been granted to every human being, who possess a certain amount of freedom of action. He has the option of taking the right, or wrong course, for which there is no compulsion on him.

It is for him to sleet to adopt either. God has set all human brings on the right path and then left them to their discretion of course, there are restrictions and limitations placed by the environments in which a man is placed. In that sense there is a partial restraint on his physical actions, but there never is an absolute compulsion for committing any sinful act which depends mainly on his volition.

In the words of "Shams-e-Bazigha" of Mullah Mahmud of Jaunpur: "Man has determined freedom and constrained volition. But the Quran has made it perfectly clear that we all are under the eye of the Omniscient God, Who sees everything that may be hidden to human eyes, or even concealed in the inner most recesses of our minds. He foresees the entire future, and His Prescience as to what will happen involves no interference with human volition, as knowledge of the future does not imply any compulsion or forced action."

In order to understand the "Will of God" and "Divine Decrees" it seems imperative to turn to the life of the Prophet Muhammad (SAW) and seek an answer, as Prof. Ardaser Sorabjee N. Wadia has with clarity attempted to deal with the charge of Fatalism against Islam in his "Message of Muhammad":

"If it were so, it is obvious that nowhere would we, or ought we to find a better exemplification of this creed of Fatalism than in the life and activities of one who originated and propounded it namely, of Muhammad (SAW) himself. Yet, what do we find in the recorded events of Muhammad's (SAW) life? A buoyant childhood; an active boyhood; an enterprising period of youth, during which he took part in two commercial ventures necessitating long wearisome journeys of months though the dreary, scorching deserts, a restless manhood given wholly to thinking out the deepest problems of life and destiny, involving an endless travail of the soul and a protracted middle-age which commenced in comparative calm and ended in perhaps the most strenuous period of his life made up of battles, sieges and expeditious."

"Such a long and vigorous career, crossed and re-crossed by the varied moods and tricks of fortune, does not look like one given to mere passive acceptance of things as they are or to sheer indolent acquiescence in events as they happen, which Fatalism rightly so called, presupposes and enforces. Rather, it has the appearances of a career which believes in actively and courageously working out solely and remaining absolutely resigned to the inscrutable will of God."

REALITY OF A MUSLIM

Islam is a religion that is essentially rationalistic in the widest sense of the term. Considered etymologically and historically, therefore its rise is remarkable and most amazing in the annals of human history. It miraculously spread its light within a century over half the earth, shattering powerful empires and remoulding the souls of races, reconstructing and revitalising world of Islam. This surge of religion (Deen) was made possible by the revibrating spirit of self-consciousness, strong Faith (Iman), Submission to Divine Will (Itaat) and Self-Control (Zabt-e-Nafs).

The idea of "Thee alone We worship," lays the foundation of individual consciousness and the unique part man has to play in this universe. With this impregnable rock of Faith and submission to Divine Will the individual marches forward and judges to himself the actions of right and wrong, good and bad. It makes him bold and courageous to carve out his own personality and become his own architect in which transcendent idealism, indomitable courage, the highest sense of justice (Adl) and a dignified attitude of Faqr (discipline of body and mind) dominate.

With Faith and submission to Divine Will right actions follow, for right actions are the outcome of right thinking and right ideas. Endowed with all the qualities of a Believer or man of God (Banda-e-Haq) the man pays no heed to worldly fears save that of Allah and becomes quite at home with the essence of Tauhid (Monotheism), which in practice consists of equality, solidarity, freedom and justice. The inculcation of these virtues (Iman and Itaat) endow the person, individually and collectively to rise to higher levels of human character and achieve wonders. Allama Iqbal portrays the character and personality of a true Momin in Bal-e-Jabriel.

> The hand of the Momin is the hand of Allah
>
> Dominant, resourceful, creative, ensuring success,
>
> Born of clay, he has the nature of light,
>
> A create with the attributes of the Creator,
>
> His Heart is different to the riches of the two words;
>
> His desires are few, but his purposes are great;
>
> His ways are graceful, his glance fascinating,
>
> He is soft of speech but warm in his quest,
>
> In war as in peace his heart and mind are pure.

In another poem he portrays the character thus:

> He is a flashing sword against untruth.
>
> And a protecting shield for Truth;
>
> His affirmation and negation,
>
> Are the criteria for good and Evil,
>
> Great is his forgiveness, his justice, his generosity and his grace,
>
> Even in anger he knows how to be kind.

The Mard-i-Momin is also fully armed with courage, tolerance and Faqr or Istighna besides Faith, submission to Divine Will and self-discipline. And he emerges out as "God's Vicegerent" who identifies his will with Divine Purpose.

Courage alone cannot give strength to an individual. Tolerance also plays an important role and is an essential constituent of man's high character. Others views and manners are to be respected if the personality of a Momin has to be developed to the highest extent. In Javed Namah, Allama Iqbal[39] clearly emphasised:

> "What is humanity? Respect for man!
>
> Learn to understand the dignity of man,
>
> The man of Love learns the ways of God
>
> And is benevolent alike to the believer and the unbeliever."

In order to emerge as an ideal or perfect man, the individual has to fortify himself with the remarkable quality of Istighna, which implies the presentation of an attitude of detachment and superiority to his worldly possessions to avoid enslavement to them and use them for productive purposes to alleviate the miseries and hardships of the suffering humanity.

A God-fearing and righteous man wields his Faqr or Istighna as a shield to protect himself from becoming contaminated by the corruptions and allurements which surround him at every stage of life. This shield of Faqr becomes a fountain of unimpeachable idealism and endeavour to shun luxury and glamour and inculcate a right intellectual and emotional tone in the individual, as Allama Iqbal expresses:

> Even if you belong to the lords of the Earth,
>
> Do not forego the grace of Faqr,
>
> Many a man who understands, truth and possesses vision,
>
> Becomes corrupted by an excess of riches;
>
> The excess of riches steals compassion from the heart;
>
> And substitutes pride of humility.

There is no denying that right action is the real source of life and "Ego." Intellect creates understanding and perception, but purposive and creative activity revitalises and transforms the forces of environment. It is through the happy blending of Intellect and Action that man ascends to higher levels of dignity and refinement.

Man is the noblest creation in the universe and is the Vicegerent of Allah. Ibn Arabi and Sheikh Abdul Karim al-gili, in his book "Perfect Man" has expounded the concept of "Insan-i- Kamil" and expressed that man is himself a world and is the mirror of God. Man's personality is the outward prototype of God and is the connecting link between God and nature.

Man performs a most significant role in this dual task and therefore the real purpose of creation of this universe is the "Perfect man", who is a reflection of the attributes of God and the personality of Prophet Muhammad (SAW); we find the Ideal man or the Perfect Man, who slakes his thirst through the Divine Love and Intuition and direct revelation.

The Prophet of Islam has rightly said: (1) "Show kindness, and kindness will be shown to you; forgive, and you will be forgiven." (2) "They will not obtain the mercy of God in whose hearts there is no feeling of kindness for others." (3) "God will have mercy upon them that are merciful. Treat Kindly the dwellers of the earth, He who dwells in the heavens will treat you kindly."

Affability, self-restraint and the ability to control one's temper and overlook the disagreeable things are the fine moral qualities held in the estimation of God. Allah showers His blessings to such people: "Those who spend (of that which Allah hath given them) in ease and in adversity, those who control their wrath and are forgiving towards mankind; Allah loveth the good."

Fulfilling the pledges has been greatly impressed by the Quran for all believers: "And fulfil every engagement, for every engagement will be enquired into (on the Day of Reckoning)." There is a Hadith also: "He who does not fulfil promises made by him, has no share in the faith." Further the Quran enjoins: "God commandeth you that ye restore deposits to their owners."

Steadfastness and fortitude have been acclaimed as extremely noble qualities of a true Momin. The Quran has assured them that they are highly held in the eye of God. There are several verses which clearly speak of it: "Allah loveth those who are the steadfast. "Verily Allah is with the steadfast."

With all the virtues mentioned above, the individuals and nations tread on the path of unity — which are conducive to the interest of the Muslim Ummah. Unity on the national and international scales will bless with social, economic, cultural and political advancement, and usher in an era of scientific and technological developments.

According to Al-Quran the true Believers will be successful, who are humble in their prayers, who shun vain conversation, who are payers of the poor-due (Zakat); who guard their modesty, and those who fulfil their trusts and keep their promises and who pay heed to their prayers."

In Surah "Al-Anfal", the believers are portrayed thus: "They are the true believers whose hearts fill up with awe when Allah is mentioned, and when the revelations of Allah are recited unto them their faith is, strengthened; and those who place their trust in their Lord."

OBJECTIVES OF ISLAM

It cannot be denied that man has propounded different views of life generally confined to the gratification of ignoble desires and glamour of mundane environment. But the most Omnipotent and Omniscient Allah has proclaimed a very lofty and sublime aim of man's existence.

He clearly declares in the Quran, "I created the jinn and humankind only that they might worship me." The real objective is a complete knowledge and understanding of the Almighty God and the service as ordained by the Quran. This service comprises all phases of human life, in religious, social, economic, cultural, scientific and technological fields. Man according to Islamic viewpoint is the vicegerent of the Creator of the Universe. He is neither sovereign nor a mere helpless animal. He is endowed with vast talents and potentialities to function as an agent of Allah and create facilities and environments for the performance of noble deeds.

NOBLE EXAMPLES

The Quran says: "Lo! I am about to place a viceroy in the earth." "Verily We have created the children of Adam. We carry them on the land and the sea, and have made provision of good things for them, and have preferred them above many of those whom We created with marked preferment." "Hast thou not seen how Allah hath made all that is in the earth subservient unto you? And the ship runneth upon the sea by His command, and He holdeth back the heaven from falling on the earth unless by His leave. Lo! Allah is, for mankind, compassionate, and most Merciful."

These verses express with clarity the significant position of man in the universe. He has been sent to this world for very lofty and sublime ideals. He is the prototype of the Creator and has to remodel his life in consonance with a pattern designed by the Almighty. But he has become very arrogant and haughty, unmindful of his real role as a vicegerent of Allah.

So long as man is aware and fully conscious that he is neither an independent entity nor a purposeless creation, but he should tread upon the right path and have absolute faith in the unity of God and His Majesty, His Grandeur and His other lofty attributes, he will be crowned with success (Falah). The Quran states, "Say: He is Allah, the One! Allah, the eternally Besought of all! He begetteth not nor was begotten; and there is none comparable unto Him."

The Quran is replete with verses declaring the Omnipotence, Omniscience, Majesty, and Glory of Allah. It presents an Absolute God who attracts the heart on account of his Majesty, Wisdom, Magnificence and rejects the dead, weak, unmerciful and powerless gods of false religions. Therefore, the Almighty Allah directs the believers to pray to Him thus: "Thee (alone) we worship; Thee (alone) we ask for help, show us the straight path, the path of those whom thou hast favoured." Again, in another verse He emphasises the same: "Ye are the best community that hath been raised up for mankind. Ye enjoin right conduct and forbid indecency; and ye believe in Allah" Being vicegerent of Allah man is bound to take actions and carry out the commands of Allah. He cannot ignore or overrule the orders of his Master. He has to follow the whole Divine scheme and master the forces of nature for the benefit and amelioration of human beings as He has enjoined in the Quran:

"The true servants of Allah are those who, if we give them power in the land, establish worship and pay the poor-due (Zakat) and enjoin kindness and forbid iniquity."

"God is glorified at morn and evening by men whom neither trade and commerce nor buying and selling beguileth from remembrance of Allah and constancy in prayer and paying to the poor their due, who fear a day when hearts and eyeballs will be overturned."

A true believer is very strict on the fundamentals and never compromises on principles, but in his behaviour he is humble and modest. He is always animated with a spirit of upholding good and uprooting evil and makes it his mission of life. "And the (faithful) slaves of the Beneficent are they who walk upon the earth modestly and when the foolish ones address them answer; peace."

Perfect Life

The Islamic society comprises a very balanced system of rights and duties. No one has the right to violate the sanctity of the laws ordained by the Quran and the Sunnah. There are the rights of Allah (Huquq-ullah) which are to be observed and respected by every Muslim. In the Islamic code of conduct these have been mentioned in detail.

Allah's rights are binding on every human being. He is the Creator, Sustainer and Cherisher of the universe. He is Omnipotent, Omniscient, Most Wise, Most Knowing and Most Merciful. His sovereignty is Absolute and none can be associated with Him. Man's duty is to follow all his commandments with perfect submission, because His blessings are vast and perennial.

The rights of people in Islam are of considerable significance and greatest emphasis have been put on this by the Quran and Sunnah. The Prophet of Islam said that Allah would forgive a man for his carelessness in performance of His rights, but the rights of other people violated by an individual would not be forgiven, until and unless the aggrieved person himself forgives.

In an Islamic society every Muslim has to observe the rights of other members. The parents have to look after, educate and create discipline and behaviour among their children. The children must obey, pay respects and follow their advice unless there are some orders against the Quran and Sunnah.

Relatives, neighbours, friends and even strangers have their rights. And all these rights are to be fully observed by every Muslim. The Quran says:

"Slay not your children, fearing a fall to poverty. We shall provide for them and for you. Lo! the slaying of them is great sin."

"Thy lord hath decreed, that ye worship none save Him, and that ye show kindness to parents. If one of them or both of them attain old age with thee, say not "Fie" unto them nor repulse them, but speak unto them a gracious word."

"And lower unto them the wing of submission through mercy, and say; My Lord! Have mercy on them both as they did care for me when I was little."

"Your Lord is best aware of what is in your minds. If You are righteous, then Lo! He was ever forgiving unto those who turn (unto Him)."

Maryam Jameela Begum[40], a distinguished scholar, has very lucidly expressed her views in "Islam in Theory and practice" thus: "What will the world be like under the Islamic rule? When men recognise the sovereignty of God and the supremacy of His Law, all false values will be automatically swept away. It will be automatically swept away. It will be a world where men are slaves of God and not to each other. It would mean freedom from all forms of tyranny. It will be a world where a man is judged by his character and not by his worldly success. There will be no place for racial discrimination or class hatred."

References

1. *A famous and world-known scholar working on Islam.*
2. *Four beloved Caliphs of the Prophet Muhammad (Pbuh), i.e., Caliph Abu Bakr, Caliph Umar, Caliph Uthman and Caliph Ali (R.A.A.).*
3. *Reciters of the Holy Quran who learn it by heart and recite it with melodious voice.*
4-9. *Companions after Prophet Muhammad (Pbuh).*
10. *A Companion of the Prophet.*
11-15. *Famous reciters of Quran who were enjoined the task of teaching Quran in Syria.*
16-31. *All these names are attributed to Holy Quran.*
32. *A record in which destiny of the universe is preserved.*
33. *A European philosopher who worked out a regular system for the first time.*
34. *A grammarian and linguist also introduced irab (Zabar, Zer, Pesh) for the first time.*
35. *The man who introduced dots (nuqat) on the Quranic words.*
36. *A great philosopher and thinker of the Islamic History and works.*
37. *Do's and dont's.*
38. *An internationally known great philosopher and thinker of Islam.*
39. *The most respected and known poet of Urdu; popularly known Shair-e-Mashriq.*
40. *A prominent thinker and scholar of the Islamic studies.*

4

LESSONS FROM QURAN

At a time when the world was totally enveloped in darkness, ignorance, barbarism, fetish and dogmas, diverse beliefs, obscurantism, and countless enigmas and mysteries, God revealed glad tidings through His Divine Revelation which was of a sublime and unique character never seen and heard by human beings.

It revolutionised and transformed the whole thinking and living of man. It gave a glittering face to human action and elevated man and woman alike to perform their duties with honesty, vigour, zest and verve.

Man's greatness and his superb position in the universe was clearly defined and established in the Quranic Chapter 16, entitled the Bee[1] (*An-Nahl*), where the activities of the Bee are mentioned as a type of duty and of usefulness. It calls attention to God's providence for creation, and to His guidance to mankind as a necessary part of it, and warns disbelievers in the guidance of a folly in rejecting it as great as would be the rejection of food and drink.

The first section of this Surah deals with the animal kingdom which is already subservient to mankind, but the second portrays most remarkable vast phenomena in the expense of creation and nature. It tells mankind that the rain that drops from clouds and revives the lives of the trees, plants, herbage and vegetables, descend from the firmament for the service of human beings; that night and day, the sun and the moon and all the heavenly bodies had been created by Allah for the service of man.

Deep oceans, wide and flowing rivers, lofty mountains have been put under man's service who must comprehend new ways of getting benefit from them. The greatest luminary was not made for nun's adoration and worship, but manifestations of His Omnipotence and Omniscience and are in man's subjection and subservience. Let the worldly wise people with latest sincere and technology pause and ponder over it in the light of history whether this idea of man's superiority and sublimity had ever dawned on the human mind before the Quran?

Man had been made conversant with a great reality. Since the entire Muslim Ummah have neglected and ignored this teaching, they are groping in darkness and stumbling here and there with the great world powers. We have to understand nature in order to discover the utility to ourselves of its various components. We have to think and learn the fundamental and basic laws under which we can decipher the properties, ingredients and component parts to make full advantage.

To perform these duties and achieve success, the Quran stresses to follow Tafaqqoh, Tadabbur, Tafakkur and Taaqqul, which signify pondering, observation, thinking and consciousness in general. But in Quranic terminology their significance is very comprehensive.

Tafaqqoh stands for the knowledge of the features in a thing which enables man to discern it from others; with Tadabbur, man will discover the object for which they have been created; and by Tafakkur, the properties and proportions of objects in which their varied elements have been mingled, will be traced out. Taaqqul is the rational power to create things for the general benefit of human race. With these objectives and ideals the Muslims established most scientific laboratories to make experiments and researches in all fields of knowledge. To inculcate and stimulate man's interest for such studies the Quran has emphasised as under:

(1) "Who had made the earth a resting-place for you and the heaven a canopy;; and Who sends down rain from the cloud then brings forth with it subsistence for you of the fruit; therefore do not set up rivals to Allah which you know better."

(2) And He has made subservient to you the sun and the moon constant in their courses, and has made subservient to you the right and the day.

(3) "And the earth have We spread out, and placed therein firm hills, and caused each seemly thing to grow therein. And We have given unto you livelihoods therein, and unto those for whom ye provide not."

(4) No labour is wasted as Quran says: "Those who believe and do good works, them verily We shall house in lofty dwellings of the Garden

underneath which rivers flow. There they will dwell secure. How sweet the gardens of the toilers."

(5) Right actions would receive ample reward, as the Quran states: Whoso bringeth a good deed will receive tenfold the like thereof."

(6) "Still toil and strive to please thy Lord"

(7) The whole world is linked by law. Everything in it follows certain laws, and we can turn everything in it to our advantage if we discover and apply the said law. The laws of nature are none other than the Will of the Almighty Allah, as the Quran reveals: "So set thy purpose (O Muhammad) for religion as a man by nature upright —the nature (framed) of Allah, in which He hath created man. There is no altering (the laws of) Allah's creation. That is the right religion, but most men know not."

(8) Human nature possesses the best talents, but we need divine guidance for progress. The Quran states: "Verily We created man of the best stature."

God has repeatedly emphasised in the Quran that man should have the power of obtaining control and utilising the forces of Nature that exist between the heights and surface. How with clarity these verses reveal: "Allah it is Who hath made the sea of service unto you that the ships may ply thereon by His command, and that ye may seek of His bounty, and that happily ye may be thankful."

"And hath made of service unto you whatsoever is in the heavens and whatsoever is in the earth; it is all from Him, Lo! Herein verily are portents for people who reflect."

"Hast thou not seen how thy Lord hath spread the shade? And if He willed He could have made it still then We have made the sun its pilot." Then We withdraw it unto Us, a gradual withdrawal?"

"And He it is Who hath produced you from a single being, and (hath given you) a habitation and a repository"

THE FUNCTIONING

It cannot be denied that one of the most significant factors of modern civilisation is Mechanism —the theory or doctrine that all the phenomena of the Universe, particularly life can ultimately be explained in terms of physics and chemistry, and that the difference between the organic and the inorganic is only in degree. The early Muslims dedicated themselves to the observation, experimentation and deep pondering of mechanism of the Universe through the inspiration of the Quranic verses and became the pioneers of knowledge and learning.

The Quran tells us that the whole Universe is in a measured order. Everything in it follows a course. Therefore, the Book of Allah emphasises that man must learn the various measures and course that he "may not be inordinate in respect of measure." The first nine verses of Surah, "Al-Rahman," the Beneficent, bring home to us this truth." He hath created man. He hath taught him utterance. The sun and the moon are made punctual, the stars and trees adore, and the sky He hath uplifted; and He hath set the measure (Mizan), that ye exceed not measure, but observe the measure strictly, nor fall short thereof."

Great emphasis has been laid on measure (Mizan), which has to be followed strictly, as the principle of measure works not only in the physical plane, but in the moral and spiritual order as well. The whole solar system worked under a prescribed reckoning and all the orbs travel along swiftly in their respective spheres. All things of physical nature work according to some laws and measure. This Quranic suggestion made the Muslim scientists cognizant of the fact that the winds also blow in prescribed ways. It led to the discovery of the meteorological laws, which with the laws of navigation, saved ships from the buffetings of wind and storm.

Philosophy of Islam

A large number of religious teachers were sent to this world in every age to uplift mankind from moral degradation and frightful ignorance. But their messages were mostly confined to social or tribal predilections. They were not imbued with the spirit of universalism, liberalism, tolerance and fraternity. It was from the cave of Hira that the first message of Islam was delivered by the Prophet Muhammad (SAW) which was couched in the most superb and transcendent diction: "Read: In the name of thy Lord who createth. Createth man from a clot. Read: And thy Lord is the Most Bounteous, who teacheth by the pen, Teacheth man that which he knew not"

This was the most majestic and magnificent message for the edification of mankind. Moses was deputed to emancipate the people of Israel from the bondage of Pharaoh. Jesus Christ was also sent to dispel darkness and tribal aggrandisement and degeneration. But the Prophet of Islam was bestowed with the message of different character, higher and nobler than the individual and racial interest.

It was the highest ideal and objective which the man has to accomplish and make ceaseless efforts to reach the peak. The message of Allah emphasises "Reading and writing —who taught with the Pen" — and of acquiring sciences unknown to the world— and taught man what he knew not. The character of this teaching is universal and draws the human race within its orbit.

Lessons from Quran

The morality of the world was at its lowest ebb and it was but natural that the sun of universal message must shine to vanish all darkness, barbarism, ignorance, fetishes and dogmas. The supremacy of wickedness and mischief has to be demolished and the rise of discipline, self-respect, integrity and service to mankind has to be re-established and recreated. The Quran clearly states that Allah has raised a wonderful creature like man out of a clot, but He vehemently contemplates to enhance him to the apex of mental, moral and spiritual culture. He (Allah) reveals this lofty message in this first revelation and clearly discloses the light and glorious path leading to that goal.

The message coming from our Lord (Rabb), "Read: In the name of thy Lord—Read and thy Rabb is Most Bounteous." Here the word "Rabb" is of far-reaching significance. It conveys not only the idea of fostering, bringing up, or nourishing, but also that of regulating, completing and accomplishing *i.e.* of the evolution of things from the crudest state to that of the highest perfection.

According to Imam Raghib, Rabb signifies the fostering of a thing in such a manner as to make it attain one condition after another until it reaches its goal of completion. Hence Rabb is the fountainhead of all existence, Who has not only given to the whole creation its means of nourishment but has also beforehand ordained for each a sphere of capacity, and within that sphere provided the means by which it continues to attain gradually to its goal of perfection.

The word "Evolution" does not convey the real Quran. The Divine Book uses the word 'Falah; to give a wider concept for unfolding the latent faculties of man. The revolution was made with the sole purpose of guiding mankind to follow the prescribed course in order to develop to the fullest extent the innate faculties of man. The emphasis on science and knowledge infused creative thinking and founding of various universities which led the world in learning and research. All knowledge was their field, and they took in, and they gave out the utmost knowledge, attainable in those days. The universities of those days were, of course, different from those of modern times, but they were then the most enlightened institutions of the world. The German scholar Professor Joseph Hell in his book Arab Civilisation has rightly remarked:

> "Even at the universities religion retained its primacy, for was it not religion which first opened the path to learning? The Quran, Tradition (Hadith), and jurisprudence, therefore all preserved their pre-eminence there. But it is to the credit of Islam that it neither slighted nor ignored other branches of learning; nay, it offered the very same home to them as it did to theology — a place in the mosque. Until the fifth century of the Hijrah the mosque was the university of Islam; and to this fact

is due the most characteristic feature of Islamic culture—perfect freedom to teach. The teacher had to pass no examination, required no diploma, no formality, to launch out in that capacity. What he needed was competence, efficiency, mastery of his subject."

These treacheries of the Arab universities were the most outstanding scholars of their time; they were really the teachers of Modern Europe. It was one of them, an eminent chemist who wrote: "Hearsay and mere assertion have no authority in chemistry. It may be taken as an absolutely rigorous principle that any proposition which is not supported by proofs is nothing more than an assertion which may be true or false. It is only when a man brings proof of his assertion that we say: "your proposition is true."

Muhammad Marmaduke Pickthall[2] has correctly said: "These Ulama were no blind guides, no mere fanatics. The Professors of those universities were the most enlightened thinkers of their time. In strict accordance with the Prophet's teaching, it was they who watched over the welfare of the people and pointed out to the khalifah anything that was being done against the rights of men as guaranteed by the Quran.

It was they, indeed, who kept down the fanatic element, discouraged persecution for religious opinion, and saved Islamic culture from deteriorating in a thousand ways. They even forced ambitious Muslim rulers, in their unIslamic strife, to refrain from calling on the people to assist them, to fight only with the help of their own purchased slaves and to respect all crops and cattle and non-combatants. They were able, by the enormous weight of their opinion with the multitude, to punish even rulers who transgressed the Sacred Law, in a way which brought them quickly to repentance; and they exacted compensation for transgression."

Who can deny that in the great centres of learning during the heyday of Islamic civilisation in Europe, in Cordova, Granada and Seville, students flocked from various corners of the world to slake their thirst for knowledge. They were much impressed by the new researches and discoveries of the Muslims and their disciplined observations of nature; laboratories for detailed analysis and experimental testing of hypothesis; systematic use of scientific and scholarly literature; critical evaluation of the work of colleagues; a dedication to, and an elaboration of the methods for investigation into the nature of the universe and of human phenomena.

This inductive and experimental method of research and inquiry and the critical spirit exercised a remarkable influence and created tremendous confidence on the oncoming generations of Europe and other countries, who subsequently built up the noble structure of their educational edifice on the foundations laid by the Muslims in Europe. The inspiration given by the Muslim universities ultimately led to the setting up of numerous colleges and seats of learning in Europe imbued with the spirit of scientific approach to knowledge.

Dr. Tara Chand[3], a distinguished scholar and historian of India, has rightly remarked: "For a thousand years this civilisation was the central light whose rays illumined the world. It was the mother of European culture, for men reared in this civilisation were the masters in the Middle Ages at whose feet the Spaniards, the French, the English, the Kalians and the Germans sat to learn philosophy, sciences of mathematics, astronomy, chemistry, physics, medicine and industrial techniques. Their names are household words."

H.G. Wells has correctly said: "And a century or so in advance of the West, there grew up in the Muslim world at a number of centres, at Basra, at Kufa, at Baghdad and Cairo, and at Cordova, out of what were at first religious schools dependent upon mosques, a series of great universities. The light of these universities shone far beyond the Muslim world, and drew students to them from east and west. At Cordova in particular there were great numbers of Christian students, and the influence of Arab philosophy coming by way of Spain upon the Universities of Paris, Oxford and north Italy, and upon Western European thought generally, was very considerable indeed.

The name of Averroes (Ibn Rushd) of Cordova (1126-1198) stands out as that of the culminating influence of Arab philosophy upon European thought....Another great name is that of Avicenna (Ibn Sina), the Prince of Physicians (980-1037) was born at the other end of the Arabic world at Bukhara and who travelled in Khorasan. The book-copying industry flourished at Alexandria, Damascus, Cairo and Baghdad, and about the year 970 AD, there were twenty-seven free schools in Cordova for the education of the poor."

Mention may also be made of Allama Iqbal's thinking on potentialities of human mind. He writes: "Western thinkers preached priesthood in religion and autocracy in politics. The Middle Ages in the history of Europe drove this Dogma of Romanticism to its political and religious consequences, and the result was a form of society which required terrible revolution to destroy it-and to upset the basic pre-suppositions of its structure.

Martin Luther, the enemy of despotism in religion, and Rousseau, the enemy of despotism in politics, must always be regarded as emancipators of European humanity from the heavy fetters of Popedom and Absolutism, and their religious and political thought must be understood as a virtual denial of the Church dogma of human depravity. The possibility of the elimination of sin and pain from the evolutionary process and faith in the natural goodness of man are the basic propositions of Islam, as of modern European civilisation, which has, almost unconsciously, recognised the truth of these propositions, in spite of the religious system with which it is associated. Ethically speaking, therefore, man is naturally good and peaceful.

Metaphysically speaking, he is a unit of energy, which cannot bring out its dormant possibilities, owing to its misconception of the nature of its environment. The ethical ideal of Islam is to disenthral man from fear, and thus give him a sense of his personality, to make him conscious of himself as a source of power. This idea of man as an individuality of infinite power determines, according to the teachings of Islam, the worth of all human action. That which intensifies the sense of individuality in man is good, that which enfeebles it is bad. Virtue is power, force, strength; evil is weakness. Give man a keen sense of respect for his own personality, let him move fearless and free in the immensity of God's earth, and he will respect the personalities of others and become perfectly virtuous."

REALITY OF ISLAM

In order to understand the complete and comprehensive concept of Islam, it is necessary to define the significance of the word "Islam."

(1) Etymologically the word "Islam" is derived from the Arabic root Salama, which signifies to be tranquil, at rest, to have done one's duty, to have paid up, to be at perfect peace, and finally to strive after righteousness with one's own strength. In Islamic phraseology this idea stands for submission to the will of Allah, which leads to a state of peace — the end and aim of all human endeavour.

(2) To a historian the word "Islam" suggests more than a system of theology. It stands for a distinctive civilisation and a socio-politico- economic order, based on a form of practical way of life. It has been evolving since the days of the Prophet whilst spreading into countries around Arabia, on the shores of the Arabian Sea and beyond.

(3) To an ordinary Muslim the word "Islam" is thought to be the name of his religion (Deen) and as such comprises a system of life, guiding its followers individually and socially, whilst binding its members into a fraternity transcending the boundaries of state race, colour, language and traditions.

(4) The Quran teaches that all bonafide religion or true communication with Allah, is Islam. "This day I have perfected for you your religion, and bestowed My favours on you, and chosen for you Islam as a religion." The very spirit of religion is submission to the will of Allah (Radai Illahi). The Glorious Quran emphasises:

> "Those who keep away from evil and follow the straight path will have a higher place than they (unbelievers) on the Day of Rackoning for God gives in measure without number whomsoever. He will."

Every Muslim must submit to the Divine commands and seek guidance and enlightenment from His fountain (Samadiat).

All his actions are disciplined by the laws of the Quran which enjoins ceaseless endeavour, righteous action (Amal-i-Saleh). Creative thinking, common sense, discernment and a deep sense of mental discipline and balanced judgement, which in the terminology of the Quran is Furqan. Furqan is the fundamental principle on which man should base his whole edifice of purposive activity and his forward movement. Idleness and stagnation is the very negation of Islamic teaching.

GLOBAL FRATERNITY

In Islam, all humanity is one vast brotherhood, with Allah as their Creator and Master who looks upon them all as equal. All the barriers, racial and others, raised against it by the self-interest of man are destroyed, and divisions on the ground of religion merely are not recognised; its teachings being directly opposed to all sectarianism and based on the broadest principle.

> "Such was the Divine message which Muhammad (SAW) brought to his people: "O mankind! Lo! We have created you male and female, and have made you nations and tribes, that ye may know one another; Lo! The noblest of you, in the sight of Allah is the best in conduct. Lo! Allah is Knower, Aware."

> God looked towards the people of this earth: the Arabs hated the non-Arabs, except the best among them of the people of the Book.

> He says, "I have only raised thee up that I may prove thee, and prove (others) by thee." "Man is only a pious believer or a wicked sinner.

> "Be ye all worshippers of Allah and brothers to one another, as Allah has commanded you."

QURANIC WISDOM

The first Surah of the Quran, "Al-Alaq" revealed to Prophet Muhammad (SAW) in the cave of Hira laid greatest emphasis on learning and knowledge:

> "Read: In the name of thy Lord who createth, Createth man from an embryo; Read, and thy Lord is the most Bounteous, Who teacheth (to write) by the pen. Teacheth man that which he knew not."

With the creation of this universe Allah enlightened Adam with new treasures of knowledge to shoulder the responsibilities and perform the duties as His Vicegerent and disseminate knowledge to all the created things and the humanity at large.

As a seeker of knowledge a Musalman should travel to far off distances like China..... "He who leaves his home in search of knowledge walks in the path of Allah; seek knowledge from cradle to grave. The learning and education is compulsory for every Muslim man and woman. He who travels in search of knowledge to him Allah shows the way to Paradise."

There is no denying that all the great fountains of knowledge and science and gushed out with the teachings of Prophet Muhammad (SAW), who emphasised the search for knowledge and learning and incessant devotion to harness the forces of nature to set forth new rays of knowledge and discovery for ameliorating the lot of the suffering humanity.

The Prophet of Islam said: "Teach Science: whoever teaches it fears Allah: whoever desires it adores Allah; whoever speaks of it praises Allah; whoever diffuses it distributes alms; whoever possesses it becomes an object of veneration and respect. Science preserves us from error and from sin; it illuminates the road to Paradise; it is our protector in travel, our confidence in the desert, our companion in solitude. It guides us through the pleasure and the sorrows of life; it serves us alike as an ornament among our friends and as a buckler against our enemies; it is through its instrumentality that the Almighty raises up those whom he has appointed to determine the good and the true.

The memories of such men are the only ones which shall survive, for their noble deeds will serve as models for the imitation of the great minds that shall come after them. Science is a potent remedy for the infirmities of ignorance, a brilliant beacon in the night of injustice.

The study of letters is as meritorious as fasting; their communication is not inferior in efficiency to prayer; in a generous heart they awaken the most elevated sentiments, to the wicked they impart the corrective and humanising precepts of virtue.

These noble and lofty teachings of the Prophet bear eloquent testimony to the fact that in the socio-economic structure of Islam illiteracy and ignorance have no place. Every Muslim must be enlightened to contribute to development and progress of human knowledge, scientific research and technology. The whole Ummat-i-Muslima[4] must be educated in order to understand the religious, social, economic and political problems of the world and be able to lead the Islamic way of life imbued with the spirit of the Quran and the Sunnah.

ISLAMIC CODE

The code of Islam is thus given "Come," says the Glorious Quran, "I will recite unto you that which your Lord hath made a sacred duty for you; that ye ascribe nothing as partner unto Him and that ye do good to (your) parents and that ye slay not your children because of penury —We proud of you and of them— and that ye draw not nigh to lewd things whether open or concealed. And that ye obey not the life which Allah hath made sacred. This He hath commanded you that ye may discern."

This was the life according to the Original Religion, and any one who broke away from it was regarded as "going astray." In the Quran such people are called an "unjust people" and "transgressors." But those who do wrong follow their lusts without knowledge.'

> "Shall We treat those who believe and do the right deeds, as those who spread corruption in the earth? Or shall We treat the pious as the wicked"?

> "Unto Allah belongeth whatever is in the heavens and the earth, that He may reward those who do evil, in accordance with their deeds, and He may reward those who do good with goodness."

> "And forsake those who take their religion for a pastime and a jest, and whom the life of this world bequiteth. Remind them hereby lest a soul be destroyed by what it earneth (of good or evil). It shall have no patron or intercessor beside Allah: and if it could atone with the fullest atonement, it would not be accepted from it."

PRACTICAL LIFE

Islam, above all, is a religion of action (Amal). The service of man and the good of humanity constitute pre-eminently the service and worship of Allah:

> "All creation is the family of Allah and of all creation the most beloved of Allah is he who does most good to His family."

Allah will not be merciful to him who is not merciful to ye, then be merciful to those who are on the earth, so that He who is in the heaven may be merciful to you." Allah is always ready to help His worshipper so long as the worshipper is ready to help his brother." A selfless life of love is the life of a Muslim. Being asked as to the best part of faith, Muhammad (SAW) said:

> "That thou love for the sake of Allah, and that thou love for men what thou lovest for thyself, and hate for them what thou hatest for thyself."

The essence of religion is declared to be the service of afflicted humanity: "Hast thou observed him who belieth religion? That is he who repelleth the orphan? And urgeth not the feeding of the needy."

And the following is conveyed to a heartless worshipper: Ah, woe unto worshippers who are heedless of their prayer; who would be seen (at worship) yet refuse small kindness."

Work, and work alone, is the true test of a believer in the sight of Allah: "Verily! Those who say: Our Lord is Allah, and thereafter walk aright, there shall come no fear on them, nor shall they grieve. Such are rightful owners of paradise, immortal therein, as a reward for what they did."

And what is the duty of man in Islam?

> "Verily," says the Quran, "Allah enjoineth justice and doing of good (to others), and the giving to kinsfolk (their due), and He forbiddeth lewdness and abomination and wickedness.

> "When one of you sees wrongdoing," said Muhammad (SAW): "Let him undo it with his hand and if he cannot do this, then, let him speak against it with his tongue; and if he cannot do this either then let him abhor it with his heart— and this is the least of faith."

But help ye one another unto righteousness and pious duty. Help not one another unto sin and transgression, but keep your duty to Allah. Lo! Allah is severe in punishment.

There is no good in much of what they talk in private, unless (in the talk) of him who bids charity, or what is reasonable, or concord among men.

SAINTHOOD NOWHERE

There is no Brahminical aristocracy, papacy and priesthood in Islam. Man has got a direct approach to Allah who is the Creator and Sustainer of all the Universe. He needs no mediator. He is All-Seeing, All-Hearing and All-Knowing and is "closer to us than our own jugular vein,." Every Muslim is his own priest and supplicates to the Almighty for mercy and forgiveness. Thee (alone) we worship; Thee (alone) we ask for help. Guide us on the right path; the path of those upon whom Thou hast bestowed favours; not those who have earned your anger, nor those who go astray."

Islam has laid great stress on the dignity of man endowed with tremendous intellectual, physical and spiritual potentialities to conquer the forces of nature and understand the meaning of time and space.

The Glorious Quran repeatedly emphasises the significant value of Ta-aqqaloon, Tadabbaroon, and Tafakkaroon, *i.e.* the practical application of mind, cogent reasoning, deep thinking and scientific planning in order to arrive at correct results and conclusions from the "Ayat-i-Ilahi"[5] *i.e.* the symbols of Allah. It is these scientific teachings of the Quran that Muslims rose to great heights during the heyday of their civilisation and wiped away all fetish and dogmas prevalent in those days.

POWER OF BEARING

Prophet Muhammad (SAW) looked upon slavery as altogether inhuman. The Glorious Quran says: What the Ascent is! It is to free a slave.

He enacted a law that slaves should be allowed to purchase their liberty by the wages of their services, and that in case the unfortunate beings had no present means of gain and wanted to earn in some other employment enough for the purpose, they should be allowed to leave their masters on simply making an agreement to that effect. He also provided that sums should be advanced to the slaves from public treasury to purchase their liberty. There is no doubt that the greatest religious toleration has been introduced by the Prophet of Islam:

> "Say thou; O ye who believe not, I worship not what ye worship, and ye worship not what I worship, nor will I worship what ye worship, nor will ye worship what I worship—Unto you your religion, and unto me my religion."

Let there be no compulsion in religion; the right direction is henceforth distinct from error.

References

1. *Honey-bee.*
2. *A famous translator and commentator of Holy Quran.*
3. *A great scholar and historian who wrote on India.*
4. *The entire followers of Islam as a whole.*
5. *Signs of Allah.*

5

LEGAL PRINCIPLES

THE JUDGES

Allah is the True Source of all Laws : The source of all laws in Islam is Allah and Allah alone. The verse of the Quran, "The *hukm* belongs to Allah alone," [Quran 6:57] is often cited in support of this. This basic rule determines the character of Islamic law and gives direction to all interpretation and *ijtihad*[1]. The rule says that it is Allah's laws alone that are acceptable to the Muslim. No temporal authority can command a Muslim's obedience, unless the authority is based on the commands of Allah. This is the essence of social contract within a Muslim community.

Each Muslim is a Muslim not only because he believes in the existence of one God and the truth of the mission of His Messenger, but also because the laws are prescribed by the Wise and Just Lord. It is these laws that grant him security from oppression and ensure justice and fair play in all dealings. A Muslim surrenders his will to Islam so that his life may be regulated in accordance with the *hukm* of Allah.

What, then, do we mean when we say that Allah is the True and Ultimate Sovereign? What is the general nature of the laws laid down by Allah? In other words, can we see a broad intention of the Lawgiver when we look at all the laws? We, therefore, ask the question: Are these laws laid down in the interest of Man? Thus, if we make a law that serves the interest of humanity (say based upon utilitarian principles), can this law be assumed to be valid and in accordance with the dictates of the *Shariah?*

Further, an extension of the above inquiry pertains to the independent use of reason. If the assumption is that Allah's laws are always in conformity with human reason, then, can we also assume that all laws that appear reasonable to humans must be in conformity with the *Shariah?*

There are a number of other questions that pertain to the methodology to be adopted to ensure that laws conform with the injunctions of the Quran and the *Sunnah,* but these require exhaustive analysis and will not be taken up in this chapter.

The Fundamental Norm of the Legal System : The fact that ultimately Allah alone is the source of all laws indicates to us the fundamental rule or norm of the Islamic legal system. The other rules of the legal system are all referred to, or checked against, this norm for their validity.

The fundamental norm is repeated several times each day by every Muslim. It is contained in the declaration: "There is no god, but Allah, and Muhammad is the Messenger of Allah." As the Muslim is ready to accept the laws of Allah, he will accept only those laws that were revealed through His Messenger. The revelation granted to the Messenger is in the form of the Quran.

Once this is accepted, we find that the Quran itself declares the *Sunnah* of the Messenger of Allah to be a source of laws. Some say that the *Sunnah* is itself a form of revelation, that is, revelation in meaning alone as compared to the Quran, which is revelation in both word and meaning. Starting from the other end, the Muslim may say:

- I am ready to obey such and such law as it has been communicated to me by a qualified jurist.
- I follow the opinion of the jurist as it is in conformity with the sources of Islamic law.
- I obey a law based on the sources as they are the sources revealed to Muhammad. I obey Muhammad for he is the Messenger of Allah, and
- I believe in Allah.

In this way the validity of all laws is traced to Allah. This basic norm or rule does two things. First, it provides a standard or criterion with which we can judge whether or not a law is valid law. Second, it creates for each Muslim an obligation or duty to obey the law. A subject of an Islamic state does not have to look for some external rule of morality or justice for his duty to obey the law.

Legal Principles

The Law and the Interest of Man : Has the Lawgiver laid down laws in the interest *(maslahah)* of Man? If this is true, can the interest of Man be an independent source of laws? Is Man free to determine his own interest, or is it predetermined by the Lawgiver? These questions have always been at the forefront of Islamic legal theory. The answers form the basis of the principle of *istislah* that seeks to secure the interests *(masalih)* preserved and protected by the Islamic legal system. This issue is extremely important for *ijtihad* and the framing of new laws in the present times The reason is that in the absence of a direct and express evidence in the Quran and the *Sunnah*, laws are to be framed in the light of the interest *(maslahah)* of Man as determined by the Lawgiver.

The majority of the Muslim jurists agreed that the Lawgiver lays down laws in the interest of Man. There have been some voices against it too, notable among them being the objections of the illustrious Imam al-Razi[2] (d. 606 A.H./1210 C.E.). He gave extremely powerful arguments against this idea. Al-Razi did concede though that whenever we consider the laws and the interests of Man, we find them lying side by side, or existing together, yet we cannot establish a causal relationship between them, that is, the laws are laid down because they serve the interest of Man. The problem may be explained in a simple way.

Is Man the Sole Purpose of Creation? : Take the case of a factory producing something. The sole purpose of the existence of this factory is the creation of a product. Every directive that is issued to the workers is intended to enhance the quality of this product or to create it on time, or to create a product that is more useful. The factory does not exist for the workers, but for the creation of that product. The effective production of goods, however, requires that the interest and welfare of the workers be kept in view, for that will lead to a better product. If the worker performs well he is rewarded or promoted, because he is in harmony with the process leading to the ultimate product. If he does not perform well, he will not be rewarded and may also be penalised for a breach of discipline. The factory does have laws to regulate the activity of the workers. These laws are laid down primarily to ensure an effective production of goods, though the laws may indirectly serve the interest of the worker.

Is Man the final product of this universe created by Allah, or is the purpose of this universe something larger, larger than Man?

> What! Are ye the more difficult to create or the heaven (above); (Allah) hath constructed it. [Quran 79 : 27]

If Man is the sole purpose, then, all laws must have been made to serve his interest. On the other hand, if the purpose of the creation of the universe is something other than Man as may be understood from the above verse, then, is

Man in the position of the worker, a servant of Allah *(abd Allah),* who is to be rewarded if he performs well and punished if he misbehaves? The laws in this case would appear to be lying side by side with the interest of Man, as al-Razi maintains, because they are actually serving some larger purpose. Again, if Man is the sole purpose of the universe, the laws would be laid down to serve his interest alone.

Thus, there would be a causal relationship between the laws and the interest of Man. In such a case, would he be called the vicegerent of Allah *(khalifat Ullah)?* Some jurists have conceded that it is proper to assign this title to Man, for the Quran mentions it too, while others consider it as heresy and maintain that the reference in the Quran is to some previous creation to which Man is a successor *(khalifa).* The latter jurists prefer to use the title "vicegerent of the Messenger" or *khalifat al-Rasul.* The answers to these questions are known to Allah alone. That is where the jurists leave the discussion, and we should do the same.

Can we Employ Maslahah (Interest) for New Laws? : Whichever approach we take on this issue it does not alter the decision on the interest of Man. There is some relationship between the interest of Man and the *hukm* of Allah. It does not matter if this is a causal relationship. The majority of the jurists, therefore, agree that *maslahah* or the interest of Man may be employed for the derivation of new laws. This in no case means that the Muslims are free to make laws in accordance with whatever they deem to be their interest. The interest of Man is determined by the Lawgiver Himself, and there is a determined methodology for identifying this. The jurists have taken great pains to lay down this methodology in a way that the laws derived through it may still be termed as the *ahkam* of Allah. It would not be an exaggeration to say that the key to the future development of Islamic law is through the doctrine of *maslahah,* as will be shown later in this book.

Are the Shariah and Natural Law Compatible? : Can the *ahkam* (legal rules) be discovered by human reason independent of the sources of Islamic law? This is a question that pertains to natural law or to the use of reason independent of the *Shariah*[3]. There have been heated debates among the early Muslim jurists over this issue, though the terminology used by them was different. The terms they used were *Hasan* (good) and *qabih* (bad or evil).

Natural law has a very long history beginning in ancient thought and continuing right up to our times. The classical theory of natural law, as Hart puts it, is that "there are certain principles of human conduct, awaiting discovery by human reason, with which man-made law must conform if it is to be valid." It should be made clear that natural law has not always been associated with God, and even

Legal Principles

when it has been its basic assumptions have not been dependent upon a belief in God.

Our discussion, however, pertains to a much restricted version of natural law in which belief in Allah as the Lawgiver and Master of the Universe is essential. Even in the West, the real developments in natural law came through the writings of Thomas Aquinas[4]. Some of his views, it is acknowledged in the West, were based on the works of Ibn Sina and the Spanish jurist-philosopher Ibn Rushd (Averroes), especially his commentaries on Aristotle. To describe what we mean by natural law in this context, let us borrow a definition provided by John Austin. He says:

> Of the Divine laws, or the laws of God, some are *revealed* or promulgated, and others are *unrevealed.* Such of the laws of God as are unrevealed are not unfrequently denoted by following names or phrases: 'the law of nature;' 'natural law;' 'the law manifested to man by the light of nature or reason.'
>
> Paley and other divines have proved beyond a doubt, that it was not the purpose of Revelation to disclose the *whole* of those duties. Some we could not know, without the help of Revelation; and these the revealed law has stated distinctly and precisely. The rest we ' may know, if we will, by the light of nature or reason; and these the revealed law supposes or assumes. It passes them over in silence, or with a brief and incidental notice.

Austin also says that these "unrevealed" laws are the only laws which God makes for that portion of mankind who are excluded from the light of revelation. We may qualify Austin's description of natural law by saying that these are laws that are to be discovered by mankind through reason prior to revelation, that is, before the arrival of the light of revelation amidst a particular community. Once revelation has come, such laws may only be discovered in the light of revelation, because revelation does not pass them over in silence; it indicates them through general principles. We are now ready to look briefly at some of the discussions of Muslim jurists.

There was complete agreement among Muslim jurists about the meaning of the words of the Exalted, "The *hukm* belongs to Allah alone." [Quran 6 : 57] The Mutazila agreed with the majority that the source of all laws is Allah, but they disagreed with them about the identification and discovery of these laws prior to revelation. They maintained that reason can discover the laws of Allah, that is, the *shari ahkam*[5], in the absence of revelation. The Mutazila were not alone in holding these views and there were other sects who held the same or similar views, especially the Maturidis, some of whom were Hanafis, though their views were slightly different. Sadr al-shariah has the following to say :

The term *shariyyah* (legal according to Islamic law) includes all that would not have been known had the communication from the Law not been issued. This is irrespective of whether this communication pertained directly to a particular *hukm* or was issued in a manner that the *hukm* was dependent upon it, as in the issues based on analogical deduction. The rules for these too would be legal for had the communication not been issued for the original case, the rule extended for analogy would not have been known either. This stipulation (of the term *shariyyah*), therefore, includes the goodness *(husn)* and badness *(qubh)* of all acts according to those who deny that this can be discovered through reason.

Know that, in our view (Hanafi), and that of the majority of the Mutazila, the goodness of some acts as well as their badness can be discovered through reason, but in certain acts they cannot be discovered and are dependent upon the communication from the Lawgiver. The first type of acts are not part of *fiqh;* they belong to the domain of ethics. The second type are part of *fiqh* and the definition of *fiqh* remains sound, comprehensive and precise (with the stipulation of the term *shariyyah*) according to this view.

According to al-Ashari and his followers, on the other hand, the goodness and badness of every act is known through the *Shariah* (even those of purely moral acts) and all these acts would, therefore, be part of *fiqh* (according to the definition under discussion). The Asharites held the view that the laws of Allah can be discovered through revelation alone and there is no way in which reason can discover these laws. The basis of this disagreement is the debate over *husn* and *qubh* or good and evil or right and wrong.

The basic question was whether an act recognised by reason as good or right in itself became binding on the subject? Was he to act upon it even in the absence of revelation or prior to it? The Asharites maintained that even if reason could identify such an act there was no obligation to obey it or act according to it, the sole criterion for right and wrong being revelation. An extreme view of the Mutazila appears to be that the laws of Allah must conform with reason, in fact, some of them appear to have gone so far as to say that it is binding upon Allah to lay down laws that conformed with reason. This was objected to by many as it amounted to restricting the attributes of Allah.

The essential point in all this is whether reason can be used as a source of law for those things on which the *Shariah* is silent? In other words, if something is not expressly prohibited or commanded by the Quran and the *Sunnah*[6], can the law for such a thing be discovered through reason? The answer of the majority appears to be a clear "No!"

Legal Principles

This, however, does not mean that reason has no part to play in the discovery of laws in Islam. The requirement is that all reason and reasoning must proceed from the principles in the Quran and the *Sunnah*. The process is the same in many other legal systems and judges are required to apply the general principles of law rather than those of natural law.

The fundamental position of Muslim jurists is that there is no such thing as natural law outside the realm of the *Shariah* on which we can rely as soon as we discover that a rule of law is not directly discoverable from the texts. Such a rule, they insist, needs to be discovered directly or indirectly from the principles of Islamic law, and not from some "ominous brooding in the sky."

In the few issues discussed above, we have tried to examine some factors that can intrude upon the concept that the *hukm* belongs to Allah alone. This is a very important, interesting, and fertile area. Many conceptions of, and misconceptions about, Islamic law can be cleared up if they are discussed in the light of this concept. The conclusion we may draw is that a *hukm* or a rule of law in an Islamic state is only that injunction that has either been directly stated in the texts of the Quran or the *Sunnah* or in which the intention of the Lawgiver has been ascertained and verified through methods accepted as valid in Islamic law.

THE PROVISIONS

The *hukm shari*, as stated earlier, has three elements, which interact, with each other to give rise to liability and to the obligation to obey the law. The three elements of the *hukm* or a rule of law in the Islamic legal system are: the Lawgiver *(Hakim)*; the act to which the *hukm* is related *(mahkum fih*, also referred to as *mahkum bih*[7]*)*; and the subject who performs the act *(mahkum alayh)*, that is, the person who is under an obligation to obey the law. The first element has already been discussed. In this chapter, the second element will be examined briefly.

The Mahkum Fih is the Act to which the Hukm is Related: The act is always the act of the subject if the communication from Allah is related to this act by way of *taklif*, that is, when it creates an obligation. If the communication *(khitab)* is related to an act by way of declaration, that is, through a secondary rule, the act may or may not be the act of the subject. For example, when there is a command to pay the *zakat*, the obligation it creates is linked to the act of the subject. On the other hand, when there is a command to fix the minimum *nisab*[8] for *zakat*, there is an obligation to obey a secondary rule *(hukm wadi)*, which is in the nature of a declaration supporting the imposition of *zakat*.

Muslim jurists discuss the *mahkum fih* from two aspects: the conditions of *taklif* and the nature of the act.

The Conditions for the Creation of Obligation (Taklif) *:* The jurists mention a number of conditions for the existence of obligation *(taklif)*. A person acquires an obligation, and is placed under some kind of duty, when all these conditions are met. Two important conditions are noted here.

The Act to be Performed or Avoided must be Known *:* The first condition for the creation of an obligation is that the subject must be asked to perform a known act. There is no obligation to perform an unknown or uncertain act. The reason is that the subject has to conceive the act in his mind and usually formulate an intention for its performance. There is a tradition to the effect that the performance of acts is determined by the nature of the intention (Verily the (nature) of acts is determined by intentions). The knowledge of the subject about the act here implies either actual knowledge or at least potential knowledge, that is, he should either be aware of the nature of the act or be in a position to find out about it either directly or indirectly. For knowledge about the nature of the act, the existence of the subject within the Islamic territory *(dar al-Islam)* is considered sufficient. Thus, the rule within the *dar al-Islam* is the same as that in law: "ignorance of law is no excuse even in a layman." Islamic law, however, makes an exception in the cases of *shubhah fi al-dalil* (doubt in the case of conflicting evidences). These are equivalent to mistake of law and mistake of fact in the positive law.

There is a disagreement among the Hanafis and the Shafiis about the presence of the subject within the *dar al-Islam* for acquiring a legal obligation. It rests on whether the world is one with respect to the *ahkam* of Allah or is divided into two worlds, that is, obligation exists where the Islamic state has jurisdiction.

The Subject should be Able to Perform the Act *:* The second condition is that the act should be such that it can be performed by the subject; it should not be an impossible act. The purpose of creating an obligation is to command the obedience of the subject. If the subject is not able to perform the act, the creation of the obligation becomes futile. This condition is split up into two sub-conditions:

(1) there is no obligation to perform an impossible act; and

(2) the performance of the act should be dependent on the will of the subject.

The former case is obvious. The latter includes such acts that involve the subject's inner emotions over which he may have little control. Thus, the tradition that requires the subject not to feel angry is not in the nature of an absolute command creating a binding obligation. It is more in the nature of a recommendation or an advice. The same would apply to a father loving some of his children more than the others, though he is not permitted to let this love interfere with his other legal obligations towards his children whom he is supposed to treat equally.

Further, the ability to perform the act may be relative to the nature of the act. What, then, about acts in which hardship is excessive? The answer depends upon the act itself. For example, hardship involved during a journey while fasting is more than normal, and here the Lawgiver has provided relief.

In other cases, where the act relates to a communal or collective obligation and has to be met by some persons and not everyone, the act must be performed even with the accompanying hardship, as in the case of *jihad.* There are cases where the subject invokes the hardship himself, because of his eagerness to please the Lawgiver or for some other reason. Consider the case of the person who used to stand constantly under the sun while fasting. He was ordered to stay in the shade and to sit down to complete his fast. There were several other incidents like this during the period of the Prophet (peace be on him).

The Nature of the Act (Mahkum Fih) : The structure of Islamic law, its classification, and the consequential obligations and duties, revolve around a set of rights. The classification of laws in Islam can generally be gleaned from the writings of Hanafi jurists.

Each act affected by an obligation creating rule *(hukm taklifi)* is based on a right. There are three kinds of basic rights in Islamic law: the right of Allah, the right of the individual, and the rights of the individuals collectively or the right of the state. The third category of rights is mentioned rarely by jurists, because it relates to the area of law with which they did not deal directly. This is the area left to the ruler *(imam)*. This kind of right is sometimes designated as the right of the ruler *(haqq al-sultan)*[9] or as the right of the state *(haqq al-saltanah)*. Modern writers consider the right of Allah and the right of the state or that of the *saltanah* to be the same thing, because both are related to social interests. A thorough analysis of the Islamic legal system shows, however, that the right of Allah is Distinct and Independent of the Right of the State. This is of crucial significance in understanding the structure of Islamic law.

In fact, when we use the term *huquq al-ibad* in the plural we may mean the rights of individuals generally, or we may mean the collective rights of the individuals, that is, the rights of the community as a whole. In this latter sense, that is, the rights of the community, the implication should be the same as the rights of the state or *saltanah*. Again, the rights of the state should not be merged with the rights of Allah.

Once this has been understood, we may say that sometimes the right of Allah may coexist with the right of the individual. In these cases, it is either the right of Allah that is predominant or it is the right of the individual that is at the forefront. This gives rise, in all, to the following kinds of rights:

1. The right of Allah (*haqq Allah*).
2. The right of the individual *(haqq al-abd)*.
3. The right of Allah lying side by side with the right of the individual. These are of two types:
   (a) Those in which the right of Allah is predominant.
   (b) Those in which the right of the individual is predominant.
4. The collective rights of the individuals or of the community, also referred to as *haqq al-saltanah*.

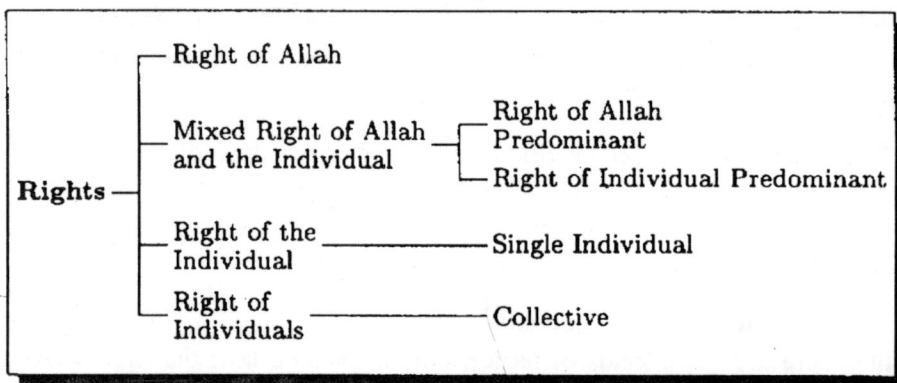

The classification of rights is of great significance in understanding the structure and operation of Islamic law. There are many practical consequences attached to these rights. It is said that where there is a right there is a corresponding duty. The Muslim jurists also deal with duties with reference to rights. The classification of laws on the basis of rights is explained below.

Classification of the Hukm Taklifi on the Basis of Rights : The proper classification of laws, perhaps, was first provided by the Hanafi jurist al-Sarakhsi. The majority of the jurists classified laws under the heading of *mahkum fih* or the act to which the *hukm* is related.

Under the heading of the *hukm shari,* they give an account of the obligations arising from the operation of the act in relation to the *hukm*. Al-Sarakhsi combined the two. It is in this combined form that the subject is approached here.

Al-Sarakhsi says that all *ahkam* are divided into four kinds of rights. These are further subdivided as follows:

1. Rules that relate to the *right of Allah* alone. These are of eight kinds:
   - *Pure Worship :* The first of these is belief in Allah or *Iman*. The second is prayer. The third is *zakah*. The fourth is fasting *(sawm)*. The fifth is *Hajj*. The sixth is *jihad*. There are other acts of worship

Legal Principles

associated with the above like *umra* and *itikaf*[10] (seclusion in a mosque for worship).

- *Pure Punishments* : These are the *hudud* penalties that have been instituted as deterrents, as a pure right of Allah.
- *Imperfect Punishments* : The example of this type is prevention from inheritance in case of murder, that is, the murderer cannot inherit from the victim.
- *Those Vacillating between a Worship and a Penalty* : These are the *kaffara*, that is, acts of expiation made for different reasons.
- *Worship in which there is an Element of a Financial Liability* : The example for this is *sadaqat al-fitr*, which is a payment made before the *Id* following Ramadan.
- *Financial Liability in which there is an Element of Worship* : This is like *'ushr*, the ten percent charge levied on the produce of land.
- *Financial Liability in which there is an Element of a Punishment*: The example given by al-Sarakhsi is that of the *kharaj* tax.
- *Those that Exist Independently* : These are three: those laid down initially as a rule; those that are imposed as an addition to a rule; and those that are associated with the initial rule. The examples of these are the *khums* levied on cattle, minerals, and treasure-troves.

2. Rules in which the *right of Allah and the right of the individual* lie side by side, but the *right of Allah is predominant*. These are like the *hadd* of *qadhf*. It is to be noted that for the Shafii jurists this is a pure right of the individual.

3. Rules in which the *right of Allah and the right of the individual* lie side by side, but it is the *right of the individual that is predominant*. For this category the example is *qisas* or retaliation for bodily injuries or culpable homicide amounting to murder.

4. The last category is that of rules affecting the *right of the individual*. This category includes almost everything that is not included in the above categories and is beyond reckoning. The important point to consider is that al-Sarakhsi does not mention *tazir* or discretionary penalties. The reason is that the discretionary penalties fall within the category of the right of the individuals, when these are considered collectively, that is, they are the right of the state. The Hanafi jurist al-Kasani clearly states that all *tazir* relates to the right of the individual. The Shafii jurist al-Mawardi has caused some confusion by stating that some *tazir* penalties fall under the right of Allah. Al-Mawardis statement leads to analytical

inconsistencies. Some later Hanafi jurists have also given confusing opinions on the issue. For our purposes, we adopt the more detailed Hanafi view.

The classification given above pertains to obligation-creating rules and shows how each type of law is linked with a right, which is either a right of Allah, or the right of the individual, or the right of both. The most important thing to remember, however, is that each act to which a *hukm* is related must be assigned a specific right or combination of rights.

Each act, therefore, must be a right of Allah, or the right of the individual, or a combination of the two. In the classification provided by jurists, the right of the *saltanah* is not mentioned, because the further sub-classification of this right is left to the ruler. It should be obvious, however, that all acts related to *tazir* offences, to taxes other than *zakat*, and a host of other areas will all be affected by the right of the state, as distinct from the right of Allah. Acts affecting the right of Allah involve duties owed to Allah alone, while the right of the state relates to obligations created by the state. Even the ruler or the state owes some rights to Allah. As the causes, consequences, and conditions affecting the right of state vary with the passage of time, the *fuqaha* saw no need to issue permanent rulings for them.

Classification of Duties: Original and Substitutory : Each right has a corresponding duty. A right is secured when the subject who owes the duty brings about the required act, that is, performs the duty owed by him. Muslim jurists say that each duty has an original form *(asl)* and a substitutory form *(khalaf)*. For example, performance of prayer is a duty that flows out of a right of Allah requiring it. The condition for its performance is ablution *(wudu)* with water, which also becomes a duty as it completes a *wajib*. If the subject fails to perform this duty, because he cannot find water, the Lawgiver provides a substitute in the form of clean soil. In the case of *qisas* (retaliation), it is the duty of the ruler or the state to subject the offender to *qisas*. If this is not possible for some reason, the state has to ensure the recovery of compensation in money as a substitute *(badlus sulh* or *diyah)*.

Some writers, following Abdur Rahim, have called this a classification of rights: original and substitutory rights. This is possible, because where there is a right there is a duty. It is suggested, however, that it is better to focus on performance and duties, otherwise some confusion may be created. This can be seen from the example of retaliation above.

Qisas is claimed by the state as a mixed right of Allah and the individual (the heirs of the victim). When *qisas* is not possible monetary compensation is substituted.

Legal Principles

Is the right of Allah replaced by the right of the individual here during substitution? The question is answered when we think in terms of duties. Thus, when we speak of original and substitutory rights, we may not be speaking of the original claimants of these rights.

The rule for substitutory duties is that they cannot be performed unless the original duty has been created and is not possible to perform.

The Importance of the Classification for Islamic Criminal Law : There are many ways in which the classification of the *mahkum fih* into various kinds of rights and their related acts is employed in Islamic law. The explanation of the above classification will remain incomplete if we do not indicate some area of the law with respect to the operation of different rights. We have chosen the criminal law to do so, though we can deal with the topic very briefly here.

Muslim jurists classified crimes on basis of the right violated. The classification on the basis of rights is linked directly with procedure. The kind of right violated determines the procedure to be followed in courts. If the right of Allah is violated, the procedure followed is that for *hudud* and *qisas*[11]. When the right of the individual is violated, the procedure followed is that prescribed for *tazir,* which maintains the *nisab* in evidence of two females for one male. When the right of the state is violated, the procedure followed is that of *siyasah.*

Jurists like al-Sarakhsi placed *hudud* penalties, excluding the *hadd* of *qadhf* in the category of the pure right of Allah. The *hadd* of *qadhf* is classified as a mixture of the right of Allah and the right of the individual, in which the right of Allah is predominant. The offence of murder liable to *qisas* is classified as a mixture of the right of Allah and the right of the individual, but here it is the right of the individual that is predominant. It is because of the existence of the right of Allah in these categories that the procedure adopted is that determined for the pure right of Allah.

Tazir and *diyah* are classified by most Hanafi jurists as belonging to the area of the right of the individual. The *fuqaha*[12] do not mention the *siyasah* penalties, yet we know that the ruler exercised this jurisdiction right from the first century of the Hijrah onwards. The *mazalim* courts, the institution of the *amil al-suq,* and the institution of the *muhtasib* belong to this jurisdiction. This was the right of the state, and the procedure was determined by the state to ensure flexibility and ease of implementation. This classification led to the following legal rules and distinctions:

1. *Commuting the Sentence and Pardon :* The penalty for an offence against the right of Allah cannot be waived or commuted after apprehension and

conviction. However, the penalty for an offence against the right of an individual alone or against the rights of individuals, that is, the right of the state, can be commuted. The important point to be made here is that if the right of Allah and the right of the state (or the right of the community as a whole) were the same thing, the state would not be able to commute any sentence according to the system developed by the jurists, whether awarded as *hadd, tazir,* or as *siyasah.* We know very well that the state can pardon any sentence that is not a *hadd.* The reason is that sentences other than *hadd* are not awarded and applied as a right of Allah.

2. *The Operation of Shubhat (mistakes) in Hudud: Shubhah* (lit doubt) in the right of Allah has the effect of waiving the penalty of *hadd,* while it does not have the same effect in *tazir, Qisas* (retaliation) has been assigned an element of the right of Allah as it is waived due to *shubhah.* This kind of doubt is not to be confused with the benefit of a doubt that goes to the accused in positive law, which is a doubt in the mind of the judge as to whether the crime has been proved beyond doubt. Islamic law has no objections to this, as proving an offence beyond doubt is a requirement in Islamic law. *Shubhah* mentioned here exists in the mind of the accused at the time of the commission of the act on the basis of conflicting opinions about the *hukm* or because of a particular set of facts. An example of *shubhat al-milk* is, in the opinion of Malik, when the offender steals (or takes by way of stealth) the property of the *baital-mal* (treasury) under the impression that he is part owner of the property. In law the *shubhat* are referred to as mistakes: mistake or ignorance of fact and mistake or ignorance of law.

3. *Shubhah and Tazir:* All *tazir* is the right of the individual and it is for this reason that *shubhah* does not operate in it. This is the claim made by al-Kasani. Some jurists, mostly Shafiites, have said that *tazir* can also be a right of Allah. This is an inconsistent statement, for *tazir* as a right of Allah would prevent pardon (*afw*), which is an acknowledged attribute of *tazir.*

4. *Criminal Proceedings and Evidence:* The evidence of women is not admissible in the right of Allah, that is, in *hudud,* while it is in the case of *tazir,* which is the right of the individual, but the *nisab* of one man and two women has to be maintained, as in the case of other rights of the individual. No such restriction is applicable to the right of the state and a single woman can furnish evidence that is admissible in cases falling under *siyasah,* just as circumstantial evidence is admissible whenever the *haqq al-saltanah* is in issue. In other words, the criminal

proceedings and requirements of evidence change according to the right involved. In modern Muslim writings and in the application of the law in Pakistan today, *tazir* and *siyasah* are both classified under the heading of *tazir*.

If one ponders over these classifications of crimes and the statements of the jurists about the various associated rules, the only conclusion that can be drawn is that the right of the state is distinct from the right of Allah. The main point that we wish to make here is that one use of the classification of acts into rights is that it governs the rules of evidence and procedure in the criminal law.

Modern jurists have ignored the significance of *siyasah* in crimes, and they appear to have merged the two areas of *tazir* and *siyasah*. This is a wise step, but only if the contradictions resulting from this merger are resolved. For example, after the merger, they appear to have forgotten that according to the earlier jurists the *nisab* of witnesses has to be maintained in *tazir*.

The second point that needs to be emphasised here with respect to contradiction is that this area, whatever the name chosen for it, *cannot be designated as a right of Allah*, as this would invoke *shubhah* and its consequences along with other the other rules that operate exclusively within the right of Allah.

Finally, if the condition of the *nisab* of witnesses imposed by the jurists has been removed arbitrarily for *tazir* and a single woman is permitted to testify in such crimes, a logical problem pertaining to the evidence of women in commercial law is raised.

The question is: If the *nisab* of two female witnesses for one male witness can be eliminated in the case of *tazir*, which is the right of the individual, should it not be waived in the case of other rights of the individual, i.e., commercial transactions? A solution would be to interpret the Quranic text as a recommendation *(nadb)* rather than as an obligation *(wujub)*. In short, these are not matters for picking and choosing according to convenience; the whole system has to be checked for analytical consistency.

RIGHTS OF MANKIND

It is possible to classify rights in other ways in Islamic law. One such classification can be seen in the public and private interests into which the *maqasid al-shariah* or the purposes of Islamic law are divided. It is from this classification that human rights recognised by Islamic law are also derived. The division into public and private interests is discussed briefly under the topic of *maslahah* in the next part of this book.

Developing the Islamic Theory of Rights and Duties : After having discussed rights and duties in the traditional sense, it must be pointed out that these concepts need to be elaborated and analysed further so as to enable the modern legal system and the members of the legal profession to make use of them. Here we can only briefly indicate the areas in which research is required by Muslim jurists and scholars.

Some ideas from the works of different thinkers and writers are given below to indicate the different issues that may need to be given importance. The purpose is to show that while there are some jurists who have criticised the very idea of rights and their utility for the legal system, others have deemed rights to be essential for the smooth functioning of the legal machinery and the protection of interests. What is clear, however, is that there is scope for such discussions within the area of rights called the right of the state and the area that is purely the right of the individual. The category designated as the right of God is clearly settled by the *Shariah,* yet the relationship of such rights with individual and public interests needs to be developed in greater detail.

According to Dias, conduct is regulated by the imposition of duties. Claims [or rights in the strict sense] may assist in achieving this end, but if it can be otherwise achieved, there is no reason why the mere fact that Y is under a duty with regard to X should confer upon X, or anyone else for that matter, a corresponding claim. There is nothing to prevent it being the law that every breach of duty, of whatsoever sort, shall be dealt with by the machinery of the state.

Such a state of affairs, though possible, would be inconvenient, for it would stretch state machinery to breaking point. Where duties are of private concern, the remedies are best left to individuals to pursue in the event of their breach. Above all, it is expedient to give aggrieved persons some satisfaction, usually by way of compensation. Every system of law has to decide which breaches of duties shall be taken up by the public authorities on their own motion; and which shall be left to private persons to take up or not as they please. The distinction between "public" and "private" law is quite arbitrary. It would seem, therefore, that there is no intrinsic reason why claims should be a necessary concomitant of duties. Indeed, some modern writers, for different reasons reject the whole idea of claims or rights as redundant.

One such writer was Leon Duguit (1859-1928), although similar ideas in a somewhat altered form may be found in the writings of Scandinavian jurists as well. According to Edgar Bodenheimer, Duguit[13], a French jurist, presented a new type of natural law theory. This doctrine was diametrically opposed to other natural law doctrines.

Duguit repudiated any natural or inalienable rights of individuals. His objective was to supplant the traditional system of legal rights by a system which would recognise only legal duties. Every individual has a certain task to perform in society, Duguit said, and his obligation to perform this function may be enforced by the law. The only right any man might be said to possess under this theory is the right always to do his duty.

As Corwin has aptly said, "this theory is that of Locke stood on its head."

Notwithstanding his emphasis on social duties, Duguit rejected any absolutist conception of state power. He proposed to strip the state and its organs of all sovereign rights and other attributes of sovereignty with which the traditional doctrine of public law had endowed it. Duguit taught that the governing authorities, like citizens, have only duties, and no rights.

Their activity is to be confined to the performance of certain social functions, and the most important of these functions is the organisation and maintenance of public services. It is the duty of governmental officials to guarantee a continuous and uninterrupted operation of the public services. This aim, Duguit believed, would be most effectively realised by a far-reaching decentralisation and technical autonomy of the public utilities under a syndicalist structure of the state.

According to J.W. Harris, on the other Hand, Correlativity is Essential : Correlativity is essential, as part of the law's lowest common denominators, because every judicial question concerns two people. The notion of tax law imposing duties without correlative rights does not arise because, in court, someone or the other (some revenue officer perhaps) must be claiming that a man ought to have paid so much tax. The only question the court has to decide is: Did this defendant owe a duty to this plaintiff?

Thus, in accordance with this reasoning, the answer would be that if there is someone in court to claim the breach of a duty, a correlative right exists. As long as there is someone to enforce the performance of a duty, a right exists; the right vests in the person undertaking the enforcement. The idea of rights in Islamic law clearly includes this function, because the function of the legal system is the adjudication of rights, and this makes it necessary that there be someone to claim the right.

It is obvious that the concept of rights in Islamic law is much wider than this. First, there are certain duties that the state owes to God. An example is the implementation of *hudud (iqamat al-hudud)*.

Such duties of the state emerge from the negative or defensive component of the purposes of law. Further, there are the duties of the state that emerge from the positive component of the *maqasid:* the establishing of *din,* the creating of conditions for the healthy flourishing of life, the strengthening of the family system, the creation of conditions for the development of the mind, and the striving for the growth of communal and individual wealth.

All these duties are justiciable. Any Muslim can go to a court of law and enforce these duties of the state. The right belongs to God, but the claimant is an individual. All this will conform with what Harris has said above, but the idea needs to be developed in detail along with a discussion of fundamental rights.

Besides these there are duties owed to God by individuals: like praying, fasting, paying *zakat* and the like. Out of these the payment of *zakat* is justiciable and the claimant will be the community or the state. The other rights may become justiciable when neglected by the entire community.

In Islamic law the idea of rights has another important dimension, a dimension that is usually overlooked. Different classes of rights in Islamic law determine the procedure to be adopted even within categories like criminal procedure, for example. Each matter brought before the court is adjudicated on the basis of the right claimed. This is evident in the criminal law and should be explained through its procedure. We have already discussed this above.

Assessment of Rights

Western jurists have contributed tremendously to the analysis of rights. Their efforts sharpen our understanding of the idea of rights and help us identify certain jural relations. The word "right" in ordinary speech or in a "wider sense" includes the following terms: claims, liberties, powers and immunities. It is only the word "claim" that conveys the meaning of right in the strict sense. For example, when we speak of having a right to appoint an agent or to enter into a contract, it is not a right we are speaking of but a power given to us by the law. At other times the term right is used to convey the meaning of liberty to act or not to act.

This type of analysis of rights has led to what is called the Hoffeldian scheme. The subjection of the idea of rights in Islamic law to such a scheme would lead to a better understanding of jural relations within this legal system. Such an understanding in turn will lead to a better adjudication of rights.

Traits of Duties

The analysis of duties within Islamic law is no less important. A duty is an obligation to do something. In other words, it is better to view it from the point of view of performance, as compared to obligation, which may be viewed from the perspective of acceptance and imposition. We have already stated that the jurists attempt to make this distinction by treating *ijab* in a different sense from *wujub*. The analysis of duties in Islamic law must answer the fundamental question: why does a duty continue to exist, that is, continue to be law? The answer lies in the examination of the changing purposes of duties.

We have to examine the issue whether "[t]he morality of yesterday has perpetuated itself as an anachronism in legal form. Or it may be that considerations other than morality gave rise to a duty, in which case the duty is independent of morality." Is there something binding in the sources and morality must conform to it? For example, how is it that the earlier jurists could perceive such wide rights for the guardian *(wali)*, but modern jurists may be inclined to be lenient today, especially when the system of tribal morality has collapsed? How is it that the earlier jurists could see a duty on would-be spouses to observe the rules of proportionality in status and modern writers do not see such a duty? The same can be said about slavery and other matters.

These questions require that the nature of duties be analysed in depth. The broad general features of duties in Islamic law must be identified, features that help us identify the law as well as accommodate the changes in the environment.

Natural Rights and Rights Given by the Law : Above all, the question has to be answered whether Islamic law recognises certain natural rights or whether it looks at rights granted by the *Shariah* alone. These two types of rights would be different from the rights granted and taken away by the state. In fact, the state it appears has a limited role to play in the granting of rights. This means that if the rights are given by the *Shariah*, they can only be taken away by the *Shariah*. In such a case, the rights will exist whether or not they are stated in the constitution of a Muslim state. The courts will have to enforce these rights under all circumstances and no emergency can justify the suspension of such rights. Yet, more research is needed to develop the theory of these rights. In our view, however, a deeper research may reveal that such rights are not only individual rights guaranteed by the *Shariah*, but they may turn out to be rights that have been guaranteed to the individuals and are claimed as the right of God.

ROLE OF THE SUBJECTS

The subject or the *mahkum alayh* forms the third element of the *hukm shari*. He is the person whose act invokes a *hukm*, or a *hukm* requires him to act in a prescribed manner. In legal parlance, he is known as the *mukallaf* (subject). A *mukallaf* is a person who possesses legal capacity, whether he acts directly or through delegated authority.

The first requirement for legal capacity is the ability to understand the communication that creates the obligation. In addition to this, there are a number of other conditions that must be fulfilled before the law can operate against or for a person. These conditions are all related to legal capacity, known as *ahliyyah*[14] in juristic terminology.

This topic is important for understanding Islamic law generally, but it has special significance for criminal law and the law of contract. All the general defences, for example, under criminal law are covered under this topic. Further, possession of contractual capacity is an essential element of each contract.

Strength of Law

The literal meaning of the word *ahliyyah* is absolute fitness or ability. *Ahliyyah* is "the ability or fitness to acquire rights and exercise them and to accept duties and perform them." This meaning indicates two types of capacity: the first is based on the acceptance or acquisition of rights and the other on the performance of duties. These are called *ahliyyat al-wujub* and *ahliyyat al-ada* or the capacity for acquisition (of rights) and the capacity for execution or performance of duties. Capacity for acquisition enables a person to acquire both rights and obligations, while capacity for execution gives him the ability to exercise such rights and perform his duties.

In the opinion of some jurists, the term *dhimma* also means the ability to acquire rights and obligations. The majority of the jurists consider *dhimma* to be an imaginary container or receptacle that holds both the capacity for acquisition and the capacity for execution. It is the location or place of residence for the two kinds of capacity. In short, *dhimma* is the balance-sheet of a person showing his assets and liabilities, in terms of his rights and obligations.

In Islamic law, *dhimma*[15] is deemed a requisite condition for the existence of *ahliyyah*. According to al-Sarakhsi, *dhimma* is the "trust" that was offered to the mountains, but they refused; Man accepted it. Thus, *dhimma* is an attribute conferred by the Lawgiver. It is a trust resulting from a covenant *(ahad)*. The fact that *dhimma* is a covenant between the Lawgiver and the *abd* (subject) means that *dhimma* can be assigned to a natural person alone. In Western law, the term *dhimma* conforms with "personality," which is an attribute conferred on a natural person as well as an artificial person.

The Underlying Bases of Legal Capacity : Legal capacity, as stated, is of two types: *ahliyyat al-wujub* and *ahliyyat al-ada*. *Ahliyyat al-wujub* is defined as the ability of a human being to acquire rights and obligations. It may, therefore, be referred to as the capacity for acquisition.

Legal Principles

Manat is a thing from which another thing is suspended. The *manat* or basis for the existence of the capacity for acquisition is the attribute of being a human or natural person *(insaniyyah)*. There is complete agreement among jurists that this form of capacity is possessed by each human being irrespective of his being a *mukallaf*.

Capacity for execution, on the other hand, is defined as the "capability of a human being to issue statements and perform acts to which the Lawgiver has assigned certain legal effects."

The *manat* or basis of the capacity for execution is *aql* (intellect) and *(rushd)* discretion. *Aql* here implies the full development of the mental faculty. As there is no definitive method for checking whether this faculty is fully developed, the Lawgiver has associated it with *bulugh* or puberty.

Thus, the presumption is that a pubescent person is assumed to possess *aql* necessary for the existence of the capacity for execution. This presumption, however, is rebuttable, and if it is proved that though a person has attained puberty, he does not yet possess *aql,* capacity for execution cannot be assigned to such a person. This is the view of the majority of the jurists.

The Hanafis acknowledge a deficient capacity for execution for purposes of some transactions for a person who has attained a degree of discretion, even if his mental faculties are not yet fully developed. Thus, a minor *(sabi)* who possesses discretion, or exhibits "mental maturity" may be assigned such a capacity, for the *khitab* of *muamalat*. Again, there is no way here of determining whether the minor has attained discretion.

The Hanafi jurists have, therefore, fixed the minimum age of seven years for assigning such a capacity; anyone over seven years of age who has not yet attained puberty may be assigned such a capacity, but the law makes this dependent on the guardian's will and discretion. Accordingly, this type of capacity is divided into three kinds on the basis of the type of liability associated with an act:

1. Capacity for the *khitab jinai* or legal capacity for criminal liability. It is based on the ability to comprehend the *khitab jinai, i.e.*, the communication pertaining to criminal acts.

2. Capacity for the *khitab* of *ibadat* or legal capacity for *ibadat*. It is based on the ability to understand the *khitab* of *ibadat, i.e.*, the communication from the Lawgiver pertaining to acts of worship.

3. Capacity for the *khitab* of *muamalat* or legal capacity for transactions. It is based on the ability to understand the *khitab* of *muamalat, i.e.*, the communication from the Lawgiver pertaining to the *muamalat*.

Two of these are civil and criminal liability, while the third is an addition because of religious law. The reason for separating the capacity for execution into these three types is to indicate that a person may, for example, be in possession of the capacity for transactions, but not the capacity for punishments. To put it differently, all three kinds of capacity may be found in the person who is sane and a major, but one or more of these may be lacking in other persons.

TOTAL STRENGTH

Muslim jurists divide legal capacity into three types: complete, deficient and imperfect. The terms *kamilah, naqisah* and *qasirah* are used to distinguish between such capacities. Complete capacity for acquisition is found in a human being after his birth. This makes him eligible for the acquisition of all kinds of rights and obligations.

Complete capacity for execution is established for a human being when he or she attains full mental development, and acquires the ability to discriminate. This stage is associated with the external standard of puberty. The physical signs indicating the attainment of puberty are the commencement of ejaculation in a male and menstruation in a female.

In the absence of these signs, puberty is presumed at the age of fifteen in both males and females according to the majority of the jurists, and at the age of eighteen for males and seventeen for females according to Abu Hanifah[16]. Attaining *bulugh* (puberty) alone is not sufficient, however. For a person to acquire complete capacity for execution, in addition to puberty, the possession of *rushd* (discrimination; maturity of actions) is stipulated as well. The *dalil,* or legal evidence, for this is the verse of the Quran:

> Make trial of orphans until they reach the age of marriage; then if ye find sound judgement in them, release their property to them; but consume it not wastefully, nor in haste against their growing up.
>
> [Quran 4 : 6]

This verse lays down clearly that there are two conditions that must be fulfilled before the wealth of orphans can be handed over to them. These are *bulugh al-nikah* and *rushd.*

The term *rushd,* according to the majority, signifies the handling of financial matters in accordance with the dictates of reason. The *rashid* is a person who can identify avenues of profit as well as loss, and act accordingly to preserve his wealth. *Rushd* is the opposite of *safah* (foolishness), which implies waste and prodigality. Shafii jurists define *rushd* as maturity of actions in matters of finance as well as of *din.* In their view, a person who has attained puberty and is adept

Legal Principles

in dealing with financial matters cannot be called *rashid,* unless he obeys the *ahkam* of the *Shariah* in matters of *ibadat* as well.

A person, then, is eligible for taking over his wealth if he is both a *baligh* and a *rashid.* This is the general view. Abu Hanifah, however, maintains that a person who attains the age of twenty-five years, must be delivered his property irrespective of his attaining *rushd.* In addition to this, he maintains that if a person attains *bulugh* and *rushd* and is given his property, but subsequently loses his *rushd,* while yet under twenty-five, he cannot be subjected to interdiction *(hajr).* Abu Hanifah appears to be giving preference to life and freedom of the individual over his wealth in these cases. The majority of the jurists *(jumhur)*[17] subject a person to interdiction if he has not attained *rushd* or even when he loses it subsequently, irrespective of his age.

On attaining complete capacity, an individual comes within the purview of all the different kinds of *khitab* (communication from the Lawgiver). He, therefore, becomes liable to punishments because of the *khitab Jinai* being directed towards him, just as he becomes liable because of the *khitab* of transactions and *ibadat.*

Stages Leading to Complete Legal Capacity : The conditions laid down by the Hanafi jurists indicate that there are three stages through which an individual passes with respect to his capacity for execution.

1. The first stage is from birth till the attainment of partial discretion, which is considered to be the age of seven years. During this period, the child is assumed to lack *aql* and discretion completely, and is ineligible for the assignment of a capacity for execution.

2. The second stage commences from the age of seven and continues up to actual puberty or the legal age of puberty, whichever is earlier. Deficient capacity for execution is normally assigned during this stage, as the individual possesses a certain amount of *aql* and discretion.

3. The final stage commences from actual physical puberty or the legal age determined for it, whichever is earlier. On reaching this age the individual is assigned complete capacity for execution, and becomes eligible for each kind of *khitab.* An exception arises in the case of *safah* and the individual may be placed under interdiction for some time. *Rushd* (discretion) is a condition for attaining this stage, in addition to puberty.

Deficient and Imperfect Capacity : Deficient capacity is assigned in cases where the *manat* or basis of legal capacity is not fully developed. Thus, a person may not have been born as yet or he may not have reached full mental development. In other cases, the attribute of being a human may be missing altogether.

Imperfect capacity is assigned in cases where the bases of capacity, being a human and possession of discretion, are present, but an external attribute has been introduced that does not permit the recognition of the legal validity of certain acts.

Deficient and imperfect capacity is understood through the study of different cases falling under each. A brief look at these cases follows.

Cases of Deficient Legal Capacity

The Unborn Child (Janin) : *Deficient or incomplete capacity* is established for an unborn child or the foetus *(janin)*. Deficient capacity implies that only some rights are established for the *janin* and no obligations are imposed on it. The reason is that the *janin* is considered part of the mother in some respects. Thus, it is set free with the mother and is also sold as a part of her (in the case of the *umm ul-walad)*. An independent personality is, therefore, not assigned to it. In other respects, the *janin* enjoys a separate life and is preparing for separation from the womb. Its personality is, therefore, considered deficient or incomplete. By virtue of this deficient capacity, the *janin* acquires certain rights: freedom from slavery, inheritance, bequest, and parentage.

On the other hand, the *janin* cannot be made liable for the satisfaction of rights owed to others. A purchase made by the would-be *wali* (guardian) on behalf of the *janin* cannot make the *janin* liable for the payment of the price. Likewise, the maintenance of close relatives and the membership of the *aqilah* cannot be enforced against the *janin*. Once the child is born, these rights can be enforced against it, but not when the obligations were acquired during the gestation period.

Capacity of a Dead Person : A deficient capacity for acquisition is also assigned to a *dead man or to a corpse*. Thus, amounts due on account of debts, bequest, and funeral expenses are taken from the wealth of the dead man. For example, if a person had thrown a net into the water immediately before his death, the fish caught in the net after the person's death belong to him. Likewise, if he had dug a pit before his death with the intention of trapping someone in it, then the *diyah* due as a result of someone falling in it is to be recovered from such a person's wealth. Further, any compensation due for property destroyed by acts commencing before his death shall be recovered from his property. As in English law, the estate of the deceased is not assigned legal personality. The Roman law and the French law do assign a personality to the estate.

Capacity of a Fictitious Person : Modern Muslim writers being faced with the need to acknowledge the existence of a fictitious personality, as it forms the basis of the present socio-legal structure, have claimed that such a concept does exist in Islamic law. They rely for this on instances like *waqf, bayt al-mal,* and the estate of the deceased. These assertions seem to be misplaced. Islamic law as expounded by the jurists does not acknowledge the concept of a fictitious person. It will be found to clash with the provisions of this law, whether the area is that of contracts, *hudud,* or constitutional law. In other words, the idea of a fictitious person is incompatible with Islamic law as expounded by the jurists.

This does not mean that the jurists were not aware of the concept. They were aware of it, but did not acknowledge it for Islamic law. The main reason appears to be that *dhimma* is an *ahd* (covenant) with the Lawgiver (see p. 110 above), and a fictitious person cannot be expected to enter into such a covenant primarily because it cannot perform religious duties.

In other words, the law derived by the jurists does not need this concept and will reject it. Nevertheless, the modern world is organised around the concept of the corporation or the fictitious personality. Modern scholars will, therefore, have to work hard to accommodate this concept into the fold of Islamic law. This means that adjustments will have to be made in the law wherever this concept clashes with it.

The fictitious person may be deemed to have deficient capacity that is not fit for the performance of religious duties, like the payment of *zakat*. It is important to note that justifying the legal validity of a fictitious legal personality under Islamic law may not be very difficult if the general principles of this law are applied. It is what comes after such justification that is important. Take the case of the state. When we admit the state as a person within Islamic law a number of traditional concepts prevalent within Islamic constitutional law appear to need alteration.

For instance, the state owns all the land within its territory. The stipulations regarding revival of barren land *(ihya al-mawat)* become meaningless, because the primary condition is that only that land can be revived that is not owned by anyone. Here all the land is owned by the state as a person, and this excludes the possibility of any revival. Yes, the state may grant land to landless peasants, but that is not the issue here; here we are talking about the clash of concepts. Further, Islamic law contemplates a personal relationship between the head of the state or the chief executive and between the members of the community, that is, the relationship is governed by the contract of *wakalah* (agency) where the head of state is an agent of the citizens.

When the state intervenes, these relationships are altered. In the case of corporations, when the juristic person steps in, the traditional concepts of *sharikah* lose their significance. In short, what we mean is that accepting this concept is not a question of saying "yes" or "no," a number of changes will have to be made to the existing Islamic law of contract, changes that may wreck its whole structure and violate the fundamental principles upon which it is based.

Capacity of the Minor (Sabi) : A child possesses a complete capacity for acquisition of rights and obligations, but until he attains the age of actual or legal puberty, he lacks the capacity for execution. To facilitate matters, this child is made liable by the *Shariah* only for those obligations that he can meet. Deficient capacity for execution is assigned to a non-pubescent who possesses some discretion, or to a *matuh* (idiot) who has attained puberty yet lacks complete mental development.

The person who possesses deficient capacity is not subject to the *khitab jinai*; he cannot, therefore, be held criminally liable. The minor, however, is subjected to *tadib* (discipline)—the reason being that the *khitab jinai* is applicable to that person alone who comprehends the *khitab* fully.

This is based on the principle of legality in Islamic law. With respect to the *ibadat,* there are detailed discussions whether the *khitab* is addressed to the *sabi* and *matuh* by way of *nadb* (recommendation) or *khiyar* (choice), or whether it is addressed to them at all. There is no dispute that there is reward *(thawab)* for such a person for the performance of the *ibadat.*

The Hanafis treat the issue of legal capacity of the minor in a somewhat different way. Our major concern here is for the capacity of such a person for the purpose of transactions.

1. *Financial Transactions are Established Against the Dhimma of the Sabi:* Though he cannot meet them personally due to the absence of the capacity for execution, the Lawgiver allows his *wall* (guardian) to stand in his place and represent him through a substitutory duty. The *sabi* is also liable for any damage caused to another's property, and for the maintenance of his wives and near relatives. He is also liable, except in the opinion of the Hanafi school, for the payment of *zakat.* All financial transactions are divided into three types for determining the liability of the discriminating minor.

    (a) *Purely Beneficial Transactions :* The transactions falling under this category are the acceptance of a gift or of *sadaqah*. These are allowed to the person who has not attained puberty, but who can discriminate and has been permitted by his *wali* (guardian) to exercise such acceptance.

Legal Principles

(b) *Purely Harmful Transactions* : The granting of divorce, manumission (*itq*), charity *(sadaqah)*, loan *(qard)*, and gift *(hibah)*, as well as the making of a trust *(waqf)* and bequest *(wasiyyah)* are considered transactions resulting in pure financial loss. These are not permitted to the *sabi mumayyiz*[18] (discriminating minor).

(c) *Transactions Vacillating between Profit and Loss* : Sale, hire, partnership, and other such transactions are considered valid if ratified by the *wali*.

2. Criminal liability does not exist in the case of a person who has not attained puberty, because he is not a *mukallaf,* and the *wali* cannot stand in his place for criminal offences: punishments being deterrents for the offender himself and not for those who represent them. This, however, holds true as far as *hudud* and *qisas* penalties are concerned; a child over seven may be liable to some suitable form of *tadib*. Yet, this may not be interpreted to mean that a minor can be awarded penalties other than the *hudud* if he is over seven, as is done in the law.

3. The *ibadat* are not obligatory on the *sabi,* as he does not possess the capacity for execution.

The deficient capacity granted to the discriminating minor by the Hanafis is also granted to the *matuh* (idiot). The majority of the jurists *(jumhur)* oppose the Hanafis and refuse to acknowledge any kind of capacity for the discriminating minor. They maintain that the communication *(khitab)* is not directed toward such a minor at all, and it is of no consequence whether the transactions are beneficial or harmful. In practice, however, we find young boys minding stores on behalf of their fathers, and often handling the transactions exceptionally well.

Cases of Imperfect Capacity : Capacity for acquisition may be perfect or imperfect. Imperfect capacity is attributed to women and slaves.

Legal Capacity of a Woman : A woman is said to possess imperfect legal capacity. Those who hold this view deny her the right to be the head of state, the right to be a *qadi* (judge), and the right to testify in cases being tried under *hudud* and *qisas* provisions (that is, duties where the right of God is involved). In addition to this, she does not have the right to divorce, like the right given to a man, she is given a share in inheritance that is equal to half the share of male heirs, and the *diyah* paid in compensation of her death is half that of a man. These provisions have led certain Orientalists, like Joseph Schacht, to observe that in Islamic law "a woman is half a man."

Women who are struggling for the emancipation and acceptance of their rights in Muslim countries have objected seriously to such a status granted to them.

Demanding equality with men, they maintain that the status of women should be the same as that of men, by which they mean that their legal capacity should not be considered imperfect or deficient in any way.

The purpose here is not to argue from one side or the other, but to identify the legal issues involved. Reasons or solutions will become obvious once these issues are grasped.

Evidence of Women : The most important issue appears to be that of the evidence of women. This is split into two sub-issues. The first is whether the evidence of women is excluded by the texts of the Quran and *Sunnah* in cases of *hudud?* The usual answer given in reply is that the evidence of women is excluded in such cases on the basis of the *Sunnah,* which is also a source of law. These are cases involving the right of Allah. The approach to this issue is that somehow women have been deprived of a right. This is incorrect. Evidence in these cases, and in others too, is a duty and not a right.

Women have been spared the burden of this duty. The purpose is to waive the penalty of *hadd,* which is usually an extreme punishment, and to show mercy to the accused in an indirect way. This, perhaps, is the intention of the Lawgiver. Related to this is a misconception that the offence of rape cannot be proved and punished with the evidence of one woman. It is true that *hadd* cannot be awarded upon the testimony of one woman, but that does not mean that no other punishment can be awarded to the rapist on the basis of such testimony.

The ruler or the state has wide powers under the doctrine of *siyasah* to award an equally stiff penalty. The Federal Shariat Court of Pakistan has ruled that this will be possible.

The second sub-issue is about the evidence of two women being equal to that of one man. This requirement is derived from a verse of the Quran, and is supported by the *Sunnah.* The details of this problem cannot be discussed here. It is suggested, however, that the scholars of this age may try to interpret the relevant verse of the Quran as implying a recommendation rather than an obligation. It should be remembered again that rendering testimony is primarily a duty and not a right, though it leads to the protection of rights.

A Woman's Share in Inheritance : The next issue is whether it is justified in the present times to give a woman half the share of a man. The answer is that the Quran has laid down the law on this in explicit terms. The justification provided by scholars is that the Islamic legal system places a much greater financial burden on the male in terms of maintenance of his family and near ones. Such a burden has not been placed on a woman. Further, a woman is paid dower upon her marriage by the husband. This increases the financial liability for males. The argument from the other side may be that Islamic law, like any comprehensive legal system, especially one that is a complete code of life, is to be applied as a whole, in toto, not in pieces. In such a situation, is it possible for a woman who is left all alone to go to a court of law and enforcing her rights ask her brother, uncle, or cousin to support her? It is obvious that many such rights that the law provides her may not be enforceable today.

Right to Divorce : As to the question of a woman not having a right to divorce the husband, the jurists unanimously agree that such a right has not been granted to her directly. There are, however, provisions in the law like *tafwid, takhyir* and *tamlik* through which she may be granted such a right at the time of the marriage contract, if she so desires. Perhaps, the rulers exercising their *siyasah* jurisdiction may make this provision mandatory.

Diyah : In the case of *diyah,* the majority of the jurists hold that the *diyah* of a woman is half that of a man. This view is based on some traditions and a number of reports from the Companions. Taking into account the number of reports from the Companions, some of the jurists consider it to be a case of *ijma* (consensus of opinion). There are a few jurists, however, like Ibn Ulayyah and Abu Bakr al-Asim who maintain that the *diyah* of a male is equal to that of a female.

They base their opinion upon the generality of a tradition from the Prophet reported by Amr ibn Hazm: "For a believing person a hundred camels." The generality of this tradition treats men and women equally. Few will disagree with the statement that women are working today and are equally efficient working members of the society. In fact, some of them may be earning more than men. In this issue, it is not the right of a woman that is involved, because the right to *diyah* belongs to the heirs, but it is a question of her status. The new law of *qisas* and *diyah* in Pakistan, therefore, makes no distinction between a male and female for purposes of *diyah*.

Judicial Office and being Head of State : According to the jurists, the reason why a woman cannot become a *qadi* or judge is linked to the question of evidence. A *qadi* can only hear cases in which he or she can also be an eligible witness. This is a qualification for the *qadi*. As a woman cannot be a witness in cases of *hadd,* she cannot be a *qadi* for hearing the cases and passing sentence. The question of being a head of state depends on the same reasoning. The primary duty of a head of state is the implementation of *hudud (iqamat al-hudud),* which again requires the qualification of a witness for such cases. A woman is, therefore, considered ineligible for the job. In Pakistan, women judges today are deciding cases under the *hudud* laws.

Bonded Slaves

The slave does not possess the right of ownership, but he does have a capacity for acquiring obligations pertaining to *ibadat,* and for criminal offences.

References

1. A way of solving problems of socio-religious character through consensus.
2. A prominent scholar and thinker of Islam.
3. Islamic law.
4. A western philosopher through whose writings the real development in natural law came.
5. Islamic legal injunctions.
6. Traditions of the Prophet (Pbuh).
7. That on whom/which an order is passed.
8. Eligibility for paying Zakat.
9. Special privileges for the ruler.
10. A seclusion and lonely sitting in a mosque for attaining spiritual power espl. in the month of Ramadan.
11. A punishment paid for an illegal murder.
12. Islamic jurists.
13. A French jurist who presented a new type of natural law theory.
14. Conditions related to legal capacity.
15. A necessary condition for the existence of Ahliyya.
16. One of the most learned scholars of Islam.
17. A majority of.
18. A minor who can differentiate.

6

VARIOUS ASPECTS OF LAW

For the last several years there is a great enthusiasm in the country for enforcement of Islam and Islamic system in every walk of life. Sufficient advancement has been made in this behalf in different directions and several experiments are being made. Steps towards the enforcement of *Hudud* and promulgation of Ordinances in this behalf are also in pursuance of the same policy.

In order to achieve the desired positive result, there are certain prerequisites which are as follows:

(1) Real conception of the problem in question;

(2) Determination of right goal and destiny;

(3) Determination of right time;

(4) Sincerity of purpose;

(5) Proper procedure; and

(6) Appropriate working personnel.

Presently we will deal with point number 5 only. When we examine the question of enforcement of *Hudud* and *Tazeerat* in connection with the establishment of Islamic judicial system in Muslim countries, in the above perspective we come to know that all that has been done is that Islamic *Hudud* and *Tazeerat* connected therewith which were already existing in the shape of substantive law have been codified and promulgated as the law of land.

Let us see as to what guidance we get from treatises on *Fiqh* for the formulation of procedure for enforcement of *Hudud* and *Tazirat*. It is provided in *Al-Tatarkhania* that, "No accused is liable to imprisonment in *Hudud* and *Qisas* until the witnesses give their evidence, and when the witnesses have given their evidence, the accused will he detained in custody until the truthfulness of witnesses is proved by purgation. According to Imam Abu Hanifah, the accused would be detained in custody when one truthful witness has given evidence and according to Sahibain (Imam Muhammad and Imam Abu Yusuf), the accused would not be kept in confinement except in *Hadd* of *Qazf* and *Qisas*."

The evidence is defined in *Fatawa-i Alamgiri* as, "giving of true information with the word of evidence for proving a right, in the court proceedings before Qadi is called evidence."

According to *Hidaya*, "*Zina* is proved with the evidence of witnesses or plea of guilt by accused but this proof must be before Imam (Judge) because *Zina* will not be proved in any way by statement of witnesses and plea of guilt anywhere other than before Imam (Judge)."

It is provided in *Altabieen*[1] that if a *Zani* pleads guilty even for four times before any person other than Qadi, who has no authority to enforce *Hadd*, his plea of guilt is of no consequences because evidence of such plea of guilt is not admissible.

> The learned author of *Hidaya* has quoted in Chapter on *Hudud* that "Imam Muhammad wrote in *'Asaf* (his book) that Qadi should detain that person in jail against whom evidence has been recorded till the time that purgation about witnesses is made because there is allegation of commission of offence against him and The Holy Prophet (peace be upon him) had confined a person on the basis of allegation of offence." (Abu Daud)

From above situations, the following conclusions can be deducted:

First, that every aggrieved person or complainant should present his grievances and complaint before Judge and not before police. In the existing system of administration of criminal justice, practically the F.I.R. plays the role of complaint for all intents and purposes. It is deemed to be foundation of entire case and its contents are treated to be binding on the complainant. As such the present procedure of lodging F.I.R. with police is wrong and should be done away with and every complainant should file his complaint directly before judge instead of lodging F.I.R. at police station.

Secondly, the statements appear to be unnecessary documents. The present procedural law and law of evidence also do not recognize them as evidence *per se* but in spite of that it is height of anomaly that contents of these so-called statements are deemed sufficient to nullify the evidence of witnesses in Court. Meaning thereby that statements prepared by police and mostly without consulting the witnesses are so important that they can render the evidence given by witnesses in open Court and recorded by Judge himself, ineffective.

The law enjoins upon the judge to disbelieve the evidence recorded by himself in open Court *vis-a-vis* the statement prepared by police if the evidence in Court is not in conformity with police statement. Thus, theory and practice on this point are diametrically opposite to each other and indirectly though not directly the police statements are given the status of evidence which is absolutely wrong;

Thirdly, the confessions of accused persons recorded are an exercise in futility because admission of guilt before such Magistrate who has no authority to enforce punishment is a useless thing; and Fourthly, no person should be kept in confinement without evidence before judge.

Now the question arises as to what procedure should be adopted for the initiation of criminal cases and proceedings in *Hudud* and *Tazirat*. We propose the following procedure :

> If complainant is able to produce the accused before judge then he should produce the accused himself before judge and give him in the custody of Court. The complainant should take his witnesses also with himself at the time of producing accused in Court. After producing the accused before judge, the complainant should present his complaint orally before judge in presence of accused. The judge should record the complaint in the form of examination-in-chief as in vogue in the present system, in triplicate and after recording the same should read it himself or may direct his reader to read the same loudly in presence of complainant and the accused and the complainant would be allowed to make any addition, alteration or subtraction in his statement which would be recorded with such note by the judge. Thereafter, judge will obtain signature of complainant on all the three copies of his statement. The original shall be placed in Court file and a copy thereof shall be supplied to complainant and accused, there and then.

After recording of complaint, the judge shall record plea of accused and framing of formal charge would not be necessary. In the plea form it would be sufficient to mention the name of offence alleged against the accused and it would not be necessary to specify the Section of relevant substantive penal law under which the offence is punishable. After recording of plea, the judge would obtain signature of accused on the plea form in open Court. The judge shall append a certificate on the complaint and plea form in token of having recorded the same and shall make endorsement that signature of complainant and accused as the case may be was obtained in his presence in open court.

If accused pleads guilty, the judge shall convict him on his plea of guilt. If the accused does not plead guilty and claim to be tried, the judge shall adjourn the proceeding for two hours and give opportunity to accused for engaging any advocate of his choice available within that time. The proceedings shall be resumed after two hours and trial shall start with cross-examination of complainant. After cross-examination of complainant, his witnesses shall be examined and cross-examined and thereafter statement of accused shall be recorded. The accused may cite witnesses in his defence and the case shall be adjourned for few days keeping in view the place of residence of the defence witnesses and distance from the court. In the intervening period, the judge shall try to complete purgation of complainant and his witnesses. The Public Prosecutor shall conduct cases on behalf of complainant and remain present to assist the judge.

If after completion of prosecution evidence, the judge is of the view that no case is made out for the enforcement of *Hadd,* he may dispense with *Tazkiat-ul-Shahood*[2] (Purgation Proceedings) and in doing so, he may hear the arguments of both the parties then and there or may adjourn the case according to his convenience to an early date and fix the same for arguments.

If the complainant is not able to express himself properly by oral submission then he may present his complaint in writing as well before judge in triplicate in Urdu duly signed by him. The complaint so presented shall be read over by the reader in open court loudly in presence of the complainant and the accused and after hearing the same the complainant shall state on oath that whatever is written in his complaint is true to the best of his knowledge and belief. The judge shall make such endorsement on all the three copies and shall return a copy thereof to the complainant and supply another copy to the accused. This complaint shall be treated as an examination-in-chief and further proceedings shall be the same as narrated above. If the judge feels that complainant is able to express himself properly then he will not accept the written complaint and shall record the oral complaint in Court as suggested above. Receiving of written complaint shall be in exceptional cases.

Any person who has personal knowledge about commission of any offence can be treated as complainant in Court.

If the complainant or aggrieved or affected person feels that taking of accused from the place of incident to the Court would be difficult or risky or cumbersome

Various Aspects of Law

for him or if the offence takes place at such odd hours that it is not possible to produce the accused in Court on that day in working hours, then the accused may be handed over to police and police shall be bound to take that person in custody and shall produce the accused in concerned court at the earliest opportunity. At the time of taking accused in custody, the police shall issue a receipt to person handing over accused to police in which, name, address and other particulars of accused, name, address and other particulars of the person handing over accused to police, the time of handing over accused to police, shall be written briefly. The receipt shall be produced and exhibited by the concerned person at the time of his statement in Court. No evidentiary value for or against shall be attached to the facts if mentioned in the said receipt, either for the complainant or the accused. The only importance of this receipt would be to ensure that no person is kept in confinement or detention by police without any reasonable cause so that the accused persons are produced in Court at the earliest opportunity and without any delay.

Production of witnesses shall be primary responsibility of the complainant. However, in exceptional situation and conditions the assistance of Court may be sought. The court shall have full authority to summon the witnesses and compel their attendance by issuance of coercive process also if so deemed necessary.

If in any incident the medical aid is required, or hurt has been caused or murder has been committed then every person who has been assaulted or injured may go or any other person may take the injured or dead body to the nearest Medical Officer without any reference from court or police and the Medical Officer shall be bound to attend, examine and provide necessary medical aid to him. The Medical Officer shall prepare the certificate of his examination and findings for production in Court. If immediate medical aid or first aid is required then every nearest qualified doctor shall be bound to examine such person and provide necessary medical aid to him. After doing the needful such doctor shall refer the person concerned at the earliest opportunity to the nearest Medical Officer along with the prescription and other documents if any prepared by him. Normally, the unofficial doctor shall not be called in evidence as witness and the documents prepared by him along with his letter of reference, shall be produced in Court by the Medical Officer concerned. However, in special or exceptional circumstances, the court may summon unofficial doctor also. In this connection police and court shall also have power to refer any injured to Medical Officer if he has appeared before police or court without getting himself examined by the doctor.

If complainant is not able to produce accused in court or accused has absconded after the incident or he has not been identified even then the complainant should appear in Court and file his oral complaint before judge and judge shall record statement of his witnesses as well Thereafter, judge may issue such directions to police as deemed fit. As soon as the accused persons are arrested they should be produced before court at the earliest opportunity without loss of any time and the judge shall cause the attendance of complainant and witnesses procured and shall start the trial as suggested above, with a difference that complainant and witnesses shall be read over their statements and they will be allowed to resile from any part of their statement but they will not be permitted to add anything to their previous statement.

If such accused persons are arrested by police who were not identified at the time of incident then after their arrest they will be brought directly to the judge and identification proceedings shall be held in the presence and personal superintendence of the judge and such proceedings shall be treated as evidence in the Court and no further recording of evidence in proof of identification proceedings would be required.

If there are such circumstances when immediate aid or assistance of police is required and it is not possible to reach up to court in working hours or there is apprehension of accused running away from the reach of the law and police or any other compelling circumstances are existing then complainant can lodge report at police station to the extent only that at such and such place, at such and such time, such and such persons identified or un-identified have committed such report and take immediate action. On the basis of such report, the police shall be bound to arrest the persons accused and produce them immediately before court. The police shall supply one copy of such report to the complainant and other copy thereof shall be forwarded to the court concerned.

The complainant shall produce copy of such report supplied to him by police at the time of filing his complaint in Court. If police refuses or neglects to record such report, the complainant shall bring this fact to the knowledge of court at the time of lodging complaint in court and the Court may take action against police after such enquiry as deemed fit. However, the complainant shall not give entire details of the incident in his police report and shall appear before court without loss of any time at the earliest opportunity along with his witnesses and file his oral complaint in Court. If police succeeds in arresting accused persons, they shall also be produced in court and the trial shall start according to procedure suggested above.

The police report shall have no evidentiary value and it shall be deemed to be a source of seeking police aid only. The police should submit entire report of progress in the investigation immediately and day to day before judge.

The entire proceedings of police investigation, concerned with the cases before court shall be brought to the knowledge of court and judge shall have complete control over such matters. If in any case two or more accused persons are required and out of them one or more than one have been arrested and other are absconding then the accused person or persons as the case may be who are arrested shall be produced before court and trial shall commence without waiting for absconding accused persons, and proceedings shall be completed. When absconding accused persons are arrested then the complainant and witnesses shall be called again and the absconding accused shall be tried afresh. In the existing system, the arrested accused and witnesses attend court hearings unnecessarily in such situations and warrants of arrests are issued, and repeated time and again against the absconding accused persons.

After issuance of warrants for several times, the statement of process server is recorded. Thereafter, the absconding accused is declared as proclaimed offender and proclamation for his arrest and attachment of his property is issued. Thereafter, it is ordered that the case may proceed in the absence of absconding accused. This entire procedure causes delay and the waste of time. It is a sort of harassment also to the arrested accused persons and the prosecution witnesses. This procedure should therefore be done away with and court shall issue proclamation for arrest and attachment of the property of absconding accused on the very first date of hearing and shall complete trial against the arrested accused so that the delay and its consequences be avoided.

In the cases of *Hudud* particularly, and *Tazirat* generally, the procedure of, obtaining opinion from Chemical Analyser and Serologist and Ballistic expert should be discontinued and as far as possible the prosecution should depend on the ocular testimony or such circumstantial evidence which can be proved by the evidence of witnesses at the spot or conversant with the facts of the case and in any case other than the so-called expert witnesses.

The trial of cases shall start immediately on the production of accused before court as suggested above and there shall be no adjournment at all. If any trial is not concluded in one day then it shall be compulsorily posted and fixed to the next working day and the cases shall proceed day to day till the conclusion of trial without any adjournment. In the proposed procedure, the prosecution evidence would normally be completed on the very first day of trial and if accused is arrested on the spot, practically the actual trial would concluded on the very day and thereafter only formalities shall remain to be completed.

If the judge thinks fit and proper to inspect the site, he can visit the place of incidence before or after the evidence of prosecution witnesses or at any stage according to the circumstances of each case. If accused is also present at the time of site inspection, it would be more better. For this purpose the judge should be provided official facilities. The judge can appoint Commissioner also in his behalf who will normally visit the site in presence of both the parties and shall obtain their signature on his report which he will prepare at the spot. However, presence of both the parties would not be necessary always.

If any witness being injured is not feeling well and the Medical Officer issues certificate to the effect that the witness is not able to attend the Court, but he is able to depose, then the judge shall appoint Commissioner at the earliest opportunity to record his statement in the hospital or wherever such witness may be. If accused is not arrested then examination-in-chief shall be recorded only and after his arrest. The cross-examination-in-chief shall be conducted in his presence.

If the accused is before court then he shall be sent with the Commissioner so that evidence of such witness shall be recorded in the presence of accused and his advocate, if any. Doing so shall be in consonance with the entire scheme which aims at getting the original version of witnesses recorded at the earliest opportunity in order to avoid the concocted versions. In our present society there is general tendency of falsely implicating innocent persons, due to enmity, taking of vengeance or for deriving some other benefits. There is another tendency of roping in a large number of innocent persons with the actual culprits. This tendency needs to be checked and curbed strictly. The existing laws and the procedure in this behalf are so complicated that the false complainant and witnesses are not punished at all. In spite of committing perjury at trial they have sense of security and their respect and status in the society remain unaffected.

There is the saying of Imam Abu Hanifah about the false witnesses that "I will make public announcement in Bazar about the falsehood of a witness who has given false evidence intentionally, but I will not punish him by way of *Tazeer.*" On the other hand there is saying of Sahibain (Imam Muhammad and Imam Abu Yusuf) that we will beat him and keep him under imprisonment. Imam Shafii, Imam Malik and Imam Ahmad bin Hambal are also of the same view. Hadrat Umar[3] imposed punishment of 40 stripes on a false witness and blackened his face. He issued directions to the Administrator of Syria in connection with false witnesses that they shall be given punishment of 40 stripes, their faces should be blackened, their head shall be shaved and they shall be awarded sentence of imprisonment for long period.

Thus it is proved that punishment can be inflicted on a false complainant and a false witness by way of *Tazir.* Therefore, if at the time of delivering judgement, the judge is satisfied that the complainant has filed false complaint against one or more of the accused persons then by the same judgement he shall suitably punish such complainant. For this purpose the procedure of issuing show cause notice, should be done away with. Likewise, if the judge is satisfied that any witness has intentionally deposed falsely he should also be punished adequately in the same manner.

The minimum punishment should be the making of publicity by the bailiff of court of the complainant or witness being held and declared false by the court with his showing to public in Bazar or at a place where he is generally known, with the message of judge that everybody should be aware of him. The maximum punishment shall be 40 stripes or imprisonment which may extend to 5 years or both. The judge may impose fine only also according to the circumstances of the case, complainant and witnesses.

If any party to the case is not willing for trial in certain court then that party may inform the trial court immediately after the filing of complaint by the complainant and before recording of plea of the accused that he intends to file transfer application. On receiving such intimation, the trial court shall postpone further proceedings and shall take bond of suitable amount from the applicant to the effect that he will file transfer application within two days before the competent authority. If transfer application is not filed within two days then the bond shall be forfeited and trial shall start. If the transfer application is filed, the applicant shall simultaneously supply a copy of the said application to the trial court. He shall send a copy of transfer application to his adversary also before filing of same in the competent court.

The applicant shall produce receipt from the Reader or C. O. C. of the trial court and postal receipt along with the transfer application, otherwise the transfer application shall not be accepted. The trial judge shall submit his remarks to the Court competent to hear the transfer application within two days of receiving the copy of transfer application. The transfer application shall be heard invariably on the 5th day of filing of application and the other side shall be bound to appear on the 5th day of filing of transfer application without any further notice from the said court.

Receiving of copy of application by him shall be deemed to be sufficient notice. If he fails to appear the application shall be heard in his absence. There would be no necessity of the filing of counter-affidavit and rejoinder. The final arguments shall be heard on the application and the parties shall be allowed to submit their respective point of view without formal written objections on record. The court competent to hear the transfer application shall be bound to decide the same within a week of the filing of same.

If none of the parties have given any intimation as above then the proceeding shall not be postponed or adjourned at all till the conclusion of prosecution evidence, on the ground that any party wants to move transfer application. However, after the conclusion of prosecution evidence any party to case may intimate to the court that he intends to move transfer application and on receiving such intimation at this stage, the trial court shall not deliver the final judgement within 12 days of receiving such information, but purgation of complainant and witnesses shall be completed. If the case is transferred then the transferee judge may rely on the same purgation or hold fresh purgation according to his satisfaction.

If the competent judge (who would be Sessions Judge) to hear transfer application rejects the application and feels that there were no reasons at all for the transfer application or feels that it was moved for gaining time or causing delay in the trial then he may impose suitable fine on the applicant which will be recovered as arrears of land revenue.

In the existing system of procedural law all the punishments of *Hadd* become barred by time. If the proposed procedure is adopted then the cases shall be decided within few days and punishment shall not become barred by time. The period allowed for transfer application has been fixed keeping the period of limitation in view.

The requirement of recording of evidence in cases of *Hudud* within one month and in the event of failure punishments becoming barred by time is peculiar to the Islamic system of criminal administration of justice. This practice is alien to all other judicial systems and it is pertinent to keep this provision in view at the time of framing of criminal procedural law for carrying into effect the penal law of *Hudud*.

In addition to adoption of proposed procedure at trial stage, it is also necessary to annul the present provision of appeals and confirmation of sentences. In order to reduce the percentage of wrong judgements it is necessary to appoint such persons as judges whose integrity, honesty and efficiency is above Board. However, it is not possible to get cent per cent right judgements from human beings in any system, under any procedure and by any number of appeals, as such reliance should be made on the understanding, knowledge, efficiency, honesty, impartiality and integrity of judges.

However, if the provision of appeal is deemed necessary as a matter of precaution then the right of one appeal only should be given. For this purpose, the procedure should be like this, that in the cases other than involving death sentence the appeal should be filed within 7 days of the judgement and appeal should be decided within 15 days without fail. In the cases involving death sentences the appeal should be filed within one week of the judgement of trial court and the appeal should be decided within one month without fail.

If any accused is convicted, the trial court shall supply a certified copy of the judgement to him at the time of announcing judgement. After announcement of judgement the file shall be immediately sent to the Appellate Court so that when the appeal is preferred the case file is already available in the Appellate Court. The trial court should send a copy of judgement of conviction to D.P.P. or Advocate-General also as the case may be and inform him about the sending of case file to the Appellate Court.

The system of preparation of paper book in the Appellate Court, in the appeals relating to *Hudud* and *Tazeerat* should be discarded instead of doing so, three photostat copies of entire file (which will not be very bulky in the proposed procedure) should be prepared at the expense of Appellant. The approximate expenses of photostating should be deposited by Appellant at the time of filing appeal. The Appellate Court should arrange for supply of photostat copies of entire file to the advocate for appellant and Government Advocate both within 3 days of filing of appeal. The appeal in *Hudud* and *Tazeerat* should normally be heard in the cases involving sentences other than death penalty on the 10th day of filing of appeal and the appeal involving death sentences should normally be heard on 20th day of filing of appeal However, the Appellate Court and Advocates may make adjustment in this behalf in such a manner that the time schedule for disposal of appeal is not disturbed.

The trial court and the Appellate court may release any accused in custody, on bail, if the court is satisfied that there are sufficient reasons and grounds for doing so. Both the courts shall have authority for granting bail before arrest also.

The courts which will try *Hudud* and *Tazeerat* cases shall not deal with the pending cases under the laws other than *Hudud* and *Tazeerat*. Such other cases shall be tried, heard and adjudicated upon by other courts.

Various Traits

The Methodology : The belief in Islam as an evolved culmination of the process of divine revelation finds authentication from the Islamic Scripture. Therefore, as an article of Faith, the authenticity of other revealed religions is upheld in Islam." This affirmation of the multiplicity of religious revelations allows an important inference of revealed law or Shariah to be common to all divine religions, irrespective of its extensiveness in any instance.

To avail the other revelations as a source of law will become a means of legal development, besides adding a dimension to law in making it commensurate with the universality of Islam. The criteria for such adoption from other revelations will be the need for revealed law not being fulfilled from the Islamic sources, and that such an adopted law is in uniformity with Islamic precepts of legal value as confirmed by its validation with the application of the Legal Method.

The specific reiteration of this latter criterion will be that the provisions of such an adopted law are not in contravention of the general legal implications of the Supreme Principles. In this perspective, as Islam is held to be the consummation of all the antedating revealed religions, therefore, the adoption of revealed law from other divine sources merely becomes the practical manifestation of this prominent religious tenet. Due relevance is accordable to the fact that no other revealed religion maintains its completion, in terms of a culmination of religious evolution, and its universality, in the sense of a source for guidance in all stages of social change and advancement.

This utilisation of the other revealed religions as a source of Islamic Law has dual legal justifiability. One, as a form of analogous reasoning in the event that the primary sources of Muslim Law are discovered not to afford applicable analogy. And, secondly, in the event of Shariah's "silence" in the instances where no immediate cause for issuing a command is ascertainable and, as a result, the Scripture remained silent, the acceptance of relevant explicit proclamations in the revealed laws prior to Islam is justifiable.

This juristic measure is called as "*Istishab*" and it is to be differentiated from a situation where the cause for issuing a proclamation existed with the coexistence of Scriptural silence, for then it connotes prohibition. Ibn Khaldun[4] described Istishab in these words: "It is the attempt to associate the present legal situation with the past by judging the present in the same way as the past is judged with the result that the legal situation is left as it had been, because no evidence to change it has been found.

Method of Selection : A closely allied and invaluable Islamic juridical approach will be the selection of rules, or even parts of rules, from different Islamic schools of law in order to frame a superior statute. In general, as a part of the juristic principle of Ijtihad, that is, in the nature of further juristic exposition and development of Islamic Law, the principle of selection, designated as "takhayyar," has been adopted in some Islamic nations such as Saudi Arabia[5]. This composite formulation of a statute is explainable on the premise that the legal validity of two or more rules itself validates the combination of their provisions. Now a systematic application of these invaluable principles can open new vistas of legal development due to the eradication of legal "sectarianism" in Islam, the tangible enhancement of the sources of law, and the reinterpretation of the Islamic Law or Fiqh with the methodical application of the juristic principle of Ijtihad, considered dormant in Islam.

Method of Induction : An abbreviated view of a beneficial subject would allow the identification of the common denominator, among the real basis of Faith and the spirit of the Quran, analogous reasoning and scientific method, to be the principle of induction. The comprehensiveness of the source of law that encompasses the inclusive view of revealed law, and the composite structure of legal statutes on the basis of "selection" from different Islamic schools of law, as a part of the legal formulation for the Islamic legal system in the envisaged new era, is remarkably complemented with the adoption of inductive approach. The principles that become ascertainable from the generalisation of the particular instances in revealed laws, and the rules or even juristic elements from various schools of law, have the potential of becoming an inestimable source of law *per se*.

Other Methods : The consideration for conscientious interpretation is of pivotal significance in the evolution of law, in general, and this observation is obviously in demand of further emphasis in the instance of religious law. Avoidance of a few evident drawbacks in the interpretation of law is facilitative in the attainment of that purpose. In Shatibi's view, the appreciation of the demand for the right understanding of the purpose of Shariah should bring to notice the relationship between intention and act.

According to the conformity of intention and act with that purpose, four situations are identified. In addition to the two concordant situations of intention and act, the discordant situations are described as "bida" and "hypocrisy" in the presence of sole conformity of intention with the purpose of Shariah without the association of act, and the conformity of act without the correspondence of intention, respectively. Another classification is established on the basis of rational understanding of the meanings as to the usefulness or unwholesomeness from the act itself. "Taabudi," or that pertaining to religious worships, are those acts whose meanings are not rationally understandable, and this is in diametric contrast with "adi," for instance, the penal prescription for crimes and other laws related to the regulation of human conduct.

Now, against this perspective, the tendency of the mechanical observance of the incidents of a legal rule, that neglects completely the purpose which the rule was designed to serve, requires justification. And, thus, the consideration of the relation between the reasons which gave rise to a rule, and the rule itself, acquires legal relevance. A simple reason for this is the continuation in force of a legal rule, long past the original reasons for the rule have ceased to exist. The illustration of the legal value of these distinctions is affordable with the example of the levying of new wealth and property taxes in a specific proportion, that resembles the Islamic tithe, in addition to those prescribed in the original sources of Muslim Law.

The act of levying the taxes alongwith the corresponding intention are construed to be in conformity with the purpose of Shariah and, hence, it retains the legal validity. This legal conclusion is further fortified with the instance of the performance of religious observances, in excess of the obligatory demands laid by Shariah, as perfectly falling within the ambit of law, and it cannot be called "bida" because the act of maintaining the excessive religious observances and the underlying intention are in full accord with the purpose of Shariah.

From the practical standpoint, the legal principles inferred from the preceding discourse can find rewarding application, particularly, in relation to Islamic laws of inheritance of property and family laws.

The word conscience connotes the perceptions of, and compulsion to, doing right. A necessary identifying characteristic of the conscientious interpretation will be the discovery of the intention of the Law-giver in relation to law and the ascertainment of the sufficiency of law, according to the well-established juridical principles, with scrupulous application.

The Supreme Principles are essentially the fundamentals of Shariah law, and no law, in its legal application, can concurrently circumvent the jurisdiction subtended by the principles and retain its legal validity. These fundamentals also necessarily incorporate the intention of the Lawgiver concerning the Shariah law. In addition, specific intention in relation to a particular law is to be identified. It is obviously inferable that the legal methodology is the judicial province, and the onerous responsibility for the interpretation of law mainly devolves upon the Muslim jurists. And the aspiring enterprise for the constitution of a new legal system lies within their domain of expertise.

The fact of indispensable interrelationship that exists between law and religion, as well as society, transforms the last two entities as an unimpeachable Islamic Judicial concern equal to that of any other social group. The consciousness that the comparability of the envisioned legal system will depend upon the juridical excellence, such as is identifiable with originality, forms an integral part of the juristic approach.

As its antecedents, a breadth of knowledge about the legal history concerning the development of legal systems in general, profound insight into the nature of Islamic law-making and an abiding belief in the inspiring instance of an original legal system will be necessitated. In this perspective, the combined genius of Muslim jurists will reflect from the conscientious interpretation of the wide-based sources of law. This requirement is contingent upon the subscription to the legal value of the Supreme Principles to impart universality and permanence to Islamic Law.

The issue of more than one injunctions concerning a particular subject is resolvable through a legal measure that can lay claim to unanimity. In the case of incompatibility of two injunctions, the later injunction will abrogate the earlier one. The injunctions concerning the subject of polygamy are citable as an instance. The later injunction is a legislative denial of polygamy, which becomes manifest upon conscientious interpretation alone, despite the fact that it is framed in a subtle language for understandable social reasons then current.

Similarly, the general subject of the status of women in society, in particular, the married women, comprises an important area of the revealed legislation. Without the complete realisation of the fact that injunctions concerning marriage and divorce are multiple and do not preclude mutual variations, hence, any superficial treatment of these subjects in law-making can result in the fostering of imbalance in the social status of women.

This outcome is compounded in case the piecemeal nature of the revealed legislation due to the special circumstances involved, and the general objectives of the legislation for the improvement in the status of women, in divergence from the pre-Islamic customary law, are not allowed to register their proper influence during interpretation. Legal history is a testimonial to the fact that the social ethos left its imprint upon the early Islamic jurisprudence.

This particular situation is illustrative of the vital correlation between the intentions underlying the revealed legislation and the law prevalent antedating it. The importance of this observation is enhanced due to the well-recognised fact of the revealed legislation not being a complete code of law.

But, perhaps, a single instance that can epitomize the necessity for conscientious interpretation is the revealed legal concept of "waiting period" or "idda." Its rationale is none other than the improvement of the chances for reconciliation between the spouses, before the divorce is finalised at the end of stipulated period. By taking this into legal consideration, and contrary to the general misconception prevalent concerning revealed Islamic laws, the repudiation of marriage in Islam is anything but an instantaneous act.

These legal instances adequately emphasize the juridical necessity for the conscientious interpretation of law, which is to be contrasted with the construction of law according to subjectively determined standards, such as the consideration for legal tradition or social approval.

Role of the Caliphate

The revealed dictum of the human vicegerency, with its implications ranging throughout the Scripture, is a Supreme Principle and, in Kelsen's term, adoptable as a "groundnorm" to "derive the whole legal system!" However, the definition and legislation of the vital concept of vicegerency, especially, pertaining to the realm of jurisprudence, have not been painstakingly ascertained. The observation that no legislation independent of the original sources of law is feasible, however, the people as the delegates of divine sovereignty are entitled to formulate required laws, has not been translated into a legal formulation, owning the lawful authority of consensus (lima). The present treatise endeavours to compensate for this legal lapse. A functional analogy for the Supreme Principle of human vicegerency, or people as the delegates of the divine sovereignty, in its legal expression, is inclusive of the latter-day juristic principle of "residual jurisdiction. In a federal-type constitution, the federal legislative power is not altogether exclusive of the legislative jurisdiction of the component political entities. The entitlement to residual jurisdiction allows the latter to legislate in areas related to federal legislative power. However, the prohibition from enacting measures which would "conflict" with the provisions of federal law, exists. On the contrary, the jurisdiction of passing such measures as would complete the lacuna left by federal legislation, or serve as addition thereto, is available.

The important limitation upon the residual jurisdiction is imposed by the legal requirement of not permitting the constituent political units to legislate against the spirit of the constitution in an allowable legislative situation, in the absence of relevant federal legislation. The consideration for already existing sufficiency of federal law also has important bearing upon the area of residual jurisdiction. In summation, then, the constitutional measure of residual jurisdiction allows adequate legislative opportunity to the constituents to enact additions to federal legislation.

The engaging subject of the Quran and the authority of human legislation can be dealt with along the conceptual lines of the vicegerency in the perspective of present-day jurisprudential knowledge. In consonance with the legal formulation, the vital legal considerations for the "spirit of the constitution" and the "sufficiency of the law" discover their legal effectiveness. The intention and the direction of legislation have similar, but not the same, jurisdiction, hence, the legal identities of the intention and direction of legislation retain their differentiating features. The legal implications of these particular concepts have the potential for the legal expression of the principle of vicegerency.

The legal analogy of the levying of taxes upon personal wealth and property, in excess of the originally prescribed proportions in Islamic Law, supplemented by the religious instance of the maintenance of observances in addition to the obligatory requirements, is a prototypical illustration of the legal concept of vicegerency in the areas of already existing revealed legislation. The explanation for an historic avoidance in the extrapolation of this legal analogy upon the Islamic laws in relation to those of the inheritance of property concerning women is inconceivable. And not too dissimilar is the revealed issue of equality in relation to polygamy, which has been accorded a moral value in the traditional Islamic Law, whose conversion into legal terms is in conformity with the definition of law, as well as within the legal jurisdiction of vicegerency.

The Muslim laws dealing with the inheritance of property are in obvious want of the extension of the same legal jurisdiction by not allowing the bequeathing of property to remain a matter of mere conscience. An inducement to moral degeneracy, casting of a slur upon the faith of Islam, and paving a way for the unsuccess of the Islamic Law-a view that finds substantiation from Fuller's observations are the drawbacks in the relevant law, which will be rectified by the use of legal jurisdiction pertaining to the Supreme Principle of vicegerency, as proposed in the Legal Method.

LAW IN PRACTICE

The causes affecting capacity are found in those factors that prevent *capacity for acquisition* and *capacity for execution* from taking full effect. The existence of these factors may result in the total absence of capacity or in deficient or incomplete capacity. For purposes of the present discussion, we may refer to all such forms as defective capacity.

The *manat* (legal basis) for the capacity for acquisition, as we have said, is being a natural person *(insaniyyah)*[6], and it is death alone that can cause a change in this kind of capacity. We have seen, however, that under certain circumstances a corpse may have such a capacity. Reason *(aql)* and discretion *(rushd)*, on the other hand, are the bases for the capacity for execution, and each factor that has the power to influence and affect the normal functioning of the human mind can become a cause for defective capacity. It is pertinent to note that many of the causes of defective capacity mentioned here will appear to the reader to be the same as the general defences in criminal law, or as other grounds for waiver of liability in civil or ritual matters. The jurists divide the causes of defective capacity into two kinds: natural causes *(samawiyyah)* and acquired causes *(muktasaba)*.

We may designate these as natural and acquired causes.

Natural Causes of Defective Capacity : These are causes that are beyond the control of the subject *(mukallaf)*, and result from an act of the Lawgiver and

Creator. Under this heading, the jurists list ten causes: *sighar* (minority); *junun* (insanity); *atah* (idiocy); *nisyan* (forgetfulness); *nawm* (sleep); *ighma* (unconsciousness; fainting; epilepsy); *riqq* (slavery); *marz* (illness); *hayd* (menstruation); *nifas* (puerperium; post-natal state of woman); and *mawt* (death). We shall discuss a few of these here, the rest are either obvious or have a greater bearing on *ibadat*.

LAW FOR MINORITIES

It is the state or condition of a human being after birth and before puberty. This, in fact, is not a cause of defective capacity or even an obstacle in its way, but a necessary stage in the growth of the human being. It is considered as a cause for noting its effect upon capacity or *ahliyyah*.

- Minority does not affect capacity for acquisition or *ahliyyat al-wujub*. All rights and obligations are acquired as their establishment requires merely a *dhimma* and the *manat* (being a natural person), which is the basis for the capacity for acquisition. Minority does not oppose this *manat*. The jurists, therefore, maintain that the minor is liable for compensation of property destroyed by him, for goods and services bought, for maintenance of relatives, and also for *zakat* according to some.

- Capacity for execution or *ahliyyat al-ada* requires *aql* (reason) for its fulfilment, and this the non-discriminating minor *(sabi ghayr mumayyiz)* lacks, because he does not understand the *khitab*. He is, therefore, not liable for the *ibadat*, for financial transactions, or for punishments. The Hanafis make an exception in the case of the *sabi mumayyiz* or one who has attained some discretion. The *ibadat* of such a minor are rewarded in the Hereafter, and it is a matter of controversy whether the *khitab* of *targhib* or recommendation is addressed to him. He is not liable for punishments, but financial transactions undertaken by him are valid in certain cases. Transactions that are purely harmful for such a minor, like donating his property, have no legal effect. Transactions that are purely beneficial or those that are evenly balanced between profit and loss are allowed, with the prior permission of the guardian or his subsequent ratification. The position of the *sabi mumayyiz* may be compared with the contract for necessaries by a minor under sections 11 and 68 of the Pakistan Contract Act. The freedom allowed to the *sabi mumayyiz* by the Hanafis is much wider than that under the law. In other countries, the contracts of a minor may be considered valid with an option for the minor to rescind the contract and return the property.

Law for Insanity

Junun has no effect on *ahliyyat al-wujub,* because rights and obligations are established for and against an insane person, who is deemed liable for *itlaf* (destruction of property), payment of *diyah,* and the like. The *manat* of such a capacity is *insaniyyah,* and the *majnun* is a human being. *Junun,* however, completely negates the *ahliyyat al-ada,* because of lack of *aql.* The insane person, therefore, has no liability for *ibadat* or punishments, and all his transactions are void. While the *fuqaha* consider insanity as effective in negating the capacity for performance they do not describe the meaning of insanity in detail. In Pakistan, section 84 of the Pakistan Penal Code appears to follow what are called the M Naghten Rules for insanity in England.

These rules have been criticised by lawyers as well as doctors as being inadequate. A number of other tests have also been devised, like the "irresistible impulse test," the "Durham test," and the "American Law Institute or Model Penal Code test." It is suggested here that Muslim scholars need to explore these issues in some depth. They may either accept the tests devised in different countries or devise some new tests. The same holds true for idiocy and death illness. Such questions must be answered on the basis of empirical evidence.

Law for Idiocy

It is a state in which a person at times speaks like a sane and normal person, while at others he is like a madman. It is also described as a state in which a grown-up has the mind of a child. The capacity of an idiot is deemed equivalent to that of a *sabi mumayyiz,* who can be permitted by his guardian to undertake some transactions.

Sleep and Fits of Fainting (Nawm, Ighma) : Sleep and fits of fainting have relevance for purposes of *ibadat,* as well as for crimes and torts. They do not affect *ahliyyat al-wujub,* because the attribute of *insaniyyah* is intact. Persons in such a condition, however, do not understand the *khitab.* Their capacity to understand things is temporarily affected and prevented from normal functioning.

The liability for missed *ibadat* lingers against such a person and these have to be performed as *qada* (delayed performance). There is no liability for punishments and transactions. If a person, while sleeping, falls on a child during sleep and kills it, there is no liability for punishment, but compensation is another matter for which there may be strict liability.

Law for Forgetfulness

This is a state in which a person is not very careful about things though he has full knowledge of them, as distinguished from sleep and fits of fainting in which such knowledge is lacking. Forgetfulness does not affect *ahliyyat al-wujub* nor does it affect the capacity for execution. The *khitab,* however, becomes operative as soon as the person remembers. Transactions undertaken by such a person are valid and enforceable against him.

LAW FOR DEATH-ILLNESS

This is a condition in which the mind of a sick person is dominated by the fact that he will die because of his illness. It is of no consequence whether the person actually dies from this illness or from something else and whether the illness is in fact a terminal illness. Two conditions must be met before an illness may be declared a death-illness:

- The deceased person must be convinced that he is approaching death, irrespective of the nature of the disease. Diseases like common colds and headaches, however, are not taken into account for such purposes. Some jurists associate other circumstances with this state, like a person on a ship that is caught in a storm, or like a person facing a death sentence.
- Death should follow such a conviction, even if it is not caused by the feared illness.
- Some jurists stipulate a third condition here by saying that death must occur within one year of the commencement of illness, because any period above this would mean that the person is accustomed to his illness and that the fear of death is remote.

Marz ul-mawt (death-illness) has no effect on the capacity for acquisition or on the capacity for execution, and it is in fact a condition of *taklif,* because it is the capacity to perform an act that is affected here and not the capacity to understand it. A person suffering from such an illness is prohibited from entering into transactions that are in excess of one-third of his wealth. In other words, it takes the *hukm* of *wasiyyah.* This condition is stipulated to protect the rights of the heirs. The reason assigned is that the rights of the heirs get linked to the estate as soon as *marz al-mawt* takes hold.

The Lawgiver has laid down that such rights are to come into play after the death of the person, but to protect the rights of the heirs and creditors it is assumed that death has already occurred. The justification provided is that the transactions of such a person are not those of one who wishes to live, but of one who is ready to depart.

The Following Rights are Attached to the Estate of the Person Suffering from *Marz al-mawt:*

Various Aspects of Law

- *Rights of Creditors* : The creditors have a right prior to all, even if the debts consume all the estate.
- *Rights of Beneficiaries* : The rights of beneficiaries restrict the transactions to one-third of the estate, however, amounts in excess of one-third will be valid if permitted by the heirs.
- *Rights of the Heirs* : These rights are linked to the estate from the time of the commencement of illness, and any transactions undertaken by the sick person will be assigned *ahkam* as follows:
    1. *Transactions with a Counter-value* : If the person suffering from death-illness concludes a contract of sale with no apparent loss in it, that is, at the market value, then the creditors or the heirs cannot have it set aside. It is to be assumed that such a sale was undertaken to fulfil his genuine needs and not with the intention to deprive his creditors or heirs. Abu Hanifah maintains that if such a sale is made to one of the heirs, it is to be declared as void even if it is at market value. The two disciples maintain that the sale is valid. The difference of opinion is due to the question whether the right of the heirs is linked to the *ayn* (substance) of the thing or to its value.
    2. *Transactions without a Counter-value* : If the transaction is a *hibah, waqf, sadaqah,* or a sale at less than the market value, or a purchase at more than the market value, then such a transaction will be restricted to one-third of the value of the estate, after the creditors have been satisfied.

Three Conditions must be fulfilled before the Rights of the Creditors can Come into Play:

(a) That the transaction was without a counter-value or without adequate counter-value. This would cover transactions like gift, charity, *waqf,* sale at a discount, or purchase at a premium.

(b) That the transaction involves the transfer of a thing (*ayn)* itself and not its use, provided that the benefit conferred through use will terminate upon the death of the owner. Some Hanafis do not consider the benefits arising from the use of a thing as *mal.* The use of land, or of a house, or of an animal are examples that explain this case. The majority *(jumhur),* however, consider the use of benefits as *mal.*

(c) That the transaction must be in *ayan* (substance of things) and not in the revenue or profit derived from them. Any assignment of profits arising from a *sharikah* or *mudarabah* will not be affected by this condition.

Besides transactions, any admission or acknowledgment of debts by the person suffering from *marz al-mawt* may also invoke the rights of creditors and heirs. Al-Shafii is of the opinion that acknowledgment by a person suffering from death-illness is valid and is not affected by the rights of the creditors or the heirs. The reason he assigns is that a person approaching death would normally tell the truth, even if he is a habitual liar. The Hanafis, on the other hand, make a distinction between two cases:

(a) *Acknowledgment* of debt in favour of an heir: An *acknowledgment* in favour of an heir can have legal effects if the rest of the heirs permit it. This is due to the apprehension that one heir may have been preferred over the others.

(b) *Acknowledgment* of debt in favour of a stranger: An *acknowledgment* favouring a stranger is valid. These debts are called *duyun al-marz* and are to be paid after all other debts, called debts of health, have been satisfied.

The Malikis distinguish between cases where an allegation of a "bond of affection" can be made, that is, where a possibility of undue influence is likely. For example in the case of a wife, close relative, or friend. The basis is the bond existing between them and not the blood relationship.

Acquired Causes of Defective Capacity : Acquired causes are those that are created by Man or in which human will and choice are the basic factors. Muslim jurists list seven such causes: ignorance *(jahl)*, intoxication *(sukr)*, jest *(hazl)*, indiscretion *(safah)*, journey *(safar)*, mistake *(khata, shubhah)*, and coercion *(ikrah)*. We will discuss some of the important causes, noting their effects on the capacity for acquisition and on the capacity for execution.

LAW FOR INTOXICATION

Drunkenness is a state caused in a human being due to the use of an intoxicant, which temporarily suspends the proper functioning of the mental faculty. Intoxication does not cause a change in the capacity for acquisition, as its basis is the attribute of being a human. Thus, a drunken person possesses a *dhimma* (legal personality) with a complete capacity for acquisition, and he is held liable for destruction of life and property, and also for all obligations, for maintenance, and even for *zakat*. All these duties and obligations require the existence of the capacity for acquisition alone, and intoxication does not negate it. The basis for the capacity for execution, on the other hand, is *aql* (reason) and *rushd* (discretion); these are negated in the case of the drunken person by the state of drunkenness.

The *khitab* is not addressed to the drunken person, because he does not comprehend it. The state of such a person is worse than that of one who is asleep, for the latter can be awakened; it is worse than that of an idiot, who may understand parts of the speech addressed to him.

The jurists agree unanimously that the *khitab* is not directed toward the intoxicated person if such intoxication has been caused by the legal use of intoxicants. For example, the person who has consumed liquor without knowing what it is or when he has done so under coercion or under duress to save his life. In such cases, the *hukm* for this person will be the same as that of the person under a spell of fainting.

Muslim jurists disagree about the person who is intoxicated when such intoxication is caused by prohibited means. The Hanafis and some other jurists do not consider such a cause to have any effect on the capacity for execution and on the understanding of the *khitab*. Thus, the *ibadat*[7] are established against such a person and he will be held liable for delayed performance *(qada)*, along with the accompanying sin. Any transaction or *acknowledgment* he makes is valid and enforceable against him. He acquires criminal liability for acts committed in such a state, though he can retract his confession made in this state regarding a case of *hudud*, as these are pure rights of Allah.

The argument provided by the Hanafis is that intoxication is a crime and as such cannot be an excuse for waiving punishments. Further, one reason why intoxication has been prohibited is that it leads to other *khabaith*. Moreover, if the acts of the drunken person are to be exempted from liability, it will become a means for the commission of offences, and for evading liability. Relying on the verse, "O you believers, approach not prayer when you are intoxicated, until you know what you say," [Quran 4 : 43] they maintain that it is obvious that the *khitab* is addressed to the drunken person and he is expected to understand the meaning and import of the verse even when he is intoxicated. If this is not the interpretation, it would amount to saying to a person under a spell of madness, "Do not commit such an act when you are insane." It is for this reason that the drunken person is held liable for his acts.

Some jurists are of the opinion that an intoxicated person has no capacity for execution, because his *aql* (reason) is completely impaired by the state of intoxication. They maintain that the Lawgiver has already provided a penalty for the offence of intoxication and holding him liable for his transactions as well, that is, those undertaken in such a state, would amount to punishing him twice for the same offence, a kind of double jeopardy. They argue that the verse about avoiding prayers in an intoxicated state is actually addressed to a sober person telling him to avoid becoming intoxicated before the time of prayer, an act over which he has control, as compared to the person subject to fits of madness over which he has no control.

Modern jurists try to prefer the second opinion as it may be closer to some forms of Western law. It must be noted, however, that consuming liquor is an offence in Islamic law and it may not be so in the law.

LAW FOR JEST

When a person uses words without intending to convey either their primary or their secondary meanings, that is, their denotations or their connotations, he is said to speak in jest *(hazl)*. Such a person may, for instance, use words employed for the contract of marriage, but does not intend the *hukm* (effect) of such a contract.

Speaking in jest has no effect on the capacity for acquisition; rights as well as obligations will, therefore, be acquired. The basis of *insaniyyah* required for this kind of capacity is not altered by jokes.

Hazl or jest cannot negate the capacity for execution either, because such a person has not lost his intellect or discretion. Contracts, on the other hand, require consent and willingness to give rise to legal effects. The person speaking in jest does bring about the apparent form *(sighah)* of the contract, but has not given his consent in reality. The Hanafis, therefore, consider the transactions of such a person as invalid, except transactions like marriage, divorce, manumission, *ruju* (retraction), and the like. This is based on the tradition that says, "Three things intended seriously are taken seriously, and if intended in jest are also taken seriously: marriage, divorce, and the freeing of a slave."

Some jurists do not maintain this exemption, and treat all statements made in jest as being ineffective. The Shafiis maintain that statements made in jest are to be considered valid at all times, because the person has brought about the cause—the *sighah* (form)—and must, therefore, bear the consequences. This is based on the objective theory of contracts that is followed in Islamic law by most schools.

LAW FOR INDISCRETION

This defect concerns financial transactions, that is, transactions undertaken carelessly and in a manner that a prudent person is likely to avoid. The result is foolish waste and squandering of property.

The tendency in a person to waste his property affects neither his capacity for acquisition nor his capacity for execution. The effect of *safah* is that a person, who has attained puberty, is subjected to interdiction *(hajr)* till such time that he mends his ways. This view is upheld by the majority. It is based upon the necessity *(darurah)* of preserving his wealth, because preservation of wealth is an acknowledged purpose of the law. Abu Hanifah maintains that interdiction can last only till the age of twenty-five, after which the property of the individual is to be delivered to him, because at this age the individual is to be preferred over property.

LAW FOR COERCION/DURESS

Ikrah is a situation in which one is forced to do something without his willingness. It has no effect either on the capacity for acquisition or the capacity for execution, because this state does not affect life or reason and discretion. It does, however, negate free consent and willingness.

Effect on Free Will : The jurists disagree about the extent to which *ikrah* can affect free will. The views of these jurists may be classified into two opinions:

1. The first opinion maintains that *ikrah* is an obstacle in the way of *taklif* (creation of an obligation). Thus, the *khitab* is not directed toward a person under coercion or under duress, because this person is prevented from understanding the *khitab*. Among those who hold this opinion are Shafii jurists, who maintain that free will is a condition of *taklif*. *Ikrah*, according to the Shafiis, arises under a threat of death, hurt, perpetual confinement, and the like. It does not arise for causes of a lesser gravity, like a threat to property. *Ikrah* defined this way is, in their view, divided into two kinds:

    a. *Justified Coercion :* This is like the order of a *qadi* directing a debtor to pay his debts to his creditors, or his command to a man to divorce his wife after the passage of the period of *ila,* as required by Shafii law. This kind of *ikrah* does not affect the free will of a person, as the duty is imposed by the Lawgiver. Thus, any transaction in property undertaken under coercion for paying off creditors shall not be declared void.

    b. *Unjustified Coercion :* Coercion without justification is again of two types. The first type is where acts committed are legally permissible under coercion. Such acts, if committed through words or deeds, have no legal effect and are considered void. If these acts can be attributed to a third person, then, they are attributed to the person coercing or threatening another. For example, compensation for property destroyed through coercion shall be paid by the person who coerces the other. The second type are acts that are legally prohibited, like murder and rape. In such cases the person coerced shall be fully liable along with the person who coerced him.

2. The second opinion is held by the Hanafis, who divide *ikrah* into three types:

   a. First is coercion that negates free will or choice. This is coercion under threat of death or loss of limb.

   b. The second type is coercion that negates consent, but makes free will irregular or *fasid*. This is brought about by confinement for a long period or by beating and torture that does not lead to loss of life or limb.

   c. The third type is *ikrah* that does not negate consent nor does it make free will *fasid*. The example is confinement of close relatives. Some Hanafi jurists do not accept this third category, and link it with one of the categories above, depending upon the nature of the threat to dear ones.

Effect of Coercion on Legal Capacity : The Hanafis maintain that the condition of *taklif* is the existence of the right to choose and not its validity *(sihhah)*. Irregular or *fasid* free will, they say, is sufficient for the existence of *taklif*. In all the above cases of *ikrah*, free will is not invalid *(Batil)* though it may be irregular. *Taklif*, therefore, may accompany *ikrah*.

To Facilitate the Understanding of the act, for which Coercion is Taking Place, the Hanafis Divide it into Three Types:

1. *Transactions :* These are divided into two kinds, on the basis of the effect of *ikrah:*

   a. First are transactions that do not accept rescission, and do not depend upon consent, for example, divorce, manumission, marriage, retraction of divorce, *zihar, ila, afw* (forgiveness) in intentional murder, and oath *(yamin.)* All these transactions are valid under coercion, because they amount to a termination *(isqat)* or relinquishment of a right, and relinquishment cannot be reverted, because these transactions are not dependent on consent.

   b. *Second are Transactions that Accept Rescission or Revocation and Depend upon Consent:* These are like sale, mortgage, hire, and other commutative contracts. These contracts accept rescission and depend upon the existence of free consent. The *hukm* of such contracts concluded under coercion is that they are irregular *(fasid.)* They can be ratified by the coerced party, after coercion has ceased to exist, in which case they are declared as valid *(sahih)*.

2. *Admissions and Confessions:* All admissions and confessions, in order to be valid, must be accompanied by free will.

3. *Acts in General:* Acts, for this purpose, are divided into two kinds by the Hanafi jurists.

   a. First is the case when the coerced is a mere instrument in the hands of another, like a person picking up another and throwing him upon another thereby causing death, or hurt, or causing damage to property. If A causes B to fire at a bush knowing that C is hiding behind it, thus, causing the death of C, then, A shall be guilty of murder, while B will be an instrument in his hand. Other cases can be imagined. In such cases the act is attributed not to the instrument, but to one who caused him to move.

   b. Second is the case when the coerced cannot become an instrument in the hands of another, for example, in the commission of *zina* or eating of food. In such a case, the person coerced is fully aware of his actions. Here the person coerced is guilty of *zina* or for compensating property consumed. In the case of drinking of *khamr,* however, *hadd* is waived on grounds of *shubhah.*

Mistake and Ignorance (Khata, Shubhah, and Jahl) : The topics of *jahl* and *khata* are usually discussed separately, while the topic of *shubhat* is not discussed under defective legal capacity. All three are interrelated and deal with concepts that are similar to what in Western law are called mistake of law and mistake of fact.

The word *shubhah* is usually translated as doubt. The most important evidence in this respect is the tradition of the Prophet (peace be on him) in which it has been said that the *hudud* penalties are to be waived in case of *shubhah.* This is usually taken to mean "benefit of doubt" given to the accused. While this meaning may be covered by the tradition it is not its primary concern. The rule of giving benefit of doubt to the accused is generally accepted as a rule of evidence in Islamic law.

Further, this rule deals with the doubt in the mind of the judge as to whether an offence has been proved beyond doubt. The tradition, according to the jurists, deals with doubts in the mind of the subject at the time of commission or omission of an act. These are of several types: *shubhah fi al-dalil* (mistake of law); *shubah fi al-milk* (mistake as to ownership); *shubhah fi al-fil* (mistake in the commission of the act); and *shubhah fi al-aqd* (mistake as to the governing law in the contract).

For example, assuming that in the early days there was a person who was under the impression that temporary marriage is permitted, that is, he may not be aware of the abrogating evidence. If he entered into a temporary marriage under this impression, the marriage contract was declared void, but the law would waive the *hadd* penalty in such a case (this does not mean that *tazir* was also waived). There could have been a possibility of the occurrence of such a case in the early days when people were not aware of the law.

Today it is unlikely to happen. In any case, it is an example of *shubhah ji al-dalil* as well as *shubhah ji al-aqd*. If some of the heirs pardon the murderer, but some of the other heirs, who have not pardoned him, execute him, they will not be subjected to retaliation due to *shubhah ji al-dalil* (mistake of law). They may be awarded *tazir*. Today, these heirs are not permitted to take the law into their own hands. It should be obvious that exemptions for mistakes of law are given where the issue is subject to *ijtihad*. Where the matter is not subject to *ijtihad*, and is clearly known, or is supposed to be known to Muslims by necessity, there can be no exemption. In the early days, when slavery was permitted, a husband may be under the impression that his wife's slave girl is also within his ownership. Under this wrong impression if he were to consider her *milk yamin* and act upon it he would be under *shubhah ji al-milk*. The *hadd* penalty would be waived in such a case (though not *tazir*). If a man aiming at an animal were to hit a human being, he would be guilty of manslaughter *(qatl khata)* and not murder. This is an example of *shubhah ji al-fil*.

The law gives some exemption in such cases and lays down principles that may be applied to new cases. It can be seen with ease, however, that ignorance or mistake does not affect the capacity of acquisition at all. It does not affect the capacity for execution either, the basis for which is understanding or *aql*. The only problem here is that the understanding of the subject is hampered somewhat, but the law takes notice even of this. This shows that ignorance and mistake are not causes of defective capacity at all, but statutory grounds of defence or exemptions.

Jahl (ignorance) may, thus, be that of law or of fact. In general, ignorance of law is no excuse for a subject present within the *dar al-Islam*[8]. This, however, should not be confused with the acts of a Muslim residing in the *dar al-harb*[9]. The Hanafis make an exemption for some of the unlawful acts of such an individual, because he is not enjoying the protection of the Islamic state during his stay abroad. Submission to the Islamic state and being subject to its jurisdiction is also stated as a condition of *Taklif* by some jurists. The issue of jurisdiction of the Muslim state is expressed as a principle by the Hanafi jurist al-Dabusi:

> The principle according to our jurists is that the world is divided into two *dars*: *dar al-Islam* and *dar al-harb*. According to Imam al-Shafii the entire world is a single *dar*.

In other words, al-Shafii does not grant the same exemptions to an individual residing in enemy territory.

AIMS AND OBJECTIVES

A discussion of the *maqasid al-shariah* (the purposes of Islamic law) as well as the principle of *maslahah,* before discussing the rational sources, becomes necessary due to several reasons. The first is that the principle of *maslahah* has grown to envelope all the rational sources. Each rational source is today considered part of the larger doctrine of *maslahah.* The second is that this principle is considered the most important and the most comprehensive instrument of *ijtihad* for the modern times; its discussion must therefore precede that of the rational sources. A third reason is that the larger doctrine of *maslahah* must be distinguished from the narrower principle of *maslahah mursalah,* which is considered one type of rational source within the broader doctrine.

The meaning of *maslahah* is discussed first and is followed by a description of the purposes of Islamic law or the *maqasid al-shariah.*

DEFINITION OF *MASLAHA*

The words *maslahah* and *manfaah* are treated as synonyms. *Manfaah* means "benefit" or "utility," that is, it leads to some kind of benefit. In its literal meaning *maslahah* is denned as *(jalb al-manfaah wa-daf al-madarrah)* or the seeking of benefit and the repelling of harm. If this literal meaning is pursued further it will lead to something similar to the principle of utility expounded by Jeremy Bentham, which means securing the maximum human happiness. The seeking of human happiness in this sense may imply three things:

(i) That the happiness sought here is dependent upon human desires or reason. The pursuit of such happiness may or may not coincide with the form of benefit or *manfaah* intended by the *Shariah.*

(ii) The emphasis in this form of happiness will always be on the collective utility, that is, the happiness of the entire community and the interests of the individual may be given a back seat.

(iii) The pursuit of pure utility may ultimately lead to the economic analysis of law (as expounded by Richard Posner and the Chicago School). In other words, all legal decisions must be reduced to a cost-benefit analysis either financial or economic. This may or may not suit the goals of the *Shariah.*

Manfaah (benefit or utility), however, is not the technical meaning of *maslahah.* What Muslim jurists mean by *maslahah* is the seeking of benefit and the repelling of harm as directed by the Lawgiver. The seeking of utility in Islamic law is not dependent on human reason and pleasure. Al-Ghazzali, therefore, defines *maslahah* as follows:

> As for *maslahah,* it is essentially an expression for the acquisition of *manfaah* (benefit) or the repulsion of *madarrah* (injury, harm), but that is not what we mean by it, because acquisition of *manfaah* and the repulsion of *madarrah* represent human goals, that is, the welfare of humans through the attainment of these goals. What we mean by *maslahah,* however, is the preservation of the ends of the *shar.*

Three things are Obvious from this Statement:

(i) That the pursuit of human goals and the principle of utility based on human reason is not what is meant by *maslahah.*

(ii) That *maslahah* is the securing of goals or values that the Lawgiver has determined for the *Shariah.*

(iii) That the goals determined for the *Shariah* by the Lawgiver may or may not coincide with values determined by human reason. Thus, reasoning based upon the principle of utility or on economic analysis may sometimes be acceptable to the *Shariah,* but it may be rejected at other times when there is a clash of values.

Types of Maslahas : Muslim jurists classify *maslahah* in several ways. These classifications are expected to show us how this principle covers most of the rational sources and how the discussion of the sources is linked with the purposes of Islamic law. Some of the most important classifications are provided below.

First Classification: Maslahah Acknowledged or Rejected by the Shariah: For purposes of this classification, it is important to understand that the underlying causes of the *ahkam* present a hierarchical structure of attributes. Sometimes the *Shariah* recognises a lower level attribute as the basis for the law, while at other times it accepts a higher level attribute. The level at which an attribute is acknowledged indicates the type of rational source being used. The classification that follows is based on the recognition of attributes at different levels. Four types of *maslahah* are discussed under this heading:

1. *Maslahah Acknowledged at the Level of the Lowest Category:* The first type is *maslahah* acknowledged by the Lawgiver at the level of the lowest category *(naw).* Take the case of drinking *khamr* (wine). The underlying cause at the lower level could be "intoxication," that is, losing of one's senses. A higher level cause could be the "protection of the intellect."

    Recognition of a cause at the lower level means that the rational source invoked is analogy *(qiyas).* This means that the law can be extended to other things on the basis of analogy using the rule: whatever intoxicates is prohibited. Prohibiting intoxication is, therefore, the repelling of harm or the securing of an interest protected by the law *(maslahah)*. All those cases where the Lawgiver has identified underlying causes at the lowest level fall under the first type of *maslahah*. Further, this tells us that using analogy *(qiyas)* is one type of *maslahah*.

2. *Maslahah Acknowledged at the Level of the Genus:* The second type is *maslahah* that is acknowledged by the Lawgiver at the level of the genus, that is, at a level higher than the lowest category. Such a recognition takes us beyond the level of analogy into the realm of other rational sources, especially *maslahah mursalah*. This recognition of attributes can go up to the highest level of the purposes of law. The purposes of Islamic law at the highest level are five: Preservation of *din;* preservation of life; preservation of *nasl* (progeny); preservation of intellect; and preservation of wealth. The jurists illustrate the recognition of these attributes through a large number of examples. Thus, the Companions of the Prophet (peace be on him) were not sure whether the text of the Quran should be compiled, because the Prophet had not done so during his lifetime. In the interest of "preservation of *din"* they decided that it should be gathered and compiled. The texts clearly mention that a life is to be taken for a life in the case of *qisas* (retaliation). Where two or more persons participate in the murder of one person, should more than one life be taken for a single life? It was decided that in the interest of the "preservation of life" such a law should be made. The details of this type will be explained under the discussion of *maslahah mursalah* as well as under the discussion of the third mode of *ijtihad.*

3. *Maslahah that is Rejected by the Shariah:* The third type *maslahah* is one that is not acknowledged by the *shartah,* because it clashes with a text. The jurists have found it difficult to give examples of this type. They provide hypothetical cases. Let us assume that the *hukm* for a person indulging in sexual intercourse during fasting is the freeing of a slave. A jurist may say that this provision gives a loophole to a very rich person, because setting free a slave is nothing for him. Such a jurist may say that this option should therefore not be available to a rich man in the interest of "the preservation of *din."* The *Shariah,* however, does not recognise such a measure and the argument is without foundation and is rejected. In other words, a provision proposed in contradiction of what the *Shariah* has already provided will not be recognised or a *maslahah* that clashes with a text of the Quran or *Sunnah* is rejected.

4. *Maslahah that is Neither Acknowledged nor Rejected*: The fourth type is a *maslahah* that is neither acknowledged by the *Shariah* nor is it rejected. This type of *maslahah* is one that is strange *(gharib)* for the *Shariah*. An example will be provided under the discussion of *maslahah mursalah* for ease of understanding.

Second Classification: Maslahah According to its Inner Strength: This classification is based upon the purposes of Islamic law and their types. The types of *maslahah* according to their inner strength are three: *darurat* (necessities); *hajat* (needs); and *tahsinat* (complementary goals).

1. *Darurat (Necessary Interests)*: Necessary interests are those without the protection of which there would anarchy and chaos in society. The absence of protection for these interests would mean the loss of everything that we hold dear. These prized social interests are five in number:

    (a) Preservation and protection of religion *(hifz ala al-din)*.

    (b) Preservation and protection of life *(hifz ala al-nafs)*.

    (c) Preservation and protection of progeny *(hifz ala al-nasl)*.

    (d) Preservation and protection of intellect *(hifz ala al-aql)*.

    (e) Preservation and protection of wealth *(hifz ala al-mal)*.

2. *Hajat (Supporting Needs)*: The second type of interests are called *hajat* or supporting interests required by the necessary interests for their smooth operation and implementation. If these supporting interests are not protected by the law there would be hardship and loss in the performance of social functions. This means that the primary or necessary interests would not be lost, but there would be considerable friction and difficulty in their protection. The examples of these interests given by jurists pertain mostly to exemptions granted by the law. For example, the exemptions available due to illness or journey in case of worship serve these interests, just like the contract of *salam* (advance payment) works as an exemption to facilitate transactions. The necessary interests do not depend on these exemptions or supporting needs, but their operation is facilitated.

3. *Tahsinat (Complementary Interests)*: These interests provide additional rules that lead to the moral and spiritual progress of the individual and society. Examples are: voluntary *sadaqah* and many ethical and moral rules (like the command not cut trees or to kill animals during war). In reality, the *tahsinat* tell us that there is a moral shell around the necessities and supporting needs provided by the *Shariah*. Thus, morality goes hand in hand with the law and there is no separation as may be found in Western law.

This classification shows the types of purposes of the Islamic law and the relationship between them.

Third Classification: Definitive and Probable Interests : Some jurists, and some later writers, have maintained that there are interests that are definitive (*qati*) and those that are probable *(zanni)*. Jurists like al-Ghazzali and al-Shatibi have spent considerable time in showing that all the interests classified according to their inner strength above are definitive, because they have been constructed through a process of induction *(istiqra)* rather than deduction. Certain cases of interests that have been called strange or *gharib* may, however, be deemed to be probable. Yet, the major area of probable purposes lies in the area called *ashbah* by al-Ghazzali. This issue is found in Western law as well when values are classified according to different types of rationality, with some legal philosophers, like Kelsen, maintaining that most interests or values preserved by the law do not meet the standards of rationality that can be called definitive. These, however, are values identified by human reason. We shall have something more to say about this when we discuss the third mode of *ijtihad* in the next part of this book.

Fourth Classification: Public and Private Interests : The necessary interests, the supporting needs and complementary interests can all be divided into public interests and private interests. In fact, the settlement of legal disputes always involves some kind of conflict or clash between public and private interests or between two private interests. The problem that arises, especially in modern times, is whether public interests are based on the rights of Allah *(haqq Allah)* or on the rights of the state *(haqq al-saltanah)* or are these the same thing?

The Doctrine of Maslahah and Maslahah Mursalah: Distinction : The principle of *maslahah mursalah* was first used by Imam Malik, the founder of the Maliki school. It was elaborated and developed in the works of al-Ghazzali[10] Out of this discussion there emerged a larger doctrine of *maslahah,* which is much wider than the principle or source of Islamic law called *maslahah mursalah.*

The larger doctrine requires that during the use or employment of rational sources to discover the law, each derived law must be checked against the purposes of Islamic law or the *maqasid al-shariah.* If there is some compatibility *(munasabah)* between the derived law and the purposes, then the law is valid, otherwise it may be rejected. In this sense, all the rational sources fall under this larger doctrine. Thus, the larger doctrine covers *qiyas, istihsan* and *maslahah mursalah.* In other words, each of these rational sources has now become or is deemed a type of this larger doctrine. It is for this reason that the meaning of *maslahah* and the nature of the purposes of law has been discussed before the description of the rational sources.

***Maqasid al-shariah* or the *Purposes of Islamic Law* :** The Purposes of Law are Divided by al-Ghazzali into two Types:

- *dini* or purposes of the Hereafter.
- *dunyawi* or purposes pertaining to this world.

Each of these is divisible into *tahsil* or securing of the interest and *ibqa* or preservation of the interest. *Tahsil* is the securing of a benefit *(manfaah)* and *ibqa* is the repelling of harm *(madarrah)*. The phrase *riayat al-maqasid* (preservation of the *maqasid*) is used to indicate both *tahsil* and *ibqa.* The worldly purposes *(dunyawi)* are further divided into four types: the preservation of *nafs* (life), the preservation of *nasl* (progeny), the preservation of *aql* (intellect), and the preservation of *mal* (wealth). Each worldly purpose is meant to serve the single *dini* purpose. When all types are taken together, we have five ultimate purposes of the law:

- *din* (religion),
- life,
- progeny (may be called the preservation of the Family),
- intellect, and
- wealth.

These five purposes are designated as *darurat* (necessities) and are the primary purposes of the law. These are followed by the *hajat* (needs), which are additional purposes required by the primary purposes, even though the primary purposes would not be lost without them. The third category is that of purposes that seek to establish ease and facility *(tawassu* and *taysir)* in the law; these are called the *tahsinat* (complementary values). The relationship of the purposes of Islamic law may be seen in the figure:

The Purposes of Islamic Law

What is Beyond the Purposes? : If we move beyond the ultimate values recognised as the purposes of the law, we reach the area of weaker attributes, which are also used by the jurists for extending the law. This is the area of the *ashbah* (probable values). These too are organised in the form of the particular and the general.

This is the area of the probable or *zanni maqasid*. Thus, the purpose beyond these purposes could be the building of civilisation, security, the maintenance of equality, freedom, and many other values that are preserved and protected by each society and they are expressed as the aims of justice in Western law. The Muslim jurists did not deal with such values, because they are probable and do not fall in the area of certain rationality. An attribute depicting such values is called *wasf baid* or a distant value; it is distant in comparison with the *darurat*, each of which is a *wasf qarib* or near value.

Maqasid al-shariah and the Texts : The purposes of Islamic law have been determined from the texts through a process of induction *(istiqra)* rather than through deduction. This is the reason why the *maqasid* are considered definitive *(qati)*, and can be relied upon without a doubt, and the same pattern is to be found in the other details of the *Shariah*. He quotes a large number of verses of the Quran to show how the ultimate purposes are indicated by the texts.

The Nature and Structure of the Purposes of the Shariah : The structure of the *maqasid* is understood by appreciating the relationship of the primary purposes among themselves, and their relationship with the secondary and supporting purposes. As the *maqasid* are designed to ultimately serve the interests of the Hereafter, it is this relationship that may be examined first.

Primary Purposes in the Service of the Hereafter : The first purpose of the *Shariah* is to secure the interest of Man that pertains to the Hereafter. It is for this reason that the purposes are divided into *dini* or purposes of the Hereafter and *dunyawi*[11] or purposes restricted to this world.

The worldly purposes, in combination, seek to preserve and protect the interest of *din*. Al-Ghazzali says that the second purpose, which is the preservation and protection of life, may be considered by some to have a higher priority than *din*, because without life there would be no religion.

This argument takes collective life into consideration, and in this sense it would also hold true for the intellect too, because the existence of *aql* is considered by jurists to be a condition of *taklif* (legal obligation). He points out, however, that some provisions of the law clearly support the superiority of the interest of *din*. For example, the interest of *din* is preferred when the subject is asked to give up his life in the way of Allah, that is, for *jihad.* The relationship of the necessities or the primary purposes is seen through the following figure:

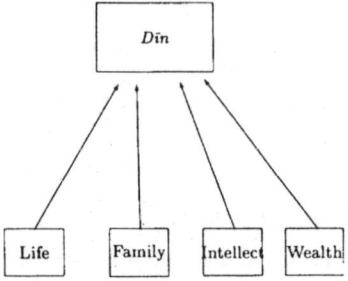

Al-Shatibi devotes three of the thirteen rules, in which he discusses the relationship among the purposes, to the discussion of the Hereafter. The most important point he makes in this context is that the identification of the interests of Man has not been left to the whims and fancies of human beings, that is, to human reason, because all the purposes seek to establish and maintain life in this world to serve the interests of the Hereafter.

He also discusses the concept of utility and points out that benefits and harms are relative; they may vary from individual to individual, and from one situation to the other. If harm and benefit cannot be established directly from the texts, then, it is to be linked to what is usually considered beneficial or harmful. The general rule that he derives is that since the *maqasid* serve the interests of the Hereafter the determination of what is beneficial and what is harmful cannot be left to human reason. He seeks support from a number of Quranic verses. One of these is:

> And if the Truth had followed their desires, verily the heavens and the earth and whosoever is therein had been corrupted. [Quran 23:71]

In his view, the role of human reason begins after the *Shariah* has laid down the essential principles. The first of the thirteen rules he expounds is devoted to this point. The primary purpose of the *Shariah,* then, as indicated already, is to free Man from the grip of his own whim and fancy, so that he may become the servant of Allah by choice, just as he is one without it. The preservation and protection of *din* is intended by the Lawgiver to achieve this.

The two Faces of the Maqasid : Perhaps the most important feature of the *maqasid* is their dual thrust. Al-Ghazzali discusses this dual nature in detail in his book called *Jawahir al-Quran.*

This point has been ignored by almost all the later jurists, except for al-Shatibi. The dual feature of the *maqasid* is evident in the use of the terms *ibqa* and *hifz,* which we may call preservation and protection. Al-Shatibi considers these the two aspects of *hifz.* The first he says is "what affirms its elements and establishes its foundations." The second is "what repels actual or expected disharmony." The focus of later jurists, and hence that of modern scholars, has been on the aspect of protection alone.

Each purpose, however, has a positive or aggressive aspect and a negative or defensive aspect. From the positive aspect, the interest is secured by establishing what is required by the *Shariah* through each of its *maqasid*. Thus, the interest of *din* is secured by the creation of conditions that facilitate worship and establish the other essential pillars of Islam. The interest of life is secured by creating conditions for the existence of life.

The interest of progeny is supported by facilitating and establishing family life. The interest of intellect is secured by promoting the means for the growth of the intellect. The interest of wealth is secured by creating proper conditions for the growth of wealth.

	Din	Life	Family	Intellect	Wealth
+ve	Establish	Establish	Establish	Establish	Establish
-ve	Defend	Defend	Defend	Defend	Defend

From the defensive or the protective aspect, interests are secured by preventing the destruction or corruption of the positive aspect. Thus, *jihad* is prescribed for defending *din,* while prayer, fasting, pilgrimage, and *zakah* help establish it. It is the duty of the *imam* to ensure proper conditions for both, while it is binding upon each subject to fulfil these duties, individually and collectively. Life is preserved through the provision of sustenance and the maintenance of good health, while it is protected or defended through the provision of penalties for those who destroy life without legal justification.

Nasl is promoted through the maintenance of healthy family life and the institution of marriage, while penalties are provided for those who would corrupt it and destroy its values. The preservation of *aql* is achieved through the provision of education and healthy conditions for its growth, while penalties are provided for the consumption of substances that destroy the intellect. Preservation of wealth is achieved by encouraging its growth, while theft or misappropriation of wealth is punished through penalties.

OTHER AIMS

The jurists break up the *maqasid* into three levels. This has already been pointed out. The first level is that of the necessities *(darurat),* which have been maintained by all societies and without which the social structure will collapse.

These are the primary *maqasid* and the jurists focus mostly on these. They are supported by the supporting needs *(hajat)*. The third level is that of complementary values and norms *(tahsinat)*.

The important point made by jurists about the significance of each level is that the primary purposes are supported by the two other levels. However, if the last two levels are abolished the primary purposes will stand by themselves. This is not true for the lower levels. Thus, the existence of *hajat* and the *tahsinat* depends upon the primary purposes and they cannot be maintained on their own.

Din	Life	Family	Intellect	Wealth
Public	Public	Public	Public	Public
Private	Private	Private	Private	Private

The importance of the individual purposes within the *darurat* is reflected in the order in which they are stated. Thus, *din*[12] has precedence over life, life has precedence over *nasl*, *nasl* has precedence over *aql*, and *aql* has precedence over *mal*. This is not all. Each of the primary purposes may divided into public and private purposes.

The public purposes seek to preserve the interests of the community as whole, while the private purposes protect the rights of individuals. Again, the purposes are divisible into those securing the rights of Allah and those preserving or protecting the rights of the individuals. There is a fine distinction between the two kinds of divisions, though many modern scholars tend to consider them identical. The distinction lies in the fact that there are three kinds of rights to be identified rather than two. These are the right of Allah, the right of the community as whole, and the right of the individual.

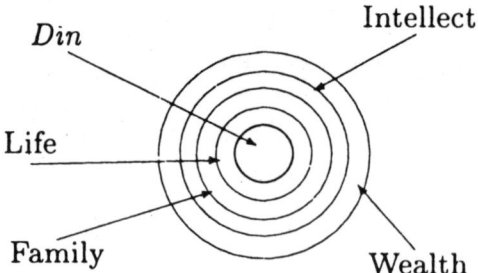

The relationship that exists between the primary purposes may be highlighted by visualising outer shells serving or protecting the inner shell or shells. Thus, the innermost shell is represented by the preservation and protection of *din*. This

Various Aspects of Law

represents the foremost purpose of the *Shariah*. The shell surrounding it is that of life, which is itself surrounded by *nasl* and so on. The outermost shell is that of the preservation of wealth that serves all the inner shells and is subservient to them.

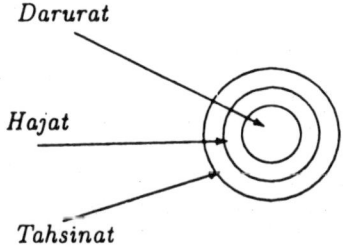

Each primary purpose considered to be a necessity has its own supporting needs and complementary norms. These are also to be viewed as shells, one inside the other. This relationship is explained by al-Shatibi through examples. Considering the example of prayer *(salat)*, he says that the essential parts of the prayer are its *arkan* (elements) and *faraid* (obligations). Whatever is besides these is meant to complete and complement it.

The parts of prayer are distributed among the *maqasid* in such a way that each outer shell forms a protective boundary for the inner shell. One who crosses the outer shell or boundary will soon demolish the inner shell. Thus, the person who gives up the *nafl* (supererogatory) prayers will soon give up the *sunan*, and will finally demolish the *faraid*.

There are many instances in the law, he says, that correspond with the analogy of *nafl* and *faraid*[13]. For example, even a drop of wine or a small quantity of it is prohibited, because it leads to the consumption of larger quantities, though it does not intoxicate or damage the intellect. A severe penalty is provided for stealing a thing of small value as it leads to the stealing of larger amounts and to robbery. In the same way, the ethical and moral norms hover around and protect the main and essential legal norms. The *Haji*[14] and the *tahsini* are, therefore, to be considered the servants of the *daruri*.

Priorities within the Maqasid : The relationships described above indicate that some purposes have a higher priority than others, that is, they would be preferred in case of a clash between two interests. This fact also highlights an important point that while deciding a legal case or while attempting to understand the position of Islamic law on an issue, one cannot look at one purpose or interest alone.

There is always a clash of two or more interests. This is achieved through the machinery of organised political society that seeks to strike a compromise between the conflicting wants, desires, and claims of individuals and between the competing interests. Looking at the purposes of law alone and identifying the priorities that exist between them would present a simplistic view of things.

The *maqasid*[15] are always used as a reference point for the general principles of the law, and this makes the situation highly complex. This will be illustrated in the third part of this book under the discussion of the third mode of *ijtihad* (see page 309). Nevertheless, the *maqasid* considered alone present a fair picture of the entire system even for the layman, who is not trained in the law.

If he observes a few rules, he can easily determine the answer to a question that he may have about the law. For the present purposes, we shall describe three main rules that govern the employment of the *maqasid*. Some other minor rules can be stated, but the idea is to avoid too much detail and technicalities.

Rule 1: The Stronger Interest Shall Prevail : The inherent strength of the interests secured by Islamic law is reflected in the order in which the *maqasid* are listed by the jurists. Thus, the preservation and protection of *din*, as we have pointed out earlier, has preference over the preservation and protection of life; life has a higher priority than *nasl*[16]; *nasl* is prior to *aql*; and *aql* is preferred over *mal*.

Din	Life	Family	Intellect	Wealth
First	Second	Third	Fourth	Fifth

In practice this would mean, for example, that *jihad* has priority over preservation of life, and if an individual is asked to participate in it and give up his life in the cause of Allah, there is legal justification for it. Preservation of life has a higher priority than the protection of *aql*.

Therefore, if a person is facing death in a desolate place due to lack of water and the only thing available to him is wine, he is under an obligation to save his life by drinking the wine. Life has priority over *mal* too and it is permitted to take the property of another person without fear of penalty during a famine, if such taking results in the saving of life or lives.

In the same way, the *darurat* have priority over the *hajat*[17], which in turn have priority over the *tahsinat*.

Rule 2: The Public Interest is Prior to the Private : The different categories of the purposes can be understood in terms of public and private interests. Whenever a public interest is in conflict with a private interest, the public interest will prevail. The example used by the jurists is that of material handed over to artisans and craftsmen. The original rule of deposit *(wadiah)* required that this material being a deposit would not be compensated by the craftsmen in case it was destroyed, and the burden of proving tort *(taaddi)* or negligence would be upon the customer, the owner of the property.

This rule was changed to conform with the public interest, because the craftsmen were misusing the facility. The burden of proof was shifted to the craftsman, who had to show the absence of negligence. The Hanafis based this change on *istihsan*. The example is expected to show that the public interest requiring security of transactions and protection of property of the general public was given preference over the interest of individuals, that is, the craftsmen.

In this case, both interests, public as well as private, lie within the same category, that is, the preservation of wealth. Does the rule that the public interest prevails over the private cut across all the categories? Can a public interest in a lower category be preferred over a private interest in a category with a higher priority? Apparently it can. Yet, the matter is not that simple; it involves the discussion of the three kinds of rights mentioned above, individual rights guaranteed by the *Shariah,* and the exact meaning of public interest. We do not have space to discuss all these issues here. This discussion will be taken up in a separate study of justice and Islamic law.

Another example used by al-Ghazzali upholds justification of taxation by the *imam* when the public interest is at stake. He permits a ruler in need of money to levy taxes in order to organise *jihad.* Here what we are calling public interest is actually the right of God, which may not be the same as the right of the state.

Rule 3: The Definitive Interest Prevails Over the Probable : This rule has been the cause of confusion for some jurists following al-Ghazzali, and the confusion is witnessed in the works of some modern scholars too. Al-Shatibi states very clearly that all the interests preserved and protected by the *Shariah* are definitive *(qati)*. He repeats this point over and over again, and it is in fact a fundamental assumption of his work.

The question, therefore, arises that if all interests are definitive, where does the probable interest come from? The answer to this issue is that the probable goals of the law belong to the area that is beyond the purposes and has been discussed above. These purposes have not been discussed by the jurists in detail. Most of the goals like building of civilisation, maintenance of security, equality, freedom and others would come under this heading. From another perspective, these goals have neither been rejected by the Lawgiver nor have they been directly acknowledged. Two cases mentioned by al-Ghazzali have been mentioned under the discussion of *maslahah mursalah*. There are, however, other possibilities too for probable interests to exist within the structure discussed, but we would like to leave this topic for the researcher here and devote adequate space to it in a separate study.

References

1. *Disciples of Companions of the Prophet (Pbuh).*
2. *Advancement or growth in the process of purgation.*
3. *Second most beloved Caliph of Prophet Muhammad (Pbuh).*
4. *A great and prominent scholar of Islam.*
5. *A member of OPEC.*
6. *Humanity.*
7. *Worship.*
8. *Under the government of Muslim rulers.*
9. *Under the government of Non-Muslim rulers.*
10. *A prominent scholar-turned sufi; called Proof of Islam.*
11. *Pertaining to this world.*
12. *Religion Islam.*
13. *Obligatory prayers or worships.*
14. *One who performs Hajj; a Holy pilgrimage.*
15. *Purposes.*
16. *Lineage.*
17. *Need or requirement.*

7

VARIOUS CATEGORIES OF LAW

CONSTITUTION AT WORK

The conception of a State in the Islamic system is, as already mentioned, that of a commonwealth of all the Muslims living as one community under the guidance and direction of a supreme executive head called the Imam or the Caliph. The responsibility of administration rests with the Imam, but for the convenience of administration, he may delegate his powers to different persons.

He may, for instance, appoint ministers to whom he may delegate practically all his powers and faculties or only particular powers, or he may appoint them merely for the purposes of consultation and for executing orders. Similarly, he may appoint a person as Governor of a particular country with such powers as may be necessary.

He may also delegate the exercise of his authority in the various departments of administration to different officers, such as the command of the army, administration of justice, revenue, Police and the like. But the Imam has no legislative powers at all though he may interpret the law if he happens to be a jurist, but his interpretation will have no special authority by reason of his position as Imam. He is bound by the law, and by the decrees and orders of the Court like any other citizen. In fact, there are many recorded instances in which Qadis passed orders against the chief of the State of the day and the latter submitted to them.

One of the best known of these is the case in which Shariah the famous Qadi decided against Ali the third Caliph a suit which the latter had instituted against a Jew. But this is possible only if the Imam chooses to submit to the order. Hence it is laid down that neither retaliation nor hadd can be ordered against the Sultan because of want of power in the Court to enforce them. It is, however, the duty of the Qadi when a suit or complaint is instituted before him against the Imam to notify the fact to the Imam with his views and to request him to redress the wrong.

He is Merely the Representative of the People; to be Elected : The Imam is merely the representative or delegate of the people, from whom he derives his rights and privileges. The office is elective being based on Ijma', as I had occasion to mention in another place, and the first precedent for it was the election of Abu Bakr as the Caliph after the death of the Prophet. But, as it is not possible for all the Muslims to take part in such election, it is deemed sufficient if the power is exercised by their chief men (*Ayan*) that is the nobility, the gentry and the learned. Once duly elected the Imam acquires supreme control over the executive administration of the State. If the Imam happens to be oppressive and to violate the injunctions of the law and religion the Muslims may, if they can, replace him by another Imam, but until then he is entitled to homage and obedience and his orders are absolutely binding. This is the meaning of what the author of Bahrur-Ruiq on the authority of Qadi Khan lays down, namely that the Sultanate is based on two facts :

(1) fealty of the aristocracy and the gentry and

(2) power to enforce orders.

If he has the homage of the aristocracy and the gentry, but has not the power to enforce orders, he does not become Sultan. If a person becomes a Sultan by acceptance of the leaders of the people and turns out to be a tyrant, he does not cease to be a Sultan by reason of this fact alone because if the law ordered that he should no longer he the Sultan, it would be useless considering that he has the power to enforce his authority as the Sultan. But if the Sultan becomes oppressive, and he has not the power to retain his position, he then ceases to be the Sultan (Yanazil).

In these passages one cannot help detecting a reluctant effort of the law to adjust the true Islamic idea of an Imam as the representative of the people pure and simple with the actual facts of later days when Kings and potentates assumed by force powers which the law did not concede to them.

The Imam ought to belong to the tribe of Quraish, but it is not necessary that he should be of the Hashimi family. If no person competent to hold the office of Imam can be found in the tribe of Quraish, then a person may be chosen as Sultan who is virtuous (*Adil*) and trustworthy and has knowledge of the conditions regarding appointments to the office of Qadi and the like. A duly appointed Imam may nominate his successor as Abu Bakr nominated Umar, but such nomination must apparently be confirmed by the people.

It is a fact of history that for a long time a number of Islamic States have existed with out a common Imam or executive chief and in fact the Islamic conception of a vast Islamic republic must be regarded in the nature of a constitutional ideal towards which some progress was made during the time of the first four 'rightly guided' Caliphs, but which has ever since been supplanted by despotic kingly governments.

ROLE OF REVENUES

The head of the State among the Muhammadan is the trustee of public property and in no sense its owner. Such public property consists first of all of revenues which when collected are to be deposited in the public treasury (baitul mal literally the house for property). The revenues are derived from the following principle sources: taxes levied on land belonging to Muslims in the shape of Ushr or tithe khiraj or land-tax, originally assessed on land belonging to non-Muslim owners, poll-tax or jiziya leviable from non-Muslims subjects in lieu of protection afforded to them, zakat or poor rate levied from the Muslims alone, and khums consisting of one-fifth of the property acquired from the non-Muslims by conquest and one-fifth of the contents of mines, escheats and forfeitures.

Of the above, the proceeds of the poor-rate and one-fifth of the booty and of the contents of mines are ear-marked for the use of the poor and the indigent. But in cases of emergency the Imam may utilize them for the protection of the Islamic community such as for religious wars. The rest of the revenues is to be spent for the purposes of administration generally.

It was at first doubted whether the Imam could take anything from the public treasury for his own maintenance and of that of his family, but when the public affairs of the community increased in complexity and dimensions so that the Imam could have no time to earn his own livelihood, the law permitted him to draw upon the public funds for the purpose.

ROLE OF IMAM

The Imam is also the custodian of such public property as rivers, public roads, waste lands and the like. He is the ultimate guardian of trusts and institutions intended for the benefit of the community or of a section of the community such as mosques, madrasas, inns and the like, and of the person and property of helpless persons such as minors, lunatics and idiots. The care and supervision of trusts and public institutions and of the person and property of minors, lunatics and idiots are generally delegated to the Qadi in addition to his ordinary duties in connection with the administration of justice.

He has besides a general disciplinary power over the Muslims so that he can enforce chastisement with a view to compel the observance of religious injunctions and public decorum. These disciplinary powers are also sometimes entrusted to the Qadi. It is also a high privilege of the Imam to lead the Friday congregational prayers, but this also he may delegate to other persons.

Zakat or Poor Rate : Jizya or Poll-tax : Of the principal sources of revenue open to a Islamic State, Zakat or the poor-rate, jizya or poll-tax, ushr or tithe, and khiraj call for a somewhat specific notice. Zakat is tax imposed on the Muhammadans alone and the payment of it is an obligatory act of worship. It may be realised by the State by enforcement of disciplinary measures as it was done in the time of Abu Bakr. But nowadays it is left to the religious sense of each Muslim even in self-governing Islamic countries whether to pay zakat or not. It is levied on a man's possessions exclusive of landed property such as on gold and silver, cattle, goods of merchandise and the like, provided they reach a certain value at the end of the year.

Generally speaking it is two and a half per cent of the aggregate. Jizya which is also a personal tax may be imposed on the non-Muslims either under a treaty in which case its amount is to be determined by agreement of the parties, or it may be imposed after conquest in lieu of the Imam confirming them in possession of their country. In the latter case, it is to be paid according to certain rates, which are fixed having regard to the means and income of each individual. This is according to the Hanafis but the Shafiis have one uniform rate for all, rich or poor. Since this tax is in the nature of reansom for a hostile non-Muslim's life and it is not lawful to kill females, children, the blind and the diseased, such persons are exempted from its incidence. The idolaters of Arabia and apostates from Islam are given the option between death and the acceptance of Islamic religion and hence jizya cannot be accepted from them. This tax is not levied on monks who have forsaken society because as they do not live in their community, it is not lawful to fight them. When a non-Muslim who is assessed with this tax embraces Islam he becomes exempt from such payment.

Ushr or Tithe : Khiraj or Land-tax : All lands of a country, the inhabitants of which have accepted Islam, are liable to pay 'ushr or tithe. The reason is that the payment of tithe is an act of worship and also least burdensome and, therefore, most fit and proper to be levied on Muslims. All land, which has been conquered after resistance or which is surrendered to the Muslims and allowed to remain in the hands of its inhabitants, is liable to the payment of khiraj, subject to certain conditions. Mecca is, however, exempted from this rule for only tithe was levied upon it when the Prophet accepted the treaty of its non-Muslim inhabitants. All the land of Arabia proper is liable only to the payment of tithe because the only option allowed to the Arabs was either to accept Islam or to fight. But Syira is subject to khiraj by consensus of opinion among the Companions. Whether land is to be assessed with Khiraj or 'Ushr, depends mainly on the means of irrigation. If a country which has been conquered by force is irrigated by stream or river, it is regarded as tributary and whatever land is not reached by such river, but is irrigated by water derived from an underground spring by digging, it is liable to the payment of tithe. If waste land is brought into cultivation then the question whether it is to be assessed with khiraj or 'ushr is determined, according to Abu Yusuf, by the character of the land in the vicinity.

According to Muhammad, if land is brought into cultivation by digging wells is it or by springs of water coming out of it or by the water of Tigris of the Euphrates or of large rivers which are not the property of anyone or by rain water then it is liable to payment of tithe. The rates of khiraj vary with the kind of crops grown on the land and its productive powers. It is not, however, to exceed half the value of its average produce. If the produce of the khiraji land is destroyed by floods or drought or blight, the revenue ceases to be payable for that year, but not if it is destroyed by the negligence of the owner. The character of khiraj paying land would bot change, merely because it has passed into the hands of a Muslim.

HANDLING JUSTICE

The powers of the Imam, not only in fiscal matters but also with regard to the appointment of Qadis and otherwise providing for the administration of justice, are defined by the law. Not only may the, Imam appoint Qadis but so also may the minister and the Governor if they have been vested with such powers. A non-Muslim Ruler or Governor may also legally appoint a Qadi to administer Islamic law.

POSTING OF JUDGES

No one can be appointed a Qadi unless he possesses the qualification of a witness, that is to say, unless he is a Muslim, free and major. According to the Shafiis he must also be of virtuous character, but the Hanafis while holding that the Qadi should be a man of virtuous character do not consider it a necessary condition of the validity of such an appointment, so that the decree of a Qadi who is not of virtuous character will not, according to them, be treated as invalid. Nor, according to the Hanafis, differing from the other Sunni schools, is it necessary that a Qadi should be mujtahid or jurist. The Hanafis[1] hold that the function of a Qadi is to redress wrongs and to enforce rights which it is possible for a Qadi who does not hold the rank of a mujtahid to do acting upon opinions of others who possesses the necessary qualifications of a mujtahid[2]. When, therefore, a Qadi is appointed who is not a mujtahid, a Mufti should be appointed to advise him on questions of law. The Mufti[3] must necessarily be learned in the law and he must also in addition to his possessing the qualifications of a Qadi mentioned above be an Adil or man of virtuous character.

Woman may be a Qadi : A woman may be a Qadi according to the Hanafis as she possesses the qualification of a witness, but she is not competent to pass orders of hadd or retaliation as in these matters her evidence is not admissible. She is altogether disqualified for the office according to Shafiis.

IMPORTANCE OF THE JUDGE

A Qadi may be appointed for a limited time or with jurisdiction over a particular area. Similarly a particular class of cases may be excluded from his jurisdiction or he may be empowered to try only particular classes of cases. For instance, a Qadi may be prohibited from hearing cases instituted after the lapse of a certain time or he may be appointed only to hear cases arising in the army or in any particular division of it. Sometimes two Qadi may be appointed to hear a particular case. The Qadi may appoint a deputy Qadi if he is empowered to do so by the Sultan[4], and he can also dismiss him. When a deputy has been properly appointed, he can pass orders on evidence heard by the principal Qadi or *vice-versa*.

The Qadi holds his office at the discretion of the Sultan who may dismiss him on suspicion or even without suspicion. Abu Hanifa[5] says that a Qadi[6] should not be allowed to hold office for more than a year. On the death of a Sultan, however, the Qadi does not, according to accepted opinion, vacate his office.

Quasi Judicial Duties of a Qadi : Among the quasi judicial duties ordinarily attached to the office of a Qadi is the protection and supervision of trust property like waqf, of the properties and interests of minors, lunatics, idiots and missing persons. The Qadi is empowered and required to supervise the management and administration of waqfs so far as it may be necessary for the preservation of the trust property and their application to the objects of the grant. The authority is quite independent of the wishes of the grantor, being exercisable for the benefit of the present and the future beneficiaries whether they be the general public or a class of individuals.

His powers in this respect are more comprehensive than those of a trustee or mutawalli[7] appointed by the grantor. For instance, a mutawalli has very limited powers of leasing, mortgaging or selling waqf property in cases of necessity, but the Qadi's powers in this respect are plenary. In fact, the trustee's general powers under the Islamic law are so limited that it is difficult for a waqf property to be properly managed or even preserved without the constant supervision of the Court.

The Qadi is to take periodical accounts from a trustee regarding the trust property and its income, and if he finds anything wrong in the way the trustee has been dealing with the property he should dismiss him and appoint another trustee in his place. The Qadi has similar power of supervision and control over the properties of minors, lunatics and the acts of their guardians. If a minor has no guardian he may appoint one for the safe custody both of his person and property and if necessary may give him or her in marriage.

Similarly the Qadi should appoint an administrator to administer the estate of a deceased person whose heirs are absent in a foreign country or whose whereabouts are not known or if some of the heirs are minors, and he should also take the necessary measures for the protection of the properties of a missing person. Shamsul Ayimma Halwai says that an administrator of the estate of a deceased person is to be appointed in three cases:

(1) if the deceased has left debts,

(2) if the heirs are minors, and

(3) if he has left a will (without appointing an executor).

MUSLIMS VS NON-MUSLIMS

The relation between Muslims and non-Muslims has several aspects, that between :

(1) the Muslim State and an alien non-Muslim State,

(2) the Muslim State and the alien non-Muslims living temporarily within its jurisdiction,

(3) individual Muslims residing or sojourning within the jurisdiction of an alien non-Muslim State and such State,

(4) individual Muslims living within the Muslim State and alien non-Muslims,

(5) the Muslim State and its non-Muslim subjects, and

(6) individual Muslims of a Muslim State and non-Muslim subjects of that State. Questions relating to (7) and (8) have already been dealt with under other heads. I propose here to notice briefly the main principles governing

the law under the remaining heads. The subject, as I had occasion to mention elsewhere, is dealt with in the writings of Arab jurists under the heading of As-Siyar or Jehad which is usually translated as religious war.

IMPOSING WAR

According to Islamic law the Imam of the Islamic State, supposing there is such an Executive Chief recognised by the Muhammadans, would be justified in declaring such a war against the non-Muslims of Darul-Harb[8] or an alien State for the protection of religion. From what the Prophet experienced at the hands of the infidels of Mecca it is presumed that Islam is liable to be exposed to trouble and danger from the enmity and prejudices of non-Muslims. Therefore, in order to ensure the safety of Islam, the Muslim State, provided it is powerful enough to do so, may wage war against an alien or hostile non-Muslim State.

That Jihad is permitted really for the protection of Islam and is limited by such necessity is in the first place apparent from the fact that the Imam is allowed to enter into a treaty of peace with the hostile State if such a treaty would secure the prevention of the evil to be avoided. Then, no such war can be waged unless the non-Muslim subjects of the hostile State have first of all been invited to embrace Islam; and if they accept such invitation, hostilities are to cease at once.

That is why, as already explained, Jihad is said to be good not in itself (Husnun li aynihi) but for the sake of something else (Husnun li ghairihi), namely, religion. If they refuse to accept the Islamic religion but accept the suzerainty of Islam by agreeing to pay a poll-tax (jizya) to the Muslim State, in that case also hostilities must cease, as there would be no more likelihood of danger to Islam. Non-Muslims so submitting are entitled to the enjoyment of all rights in respect of their lives and property like the Muslims. The underlying idea of Jihad is to maintain the predominance of power or the balance of power as it is euphemistically called in modern European diplomacy.

Life and Property of the Citizens and Soldiers of the Beligerent States : In the event of a religious war, the women, the children, the aged and the diseased among the enemies are not to be killed or maltreated, but such of them as have taken part in the fight cannot claim such consideration. The goods of the enemy that are captured during hostilities are treated as a prize in the hands of the Muslims. The head of the conquering Muslim State is entitled to divide the country which has been wrested from the non-Muslims after fight, among the soldiers or if he chooses may impose a poll-tax on its inhabitants. As regards the prisoners taken in war they may be killed or enslaved or left free to live under the protection of the Muslim State as dhimmees.

Various Categories of Law

The Imam has the discretion to determine what is to be done with them and he should do what is most politic under the circumstances. If the non-Muslim enemies triumph over the Muslims, whatever property the former may have taken in the fight become their according to the Islamic law; so that it will not be lawful for the previous Muslim owners to take the same from the captores except by recognised means of acquisition. But Muslims captured by their non-Muslim enemy cannot be enslaved, as freedom is the inalienable and inviolable condition of a Muhammadan.

Duty of Muslim Subjects of the Muslim State in Case of War : When there is a religious war between a Muslim State and a non-Muslim State, it is the duty of the Muslim subjects of the former as a body to serve in such war, but not of every individual. What is meant is that if a sufficient number of men join, the rest will be absolved, but if none join, every one would be a transgressor in the eye of law.

There is no obligation on the children, the women, the aged and the infirm to join in the fight except when the non-Muslims are the aggressors, and it has become necessary for them to fight in self-defence, because otherwise if the infidels triumphed, Islam would not be safe.

Treaties : The head of a Muslim State may, if he considers it beneficial to the Muhammadans, conclude a treaty with a non-Muslim State which it will be his duty to observe faithfully. Such a treaty is regarded as carrying out the real aim of Jihad which is to ward off injuries likely to be inflicted by non-Muslims. It is assumed that the Imam is to enter into a treaty only for the good of the Muhammadans.

The treaty may be for a short or a long period of time as the Imam may think best, and according to the accepted doctrine there is no fixed limit of time for it. If, during the term of the treaty, the Imam finds that it would be good for the Muhammadans that he should withdraw from it, he can do so, but only after giving sufficient notice of his intention to the other party, because otherwise it would be an act of treachery which the law forbids. If the other party begins hostilities in violation of the treaty, it will not be incumbent on the Imam of the Muslim State to give a formal notice before taking action.

Not only may the Imam enter into a treaty of peace with a non-Muslim State, but individual Muslims may afford protection to individual non-Muslim subjects of a non-Muslim State, in which case it will not be lawful for a Muslim to fight them. But should the Imam be of opinion that it is not expedient that those non-Muslims should continue to be under such protection, the protection will be withdrawn after notice has been given to them.

Two Important Concepts

The relations of the Muslims towards the non-Muslims are mainly determined on the basis whether the country or State of the latter is to be regarded as Darul-Islam literally, territory of safety, or Darul-Harb literally, territory of war. There can be no question but that a country go earned by a Muslim ruler according to the laws of the Islamic religion is Darul-Islam. Nor can there be any doubt that a country under a non-Muslim Government in which a Muhammadan cannot live with personal security and freedom to perform his religious duties is Darul-Harb. But it does not follow that a self-governing Muslim country passing into the hands of non-Muslim conquerors or of the dhimmis rising against the Muslim Government becomes by that fact alone Darul-Harb. It turns into Darul-Harb if it fulfils three conditions, namely, that the laws and regulations of the non-Muslims be enforced there, that it should be surrounded by other countries answering the description of Darul-Harb without any country of the description of Darul-Islam being contiguous to it and if no Muslim or Dhimmi, that is, a non-Muslim subject of a Muslim State, can live there, in the same security as under the previous Muslim Government. This is apparently the opinion of Abu Hanifah and adopted by the author of 'Durrul-Mukhtar' as representing the law on the subject.

The two disciples, however, hold that such a country would be called Darul-Harb if the laws of the non-Muslim are promulgated there so that neither hadd nor retaliation is enforced. If the laws of both are enforced, that is, non-Muslim laws for the non-Muslims and the Islamic laws for the Muhammadans, the country will retain its character of Darul-Islam. On a Muslims' country being conquered by the non-Muslims and turning into Darul-Harb it is lawful for the Muslim prisoners to oppose, and fight with them in every possible way. A Darul-Harb, on the other, hand, becomes Darul-Islam if the ordinances of Islam may validly be promulgated there.

One of the tests, as to whether a country should be treated as a Darul-Harb or Darul-Islam, is whether congregational prayers during Fridays and Eids should be held in the country. Under what circumstances then the holding of Friday prayers is allowed by the Islamic law? One of the conditions mentioned in the books is that such prayers can be said only in a town where there is a Governor and a Qadi administer the laws and to enforce the punishment of hadd and retaliation.

The author of 'Hedaya' says that this is the accepted law. According to Abu Hanifah, Friday prayers are to be held in a town where there are roads and markets, a Governor who administers laws and redresses wrongs, and learned men to whom Muhammadan can resort for the solution of the difficulties of Shara⁹ or the Islamic Code. Another condition of Friday prayers is that they must

Various Categories of Law

be held under the order of the Sultan or of some person authorised by him in that behalf. If the non-Muslims who have conquered a Muslim territory have appointed a Muhammadan Governor, he may give such sanction. If the Governor himself be a non Muslim, it may be the interests of Muhammadans to obey him. In a self-governing Islamic country when the Sultan has appointed a non-Muslim Governor, the Muslims of the place may hold Friday prayers and the Qadi of that place will be regarded, although appointed by the non-Muslim Governor, as if he had been appointed by the consent of the Muslims. But under such circumstances it is the duty of the Muslims to demand the appointment of a Muhammadan Governor.

Ibn Abidin then quotes a passage from a commentary of Sheikh Ismail[10] of Delhi to the effect that when it is said that Friday prayers can only be held in a place where the Islamic laws are enforced, it does not mean that all the laws should actually be enforced, but that the Governor or the Qadi should have the power to enforce them. It is also stated in the gloss of Abu Sawood on a treatise by Allama Nur Effendi[11] that if actual enforcement of all the laws or, it may be added, enforcement of hadd and retaliation were a necessary condition, then Friday prayers could not be held even in any Islamic country at the present day, and therefore it is regarded as sufficient if the Governor or the Qadi should as already stated have the power to enforce them. But it is necessary that most of the Islamic laws should be enforced. The substantial idea running through the discussion of the jurists on this point seems to be that Friday or Id prayers may be held in a place where the congregation will not be liable to molestation.

India is Darul-Islam : It may be observed here that the Friday and Id prayers are regularly held all over India and recognised to be validly held according to the Islamic Canonical Law. Further, the Muhammadans of India enjoy absolute protection of person and property and religious freedom and their laws relating to religious institutions and usages and those governing family relations and succession and certain forms of transfer of property are enforced by the Anglo-Indian Courts. Another convincing test that India under the present form of Government must be regarded as Darul-Islam is that those Muhammadans who strictly follow the rules of juristic law regarding Riba do not feel themselves justified in taking interest on money advanced to non-Muslims.

Duty of non-Muslims Residing in an Alien Country : As I have had occasion to point out, the Islamic law, generally speaking, has two sides. In its worldly aspect, it is enforceable by the Court and in its spiritual aspect, it affects the conscience of every individual Muslim. The head of the Muslim State can obviously enforce Islamic laws only within his own jurisdiction. A Muhammadan living within the territory of non-Muslims is required to conform, as far as is practicable for him to do so, to the rules and injunctions of the Islamic law and religion. If he violates them, he incurs religious guilt and when he finds that he cannot stay in a particular non-Muslim country with safety of person and property nor discharge his religious duties there, he is expected to retire to his own State.

If such a person finds that the non-Muslim Government actually interferes with his property and reduces his children to slavery or suffers it to be done or is guilty of other similar acts of oppression, he would be justified in interfering with the lives and properties of the non-Muslim inhabitants of the place. The reason ins that the Government itself of the country of his adoption must in such circumstance be held to have been guilty of treachery towards him for he could not have resided in an alien country without its express or implied permission and it is always lawful for a Muslim according it his law to repel oppression. But otherwise, he must forbear from interfering with the non-Muslim Government and inhabitants of the country of his as option as that would be an act of perfidy on his part which the law absolutely forbids.

RIGHTS IN ISLAM

Following the method adopted by Sadrush-Shariat, we have to study the remaining topics of the science of Usul with reference to the two main classes of law, namely, defining and declaratory laws. Defining law is that which does not derive its character as such from the fact of one thing being connected with another. It may define either :

(1) the quality of an act of the obligee, that is, the person to whom the law is addressed, for example, the law which tells us that a certain act is obligatory or forbidden, or

(2) indicate its legal effect such as ownership, and that which is connected therewith, for example, right to conjugal society, right to the usufruct, whether produce of property or services of man and the establishing of obligation to discharge of debt.

Let us now see how the objectives of law (Mahkum bihi)[12] namely, acts rights and obligations are classified.

Natural, Juristic, Physical and Mental : Acts are, first of all, classified into natural acts (hissi) and juristic acts (Shariah). Natural acts include acts of the body or physical acts (afalul jawarih) as well as acts of the mind (afalul-qalb). An act of the body consists of the motion of some limb of the human body, such as utterance of words, eating, drinking, striking, and so on. One of the obvious properties of such an act is that it is perceptible to persons other than the doer. In this respect it differs from an act of the mind such as believing, acknowledging, intending, wishing and the like.

Human tribunals cannot deal with an act of the mind by itself, for the simple reason that they cannot seize upon it. Suppose a man acknowledges in his mind a multiplicity of Gods instead of one God, the magistrate is powerless to deal with the matter and the offender can only be held responsible by God himself. On the other hand, if he expresses such *acknowledgment* in words or conduct, the law would treat him as a non-Muslim. Similarly one may intend to take another's watch, but so long as he does nothing to accomplish his purpose, the law will leave him alone.

A juristic act may be described as an aggregate of more than one natural act of one or more persons which the law treats as one act, such as iman or act of faith or belief, salat or prayer, a contract of sale or hire, an offence of sedition and the like. Juristic acts or rather their component elements must have existence in the outside world, and also separately in the contemplation of law while a natural act has no separate existence in law though the latter deals with it.

Physical acts are broadly divisible into acts of utterance (Qaul)[13] and act of conduct (amal or fil). Utterances consist of spoken words, or of such other expressions of the will as are intended to be substitutes for spoken words, such as writings gestures, etc., and acts of conduct include all other motions of the body or a limb such as walking, hunting, striking, threatening as well as acts of omission to discharge obligations (tark), such as default in fulfilling one's contracts.

TYPES OF OBLIGATION

The legal character of an act is often affected by the state of mind of its doer preceding or accompanying the act, and hence one important classification of acts is into voluntary and involuntary. But the nature of the relation between the mind and the legal character of an act is a question of considerable refinement and difficulty in the Islamic system, which I shall have to discuss at some length in dealing with the circumstances affecting legal capacity. All voluntary acts are called tasarrufat which means expenditure of one's energy or will, and tasarrufatushshari' are acts according to the shara' or lawful acts.

Originating acts, Informations and Acts of Faith : Juristic acts generally are divisible into inshaat or originating acts, akhbarat or informations and itiqadat or acts of faith. As I have already pointed out, the difference between an originating speech and an information is this: with reference to the latter it is possible to affirm whether it is true or not, but not so with respect to the former. Originating acts and informations are physical acts, while acts of faith are mental acts. The object of an originating act is the production of a legal result, such as sale, marriage, divorce manumission, etc., and the object of an information is to describe an event, such as testimony (shahadut) of a witness in Court, admission (iqrar) which is testimony against one's self narration of a tradition and the like.

Acts Creating Rights and Acts Extinguishing Rights : Lawful acts generally are again divided into ithbatat or creative acts, that is, acts creating rights, for example a sale, a lease, a gift, etc. and (isqatat or acts extinguishing rights, such as release, divorce, manumission, etc.

Acts which can be Undone and Acts which cannot be Undone; Contracts and Acts Annulling Contracts : Originating acts are of two kinds, those whose legal effect can be undone, that is, revocable acts such as sale, lease, etc., and those whose legal effect cannot be undone that is, irrevocable acts such as divorce, manumission and vow. Such originating acts as create legal relations are called uqudat or contracts and acts cancelling or annulling contracts are called rusukhat such as avoidance of a sale in the exercise of an 'option.'

Acts which are Causes of Legal Injunctions and Acts which are not Such Causes : Physical acts are divided into:

(1) acts in respect of which there is a pronouncement of the law and which are also the cause of another command of the law. Example: Whoredom is a physical act and is pronounced by the Islamic law to be forbidden (haram), and it further gives rise to the sentence of hadd;

(2) acts in respect of which there is a pronouncement of the law, but which do not form the cause of another command of the law. Example: Eating, which is regarded in some cases by the law as being obligatory (wajib) as when eating is necessary for the preservation of life and in some cases as being forbidden, for instance, eating during a fast. But eating itself is not the cause of a legal injunction.

Similar distinction holds good with reference to juristic acts. With reference to some juristic acts there is a pronouncement of the law, and they are also the cause of a further command of the law. For instance, selling is a juristic act and the law designates it as permissible and spiritually indifferent (muba)[14], and it further leads to a legal result, namely, transfer of ownership. There are other juristic acts which, though subject to a pronouncement of law, are not the cause of any further command or consequence. Salat or prayer, for example, is a juristic act and according to Islamic law it is sometimes obligatory and sometimes supererogatory (nafi); but it is not the cause of any other command.

Acts Classified with Reference to their Religious Purpose : In so far as the defining law indicates the quality of an act, its object may be mainly secular or spiritual. The secular object of a law of this class when it imposes an obligation to perform certain devotional acts is to secure the release of a person from such obligation by performance of the acts enjoined, and its spiritual object in such matters is to secure spiritual reward. All acts viewed with reference to their spiritual purpose may be thus classified.

If an act be such that the doing of it is regarded as better than the omitting of it and the omitting of it is prohibited, it is either obligatory in the first degree (fard)[15], or obligatory in the second degree (wajib). An act is said to belong to the former class if the prohibition of its omission is established by a clear and conclusive text of the Quran or tradition, but if such prohibition is established by an authority of a presumptive nature, the act would belong to the other category. A Muslim is bound to do acts which are obligatory either in the first or the second degree. If he does them, he secures spiritual merit (thawab)[16], and if he wilfully abstains from them, he makes himself liable to spiritual punishment (adhab).

The difference between the two classes consists in this, the man who refuses to believe in the binding nature of a command imposing an obligatory act of the first degree becomes an infidel, but not if he disputes the authority of an obligatory command of the second degree, although he becomes a transgressor, if he makes light of the authority on which such a command rests. The saying of the five daily prayers, fasting, pilgrimage, payment of the poor rate are, as I have already mentioned, obligatory acts or duties of the first degree.

The maintenance of one's wife, children and poor parents are examples of obligatory acts or duties of the second degree. Imam Shafii, however, does not draw any distinction between fard and wajib. Again there are certain acts which are obligatory on the Muslim community as a whole; if these are performed by a sufficient number of Muslims, the law is satisfied. Such acts are called furdun kifayatun[17] and may be described as duties of the community. Jihad or religious war is an act of this character. If an act be such that the doing of it is better than abstention from it, but at the same time such abstention is not forbidden, it is called sunnat if it be in accordance with the practice of the Prophet or his Companions or of the Muhammadans as a body, otherwise it is called supererogatory, but commended (mandub, mustahab, nafi. To create a charitable or religious endowment, to make gifts either *inter vivos* or by will, to give alms to the poor, the saying of certain prayers besides those prescribed as obligatory, fasting on days other than those of the Ramadan, attending the sick and the like are duties of this category.

There are, however, some supererogatory duties of this class, abstention from which subjects a man to blame, as absence from congregational prayers and omission to call out to prayers. If an act be such that abstention from it is better than the doing of it, it is called forbidden, if the doing of it is prohibited; otherwise, it is regarded as abominable or condemned (makru)[18]. Of the class of condemned acts there are some which approximate towards unlawfulness (makruhun kirahata tahrimin) and some towards lawfulness (makruhun kirahata tanzihin).

Further an act may be forbidden with reference to certain physical objects, such as the drinking of wine, eating pig's flesh, and carcases, or with reference to the rights of other persons, such as killing or injuring a person, appropriating to one's self another's property, defamation of a man or a woman's character. If an act be such that the commission or omission of it is regarded with indifference by the law-giver, it is, as I have already mentioned, called muba or permissible. Transactions of sale, pledge, lease and the like are acts of this class.

With reference to the secular purpose of the law acts are classified as follows:

Classification of Acts with Reference to their Secular Purpose; Correct, Valid, Vitiated and Void : A juristic act is said to exist if it possesses its essential elements, (arkan) and conforms to the necessary conditions (shariaat) insisted on by the law. If it also possesses such qualities of an extrinsic character as the law takes notice of it is said to be legally correct (sahih) otherwise it is regarded as faulty or vitiated in law (fasid)[19]. But if a juristic act be wanting in any of its essential elements or conditions it is called Batul or null and void. A vitiated or faulty act is correct in its essence and defective only so far as qualities, that is extraneous considerations are concerned, while a void act is bad essentially. A correct juristic act leads to the desired object and a void act altogether fails to attain such object. A vitiated act leads to the object in view so far as its constituting elements and necessary conditions are concerned, but not its extraneous conditions.

The difference between the three kinds of juristic acts stated briefly amounts to this: both correct and vitiated acts are legally valid and operative, but in the case of vitiated acts the law allows the parties a certain locus penitentia to withdraw from them so that they may not incur spiritual demerit for violating such injunctions in connection therewith as are of a directory rather than imperative character.

The Shafiis do not recognize vitiated acts as forming a separate class and hold that juristic acts are either valid or void, and they use the word fasid which I have translated as vitiated or faulty as synonymous with Batil or void, both being wanting in correctness. Even some Hanafi jurists, including such a careful writer as the author of 'Hedayah', sometimes use the term fasid in place of Batil and sometimes in its proper sense of vitiated or faulty in law. Used in its proper sense the word fasid or vitiated denotes an act which under certain conditions is voidable at the instance of the parties. In English textbooks on Islamic law, and in the reports

Various Categories of Law

of cases the word is sometimes translated as voidable, sometimes as invalid and at other times as vitiated or faulty.

Constituted Operative and Binding : A juristic act of the nature of a secular transaction (muamilat)[20] is said to be constituted (munaqad), if it possesses the necessary elements of such transaction. An act of this class is said to be operative (nafid), if it has the desired legal effect, otherwise, it is called inoperative. A contract of sale of an article by its owner, if duly formed, is operative, but if such a contract is entered into by a person who is not its owner, nor an authorised agent of the owner, it is inoperative even though duly made or constituted. A vitiated sale would be duly constituted though not legally correct. There seems to be no difference between a legally correct or valid act and an operative act. A void transaction of the nature of contract or disposition of property is always inoperative, and a valid transaction of this class is always operative. A transaction is said to be binding (lazim), if the person entering into it cannot get rid of its legal effect, such as a valid waqf contrary to a bequest which the testator is always at liberty to revoke.

Essential Elements of a Secular Transaction : Three things, generally speaking, are the essential elements of a secular transaction: (1) legal fitness or capacity of the person entering into it; for instance, he must be a person of understanding; (2) fitness of the subject-matter, that is, whether it can be dealt with by such a transaction and (3) consent of the parties. A gift by an infant is void in law as he lacks legal fitness to make a disposition of property without consideration. A sale of a carcase is void as it is not a proper subject-matter, not being property according to the Islamic law, so also a marriage within the prohibited degrees of relationship. As regards consent the general rule is, if a transaction is a contract consent of both the parties is necessary; if it is an act extinguishing a right consent of the owner of the right is necessary. What is the exact nature and degree of consent required in particular cases will be discussed hereafter.

Conditions : As regards necessary conditions, I mean those exclusive of the three essential elements just mentioned, they vary according to the nature of a transaction. Such conditions may relate to either of the three elements. For instance, the condition that the testimony of a witness who is not a man of rectitude is not to be accepted is one relating to the capacity of a person for that particular juristic act. As an example of a condition relating to the subject-matter, it may be mentioned that sale of gold for gold is not allowed, unless both the articles of exchange be equal in quantity.

The conditions that, in a contract with the object of alienation, the intention to part with the entire proprietary rights must be expressed, and that when a gratuitous gift is made the expression of intention must be made manifest and complete by the donor actually delivering possession of the property to the donee, are instances of conditions relating to the act itself. The question relating to conditions of legal transactions will, however, be more particularly considered with reference to the juristic ideas appertaining to the different departments of law.

As regards the standpoint from which Islamic jurists regard the legal relation of the state of mind of a person to his acts generally, we shall presently consider the subject, but it may be pointed out here that the normal act of a person is the expression of the free-will of a man, acting with full knowledge of the effect of his act. In its spiritual aspect the value of an act is measured by the state of mind of its doer, for God knows everything. But in apportioning the secular effect of an act, with reference to the mental condition of its doer, a human tribunal is under considerable difficulties. This difficulty is the main reason for the elaborate and at times too subtle, distinctions with which the matter is discussed by Islamic jurists.

Classification of Rights, Public Rights and Private Rights : Rights having regard to the person of inherence are principally classified by the Islamic jurists into rights of God and rights of men. Rights of the former class are such as involve benefit to the community at large and not merely to a particular individual. They are referred to God because of the magnitude of the risks involved in their violation and of the comprehensive benefits which would result from their fulfilment. It is not to be understood that those rights are called rights of God, because they are of any benefit to God for He is above all wants, nor because they are the creation of God for all rights are equally the creation of God who is the Creator of everything.

The rights of God correspond to public rights and since the Islamic law regards the observance of obligatory devotional acts as being beneficial to the community there is no difficulty in describing all rights of God as public rights. What chiefly distinguishes such a right from a right of man or a private right is this the enforcement of the former is a duty of the state, while it is at the option of the person whose private right is infringed whether to ask for its enforcement or not. It may be that certain acts which give rise to a public right affect some particular individuals more than the others but that fact will not entitle those individuals to condone the acts of the offender. It is, however, entirely at the discretion of the individual injuriously affected by the infringement of a private right, whether to pardon the wrong-doer or to insist upon redress.

From the above point of view the Islamic jurists make the following classification of rights:

(1) Matters which are purely the right of God, that is, public rights involving benefit to men generally. For instance, the infliction of the punishment

of hadd for theft is such a right and the person whose property is stolen is not, therefore, entitled to condone the offence.

(2) Matters which are entirely the right of individual men, that is, private rights, such as a right to the enforcement of contracts, protection of property and the like. Enforcement of such rights is entirely at the option of the individual whose right is infringed.

(3) Matters in which rights of the community and of individuals are combined but those of the former preponderate. The right to punish a slanderer who imputes unchastity to another person belongs according to the Hanafis to this class. By such imputation the right of the community is infringed by reason of depreciation of the honour of one of its members, and the right of the individual slandered is violated in as much as slander tends to destroy one's prestige in society. According to the Hanafis the right of God preponderates in this matter because the person defamed is not entitled to compound the offence nor in the case of his death, can his heirs demand punishment of the offender. The Shafiis, however, hold a contrary view. According to them the person defamed is entitled to exonerate the defamer and the right to prosecute passes on the death of the former to his heirs.

(4) Matters in which public rights and private rights are combined but the latter preponderate. Qisas or retaliation which is the punishment for murder or voluntary hurt is a right of this kind. Here the right of the community consists in putting a stop to disturbances and breaches of the peace on this earth. The private right in a case of murder arises from the fact of the offence having caused loss and sorrow to the heirs of the person murdered and in the case of voluntary hurt by reason of the pain and loss caused to the injured man. The private right preponderates in these cases because the person injured on the heirs of a murdered man may pardon the offender or accept money in satisfaction of the injury, and it is, therefore, their right to enforce punishment.

Types of Common Rights

Classes (1) and (3) are again divided under eight heads:

(i) Acts of devotion, pure and simple (ibadat) namely, faith or Imam and the consequential duties that is the saying of prayers (salat) payment of the poor rate (zakat) fasting (saum) and pilgrimage (hajj) and jihad.

(ii) Punishments (uqubat) of a perfect nature (kamilatun) attached as a consequence to the commission of certain offences, for example, punishments known as hadd, for theft, adultery, drunkenness and slander.

(iii) Punishments of an imperfect nature (qasiratun), such as depriving a man who has killed another, of his right of inheritance, if he be an heir of the person he has killed. Such a penalty is regarded as imperfect as it inflicts no physical suffering nor deprives the guilty person of anything of which he is already the owner.

(iv) Matters which partake of the nature both of devotion and punishment, such as atonements (kaffara) for the non-discharge of certain obligations. These bear affinity to acts of devotion as they mostly consist of fasting or emancipating a slave or feeding and clothing the poor.

(v) Acts of devotion involving an impost consisting in an obligation to make payments out of one's possessions such as the giving of certain appointed alms at Eid-ul-Fitr.

(vi) Imposts having the sense of worship, for example ('ushr) or tithe payable by a Muslim owner of lands of certain description.

(vii) Imposts which have the sense of punishments, for example, Khiraj or land tax originally leviable from non-Muslims.

(viii) Certain rights which exist by themselves (haqqun qaimun bi nafsihi), that is, rights in respect of which there are no active duties imposed on any particular individual. Examples: the right to one-fifth of the booty acquired in religious wards which is reserved by the law for distribution among the poor while the remaining four-fifths are to be divided among those taking part in such wars. Jihad or the waging of a religious war against hostile non-Muslims, is a public right, and therefore, its proceeds should prima facie belong entirely to the community. But the Lawgiver out of grace has allowed four-fifths to go to the soldiers engaged in the fight and reserved only one-fifth for the community, empowering the head of the State as agent of the community to take it on its behalf and distribute the same among the poor. Another instance, is the right to one-fifth of the contents of a mine such as gold and silver. As God has created all that is inside the earth, whatever is in a mine belongs to Him entirely, but He has out of grace permitted the owner of a mine or the finder of precious metals to take four-fifths, reserving the remaining one-fifth for the community.

KINDS OF RIGHTS

As we have just seen, the Islamic jurists divide rights generally into those that exist by themselves, that is to say, rights which are independent as distinguished from dependent rights. It is the characteristic of a right of the former class that it imposes no corresponding obligation on any particular individual, though it is a duty of all alike not to infringe it, while the essence of a dependent right is that it exists against a particular person, who is under an obligation to discharge certain duties towards the possessor of the right.' In short an independent right is the 'right in rem' and a dependent right is the 'right in personam' of European jurisprudence.

Nature of Rights

The Islamic jurists make a further general classification of rights into asl or original, and khalf or substitutory. For instance, the right of God to require the performance of ablutions with water before A says his prayers is an original right, but in case of sickness, ablution by rubbing one's hands and face with earth (tayammum)[21] is allowed as a substitute. Similarly, A buys certain goods from B. A's right to have the goods delivered to him is a right of the first class, and in case of default by B, A's right to recover damages belongs to the other class. Original and substitutory rights correspond to what are called antecedent and remedial, to use the language of Professor Holland.

Private Rights

The division of rights generally into independent and dependent, and original and substitutory runs through the entire group not only of public rights but also of private rights. The jurists do not, however, make an exhaustive classification of private rights as they do of public rights, and even Sadrush-Shariat is content to leave the subject with the observation that private rights are too numerous to mention. The reason for this seems to be that the science of Usul is mainly concerned with the sources of law, and the rest of the topics are dealt with as supplementary to the main subject.

But the basis for the classification of private rights has already been sufficiently indicated in connection with the purpose of law and the objectives of law. If we group private rights with reference to the purpose of law then some of them would relate to matters of primary necessity, such as the right to the protection of person and property and the others would relate to matters of secondary necessity, such as rights arising out of contracts.

But, as we have seen, it would be difficult to draw the line between the two classes. A more useful method would be to classify private rights according to their subject-matter, following the line adopted by the Islamic jurists with respect to public rights.

The direct subject-matter of a private independent right as we have seen in the case of a public independent right is some physical object, or something which the law considers as such, and that of a private dependent right is the act of another person. Viewed with reference to their subject-matter private rights may be classified as:

PERSONAL RIGHTS

(1) right to safety of person (nafs)

(2) right to reputation (hurmat), according to the Shafiis;

(3) rights of ownership;

(4) family rights, including: (i) marital rights (zanjia), (ii) rights of guardianship (wilayat), (iii) rights of children and poor relatives, (iv) right to succession (khilafat) and inheritance (wirathat),

(5) right to do lawful acts (tasarrufat)

(6) rights ex-contract.

ALTERNATE RIGHTS

The above are the most important original private rights. The substitutory private rights are treated by the Islamic jurists from the point of view of the person of incidence, that is, as part of the subject of obligations (wajub) imposed by an imperative command of the law and the performance of what has been so ordered.

Obligations having regard to their origination may be generally classified as those arising:

(1) by the implication of law (i) towards God or the State, for example, obligations to worship, to pay taxes, etc.; (ii) towards individuals, such as those arising out of family relations, namely, connubial, parental, filial, and kinship and out of constructive trusts.

(2) Out of a man's own acts of utterance that is, rights ex-contract or by the admission of another's claim;

(3) by reason of conduct infringing another's rights relating to (i) personal safety, (ii) the doing of lawful acts (iii) reputation, (iv) family rights, (v) ownership and possession.

Obligations of the classes (1) and (2) relate to acts which are designated as obligatory (fard) and those of the class (3) arise by the commission of acts which are forbidden (haram).

Obligation per se as Distinguished from Obligation to Perform Certain Acts: Most Hanafi jurists including Sadrush-Shariat and Fakhrul-Islam would distinguish obligation *per se* nafsul-wajub from obligation to do or perform certain acts (wajnbul-ada). The first consists in the liberty of the obliged being restricted with reference to certain matters, and the second in his obligation to release himself from such restrictions. That is to say, one is the incidence of an obligation and the other is the discharge of such obligation. Obligation of the last kind arises when the law demands it and not until then. On the other hand, the mere incidence of certain obligations may have existed antecedently. The obligation, for instance, to perform certain appointed acts of devotion, is said to have existed from eternity, but that it becomes ripe for fulfilment only after a man has attained the age of discretion, and is required to be fulfilled only when the hour fixed for the performance of such devotional exercises has arrived. Here the attainment of majority and the arrival of the particular time of the day are regarded as the causes for the discharge of this obligation, the former being preparatory and remote and the latter the proximate and effective cause.

Similarly if a man sells to another certain goods without fixing the price, and the buyer takes possession of the goods, the vendor becomes entitled to the price, with respect to which an obligation is imposed on the buyer. But the buyer is called upon to discharge the obligation only when a demand to that effect is made on him. Some jurists, however, fail to see any substantial distinction between obligation *per se* and the obligation to discharge such obligation. They say that obligation must have reference to the performance of some act and cannot be disconnected from it.

Discharge of Obligations, Specific Non-specific : The discharge of an obligation may be either specific (ada) or substitutory or non-specific (qada). It is specific when the very thing which is required has to be carried out, and nonspecific when what has to be carried out is something similar to what is required. This classification holds good both as to obligations which are the right of God as well as of men.

Further the specific discharge of an obligation may be perfect or defective or it may be such as to resemble non-specific performance. For instance, when the very thing sold by a man is delivered to the purchaser or the thing which a person has wrongfully taken possession of is restored to its rightful owner the obligation is performed by the obliged in each case specifically. But suppose a slave, who has been wrongfully taken possession of, is restored by the wrong-doer to the lawful master, but after such slave has incurred criminal or civil liability, the obligation of the wrong-doer is said to be imperfectly discharged If in the last case, the slave be sentenced to death or a limb of his cut off on account of his offence, or if he is sold in satisfaction of the debt, the owner will then be entitled according to Abu Hanifah to the full price, and according to Abu Yusuf and Muhammad, he will be entitled to the difference in price between such a slave and a similar slave free from such liabilities.

In some cases, specific performance of an obligation resembles nonspecific performance, for instance, A takes wrongful possession of B's slave and the former thereafter produces the slave before the latter and asks him to emancipate him, which he does in ignorance of the fact that it is his slave. According to the Hanafis not only will such emancipation be effective, but the wrong-doer will be absolved from liability. The Hanafis argue that the wrong-doer in making over the slave to his master has discharged his obligation, and any subsequent act of the master emancipating him cannot make any difference. But according to Shafiis the action of the wrong-doer would not be regarded as a valid performance of his obligation because of the fraud accompanying it.

Non-specific discharge of an obligation may be by means of something, which is intelligibly similar (mithlun maaqulun) to the subject-matter of the right both in appearance (zahirun)[22] and in essence (batinun)[23]. When that is not possible the law will be satisfied with something which is similar in essence though not in appearance, such as payment of the price of an article which has been misappropriated.

If there be no intelligible similar at all, non-specific discharge of an obligation will be ordered according to the Hanafis, only in cases for which there is the authority of some express text. Thus, as we have seen, they do not allow recovery of mesne profits from a wrongful possessor of another's property, for according to them usufruct is in the nature of a mere accident and is not capable of being valued like property. When the object of a right is of an unascertained description and, therefore, its restitution in specie cannot be ordered the law is satisfied with payment of its price.

If the thing which is the subject-matter of a right has no intelligible similar, the obligation with respect to it is sometimes discharged, that is, according to Hanafis when there is authority for it by means of property, such as in the case of non-wilful homicide. But if it has a probable similar satisfaction by means of property will not be given preference, for instance, in a case of murder the aggrieved persons, that is, the heirs of the deceased cannot be compelled to accept blood-money in lieu of retaliation. Compensating by payment of the blood-money is allowed for this offence out of mercy to the murderer and in order that loss of a life may not be altogether uncompensated for.

Origination, Transfer and Extinction of Rights and Obligations; Constituents, Causes, Conditions and Signs of the Law : The declaratory laws as already mentioned deal with the origination, transfer and extinction of rights and obligations. A declaratory law derives its character as such by reason of the connection existing between one fact and another. If the connection between the two be such that one

Various Categories of Law

is included in the other, the former is called ruku or constituent of the latter. If one fact directly brings about another fact as its legal result the former as we have seen, is regarded as the illat or effective cause of the latter. If one fact leads to another fact on the whole that is to say, no directly and immediately but remotely the one is called the sabab or preparatory case of the other. If the existence of one fact be dependent on the existence of another fact, the latter would be called the shart or condition of the former.

Until the fact which is the condition of a law happens, the effective cause will not come into operation. When the existence of a fact is indicated by, but does not depend on, another fact the latter is called the (alamat), or sign of the former.

Tasdiq or *acknowledgment* of God's unity and authority, for instance, is a constituent of Imam or faith; so that if such *acknowledgment* be wanting faith would be negatived. It may be mentioned here that the Hanafis drawn a distinction between necessary constituents and supererogatory constituents. For instance, they regard declaration of faith in so many words (iqrar) as a supererogatory constituent, so that its omission would not negative, the existence of faith.

The Different kinds of Effective Cause: An effective cause has three aspects: (1) in so far as a legal injunction is referred to it, it is effective cause by name; (2) in so far as it tends to bring about the legal injunction, it is effective cause in essence and (3) in so far as it is immediately followed by the legal injunction, it is effective cause in its effect. An absolute sale is the effective cause of transfer of proprietary rights; marriage is the effective cause of lawfulness of connubial intercourse; and murder is the effective cause of retaliation. These are instances of effective cause in all the three senses. A sale with an option and a lease are examples of effective cause in the first two senses, because completion of the legal result, namely, the acquisition of property in the first case and of usufruct in the second case are postponed until the expiry of the option and the coming into existence of the usufruct.

A divorce which is referred to a future date, such as the husband saying to the wife, 'Thou art divorced tomorrow'; death-illness, the legal effect of which in giving rise to the rights of heirs cannot be ascertained until death actually occurs, and a wound, the effect for which on the wounded person can only be ascertained at a future date for the purpose of computing compensation are other examples of effective cause in the first two senses. An effective cause of an effective cause also falls within the category according to Fakhrul-Islam, for example, purchase of a slave by his brother is the effective cause of the former's emancipation for purchase is the cause of ownership, and ownership of a slave by his brother is the cause of emancipation. But Sadrush-Shariat says this is not correct and would treat it as an illustration of effective cause in the last two senses, as the purchase in this case is only the preparatory cause while proprietorship is the effective cause of emancipation and further the legal result, that is, emancipation follows immediately and is not postponed.

As instances of effective cause in the first and the third senses are the cases in which the legal result is imputed to what is really the preparatory cause, because it embodies the effective cause. Examples: The right of the father to a child is imputed to the marriage between its parents as presumptive of cohabitation between them, which is the effective cause of birth of the child while marriage is only its preparatory cause. Another illustration is furnished by the rule fixing an interval of time between each pronouncement of divorce in the approved form. Divorce according to Islamic religion is an act to be avoided as it involves dissolution of marriage but is allowed because of necessity as sometimes the parties to it are unable to discharge their marital duties towards one another. The existence of such a necessity is not a perceptible fact, and the law, therefore, requires that a certain interval of time should elapse before each declaration is made, so that if the husband remained of the same mind at its end the necessity for separation would be established. Similarly travelling is allowed to be a good ground for non-observance of fasting, because of the hardships and inconveniences incidental to travelling, but the law has put down travelling as the effective cause of the concession in as much as travelling in most cases entails hardships and inconveniences.

IMPORTANCE OF PREPARATORY CAUSE

When two causes in the chain of events contribute to a certain result, the one which is proximate to the result is regarded as the effective cause and the more remote, the preparatory cause so that the result would be attributed to the former. But if the effective cause itself be attributable to the preparatory cause the result will be ascribed to the latter. For instance, if an animal driven by a man treads upon something and destroys it the loss will be attributed to the act of driving for that led to the treading which was the immediate or effective cause of the loss. But if it be otherwise as when the immediate or effective cause is the act of a free agent, the result will be attributed to such act. For instance, if a man gives a knife to a boy to hold it for him and the latter voluntarily cuts himself with it, the man who gave the knife would not be held liable, because the cutting which was the immediate cause of the hurt was ascribe able to an act done in the exercise of volition. But if the boy accidentally cut himself, the person who gave the knife to him would be responsible. On the same principle, a person who points out to warriors certain property of the enemy will not be entitled to a share in that property when captured, not will a person who points out property to a thief who steals it will be liable for damages.

Some causes are preparatory in a secondary sense, for example, pronouncement of a contingent divorce or manumission, as when a husband says to his wife: if thou enterest the house thou art divorced', or a master of a slave says: if I enter the house my slave is free.' In these case the cause is the declaration; it is called preparatory, because the event contemplated may never happen. If it does happen the cause will be regarded as effective.

It is to be born in mind that for each injunction of the law there must be a perceptible cause on which the injunction is based. For instance, the cause for faith or belief in God is the creation by Him of the universe, but since this cause has always been manifest in the physical and animal world, the *acknowledgment of God* by an infant is regarded as valid, although the law imposing obligation to believe in God is not addressed to infants. Similarly certain particular hours of the day are preparatory causes of certain prayers; the possession of property is the cause for payment of the poor-rate, the month of Ramadan is the cause for fasting; the existence of the house of Kaaba is the cause for pilgrimage; produce of the soil is the cause for payment of ushr and khiraj; theft and murder are the causes for punishments, the necessities of life are the causes for legality of dealings among men, and the different transactions authorised by the law are the causes of the particular results which are in the contemplation of law in each case, for example, sale is the cause of ownership, marriage is the cause of legality of sexual intercourse and the like.

When an injunction of law has been based by the lawgiver on a fact or event which is not within the control of men and the reason why the law is based on that fact or event is not intelligible to human understanding, such fact or event is called preparatory cause.

An illustration of this is furnished by the ordnance imposing the duty of saying certain prayers at particular hours of the day. Here the arrival of the appointed time is not within the control of men and the reason why that particular hour should be the cause of the obligation to say particular prayers cannot be ascertained by human understanding. The death of a person is also similarly called the sabab or preparatory cause having the sense of an effective cause, of the creation of a right in particular persons to certain appointed shares, in the inheritance.

If the cause be within the power of man, and it was brought into operation with the intention of producing the desired legal result, it is properly speaking the effective cause of that result but is also in a secondary sense called its preparatory cause. For instance, an act of sale giving rise to the transfer of proprietary rights is often called the preparatory cause of such transfer though it is really an effective cause. But if the result produced by such cause is not what was designed but incidental to the main object then the act in question would be rightly called the preparatory cause of such indirect result. If the cause be such that human reason is able to understand why it produces a particular legal result, as already mentioned in the chapter on Analogy, it is properly called the effective cause of the law in question. For instance, minority is called the effective cause of guardianship because the reason for this is intelligible.

Condition : A condition of law may be (1) a condition pure and simple or (2) it may have the force of an effective cause or preparatory cause or (3) it may be a condition in name but not its legal effect. In the first sense a condition may be proper that is one on which something is dependent in fact or in law, for instance, understanding on the part of person making a disposition of property is by law a condition of its validity and the presence of two witnesses according to the Hanafis is by law a condition of the validity of a marriage. A condition may be the creation of a person as when a man makes the operation of an act of his dependent on the happening of a certain event, for instance, a man declaring 'the woman I shall marry is divorced' separation will take place according to the Hanafis from the woman with whom he may thereafter contract marriage on the instant of such marriage taking place.

A proper condition may sometimes come into existence, before the effective cause itself and sometimes after the effective cause, while a condition which is the creation of a person always comes into existence subsequently to the effective cause.

A condition has the force of an effective cause, when there is no effective cause to which the injunction of the law may be properly referred. For instance, A digs a well in B's land without the latter's knowledge and B while walking on his grounds falls into it and is killed. Here according to Islamic jurists the effective cause of the fall was the weight of the man's body but no liability could be imputed to it as it is a fact of nature nor to walking which is a lawful act.

But the condition on which the fall depended was the destruction of a certain portion of the surface of the earth, and therefore liability is imputed to the person who brought about that condition by his wrongful act. Hence in this case the condition has the same juridical effect as an effective cause. As an example of a condition which has the legal effect of a preparatory cause: a man unfetters another man's have slave in consequence of which the latter runs away, the unlocking of the fetter is the condition on which the escape of the slave depended

Various Categories of Law

but as between the two acts the volition of a free agent, namely, that of the slave intervened, no responsibility is attached to the action of the man who by undoing the fetters brought about the escape and his act is regarded in the light of a preparatory cause. As an example of a condition, which is so nominally but not in legal effect, is mentioned the case in which a man suspends a divorce on two conditions.

Signs : Alamat[24], or sign, is really a condition which is prior in existence to an effective cause. It has not the force of an effective cause, because the legal result is not imputed to it. For instance, the fact that a man or a woman who is guilty of whoredom is legally married (ihsan) is called a sign of the particular punishment laid down for such offence. But ihsan is also often called a condition of such punishment.

VARIOUS CRIMES

Distinction between Torts and Crimes : The line which divides the two kinds of wrongs, torts and crimes, is sometimes very narrow or as the Islamic jurists put it there are some matters in which the rights of the public and of individuals are combined. The test is, to whom does the wrong grant the remedy, the public or the individual. If to the latter, the wrong which gave rise to the remedy will be regarded as a tort, and, if to the former, it will be called crime. I shall deal with torts first which mostly arise from infringement of a man's rights to the safety of person, to freedom of action and to protection of property.

ISSUE OF SECURITY

I may here mention that the law does not require a person whose right to the safety of person or property is attacked to wait until the harm has been done, but allows him under certain conditions to prevent and to repel the attack by defending himself or his property. The principle on which the right of self defence is based in Islamic Law is that, when a man takes up arms against another, he loses the protection of law. This right is available not merely to the person whose life or person is threatened, but also in certain cases to the bystanders.

The extent, of the right is measured by the necessity of the occasion, so that a person exercising it is not allowed to inflict, if he can avoid it, more harm than is required for warding off the threatened injury. Similarly, if the person threatened can have recourse to the assistance of law in time to prevent the harm, he cannot take the law in his won hands. Otherwise, the law allows a man even to inflict death for the protection not only of his life and limb but even property; for instance, if a thief runs away with the stolen property at night the owner is entitled to follow and to kill him if necessary in order to rescue it.

On the same principle in cases of trespass or nuisance on land, the owner of the property has a right to prevent or to abate it himself. For instance, he may remove an erection made by his neighbour projecting over his land and occupying any portion of the space upwards. For similar reasons a member of the public is entitled to have any projection over a public road removed, because every one has a right to use it and no one has a right to the exclusive user of the road or of the space above it. The law also confers power on individual citizens to prevent the commission of certain offences which are punishable by the State as being an infringement of the right of the community. That is to say, when a person sees that such an offence is about to be committed, he may take the law in his own hands but only so far as it may be necessary to prevent its commission.

Various Torts

The Arabic word for torts generally, is janayat but the word janayat is mostly applied, in the parlance of layers, to injuries illegally inflicted on the human body whether such injuries have caused death, grievous hurt or merely simple hurt. Torts with reference to property may either be in the nature of usurpation or appropriation (ghasab) or destruction or damage (talaf/nuqsan). Infringement of a man's right to freedom of action is caused either by coercion of his will (ikrah) or by misleading his judgement, that is, by fraud (taghrir)[25].

These rights, subject to such modifications as may be induced by a defect in legal capacity as mentioned elsewhere, are inherent to the status of every human being and generally speaking the liability of a person violating them is absolute and unqualified.

Loss of Property

The principle is that the law looks to the loss caused to the person injured and is not, as a general rule, concerned with the moral culpability of the person by whose act it is caused. Thus if injury to a man's person or property is caused directly by an act of another person without the intervention of any other extraneous cause (al-itlaf mubasharatun), the law holds the latter responsible whether such act was intentional or accidental. Nor would it make any difference if the person who caused the loss happened to be an infant or a lunatic.

But suppose the injury or loss was the combined result of two or more causes (al-itlaf tasabbuban), the question then arises to which of the causes will the loss be attributed in law. In this connection one must bear in mind the different significances of the technical terms effective cause, preparatory cause and condition as already explained.

Various Categories of Law

THEORY OF RESPONSIBILITY

When the two causes preparatory and effective are both acts of free agents but independent of each other, the general rule applies fastening liability on the person whose act is the immediate or effective cause of the loss. For instance, two witnesses swear before the Qadi that the husband of a certain woman had conferred on her the power to dissolve the marriage and two other witnesses swear that she subsequently exercised such power, and the Qadi thereupon passes a decree declaring the marriage to be dissolved.

Afterwards if both sets of witnesses retract their testimony admitting that they swore falsely, the testimony of the witnesses who deposed to the exercise of the alleged power would be regarded as the effective cause of the Qadi's decree, and they would be liable for the wrong.

But if one of the two persons each of whose acts is the cause of the loss is morally culpable and the other acted as an innocent agent, the responsibility will be fastened on the former and not on the latter; for example, a man hires labourers to dig a well in the ground of another and the labourers do so without knowing that the ground belongs to a third person, the employer of the labourers will alone be liable; a man orders another to kill a particular animal and the latter thinking that the animal belonged to the person giving the order kills it, here, though the person killing the animal will, in the first instance, be liable, he will have a right of recourse against the person giving the order.

Coercion : If the immediate cause was not the act of a free sentient agent, but was brought about by an act of a human being, the general rule is, that the loss will be imputed to the latter. For instance, if a man collects water on his land and then discharges it on his neighbour's land causing damage thereby, the former will be held responsible for any loss which might have been suffered by the latter. The rule, however, is not absolute and is subject to certain necessary limitations.

For instance, if a person does something in the ordinary exercise of his rights, he will not be held to insure the safety of the person and property of other persons exercising similar rights and will not, therefore, be responsible for any injury which may result in consequence of the act. A Muslim suspends a chandelier in a mosque of the locality in which he lives as a pious gift, and it happens to come down and kill one of the worshippers, no liability would attach to him, because he had a right as an inhabitant of the locality to enter the Mosque and to decorate it if he so desired. *A fortiori* if a person does something on his own land, as for instance, lets his cattle graze thereon or digs a well and a person entering upon such land unaware of any danger meets with injury being hurt by the cattle or by falling into the well, the law will not ordinarily hold the owner of the land liable.

But if a person in the exercise of a right does an act which involves risk to the person or property of others who are at the place where the act is done by virtue of a similar right in themselves, he will be held to insure the safety of those other persons. For instance, if a man carries timber along a public road and the timber falls on a passer-by and causes damage to his person or property, he will be held responsible in damages. In all such cases the question to be considered is whether in its particular circumstances the man doing a lawful act was under an obligation to take care or not.

It the act in itself was wrongful, the person doing it will always be held to have been acting at his won risk. For instance, a public road is meant for traffic and any other use of it amounts to trespass. Hence, if a man makes a projection on a public road and the projection falls on a passer-by and injures him or damages his property, the owner of the projection will be responsible. But if a man rides on a public road and his horse kicks at a passer-by and kills him, he will not be held responsible; on the other hand, if a man ties his horse on a public road and it kills a passer-by, he will be liable for damages.

Sometimes injury to a person may have been due to a cause proceeding from another, but the person injured could have avoided it if he had used ordinary care. For instance, a shopkeeper sprinkles water on the portion of the public road in front of his shop, and a passer-by, who, if he wanted,' could have avoided that part of the road, chooses to walk over it and falls down and injures himself, the shopkeeper will not be held responsible, because the injury is due to the man's own act.

Coercion : Coercion whether exercised by threats of violence or confinement or by actual application of force is an infringement of a man's right to freedom of action. In another place we have considered the effect of coercion on the validity of the act done under its influence and the responsibility of the doer of the act. Let us now see how Islamic jurists regard the responsibility of the coercer towards the person coerced and any third persons who have been affected by the act. The question has to be considered with reference to acts of utterance and conduct.

The general principle according to the Hanafis is that if the act was done under duress of the extreme form, the volition of the coerced would be regarded as vitiated and if such act can be properly attributed to the volition of the coercer then the law would treat the volition of the former as if it did not exist and refer the result to the volition of the latter. In other words the person coerced would be regarded as a tool or instrument of the coercer. On the other hand, if what has been done is not capable of being imputed to the coercer, he will not be held responsible. In the last category are included all legal acts constituted by utterance, such as contracts and admissions, because it cannot be conceived that one person, namely, the coercer should pronounce them, through the mouth of another, namely, the coerced. But if loss has been caused to the doer by his being coerced to do an act of utterance, the coercer will be liable to compensate him. Suppose A coerces B to manumit his slave, the slave will be emancipated as the act is irrevocable, but A will be liable to B for the price.

As regards acts belonging to the class of conduct, that is, wrongs, there are some with respect to which it may be said that a person doing them under coercion acted as the instrument or tool of the coercer and there are others with respect to which this cannot be predicated. The principle according to Hanafis is this, if the extending of the liability for the act to the coercer, will necessarily involve a change in the subject matter of the wrong, the law will not allow such extension, otherwise it will. Take the case already cited in which X is compelled by Y to sell and deliver possession of his property to Z.

The sale itself being a disposition requiring consent is invalidated by coercion, but the delivery of property to Z cannot be imputed to Y, for he not being the proprietor delivery on his part would not be of the thing sold but of something unlawfully taken. If the imputing an act to the coercer would not involve a change in the object to which the act relates then the coercer alone would be fixed with liability.

This would be so in all cases of torts against the person or property of a third party. For instance, if A compels B to murder C the deceased C's heirs will have a right of retaliation against A alone. The reason is that a man's own life is dearer to him than that of any other's and as B killed C to save himself he cannot be said to have acted intentionally. This is the opinion of Abu Hanifah and Muhammad, while according to Zafar the person whose hand actually caused the death will be liable to retaliation. In the opinion of Abu Yusuf, however, the extreme sentence will not be enforced either against the coercer or the coerced but that the latter will be made to pay blood-money. The rule according to Shafiis[26] is that the coercer would be liable in all cases where the act is capable of being imputed to him, such as acts of conduct and not when the act cannot be imputed to him, such as acts of the class of utterance which, if done under coercion, are according to them altogether void and so no loss can be said to have been caused by the coercer.

Fraud : I have already referred to the principles governing the validity of acts induced by fraud. Here I wish to indicate the general principles on which the responsibility of the person committing a fraud towards the victim of the fraud is based. In many cases questions as to whether the conduct complained of was fraudulent or whether it influenced the action of the person complaining of it, and if so whether such conduct was the cause of any loss would not arise under the Islamic law in as much as it lays down positive rules as to the circumstances in which a party to a transaction who has suffered loss should be relieved. For instance, if in a transaction of sale, as already pointed out, one party suffers loss owing to some fact not being known to him, such as a defect in the goods bought, the Islamic law would at once relieve him without inquiring whether he acted with his eyes open or whether, the other party actively and knowingly practised any deception on him. In other cases the law is based on two principles: if any loss of property has been caused to the victim of a fraud, he is entitled to compensation from the wrong-doer, and a person committing a fraud should not be allowed to derive any advantage from his own wrong.

Remedies : The remedies for torts as recognised by the Islamic law are retaliation (Qisas, Qawd) and compensation (diat, irsh) in cases of infringement of a man's right to the safety of person; and restitution and compensation are the remedies provided for the violation of a man's proprietary rights and for other wrongs of a similar character.

Retaliation was sanctioned by the usages of the people of Arabia and of most other ancient peoples and was largely in vogue in Arabia at the time so promulgation of Islam. The principle of compensation was also recognised by the Arabs. Islam, while recognizing retaliation as the basic principle of remedial right, favours compensation as being a principle which is most consistent with the peace and progress of society, and lays down rules for the purpose of confining retaliation within the narrowest possible limits. The theory set up is, that retaliation is not solely a private right, but that the right of the public is also mixed up in it. Hence the State takes charge of its supervision and imposes strict conditions with a view to prevent the injury caused to the wrongdoer being in excess of what was inflicted by him.

Retaliation is allowed only in cases of wilful destruction of life or limb or of such bodily injury as is capable of definite ascertainment. It consists in the infliction by the person injured or by his heirs in case he is dead, of similar injury or death on the wrong-doer. Suppose A has wilfully destroyed a limb of B's, or made it useless by the injury he has inflicted on B, the corresponding limb of A may be destroyed in retaliation, that is, a hand for a hand, an eye for an eye, a tooth for a tooth, and the like.

On the other hand, if a person has caused fracture of another man's bone, retaliation will not be sanctioned, for it is not possible to be sure that the injury to be inflicted in return would not exceed what has been suffered and there is always a risk to life. No such difficulty arises in the case of murder for one life in the eye of law is equivalent to another. According to Hanafis the life of a slave stands on an equal footing with that of a freeman, of a woman with that of a man, of a non-Muslim subject with that of a Muslim.

The law, though it recognizes retaliation in theory, discourages this form of remedy in every possible way. For example, if there be the least doubt as to the wilful character of the offence or the proof retaliation will not be ordered.

Retaliation being the right of the person injured or of his heirs, they can compound with the offender for money, or, if they chose, pardon him. Whenever retaliation for murder or hurt is compounded, the money payable as consideration can be realised only from the offender himself. So also when compensation is ordered in cases where there is a doubt as to the wilful nature of the homicide. Similarly, when the hurt caused has not resulted in death, the wrong-doer alone can be called upon to pay compensation.

But when death has been caused by negligence or mistake, the offender's Akilas that is, his tribe or regiment or the inhabitants of the town to which he belongs, are to pay the blood-money to the heirs of the deceased. The reason is, that it is the duty of a person's Akilas to watch over his conduct and the law presumes that the wrong-doer would not have acted in the way he did unless they neglected their duty. On the same principle if a dead body is found in a certain locality with signs of violent death on it, the heirs of the deceased are entitled to call upon fifty inhabitants of the place whom they may select to take the oath that none of them killed him. If they take the oath then all the inhabitants will have to pay blood-money; otherwise they will be imprisoned.

Similarly, if a dead body is found at the door of a man's house, he will be given the oath and if he swears that he did not kill him, his Akilas will have to pay compensation. Here we have distinct traces of the impression left by the Arab tribal system on the Islamic law.

The scales both of blood-money and compensation are in many cases fixed according to the nature of the injury and the loss sustained and the culpability of the acts causing it.

As I have already indicated, the provisions of the Islamic law relating to retaliation have mostly a theoretical interest, showing that the Islamic Jurisprudence recognizes retaliation to be the original principle of remedial rights. Otherwise retaliation as a remedy has long been unknown in the Islamic world and having regard to the strict conditions with which the law hedges round this form of remedy, it must be in rare cases that it could be available. Further, now a days in Islamic countries wrongs against human life and body are no longer treated merely as torts, but are punished as crimes, and apparently this would be justified on the ground that by wrongs of this category the interest of the community in the preservation of peace and order is seriously interfered with.

As regards remedies for other wrongs, restitution may be either by return (radd) of the thing, subject of the wrong or by delivery of a similar article (itai mislihi). The first is the proper remedy in cases of usurpation or wrongful appropriation of all properties of the nature of dissimilaters, but if in such cases the property cannot be restored or if the article in respect of which a wrong has been committed was of the nature of similars, the defendant will be compelled to deliver a similar article to the plaintiff.

The wrong-doer is further liable for all the produce or profits derived by him from the property not only in the opinion of the Shafii and Maliki[28] jurists, but also of the modern lawyers of the Hanafi School in spite of the dictum of Abu Hanifah to the contrary already mentioned.

Then rules are laid down to meet cases in which an usurper has made improvements on the property; the principle on which such rules are based is, that both the owner of the property and the wrong-doer should, as far as possible, be restored to their former positions. Rules are also laid down for the assessment of damages in cases of destruction of, or loss caused to, property.

Various Crimes

When certain primary public rights are violated the wrong is called masiat that is, crime or offence; and it gives rise to certain substitutory public rights in the form of uqbat or punishments. Criminal offences relate mostly to property, human body, reputation, religion, the state, public peace and tranquillity, decency or morals. Punishments are divided into two classes: one of which is called hadd and the other taazir. Hadd means measure, limit, and, in law, it means a punishment, the measure of which has been definitely fixed. In taazir, on the other hand, the Court is allowed discretion both as to the form in which such punishment is to be inflicted and its measure.

Hadd : Hadd used to be prevalent in Arabia at the time of the promulgation of Islam, and the Islamic law, while confirming it as the extreme punishment for certain crimes, has laid down conditions of a stringent nature under which such punishments may be inflicted.

These rules are so strict and inflexible that it must be only in rare cases, that the infliction of hadd as of retaliation would be possible, and, in fact, there are only a few instances known in which hadd has been inflicted. The department of the law relating to hadd has merely a historical interest and is typically illustrative of the principle of Islamic jurisprudence, namely, not to interfere with the customs and usages of the people in such matters except so far as it may be necessary to safeguard against abuses and oppression and to let the new principle take the place of the old rule slowly and along with the advance of public opinion. Punishments by way of hadd are of the following forms: Death by stoning, amputation of a limb or limbs, flogging by hundred or eighty strikes. They are prescribed respectively for the following offences: Whoredom, theft, high-way robbery, drunkenness, and slander imputing unchastity.

I may here mention some of the more important limitations and conditions and conditions under which the Islamic law allows the infliction of this form of punishment. The principle underlying them, is that any doubt Would be sufficient to prevent the imposition of hadd. For instance, such doubt may arise from the nature of the authority applicable to the facts of a particular case or from the character of the evidence or from the state of mind of the accused person, that is, his knowledge of the law or facts, or the state of his will at the time of commission of the offence charged against him. If there be a show of authority though not of a sound character against the accepted law which declares a particular act to be punishable with hadd, this is treated as a doubt sufficient to prevent the imposition of such a sentence, even if the accused himself did not entertain any doubt on the point. This is called error or doubt with respect to the subject of the application of law (shubhatul-mahal). Even when an offender misconceived the law in a case where there is no foundation for such misconception, but he actually believed that what he was doing was not an offence, the sentence of hadd will not be enforced against him. This is called doubt or error with respect to the act (shubhatul-fail).

In certain cases, such as an offence of whoredom, some jurists go so far as to recommend to a man who has seen it committed not to give information or evidence, though if he chooses to do so his testimony will be admitted, provided he possesses the qualifications of a witness. I may mention that the policy of law in connection with this offence is to punish only those offenders who defy public and openly flaunt their vices. Hence it is, that four male eyewitnesses are required for its proof. Even if they are forthcoming which is hardly to be expected, the Magistrate is asked to scrutinize their testimony closely in order to see if they are not mistaken, and to allow them to retract what they have deposed to. Furthermore, if there has been any delay in the witnesses coming forward and giving their evidence, that circumstance in itself is held sufficient to raise a doubt.

Taazir : *Taazir* may be inflicted for offences against human life and body, property, public peace and tranquillity, decency, morals, religion and so on; in fact the entire criminal law of the Muhammadans (as-siasat ush-Shariah) as prevalent at the present day is based on the principle of taazir. The nature of the sentence to be inflicted by way of taazir for particular kinds of offences may be regulated by the head of the State who has absolute discretion in the matter. The objects of taazir are the correction of the offender and the prevention of the recurrence of the crime, and it is left to the discretion of the Magistrate to determine, in view of the circumstances of each case, the sentence by which the objects of the law would best be achieved. He is to take into account in awarding punishment, the nature of the offence and the circumstances under which it was committed, the previous character and the position in life of the offender and so on. The range of this form of punishment extends from mere warning to fines, corporal chastisement, imprisonment and transportation.

References

1. Followers of the Hanafi school of thought founded by Imam-e-Aazam Abu Hanifah.
2. A person who does Ijtihad.
3. A person who issues fatwa—a religious decree. In olden days, this job was done by an Imam.
4. Head of the State; Monarch or king.
5. Father of Hanifah.
6. A judge or a person who settles disputes.
7. A person who is entrusted a mosque or madarsa or any public religious building or institute.
8. A nation governed by a non-Muslim.
9. Islamic law.
10. A commentator and translator of the Quran.
11. A renowned scholar of Islam.
12. Aims and Objectives.
13. Whatever we say.
14. Allowed but spiritually not encouraged.
15. Compulsory or obligatory.
16. Reward.
17. An obligatory act which is considered 'done' if some people do that, i.e., it is no more incumbent upon everyone to do it.
18. Not preferred or liked heartedly.
19. Disgraced.
20. Behaviour and interaction in society.
21. In cases when water is injurious to health, tayammun is performed. It is done with dry clay. Dust is a must.
22. Physical or outer or external.
23. Internal or inner.
24. A sign or symbol.
25. Change or tampering.
26. A follower of Shafii school of thought.
27. Compensation of illegal murder.
28. Follower of Maliki thought of Islam.

8

SECURITY AND SAFETY

PROTECTIVE LAWS

We have said elsewhere in this book that Yathrib had no organisation, which could be called a state or any institution in the nature of an organ of a state to run its collective affairs, normally known as a government. The result was that there was no arrangement or an organisation to defend it.

The tribes had been fighting among themselves, but they had never been involved in war with outsiders. Hence lack of arrangements for defence. As a result of absence of an institution to look after their collective affairs, there was no arrangement for internal security either. The Constitutional Charter of Medina had to cater for both of these requirements. We have already studied the background of the Charter and the declaration of war by the Quraish of Mecca and as a consequence, the Prophet's undertaking, that believers will defend Yathrib and "The others," will be welcome to join in this common cause, provided they worked under the leadership of believers. This decision resulted in the issue of the charter and it gave to all governmental and defence activities a legal frame-work in which defence preparation, training and contacts with neighbouring tribes and treaty obligations could be looked after.

Preparations for war take a great deal of time and planned efforts. "It is not merely the number of able-bodied men who could be thrown into the battle line, but their training the quality and the numbers of experienced officers and equipment", that count in war.

Those who do not take adequate precautions and remain unprepared are forced in the end to follow a policy which ends in the surrender of their independence. Believers in Yathrib were new to the environment. They had sought protection, in a place, which did not have a unified defence policy, because that city, in the past, had no occasion to do so. With the arrival of Islam and *Muhajir*[1] believers, the situation, both in Yathrib and in relation to the Meccans, had altered. War had been declared and, as explained earlier, the threat of the invasion, and eventually the invasion itself demanded action. Allah had commanded, apart from other instruction that, defence and internal security arrangements were vital to the existence of *Ummah*.

"O you who believe! Take your precautions". (4:71)

The original word Hizrakum has so vast in application, that it includes all aspects of defence, internal security, foreign relations, defence production, educational policy and planning the entire life of *Ummah*[2] in a manner that it can guarantee its future Islamic Way of Life. The *Ummah*, at that time, was confined to Yathrib. Therefore the Commandment at that time meant the defence and internal security of Yathrib. Believers had accepted the responsibility, but their strength was inadequate. It was not yet known if "The Others, would join in defending Yathrib or not. Shortage of manpower demanded excellence of training and morale. Training demands time.

Readiness for war, therefore, posed very serious problems. The issuing of the Charter was, in this respect, the first step. It gave legal base to all future activities towards defence and internal security. We would now like to proceed with the clauses dealing with defence.

Clause 1.

We have so far, looked at it from the angle that it also forms the heading of the Charter. In view of the fact that it mentions 'War' and 'fighting' we feel that it very appropriately opens the Charter with the purpose for which it was being issued. It says:

"Those" (others) who followed them (the believers) and fought with them".

Defence is guaranteed only when a people are prepared to fight and accept losses in men, money and equipment. When a nation is threatened with invasion by a stronger power, the only honourable course open to them is to accept the challenge like free men who fear none, but Allah. Weakness, both physical and moral invites aggression. Philosophies, which advocate peace at any cost soon disappear. It has been rightly said that "War is perhaps the most searching test

Security and Safety

of national worthiness....nor has any nation kept its place when martial spirit died away".

The Meccans, although, at the time of the issue of the Charter, do not appear to have started hostilities, but because of the declaration of war by Mecca, a state of war had come into existence. State of war permits both adversaries to take defensive measures as though hostilities had commenced. It has been accepted at international level that, "being at war refers to a state or condition of affairs and not merely acts of force...."

Mecca having declared war, was automatically, in a "state of war," with Yathrib and the same was being reciprocated by Yathrib, by initiating defensive measures. The issue of the Charter was the first step. Through it the rights, duties, responsibilities of various types of residents of Yathrib were being announced and established by law. Events occuring after the issuing of the Charter have to be viewed and judged in the light of this document. All previous undertakings between parties mentioned in this document, and hence governed by it, stand cancelled, unless reiterated in it in some form or other. Historians have been referring to the conditions agreed upon during Baih of Aqba Thani, between the Prophet (PBUH) and men of Yathrib. This Charter does not mention the *Baih,* or conditions agreed upon at that time.

The Charter being a later document, cancels all previous undertakings between the parties. In any case, they being believers and having sworn allegiance to him would only too willingly have given assent to any decision he was pleased to take on the issue of defence of the abode of the *Ummah.* The fact that a state of war had arisen and they had sworn to defend him further strengthened the contents of the Charter. We feel, that in view of this "state of war" all future events should be judged keeping the contents of the Charter in view. As mentioned elsewhere this Charter announced the existence of an *Ummah,* which had existed, but had not been recognised. This document gave an official international recognition to Muslim *Ummah,* which has never been challenged, though efforts have been made to give it a nomenclature of religion like dozens of others in the world. It was to differ from all other denominations, which had hitherto existed, whether ethnical, linguistic, religious or geographically based nationality. It was global, universal, and beyond the boundaries set by time. It would last until time would last. Having been based on the acceptance of the principle of Sovereignty of Allah it would last until there was a single individual, who believed in His Sovereignty.

A nation has been defined as "a separate society of individuals, who possess a common government, common laws, rights, institutions, interests, common history and glory, common defences and security of the rights, riches and lives, constitute one body free and independent."

In order, eventually, to bring about unity of mankind, this document, which was being bestowed by Muhammad (PBUH) to Yathrib, was inviting others to live and endeavour alongside the believers, to bring into existence, a society of individuals, whose readiness for sacrifice, in the name of Allah, was of a standard not achieved by any human group before, with the object of bringing mankind under one flag and on one platform. This alone could put an end to perpetual wars which had plagued mankind throughout the ages.

It will be admitted that it is an unusual document. It is, therefore, important that every phrase, every sentence and every word of it must be studied with great care. For instance this very first Clause of the document says. "Those who followed them and fought with them, they form *One Ummah* to the exclusion of the others." It means, that those who fight alongside one another and maintain discipline by following those, who had set up and established the central core of *Ummah* are entitled to become *One Ummah* to the exclusion of the rest of the world. It means that those who are prepared to lay down their lives for a cause form part of *One Ummah*. There is no geographical, ethnic or linguistic barrier to their forming *One Ummah* — nation in the modern terminology. It also would mean that those who deny the principle of fighting to safeguard the basic principles on which an *Ummah* is based would surrender their right to be a part of the *Ummah*. Being outside the pale of *Ummah* they should be excluded from all assignments of trust, in the defence and administrative departments. Quran has laid down:

"O you who believe take not for intimate others than your own folk".
(3:118)

This Clause, which establishes the basis of a universal *Ummah* also lays down the disqualification for being bestowed the honour of belonging to a universal brotherhood spread out along the entire surface of the globe.

The use of the phrase "making utmost effort," has been used for "fighting in the Path of Allah." This new meaning has vast application. It covers total war in which fighting in the front lines and supporting those involved in fighting are all included. The notion of National War and Total War are special ingredients of the term *Jihad,* particularly in view of the involvement of the entire *Ummah* in it.

The opening Clause of the Charter speaks of war. To start a document with mention of war was the requirement of the situation because the document was the result of declaration of war by Mecca. It was, therefore, appropriate that the first Clause which also formed the heading of the document should refer to war. The matter does not end with Clause 1, but subsequent eight clauses also deal with one or the other aspects of the problems of war. It also shows the stress and strain under which believers must have been living during this early period after Hijra. The war, however, was not the result of their choice. It had been forced on them. This war was the result of vested interests as it had been in bygone ages, "for century after century war was the recognised method of settling international disputes. Not only was it legal, but it was the authorized court of last resort.

Frances Bacon called it the highest trial of right. As long as war was recognised as legal, there was no punishment for those responsible for it." Islam, however, holds these mischief makers responsible. The Quran has laid down that if these guilty persons who wage war but are in the end regretful, then they may be pardoned. If, however, they break their promises then:

> "And if they break their pledges after their treaty (hath been made with you) and assail your religion, then fight the heads of disbelief— Lo! they have no binding oaths — in order that they may desist". (9:12)

People guilty of dragging mankind into uncalled for slaughter must be punished.

ALMIGHTY SUPREME

The Prophet (PBUH) had to prepare believers for the "Highest Test of Right," to establish the principle that those who believe in the Sovereignty of Allah, prefer to lay down their lives rather than live under any other sovereign and laws promulgated by it. He was a man of peace. His whole life had been spent in peaceful activities, but he was now placed in a position, where he had to prepare a peace loving, people to stand for "the highest trial of right," and prove, that Allah is with the righteous, provided they prepare themselves for the task. He has ordered:

> "Make ready for them all thou caust of (armed) forces and of horses tethered, that there by ye may dismay the enemy of Allah and your enemy, and others beside them ye know not. Allah knoweth them. Whatsoever ye spend in the way of Allah it will be repaid to you in full, and you will not be wronged". (8:60)

Modern military writers have accepted this truth. A well known authority on naval matters of modern times, has echoed these thoughts very aptly, when he says, "It behaves countries whose genius is essentially not military, whose people, like all free people, object to pay for large military establishments, to see to it, that they are at least strong enough to gain time necessary to turn the spirit and capacity of their subjects into the new activities which war calls for."

War brings all human beings on the same platform. A general and soldier of rank and file are made of the same flesh and blood. The sword and the arrow or a bullet and a missile treat them alike. This was a document, which was the product of state of war. It had to bring home to mankind that those who face danger as equals must be treated as equals in day to day life as well. Islam has given to every man the same status. All are equal. All are free born. All must, therefore enjoy equality and freedom. This is the first written piece of paper which has declared that those who followed them and fought alongside them would be equal to them, because they would have become members of this the "best of all *Ummahs.*"

> "You are the best Community that hath been raised up for mankind. You enjoin right conduct and forbid indecency; and you believe in Allah". (3:110)

The world has borrowed the terms of equality, liberty and justice from Islam, but have not yet been able to understand the full meaning of these qualities, when adopted by an *Ummah* as a whole. Europe has failed to achieve equality and liberty because they have divorced day to day life from the faith they acknowledge as their guiding principle. The result is that all ethical standards fall outside the realm of daily life. That is why such statements are heard. "The two great ideas of liberty and equality are often mentioned together, but the right relation between them is far from simple.... We give the strong members of the community to have the liberty to dominate the others as they like, to acquire wealth as they like and to keep it as they like. Such a system is bound to be so ruthless that equality, in any meaningful sense, is impossible."

Clause 3.

> "They will redeem their prisoners with kindness and justice common among believers."

Clause 1 had spoken of fighting *Jihad.* Prisoners of war is a natural consequence of war. In the past and for a long time afterwards redeeming of prisoners was not thought of. As explained elsewhere a defeated army and its nation could not look after its prisoners of war or ask for their being returned to their home country. Armies used to belong to the rulers. When a ruler was defeated each soldier had to look after himself, if he was not taken prisoner. Slavery resulted from the fact that prisoners of war had to be fed, clothed and provided with other necessities, because their governments could not pay or did not care to pay war indemnities. Modern states have shown interest in their men who have been taken prisoners of war, but it is rarely thought of to redeem them with kindness and justice. It was during the later part of eighteenth century that consideration started being given to prisoners of war. Matters, however, stood still and after the First World

War, when the League of Nations came into being steps were taken to see that nations did not maltreat each other's prisoners of war. Hague Convention is the official document to which most nations have shown agreement and it governs the manner, in which prisoners of war have to be treated. Inclusion of this Clause in a document executed during the first year of Hijra, corresponding to 622 A.C. should not surprise readers. It was in line with the spirit of Islam and in conformity with other laws promulgated for believers. A point to note is, that during nine years of war fought by the Prophet (PBUH) the enemy, including the Byzantine Imperial Army, did not capture a single believer to make him a prisoner of war. It was a fight until *Shahadah*[3], that the believers believed in. In spite of it, the Prophet (PBUH) included this clause in the Charter, mainly because his Commands had to last for ever.

It is after fourteen centuries of the promulgation of the Charter, that we read in Article 118, para 1 of the report of International Committee of the Red Cross that:

"prisoners of war have an inalienable right to be repatriated once hostilities have ceased."

Islam has laid great stress on alleviating hardships of prisoners of war and redeeming them. *Zakat*, which is official collection of $1\frac{1}{2}\%$ of one year old savings of every believer has to be spent on specific needs of the *Ummah*. One of the needs specified in *Quran* is the freeing of prisoners. These naturally could be no other, than the prisoners of war in enemy's hands. Today, they would be the persecuted Muslims under foreign domination. The manner in which they can be helped through *Zakat* is a point, which should be thrashed out by the learned and the intellectuals of the *Ummah*.

If redeeming of prisoners is given the importance envisaged in this Clause, early discussions will have to be initiated so that prisoners do not have to remain in the hands of enemies too long. War is not undertaken with kindness, for the enemy, "War is a contention between two or more states through their armed forces for the purpose of overpowering each other and imposing such conditions of peace as the victor pleases."

The army which is keen to see that its personnel, which has fallen into the hands of the enemy, should be treated well and repatriated speedily, will necessarily look after enemy prisoners of war with kindness. A year after this document was promulgated a number of the enemy fell into the hands of believers. They were treated kindly and permitted to be repatriated gracefully. Those, who could not pay ransom, but could teach others to read and write they were asked to teach ten people each and were allowed to return to Mecca.

EQUALITY UNDER LAW

The words "with kindness and justice common among believers," could only be used if in the short time, that Islam had been introduced in Yathrib, these qualities of believers had been so noticeable that they were being appreciated by all who came in contact with them. These national characteristics of the believers had made them respected in Yathrib and had resulted in Abdullah bin Ubay to give up the idea of using force against believers from Mecca.

Well-knit nations both individually and collectively behave in a certain manner under certain conditions. It is difficult to analyse or define as to how a certain National Character comes into being, but the fact, that National Character does exist, is a fact, which cannot be denied. "What is National Character and how shall we define its nature." The author then asks "Is it a natural and inherent datum, or is it a growing product, which is being shaped by historic revolutions and the ongoing and pressing mind of man. If it has within itself both of these elements, how, and by what combination of nature and human art, has it been made? By what influences and in what direction it is now being shaped? What forecast we shall make of its future turns and trends?"

The answer to these questions, with reference to the National Character of believers in Allah and His Rasool (PBUH) is given in Clause 24 of this Charter, which says, "The believers, because they fear Allah, they are better in showing steadfastness..." Thus it can be said that reading clauses 3 and 24 together, to the National Character of believers is that they are kind and just in peace and steadfast in war. This would be a reflection of the Quranic verse which reads:

> "Muhammad is the messenger of Allah. And those with him are hard against the disbelievers and merciful among themselves". (48:29)

It was the result of training given by the Prophet (PBUH) to his Companions and their Faith in Allah that they developed the Characteristics of kindness, justice, bravery and steadfastness to such an extent that they surpassed those around them in these and other similar qualities.

It is said that:

> "National Character being the common traits in a million or more members of a nation, it is difficult to analyse the process by which sympathetic feelings connect the working of the minds of innumerable individuals. It is said, that "The superstructure is a mental organisation connecting the minds of all the members of national community by ties and connections as fine as silk and as firm as steel. It is a subtle spiritual cobweb of threads which are spun from mind to mind."

Security and Safety

The focal point of the National Character of believers, however centred in their belief in Allah, "When a man joins the brotherhood of Islam it is as an association of self-effacing individuals, that the community can come into being." Belief in Allah, the Creator of Universe, "not only permeates and encompasses universe, but also His Domains beyond. He is the unique Other Self, that transcends and encompasses the private personality of the finite individual self."

Training is an integral part of preparation for defence. It was entirely in the hands of the Prophet (PBUH) himself. Thirteen years spent in Mecca moulded the character qualities of this small band of devoted Companions, which were based on belief in Allah the Creator of this entire Universe. To realise the source of moral strength of these few devoted believers, it is necessary to study minutely the Verses of *Quran* Revealed at Mecca. The deep impression of the Might and Glory, Mercy and Benevolence, Wisdom and Knowledge, Absolute and Complete resulted in moulding their character. If He be the Lord of man, so insignificant to look at, but so far-reaching in his comprehension of Him, Who has no second, then what difference if I, a Muslim, His humble servant lived in this world or while giving evidence of His Omnipotence, was to step into the next world and was granted His Audience. The sooner the entrance into His Grace the better.

Experts tell us, that defence preparations cannot be completed in a short time. This is a long and tedious task, which is accomplished with great care and patience, on the part of both the trainer and the trainee, but the time at the disposal of the Prophet (PBUH) was not only short, it did not exist, and yet, when hostilities started he was ready for them. The course of the "Battles of the Prophet (PBUH) is outside the scope of this essay, but the manner in which he fought these battles is a refreshing story, worthy of being narrated again and again."

No nation can defend itself unless it has a well thought out defence policy. Based on that policy a defence organisation is brought into existence. Without a defence organisation no worthwhile achievement can be expected. A successful general of Second World War having won the severest and most expensive war of human history desired to create a more efficient organisation for his nation. He says, "We will build a national military team that will make it unavoidably clear, that anybody who endangers our Way of Life, will risk destroying himself." The Prophet (PBUH) in the short time at his disposal, created a Military Machine which destroyed the enemy, which wished to destroy the Islamic Way of Life. One of the lessons learnt from the successes of this machine was, that they were the most respected individuals of the society. Abu Bakr saying good-bye to the commander of the Army proceeding to the north was walking beside him while the commander, the son of a former freedman, was riding at the head of the Army. The Germans lost Second World War because German Army in and around 1930, "felt that they were regarded as something less than the respectable members of a modern society."

Clause 5.

"All parties will redeem their prisoners with kindness and justice according to practice among believers."

A soldier who is sure of being looked after if he is wounded and redeemed if he is taken prisoner will fight better than otherwise. The Prophet (PBUH) had dictated the Law that believers must as an *Ummah* redeem their prisoner with kindness and justice was common among believers. This must have, at first, surprised the listeners. It was something new, which had not even been heard of. On second thought people must have felt that this responsibility must be accepted by other parties as well. They, therefore, must have requested that their parties must also be ordered to redeem their prisoners in exactly the same manner as the believers were ordered to do. This request was accepted and it became legally binding on "the others" as well to redeem their prisoners "with kindness and justice according to practice among believers." It was felt, or it appears so, that the redeeming of prisoners of all parties was not being made the responsibility of the Central Government because of two factors. One, that a certain amount of autonomy was advisable in a new Federal set up. Second reason was that, as yet, no central treasury had been established. It was, therefore, more suitable if all parties bore their own expenses.

The term, "kindness and justice common among believers," needs being paid special attention to by the leaders and intellectuals of the *Ummah*. How is it, that a small group of early believers was able to have it accepted by all concerned, that kindness and justice were part of the National Character of believers. We feel that the learned Ulama of *Ummah* owe it to themselves and the *Ummah* to examine, if they can say that these qualities can still be included in the National Character of believers. If this is not so, what factors of collective life need reform so as to inculcate these qualities once more.

Could it not be that Islam, which is a Way of Life, has been equated with religion in which the basic principle is that it is a personal matter and has no place in directing collective morality. Islam has been revealed to guide human life in this world so that its followers, by conducting their lives in accordance with it, win the place of being the heirs to Viceroyalty of Allah in this world, and be near to Him, in the next. If, Islam becomes a matter of personal relations between man and Allah, and is disassociated from the conduct of its followers in public and international life, then humanity will never achieve peace and unity on the global scale.

Clause 6.

"The Banu Saeeda[4], the Banu Harith[5], the Banu Jushan[6], and the Banu Najjar[7] will be governed on the above lines."

The importance of being redeemed was so great that although Clause 5 had made it Statutory duty of all parties that they would redeem their prisoners in the same manner as the believers were duty bound to do, but all those tribes, wanted that an order should be specifically given that those tribes should also redeem their prisoners in the same manner.

This Clause confirms our view that the document was being dictated in the presence of members of all parties. The moment a duty or a concession was dictated for the believers or any other party, those not included would speak out, if they also desired to be governed by the same enactment.

Inclusion of some tribes in a separate Clause does not mean, that they were governed by a separate document which, at a later date, got joined up with one or all other similar documents. If this was so the words "on the above lines," would not have been there and the whole text would have been repeated and not in the same wordings, but in a totally new context.

Clause 7.

"The Banu Amr, Banu Auf, Bani Al-Nabeet, and Banu Al-Ass will be governed on the same lines,"

Once again, a few more tribes make up their mind to join in. Tribal habits are strange. They take time to make up their mind, in matters which are new and they have no previous experience. They, as a result of centuries of hard life, are afraid of pitfalls.

The tribes joining in the redeeming of prisoners of war confirms our view that although this was not the custom previously, the inclusion of this responsibility on the High Command of believers opened the door to the acceptance of this responsibility by elders of other parties as well. It is possible that the little hesitation shown by the late comers may have been due to the consideration whether they would be able to raise funds for the purpose or not. Second thought, however, would have prompted them not to be left out of this social service to the common man of the tribe.

Modern world has risen to this need rather late. "The axioms of international law exerted an undeniable influence on the mode and manner of warfare, before the close of the seventeenth century." One of these was the treatment and disposal of enemy prisoners of war.

The first Geneva Convention was held in 1899 and the first Geneva Conference was held in 1929. It says, "Each of these fundamental international agreements is inspired by respect for human personality and dignity." It has been proudly announced that, "whereas the 1929 text demanded respect and protection only for the wounded, Article 12, which is new, gives a list of prohibited acts, attempts on life, torture....etc."

Clause 8.

"Believers will not fail to redeem their prisoners or fail to pay blood money on behalf of one of them."

This clause and its wording clearly show that the document was not an agreement, but a Statutory and Constitutional document in the form of an Order and no less. The words, "will not fail," is a firm order, a legal binding which cannot be evaded under any circumstances. The importance of redeeming the prisoners can be judged by the number of clauses which cover the subject. It was a new subject, but extremely important from the point of view of the fighting men. Prisoners of war, until then, as mentioned earlier, remained slaves for the rest of their lives. This could not be permitted in case of a Muslim soldier, because, as a slave he could not continue to observe his duties to Allah and thus lost freedom of action to submit to the Laws of Allah. He had, therefore, to be redeemed so that he could continue to observe all the functions of a free believer. Slaves cannot continue to remain believers in Allah and His Rasool (PBUH). We see that even in the twentieth century, there are countries where they are forcibly prevented from observing Islamic practices or even to give their children Muslim names. Has not the *Ummah* forgotten to redeem them or free them. This question has to be answered by every one of us, more so, leaders of the *Ummah*.

Redeeming of prisoners becomes all the more important, when it is realised, that military service during Jihad is obligatory on all able bodied Muslim males, where ever they may be. The order, quoted as under has been addressed to all believers.

"Fight in the way of Allah against those who fight against you". 2:190 has been addressed to all believers. Believers are *One Ummah,* both according to this document and according to the *Quran.* When any part of the World of Islam is attacked, *Jihad* becomes obligatory on the entire *Ummah.* Those nearest to the area attacked, have to face the enemy first. But that does not absolve the others. The World of Islam, today, should find it much easier to coordinate an integrated defence of the entire area occupied by them. Lack of plans, however, is no excuse for not redeeming those believers, who due to ignorance or other reasons are under the domination of others and leading lives of slaves or prisoners of war.

It is said that, "From the earliest records of man, war has been his dominant preoccupation." It is, therefore, more than likely that war will be resorted to for a long time to come. It is a proper time for Muslim World to start thinking of organizing coordinated defence. Believers, have, for a long time, ignored opposition to them from various quarters. As in the case of Quraish of Mecca, the world at large does not approve the Islamic Way of Life, because of the equality and freedom it allows to poor and rich alike which is the result of belief in the Sovereignty of Allah. War against believers will, as a result, continue until such time as they remain weak, disorganised and an easy target. The only solution to this is unity. As the *Quran* says:

"And lo! this your religion is one religion"　　　　　　(23:52)

Muslim can lead an honourable life if they live as *One Ummah*.

Clause 14.

"Protection in the name of Allah will be common. The weakest among believers may give protection and it will be binding on all believers".

Protection used to be given to strangers by powerful individuals. The practical effect of such protection depended on the power and prestige of the person giving protection. Islam had, however, changed the very concept of power held by individuals and the society or organisation, in which an individual lived. Believers, irrespective of their numbers, living in a place and forming a society are an *Ummah,* apart from any other group of human beings. Each individual believer is equal to all others in his status as a believer. The task he performs in the society, the job he holds, the wealth he possesses or the rank he has achieved in the hierarchy formed for purposes of conducting affairs of the *Ummah* do not infringe on or enhance his status as a believer and member of the society. "An individual who belongs to an organisation of equals is an integral part of that organisation. This is specially so, where the organisation is based on a particular mode of thought, a distinct Philosophy of life and a Way of Life distinct from all other ways of life."

In such a society, if protection can be given to individuals or groups of people who are not believers then it stands to reason that any one of the believers should possess the right to give protection. As far as believers of other towns or areas were concerned, they were brothers in faith. They were, as believers, part of the *Ummah.* They needed no protection. On the contrary, as members of brotherhood of Islam, they could themselves promise protection and that would have been honoured. It was to unbelievers that the Clause applied. Any believer, however humble, poor or weak he may be, he was entitled to give protection and this protection was valid from the point of view of the state and government of Yathrib. The protection could not be in the name of the person giving it or in the name of the *Ummah,* but it had to be in the name of Allah. Most societies, however primitive they may be, assign certain human rights to the individual as long as he has the status of a freeman and is not a slave. Islam had given human rights to all individuals, whether free or otherwise. He had to believe in Allah in order to benefit from some of those rights. The right to offer freedom in the name of Allah, demanded his belief in Allah. This was logical. He enjoyed all other rights; rights of equality, justice and freedom to hold any views, but to give protection to a sworn enemy in the name of Allah, he had to be a believer in the Sovereignty of Allah. In this right, he held the same position as the head of state himself.

This greatness of the status of an individual in society was the greatest factor which attracted masses towards Islam. It has been remarked by a modern writer that "one can find no better key to the internal logic of a society than its conception of man and his place in nature." In Islam all men are equal. The Prophet's last address, at his Last *Hajj* is very clear. Its words still ring from millions of pulpits around the Globe. He has said," All men are descended from Adam and Adam was created from clay...." As far as man's position is concerned he is Allah's viceroy on earth (2:30) and the most balanced creation of Allah.

"Surely we created man of the best stature". (95:4)

It is due to this equality in socio-economic fields, political matters and before the law that the frontiers of Islam have been expanding throughout these fourteen centuries. European literature, whether dealing with social development, philosophical treatises or political movements in the West, have lauded the pre-Revolution philosophers of France, for having given to Europe the principle of equality of man. If French Revolution was the result of the preaching of principle of equality by French philosophers then the streams of blood which flowed as a result, show that it has not achieved much. America is said to have been affected by this French movement.

One of the critics of unchecked principle of equality says, "I attribute so many different aspects to the principle of equality; it might be inferred, that I consider this principle as the only cause of everything that has taken place in our day... many persons would take it upon themselves to inform men of the benefits which they might hope to receive from the establishment of equality, while very few would venture to point out from afar the dangers with which it would be attended." This fear of equality appears to be premature because, as yet, America has not been able to introduce equality in its society. When this happens many white Americans may decide to migrate to some other part of the Globe.

Clause 16.

"Those Jews who follow us will be helped and will be treated with equality."

The Clause deals with Jews. The reason for including this Clause under Laws Concerning Defence is that the Heading of the Charter had said, "Those who followed the believers and took part in *Jihad* with them, were to form *One Ummah* with them." The act of following was to be supplemented by taking part in *Jihad* alongside the believers. The words, "those Jews, signifies that the concession were to be restricted to those "who will follow," in future. Therefore, there was no question of having gone through the procedure of having an agreement, with the Jews, as has been suggested by certain writers.

The fact that they never took part in *Jihad* means that the situation did not arise, where they could be treated with equality and be included as a part of the *Ummah*.

Clause 19.

"The peace of believers cannot be divided."

Islam, submission to the Will of Allah, leads to peace from the level of individual man and woman to peace among entire humanity. Islam signifies absence of tensions within man and within the society of men and women, who have discarded love of all things, which take away from the Path of Allah. This gives them further contentment and determination to abide by the Commandments of Allah. He has conveyed the greatest Secret of success to believers that they are one people. *One Ummah* (21:92 and 23:52) and must remain united. That is the only way in which they can fulfil their duty of guiding mankind along the Right Path.

Allah has also Commanded believers to take all precautions so that they can avoid splitting themselves into factions, sects and parties. Allah has warned:

"Lo! As for those who sunder their religion and become schismatics, no concern at all hast thou with them. Their case will go to Allah, Who then will tell of what they used to do." (6:160)

He has clearly told believers the result of dividing *Deen* into factions:

"There is no altering (the laws of) Allah's creation. That is the right religion, but most people know not. Turn unto Him (only); and be careful of your duty unto Him, and establish worship and be not one of those, who ascribe partners (unto Him) Of those who split up their religion And become schismatic each sect exulting in its tenets. And when harm touched men they cry unto their Lord turning to Him in repentance." (30:30-33)

When having divided themselves, they suffer and then cry for the Mercy of their Lord. Even when He gives them respite, they go back and divide themselves again and again, until they are overpowered by others who deprive them of even the right to cry for the Forgiveness of their Lord. About them the order is:

"Say: He is able to send punishment upon you from above you or from beneath your feet, or to bewilder you with dissensions and make you taste the tyranny of one another." (6:65)

The world of Islam has tasted enough of the tyranny of one another and have been punished a great deal because Allah and His Messenger had Commanded them to remain united and they arrayed themselves after their nominees and were thus guilty of *Shirk*[8] (30:30-32). They had refused to Obey His Prophet's Command, that "The peace of believers can not be divided."

In their arrogance, they dared to show, that it can be divided. They divided it and they are being punished by being denied the power and freedom to proclaim the Sovereignty of Allah. How many are the lands, where they cannot call Muslims to their mosques through *Adaan* and how many are the lands where their mosques have been turned into clubs for drinking wine and. The Commandments of Allah and the Command of the Prophet (PBUH) have been disobeyed so flagrantly that one wonders if they really believed in Allah and His Prophet (PBUH). The punishment has been equally severe. Dissension among believers has been responsible for inviting comparatively small European nations to invade lands held by believers and rule over them for nearly two centuries.

The Command that "Peace of believers cannot be divided," demands that states controlled by believers must bring into existence an organisation which acts as an advisory and supervisory body, so that such situations do not arise, which lead to the breech of peace between Muslim states. If, however, inspite of it, two countries of Muslims go to war then this body can act according to Quranic injunction in *Surah Al-Hujuraat,* Verse 9. If the World of Islam was united for such an action other nations will not dare to fan such internecine warfare. The basis of weakness is disobedience of the Quran and Constitutional Charter issued under the seal of the Prophet of Allah (PBUH).

There are other aspects of this Clause as well. Fighting among themselves is the worst form of breech of this Clause of the Constitution of Medina. The other form is that when one part of the *Ummah* is invaded or attacked, some other part commits breech of peace, between Muslims, by either having friendly relations with the aggressor or taking a neutral posture. It must be remembered that at the

Security and Safety

time of second Baih of Uqba, the Prophet (PBUH) had replied to one of the questions of a member of new believers from Yathrib. The question was:

> "When Allah will have given you victory, you will return to your people and leave us?"

The Prophet (PBUH) had replied:

> "No! blood is blood. And blood not to be paid for is blood not to be paid for. I am of you and you are of me. I will war against them that war against you, and be at peace with those at peace with you."

This is exactly, what is meant by "Peace of believers cannot be divided." They are either all at war with a third power or all at peace. Their peace and war are indivisible.

Unity of the Muslim World in time of *Jihad* has so great an importance, that even when a Muslim country, which has been attacked by a non-Muslim country, and it can cope with the attack single handed, the rest of the *Ummah* is not absolved from considering it a common cause. In such cases it is necessary for them to send token forces, or observer groups. Allah has Commanded:

> "And the believers should not all go out to fight. Of every troop of them, a party only should go forth, that they (who are left behind) many gain sound knowledge in religion, and that they may warn their folk when they return to them, so that they may beware. O ye who believe! Fight those of the disbelievers who are near to you, and let them find harshness in you, and know that Allah is with those who keep their duty (unto Him)." (9:122-123)

The nearest to the enemy is the one who is attacked. He engages the enemy with determination and harshness so that it gives time to the others to go to his help. If the country attacked can defend itself then the others send token forces only as in Verse 122 above.

Importance given to the unity of Muslim *Ummah* in peace and war is so great, that even when the part of *Ummah*, which is attacked is capable of defending itself the other parts have all to send token forces. These token forces and their main body gain experience of war, learn new methods and tactics and get acquainted with new weapon used on such occasions. When they return home, they acquaint their home-forces of new defence techniques. The advantage of unity and strength being the main object and advantage in such undertakings and the satisfaction that they have obeyed Commands of Allah and His Prophet (PBUH).

The greatest tragedy in the annals of any *Ummah* is that Muslims have been dividing their peace, particularly during the last few centuries and thus enslaving themselves and their future generations. An Englishman, by the name of Colonel Lawrence, who for years remained active in dividing the peace of Muslims, writes, "Some Englishmen of whom Kitchener was chief believed that a rebellion of Arabs against Turks, would enable England, while fighting Germany, simultaneously to defeat her ally Turkey—so they allowed it (rebellion) to begin, having first obtained formal assurance of help for it from the British Government."

Abdullah, the eldest son of Sharif Hussain of Mecca, who probably was the only person, who could influence his father to embark on the path of betrayal of brother Muslims, has not been honoured, by his benefactors, the British in their writings. The same Englishman writes about him, "The Arabs thought Abdullah a far seeing statesman and an astute politician. Astute he certainly was, but not generally enough to coerce us always of his sincerity. His ambition was potent. Rumours made him the brain of his father and of Arab revolt, but he seemed too easy for that. His objective was, of course, the winning of Arab independence and the building of Arab nations, but he meant to keep the direction of the new states in the family. So he watched us, and played through us to the British gallery."

It is lack of belief in Islam and its Commandments which result in breech of peace among Muslim states. Reasons have been various and they date back to the early period. When the masses in Syria, Egypt, Iran and Central Asia, were attracted to Islam due to liberty, equality and freedom offered by it to them the upper classes and rich Jews, also accepted Islam, in order to retain their privileged positions in the society. As a result, these states and their provinces and districts remained family properties of the previous owners. During subsequent centuries families, changed ownership passed into new hands, but traditions of personal and family interests being superior to the interest of *Ummah* remained. Rulers like Shah Abbas, Taimur, Nadir Shah have been appearing and disappearing, but the passage of every one of them has been strewn with the corpses of Muslims. In most cases there are names of foreign advisers encouraging them in their follies. It is said that Shah Abbas had two Englishmen Sir Anthony and Sir Robert Shirly at his court who, "enabled him with the help of a cannon caster accompanying them," to provide the Persian Army with artillery to attack Turkey while the Turks were busy defending themselves from the European side.

In 1612 Shah Abbas, had broken off war with Turkey, but in the next year he wrote letters which reached Spain in 1614, offering to renew it if the Christian powers would fulfil their promises, adding that, it was long since the Christians had taken up arms against the common enemy. At that time a great plan was afoot for a Crusade." It is said of him that by 1618, he "was growing weary of the insincere and dilatory princes of Christendom." "Shah Abbas died in 1628, amazed to the last, it would seem, at Christian neglect of opportunities." The habit of Europe to divide the peace of Muslims has been a constant affair. The same writer says, "It should be added here that Persia was not the only Islamic power whose aid was invoked by Christendom against the Turks, at this time.

Morocco was also approached." In the nineteenth and twentieth centuries selfishness on the part of Muslim rulers has led them to seek the help of foreign powers quite frequently. A well known Englishman writes, "It is true that all the chiefs concerned were genuinely desirous of cooperation with the English in their struggle with the Turks."

Instances of breach of peace among Muslims are so many that it would be impossible to enumerate them in an essay of this nature. The numerous Muslim states of Central Asia fell into the hands of Russia because of the internecine warfare, that had been waged by them for centuries and weakened them all. The surprising part is, that the rulers of these states, their nobles and their learned did not see through the game which the invaders were playing. One of the despatches of Russian court issued on 21st of November, 1864 gives out the policy followed by Russia. It says, "Of late years people have been pleased to assign to Russia the mission of civilising the countries which are her neighbours in the continent of Asia.

The advancement of civilisation has no agent more efficient than commercial relations. The last to become developed, require order and stability, but in Asia this necessitates a complete change of customs. Asiatics must be made to understand that it is more to their interest to favour and insure the trade of caravans than to pillage them. These elementary notions can only penetrate the public conscience, when there is an organised society and a government to direct and represent it. We accomplish the first part of this task in advancing our frontiers to the limit where these indispensable conditions are to be found. We accomplish the second by endeavoring henceforth to prove to the neighbouring states by a firm system, so far as the suppression of their ill dealings is concerned, but at the same time by moderation and justice in the employment of force.

In consecrating itself to this task the Imperial Cabinet is inspired by Russian interests" Prince Gortschnakoff's excellent logic reminds of the story of the wolf and the lamb. When the above mentioned policy was put into practice in Central Asia, Colonel Venukoff, the Russian commander of Orenburg area, wrote down the way he and his compatriots had been acting on the policy formed by the benign Russian Cabinet. He writes, "In Central Asia, that is to say, where there is easy to apply the principle, divide et imperia (and rule), by making use of rival antagonism of the Bashkirs, Kirghiz and Kalmucks; the Orenburg and Siberian

Governors have taken for their guidance the rule to weaken each one of these troublesome nations by the means of the others."

Nearly all leading European nations have tried to weaken Islam by dividing Muslim countries. "To preserve its authority the Church managed to urge the Christian princes to fight Islam in the name of religion; it was able to diffuse the spirit of exaggerated fanatism and religious zeal in Christian societies for long ages."

The rulers were, at times, keener than even the Church. "The policy of Charlemagne[9] towards Islam was one of the most important elements of Frankish diplomacy. The policy was contradictory in appears. While Charlemagne was planning to crush the Muslim state in Spain, he was, as the Frankish chronicle records, in correspondence with the Abbaside Caliph and sent his envoys to strengthen the bonds of friendship and alliance with him.... His relations with the Abbaside Caliph were, from his point of view, nothing but the means to facilitate his mission to fight Islam in Spain, and to protect Christianity in the East. The fault, however, lies with the Muslim ruler who disobeyed the Prophet's order, and divided the peace of believers.

This principle of divide and rule, which had been successfully applied by the British in the sub-continent of India, proved very useful to the Russians in Central Asia. Ever since the time that the Russians had taken on the role of Saviours of Christendom, they had developed an inborn hatred for the Muslims. Travellers heard remarks pertaining to Muslims as if they were the very incarnation of Satan. One Russian talking to another was heard saying, "I would give anything to drive out those Musalmans."

The Russians had started their eastward move against Central Asia about the end of sixteenth century. By the middle of nineteenth century they had nearly accomplished their object. Khiva had put up a fairly stiff resistance. Their advance had been very calculated. They always waited for the weakest moment of the defenders. In one instance, "After crossing Oxus they attacked the Khivan town Urgench. The Khan and his force were absent. Little resistance was made and the town was destroyed, the Cossacks carrying off thousands of women, besides many carts laden with rich booty. When the Khan returned, they were given a chase and were overtaken and surrounded by the Khivans. They had to flee leaving behind the prisoners and the loot."

The peace of believers has remained divided for centuries in Central Asia, as in other parts of the world. Brave Khivans were eventually defeated by the Imperial Russian forces, "The Khan, Said Muhammad Rahim Bahadur Khan, had fled, the Russians were in possession of his palace and *harem,* and so fell Khiva, the greatest stronghold of Islamism in Central Asia, after a succession of disastrous expeditions extending over 200 years."

The disobedience of the Law promulgated by Prophet Muhammad (PBUH) has been repeated again and again by those, who proclaim him as the Last Prophet of Allah. British gold must have attracted a great number of leaders of Muslim masses, because an Englishman has said." The people of the Hijaz and large number of tribes in the Arabian desert were openly for the allied cause."

In order to profit by the folly of Muslims in dividing their peace the author puts forward an excuse. He says, "Steps had to be taken on our side to protect British interest. Accordingly when Sharif Hussain, Amir of Mecca, showed a desire to throw off Turkish sovereignty, he was strongly encouraged and given promises of material assistance by the British Government."

The story of believers, breaking peace among themselves is both sordid and long. It is also painful but it has to be referred to, if not the whole of it, at least some of the instances, where it has been broken to get a little richer or for satisfying feelings of hatred of some inconsequential belief of a ruler. Nadir Shah[10] of Iran invaded India, for no apparent reason and weakened the already decaying power of a Muslim dynasty. When in occupation of the capital, as a victor, he, a believer, or so he maintained, without verifying the report of death of three of his soldiers, he, "remained in the mosque, his sword by his side, while the work of death and destruction went on. How many persons, the vast majority of whom were guiltless of any crime against the Persians, lost their lives on this troubled occasion, will never be known."

As a result of believers dividing their peace for such earthly benefits, the Christian writers get an occasion to say, "Are we to say, that the reality of Islam is purely subjective— that it is defined strictly by the feeling of belonging to it? This would be evading the problem, which is to know to what degree belonging to Islam involves an actual solidity, a will to mutual aid, a community of custom, of interests, of aspirations." We know that the feeling of oneness was present among the people, but history points in the other direction. Is it not time, that the intellectuals of Muslim countries put their heads together to find out if political leadership of Muslim lands is voicing the wishes of the masses or not?

The present century has introduced a new form of dividing peace of Muslim societies. This happens to be on the ideological level. The generation of Muslims educated on European lines, immediately after the Second World War, had started discussing, whether Islam was suited to the demands of this Atomic age. When asked as to which were the demands of the present atomic age, which could not be met, it did not bring out any clear-cut answer. These were the very people, who due to their having received modern European education, were entrusted with the reins of the Muslim lands by their outgoing colonial mentors. The Muslims have been loyal to their erstwhile masters, but have betrayed the trust of their brothers and sisters. They have not been able to secularise the thinking of their masses, but they have succeeded in producing confused minds among the present generation, who having seen through the trap have turned to religion, but they find that the secularised education, society, culture, and law do not permit them to coordinate their activities, in this atmosphere of contradictions. If efforts had been made to acquaint the youth with *Shariah*[11] and the fact that they are the part of an *Ummah,* this confusion would not have arisen. "The two essential and primary ingredients of the Islamic political theory are the *Ummah* and the *Shariah.*" It is difficult to get a clear picture of Islamic polity, without first understanding the impact of belief in the Sovereignty of Allah and Prophethood of Muhammad (PBUH). This belief automatically leads to the acceptance and application of *Shariah*. The application of *Shariah* starts with the Command "This *Ummah* of yours is *One Ummah,"* and therefore, "The peace of believers cannot be divided."

It is a matter of time alone, because as soon as the generation left behind by colonial masters and their immediate successors have relinquished authority, Muslim lands will discard secularism. Some neutral observers feel the same. It has been remarked that, "We can be sure, despite all the secularisation, all the economic, legal and social explosions, Islam will be able, in the course of time, somehow, to recreate its active specificity and to manifest once again the power as a common primordial factor." This resurgence of Islam is frightening Europe, because its economic colonialism is still dominating the Muslim world. The Muslim lands are quite likely to go over to Islamic social and economic system on the pattern established during the Prophet's (PBUH) life-time and followed in later periods, which is quite likely to free them from western capitalistic economic domination.

It is felt by some that, "All Muslim countries, are fated, one might say, to do one of two things: to deny the Laws of Islam and opt for a secular state; or persist with the arduous task of trying to produce an Islamic state, or even more difficult, an Islamic order." The ultimate goals can be nothing else, but an Islamic Order, because an Islamic state, by itself is unimaginable and if efforts are made to bring in *Shariah* without the support of an Islamic Order, its Laws will be broken like any other Secular Laws. The fight is uphill. As mentioned earlier, the Europeanised minority now firmly established in power in these countries will not abdicate easily. A civil war will be worse. The extremists of both camps should learn a lesson from the failure of Secularists in Turkey and the Revolutionaries of Iran. It is, as yet, difficult to lay down the details of the middle course, but it will have to include equal opportunities for all in all walks of life. The basis, however, should be a sincere effort coupled with knowledge of both the word and spirit of Islam and the needs of the time and place.

It is correct to say that "the question of accession to the seat of authority has unquestionably been the most controversial subject of Muslim politics," but if the solutions found by the Companions of the Prophet (PBUH) had been kept in view, this question need not have been controversial. The first *Khalifa* of the Prophet (PBUH) was elected by common consent according to the custom of the time and place. The appointment of the second was indicated by the first *Khalifa* and accepted by the people. The third was elected by a nominated council, as is done in the case of a Pope in Christendom, and the fourth was elected according to the custom of the time, keeping in view the urgency of the occasion. The question thus devolves to the conclusion that the wishes of the people of the time and place should be the final judge of how the question of succession should be solved. The decision whether to have Islamic Law or continue with borrowed and out of place Secular Laws should also be left to the will of the people who have time and again demanded introduction of *Shariah*. "If the interpretation of the law ultimately depends on popular consensus, correct interpretation and good government are best obtained by consulting the people."

At the present moment, the reins of government in nearly all Muslim lands, except in Saudi Arabia and Iran, are held by a small westernised minority, who incidentally are ignorant of both the Islamic and Western political thought and philosophy. They are not even pseudo-intellectuals. They were trained either as clerks or soldiers and have little inclination to develop into statesmen. If they had been sincere Muslims then if not the Islamic Order, at least Islamic states would have come into existence. "Islam is the state, or should be, if those in charge of the state were true Muslims."

Islam was a Way of Life in Mecca and Medina. It still is, but those who wish it to be a religion only, and a private affair, would like it to be kept out of the Houses of Parliament of Muslim States and thus maintain the division and fragmentation of the believers. It is this class which is at the root of trouble in all Muslim lands. A young writer of Pakistan has said, "The so-called educated class of Pakistan is creating intellectual anarchy. Laws of logic and systems of reasoning are abandoned over-charged emotionism replaces the strength of calm conviction." If it is the majority, that will eventually win the battle then the hurdles" placed in the way of Islamic Order are not only a mere waste of time, but are a cause of creating confusion. We all agree that "Muslims generally do not look at social and economic issues from, what we call, a purely secular angle. Their perception of such issues is usually faith oriented."

This perception is bound to remain faith oriented as long as they claim to be Muslims. The modernist, under the influence of accidental free thinking, is like the pre-Islamic Arab, when every individual had his own little god and the idea of state or society being subject to ethical and moral restraints, was completely absent. The opposition to the implementation of *Shariah* is purely on the basis of supposed freedom, otherwise, "The regulations of the *Shariah* do not go contrary to most of the Natural Laws."

The result of these inner tensions is delay in the development of the various sectors of collective life of the *Ummah* and its peace remains divided. The conflict created by ideas borrowed from abroad and efforts to reoriented life on so-called conservative patterns has held up intellectual progress unnecessarily. These foreign oriented intellectuals forget that, "In all great movements of the human intellect the force of progression or delay should be looked for mainly from within, not from without."

As said earlier, it is difficult to convey the sense of one discipline in the terminology of another and more so when the phrases used have been coined after an internal of centuries. "Islam is a comprehensive phenomenon, making no distinction between sacred and secular: all creation is suffused with the ineffable oneness of God. This inseparability of sacred and secular is not simply pantheism, it is argued, because nature is decidedly created and God uncreated...." Islam is religion, social behaviour and statecraft all at the same time. It also cannot be denied that, "Muslims in all parts have become more devout concerned with social, economic and political application of Islamic values all the people believe that, Islam, not a secular ideology, increasingly shapes the attitudes of their actions." It is this trend towards Islam, particularly among the young generation and those living as minorities amidst non-Islamic societies, that has created the hope, that time will soon come when it will be difficult for the ruling classes to keep the peace of believers divided, Muslims who have come in contact with the free thinking Western society are keen to get organised so that they find it easier to live by their Islamic values. One report says, "Finally there are those, who are highly organised, with international connections and specific identifications of what constitutes right practice. They are committed to an Islamic vision, striving to realise an Islamic Order and an Islamic state where religious laws are implemented and where a just government rules equitably."

This may be due to having been exposed to unbearable pressures in the middle of an alien surrounding. It has been generally observed that once a Muslim finds himself in a non-Muslim environment it becomes his Islamic duty to get organised with other Muslims. Inspite of these observations it is important that Muslim intellectuals get together and try to chalk out a programme for bringing about concerted efforts against forces trying to create ideological confusion amongst them. This is the only way to see, that the *Ummah* itself is no more guilty of dividing the peace of *Ummah*.

It would not be out of place to lay a part of blame of "dividing the peace of believers," on the intellectuals and learned men of the *Ummah*. They equally share this blame with the rulers and courtiers of the rulers. "Nasiruddin Toosi, who after having served the Assassins, then acted as counsellor to Halaku, on the Baghdad campaign, and ended up happily in the observatory built with funds furnished by his new protectors. Such a flexibility allowed the Persians to come through many trials, but it has not been without its effect on national character," His ability in Mathematics and Astronomy cannot be denied but it was Nasiruddin Toosi[13], the great mathematician, "who continuously urged him (Halaku), to march against Baghdad, and to accept the invitation of Mohiuddin bin Abdul Malik Alkami, who as Wazir, administered the affairs of the *Khalifate*[14] with unlimited power, and by the blackest treachery, caused its fall, is stigmatised ignominiously as traitor throughout the whole world." Their sectarian prejudices were so intense that they invited non-Muslim against a Muslim ruler who had placed his trust in them.

> "Say! He is able to send punishment upon you from above you or from beneath your feet, or to bewilder you with dissensions and make you taste the tyranny of one another." (6:65)

> "So learn a lesson, O you who have eyes" (59:2)

Clause 20.

> "No separate peace will be made when believers are fighting in the Path of Allah."

This Clause has wide implications. The preceding Clause has laid down that the peace of believers is indivisible. It follows that believers, who are fighting a common enemy have to remain at war with that enemy until the end. One of the parties from among the believers, cannot make a separate peace treaty and get out of the war, thus in a way stabbing its believer allies in the back. This Clause had very little significance, as far as the believers, of that period, were concerned, but, like Clause 19 it has a great significance under the present state of affairs. The Commandment "Obey Allah and obey His Prophet (PBUH)," still stands and when believer states go to the aid of another state of believers which has been attacked, one of them, under pressure from the enemy, cannot sign a separate peace treaty with the enemy. Such a treaty will be rejected by all Muslim states and the people of that state will be justified in demanding the abrogation of such a separate peace treaty.

As far as the situation, that existed in Yathrib itself the Clause had a certain amount of possible application, if it was assumed, that those who "would follow the believers and would fight alongside them," did avail of the status of equality and become a part of the *Ummah*. In that case any separate peace agreed by them with the enemy would have been considered as null and void, in view of this Clause.

The others did not decide to help the believers in the defence of Yathrib. In case of their joining, there was the danger of their losing heart and trying to make a separate peace treaty, with the Quraish[15] or one of their numerous allies. It is just as well that "the others," thinking that the believers were weak, as compared to the Quraish, remained aloof and did not opt to benefit by the offer of becoming a part of the *Ummah*.

Information about the general contents of the document must have reached the Quraish. Throughout the period of nine years, that the war lasted, there is no evidence of a friendly document being signed between "the others" and the Quraish. The Quraish, the Jews, and even the Hypocrites are known to have been in touch with the Quraish. Before the battle of Ahzab the Jews of Khyber, including men who had left Yathrib, are known to have sent a delegation to Mecca to persuade them to join the confederacy and attack Medina, but there is no evidence of a proper offensive or defensive treaty between "the others" and the Quraish.

The links between the Jews of Yathrib like Kaab bin Ashraf, the poet, and the Quraish existed until the end. Similarly the leader of Hypocrites, Abdullah bin Ubay[16] kept in constant touch with the Quraish, but no proper treaty of friendship has come to light. It appears that although the Jews lived and led their lives, according to Arab tribal pattern of life, they had inter-tribal rivalries and never thought of putting up a joint opposition to believers. From the remarks of Banu Qainuqa after the battle of Badr, it is certain that, due to the small number of believers the Jews did not think, that the Quraish will be beaten by the believers.

This Clause, as explained in foregoing paragraphs needs to be kept in mind by the statesmen of Muslim states of today, when signing defensive pacts among themselves. They need to insert words to the effect that no separate peace will be made by any of the signatories.

Clause 21.

"Conditions must be fair and equitable to all alike."

War has peculiar effects on the ruling party and its administration. Security measures have to be adopted. The Prophet (PBUH), for instance, did not give out the destination of the Army, marching out of Medina, on numerous occasions. The patrol sent to Nakhla had been ordered to open its orders after three days march from Medina. Such security arrangements and the desire to be watchful about the elements, whose loyalty is doubtful, sometimes results in unfair and inequitable conditions for a part of the population. The Prophet (PBUH), who was always just and kind, according to the principle of "justice tempered with benevolence," made it a point through this Clause, that whether a person or a party took part in defence or not, the whole population must be made to realise, that justice was being done to them.

Pre-Islamic conditions were not equitable to all. It was, therefore, vital that equality and freedom given to mankind by Allah, had to be practised with special care in this very first state brought into existence by the Prophet of Allah and his devoted Companions.

The Prophet (PBUH) had undertaken the defence of Yathrib. Fighting men and armament were given a secondary position and a low priority. His first concern was a willing, happy and free society. Apart from the fact that free soldiers are better soldiers, he desires to infuse the spirit of equality in the society he was creating. He planned to win the war and achieve peace at home and abroad by infusing new ideas in the population of Yathrib. "The major hope of peace lies not in armament, however important they are, but rather in ideas" There could have been no better idea than the idea of equality and "conditions being fair and equitable for all.

It has to be kept in mind that Islam was being made the state religion for the first time. This period was to remain as the Ideal Period for all times. The Prophet (PBUH) has said that his period is the best of all periods. Equity, justice, kindness, compassion and forgiveness are the hall-mark of this period. Allah is the Creator of believers and un-believers all alike. The Law of Allah must, therefore, be applied with the same spirit of equity for all. If this did not happen and injustice prevailed or the followers of other Ways of Life were denied the good things of life, how could believers maintain their distinction as slaves of Allah? Conditions, therefore, had to be "fair and equitable, to all."

Even most modern societies cannot claim to have given to their nations such conditions as can be called "fair and equitable" as mentioned in this clause. "The leadership in England is drawn from a narrow class base....especially educated in England for the task."

Clause 22.

"On expeditions a rider must take another behind him."

There was a shortage of all material resources, suitable for defence, with the

Prophet (PBUH) and his Companions. He had accepted to defend Yathrib, not because he had the means to defend it. He undertook the task and responsibility to defend Yathrib because he had been ordered to do so. Allah's orders had to be obeyed. Allah alone knew, what would be the outcome. It was not for the Prophet (PBUH) to question; Why? Although the number of men available to go on expeditions was small, the number of transport animals was inadequate even for the few men available to go out on expeditions. It was essential, that there should be "Standing Orders" that men who possessed camels, must take another behind them.

The number of camels available to the first large expedition, of 313 men which moved out of Medina, was only seventy. There was less than one mount per four people. Even the Prophet (PBUH) had to share a camel with three other Companions. If two could ride a camel at a time, then every one had to walk half the distance. The Prophet (PBUH), who was over fifty years of age at that time had to walk at least forty miles to the battle-field. It was his habit to share the vicissitudes of life with his Companions. During the early days at Yathrib, when there was constant fear of Meccan night attacks, he used to perform sentry duties taking his turn along. The word, 'expedition, signifies conditions, then prevailing in Yathrib, as a result of the certainty, that it will be   cked by Meccans. The transport needs of future are being brought within the legal frame work of a Constitutional document. The problem was being viewed from a long term point of view. The *Ummah* was to fight many wars in future and it had to be brought home to the leaders of *Ummah* of the future, that they would need to remain on the look out, whether they could transport their fighting forces to the areas of selected battle-fields. The numerous lands that the Muslims were to inhabit around the Globe would certainly find that they were short of war material. Here was a precedent for mutual help and pooling of resources by them. The principles laid down by him in this document, need to be studied afresh and acted upon in planning for the Defence of the World of Islam.

Clause 23.

"The believers must avenge the blood of one another, when fighting in the Path of Allah."

The war with Mecca, which was the basis of this Constitutional Charter, was, as yet on a scale, that the blood of one another would have been avenged, when fighting in the Path of Allah, without an order of this nature having been issued. He was the Supreme Commander and he could have ordered any action felt necessary. The Charter was, however, meant to be for all times. The problems being faced by the *Ummah* today are such, that, their correct and certain solution is possible only if the *Ummah* observes the Commands given in this document. The history of the Battles of the Prophet (PBUH) show, that the blood of believers was avenged every time. It is regretted that it ceased to be avenged soon after.

The Muslims are being persecuted in more than dozen lands today. Those who are persecuting the Muslims happen to be on the friendliest of relations with other Muslim state. We are thus guilty of breaking at least two Commands is possible only if the *Ummah* observes the Commands given in this document. The history of the Battles of the Prophet (PBUH) show, that the blood of believers was avenged every time. It is regretted that it ceased to be avenged soon after.

The Muslims are being persecuted in more than dozen lands today. Those who are persecuting the Muslims happen to be on the friendliest of relations with other Muslim state. We are thus guilty of breaking at least two Commands of this document. We are dividing the peace of believers and at the same time not avenging the blood of other believers, who, risk their lives even if they demand humane treatment at the hands of ungodly regimes.

The main problem appears to be, that no one can tell the reason why the Muslim countries find it difficult to act unanimously in international affairs. What lies at the bottom of joining different camps. What benefits do Muslim countries derive by developing relations with the so-called super powers, which result in their estrangement with neighbouring Muslim countries. It is time, that some studies were undertaken to analyse the events of last hundred years to determine the causes of conflicts between members of *Ummah* of Islam, an *Ummah* which came into being to bring mankind on to one platform. Is it because the majority of us wish, like, the Quraish of Mecca to protect our vested interests and will not step on to the same platform unless forced to do so.

Zakat has to be spent according to the formula laid down in the *Quran*. One of the lawful subjects given is to free prisoners. Muslims who are held by non-Muslim regimes as virtual prisoners would seem to deserve help under this Clause. The subject, however, needs further study, and the present writer feels that such questions need to be studied at a much higher level.

War, if it is fought with an objective in view, must be multi-dimensional, because life itself is such. Believers, which ever part of the world they may be inhabiting, share the same purpose in life; to help mankind in acting and achieving good and to discourage and prevent evil to the best of their ability. This would be the only way to declare Sovereignty of Allah in a practical manner. War aims of entire Muslim *Ummah* would thus be identical. Their political aim thus becomes the unity of the *Ummah* for purposes of establishing good and discouraging evil. Any war fought with this in view would be in the words of an eminent military thinker, "War thus becomes a political instrument as much as it is a political act." He arrives at this conclusion by arguing that "War starts from a political condition and is called forth by a political motive. It is, therefore, a political act." This reasoning, however, does not apply to the war declared by Mecca against the believers. The war that had been forced upon the believers was because of the fear of Quraish of Mecca, who thought that the New Way of Life would eclipse them and they would not be able to maintain their social and economic supremacy. They did not hold any political power which could have been usurped by the believers. They were the leaders of the existing Way of Life in Arabia. They were confident of the entire support of Arab tribes, who each, in its own tribal area, held sovereign power. This power had not been challenged by the Prophet (PBUH), except through the Islamic belief that Sovereignty belongs to Allah alone and that obedience of the Laws given by Allah was the symbol and token of accepting His Sovereignty.

Man made laws had created a Way of life within a society, which denied equality and justice to a greater part of humanity. The believers in defending the New Way of Life were, in actual fact, fighting a war on behalf of the present and future generations of humanity, which were being denied their birthright of freedom. This war was in support of the weak and downtrodden of the world and not for political supremacy over the Quraish of Mecca. If the Prophet (PBUH) had desired political power he had been offered it, but under the old Way of Life, and he had rejected the offer.

The war, as far as the believers were concerned, was for the freedom of the downtrodden of entire humanity, which was the creation of Allah. It was, therefore, termed as "Fighting in the Path of Allah," by Allah Himself. Being a war in the Path of Allah, the believers had to continue it to the end and as such be ready to "avenge the blood of one another, when fighting in the Path of Allah." There could be no question of surrendering, when fighting such a war. The spokesman of Western Philosophy of War, Clausewitz, accepts that, "Wars must differ in character according to the nature of the motives and circumstances from which they proceed."

It cannot be denied, that the war had resulted from an imaginary fear of losing vested interests, which were not territorial and could be called ideological. The interests, that were being threatened, were in the possession of a particular class, which feared the New Way of Life. As it happens elsewhere, in the case of war, here also, the tribe which held the leadership in socio-cultural field was the one to start the war. As has been said, "The problem of power in international relations would not exist if it was not for the vested interests of the governing classes that created them." In this case vested interests figured on one side only. The imaginary fear of losing prestige, economic power, religious eminence and threat to monopoly of international carriage trade through the followers of the New Way of Life had initiated this declaration of war.

They had hoped, that people of Yathrib will throw out the handful of believers from Mecca. Peace among believers being indivisible and the determination to avenge the blood of other believers had brought about a solidarity among believers, which could not be splintered by such threats. They may have hoped, that threat of force will achieve what they desired. They, however, did not realise, that the threat and eventually the use of force, in this case, will start a war, which will continue for centuries. "Force, or a threat of it, may not settle argument, but it does play a considerable part in determining the structure of the world in which we live."

Commands of Allah and decisions of the Prophet (PBUH) hold inviolable position. This Clause may not have appeared of great consequence to the observers of that era. Believers were confined mainly to Yathrib and as refugees in Habsha, in addition to possible individuals scattered about in various parts of Arabia. Except those in Yathrib, the other believers were not in a position to avenge the blood of their brother Muslims. If, however, we look at this Clause to the centuries, that PBUH Muslim countries falling a prey to the domination of Christian West, we realise how significant would have been the result, if Muslims had been obeying the Commands of this document, issued by the Prophet (PBUH), whose Commands are as inviolable as those of Allah Himself.

"Obey Allah and obey His messenger, but if ye turn away, then the duty of Our messenger is only to convey (the message) plainly." (64:12)

He conveyed the message, in the best possible manner. In an age, when written orders were not resorted to, he gave a written document in as plain words as possible. How numerous, in fact, countless are the occasions, when Muslims have failed to avenge the blood of their brothers, in various corners of the Globe. Muslims have failed to visualise *Jihad* in its correct perspective, because they have failed to comprehend their own identity in circumstances, which have been changing constantly. Because they failed to comprehend the meaning and consequence of being *One Ummah,* they have failed to organize, their collective affairs in accordance with the dictates of the *Quran* and Prophet's Orders which in the case of this document is not merely *Sunnah* of the Prophet (PBUH) but an outright order, and which should not have been disobeyed under any circumstances. Muslims have for centuries ignored their correct standing and as a result could not evolve correct strategy and tactics to defend themselves. "The object which every one, who undertakes war proposes to himself, and the means he calls forth are determined entirely according to the particular details of the position."

When the *Ummah* ceased to exist as one body, its war strategy never attained that position, which alone could fully defend its interests. It has been said, that "the objective of military strategy is the creation, by military means, those conditions, under which politics is in a position to achieve the aims it sets for itself." The Prophet (PBUH), through successful defence of Yathrib, had been able to create those conditions where unity of *Ummah* could be guaranteed. Later generations have, one after the other, failed to maintain that condition of *Ummah,* with the result that they have lost the will and the means to defend themselves.

Unity of *Ummah* demands sacrifices by all in an equal measure. Separatist tendencies spring, very often, from hesitating to contribute to the common cause by members of ruling classes. This leads to hesitation on the part of the common man to sacrifice his life and wealth for common defence. When nations are threatened with extermination, as the Muslim *Ummah* has been for centuries, and they do not resolve to put up a fight and are afraid to go to war, they cannot survive as free people. In the words of a modern military thinker, "if a nation is really determined not to fight, ardently desires not to fight, and is prepared to endure anything rather than risk a decisive campaign," then that nation or *Ummah,* ends up as an acquired and conquered territory to be used as a colony by its victor. If Muslim of the present age desire to live as free people, then the first step for them is to organize themselves for defence, and act in accordance with the dictates of the Constitutional Charter of Medina. Muslims, in the past, may have defended their territories individually. They have not fought as an *Ummah,* for a number of centuries. The result has been that they have all been defeated one after the other. They have wasted their sacrifices for having failed to act as *One Ummah*.

Clause 24.

> "The believers, because they fear Allah, they are better in showing steadfastness, and as a result receive Guidance."

This Clause is more of a statement of fact, and a standard set for believers, which they must maintain in order to continue to receive Guidance from Allah. This is the standard to be achieved by all true believers. The basis of excellence in showing steadfastness has been established as Fear of Allah. It must be remembered that this document was being dictated soon after Hijra[17]. The steadfastness, which had been shown by Quraish *Muhajirin* was known to all. The manner in which they had migrated and the hardships endured by them on the way could be imagined. The short period of stay in Yathrib was also a period of patience, hard work and facing hardships in an extremely disciplined, coordinated and united manner.

The *Ansar* believers who were although new to Islam, had shown great changes in their moral qualities and had achieved character qualities not found in their other compatriots, who had not yet embraced Islam. This Clause was a reminder to non-Muslims of that period and the world at large of future generations, that belief in Allah and Muhammad (PBUH) leads to Fear of Allah, which transforms the very character of men and women who are fortunate enough to see the Light, without staunch Faith and Fear of Allah, it is difficult to remain steadfast and achieve "Calm courage in the midst of tumult and the serenity of soul in danger and cool headedness." The Companions of the Prophet (PBUH), whether from amongst the Quraish of Mecca or the *Ansars* of Medina, excelled one another in their devotions to him and faith in Allah, which had been bestowed to them, through his teachings and personal conduct. It has been said of them that, "these men formed the venerable stock of Islam, from whom one day was to spring the noble band of first jurists, theologians, and traditionalists of Muslim society." Abu Bakr, the first successor of the Prophet (PBUH), when advised by Umar, Ali, and other brave Companions, to postpone the despatch of the Army to threatened Northern Areas, refused to listen to any such advice.

He had said, "I will not revoke any order given by the Prophet (PBUH). Medina may become the prey of wild beasts, but the Army must carry out the wishes of Muhammad (PBUH)." Such strength of character was the result of faith in the Prophet's mission and belief and Fear of Allah, in which he excelled all others, and was known as *Siddiq* for such staunch faith. Faith in Allah leads to the firm belief, that death comes only once and then the eternal life of the hereafter starts for ever. This belief in life after death seems to have been the hall-mark of early Muslims. Chinese Muslims are known as *'Huyee'*[19] by others, which means, "those who believe in life in the hereafter". To a Muslim life continues after death. A Muslim soldier does not go to war merely because he desires to "die in war so that others may live," but he goes to war because he wishes, that he dies as a martyr so that he achieves Eternal Life.

"Think not of those, who are slain in The way of Allah as dead. Nay, they are living. With their Lord thy have provision". (3:169)

Belief in the hereafter presupposes the Day of Reckoning and Reward from Allah. Dangers of all kind, thus, fade, into insignificance. Steadfastness, when fighting, in the Path of Allah, is the logical outcome.

History was to prove the truth of this Clause in many a battle-field around the surface of the Globe. This fundamental truth was being brought home to those engaged in war, that Belief in Allah and fear of Him result in ignoring the consequences of the losses and injuries caused in war. As a result it is the quality and not the quantity of human and material sources that influences the issue.

Military thinkers of all ages have admitted this truth. A modern writer has to say, "Neither policies nor machines will determine the history of tomorrow. Man is the measure of all things.... This then is the ultimate battlefield: the hearts and minds of men." Life, to the believers, was one entity. They stepped from this to the next world with clear conscience. Both worlds were subject to the Sovereign Power Allah, the Creator and Sustainer of the entire Universe.

> "Have they not pondered upon themselves? Allah created not the heavens and the earth, and that which is between them, save with truth and for a destined end. But many of the mankind are disbelievers in the meeting with their Lord". (30:8)

This belief in meeting with Lord of men and all there is between the earth and the heavens, makes all the difference. He who obeys Him here, is happy, and longs to meet Him in the Hereafter.

> "Whoso looketh forward to the meeting with Allah (let him know that) Allah's reckoning is surely high, and He is the Hearer, the Knower". (29:5)

This high reckoning is measured by the sacrifices in His Path. And the sacrifice of the life He bestowed on man is, with Him, of the highest reckoning. His knowledge is Complete. The main thing is, whether a man believes in His Sovereignty both here and in the hereafter.

> "Allah! There is no God save Him. He gathereth you all upon the Day of Resurrection whereof there is no doubt. Who is more true in statement than Allah". (4:87)

When fear of death is no more, then the fighter does not hesitate to face the most powerful on earth. These Companions of the Prophet (PBUH) were the most peaceful and lovable people in peaceful surroundings, but harsh and firm in battle. Allah has said of them;

> "Muhammad is the messenger of Allah. And those with him are hard against the disbelievers and merciful among themselves". (48:29)

Thus they were more steadfast than others.

This characteristic of being hard in battle and mercifulness with companions and those who came in contact with them under peace condition, has been portrayed by a modern writer in these words:

> "War and peace is personified respectively in heroes and saints."

These Companions of the Prophet (PBUH) were all heroes in war and saints in peace. This was the result of their Faith and Fear of Allah. They knew their proper place in the scheme of things. When man realises this, he feels how close he is to Eternal Truth. As one such person who realised it in the middle of throes of war has remarked, "The discovery—that is discovery for myself that God is Universal, which is not so obvious as it sounds, was, I think, the first great step I made in finding, that within that Universal, fear shall be impossible."

Role of Holy Companions : In the final analysis, it is the determination and steadfastness, of the combatants, which decides the issue of war. In this first war between Islam and The Rest, it must be remembered that the *Muhajir* Companions were initially the product of the old Way of Life of Mecca, and the *Ansar*[20] Companions had grown up in the same surroundings, background and upbringing, as other residents of Yathrib, but both had been transformed into new beings as a result of their belief in Allah and His Messenger (PBUH). These two groups of Companions of the Prophet of Allah had shed all their earlier prejudices, fears, and taboos by becoming believers. Like the word *"Huyee"* in China, the word believers has a special meaning. It covers steadfastness, patience, forbearance, courage, bravery, and fearlessness apart from benevolence, forgiveness and mercifulness to the weak and persecuted. A modern writer thinks that, "courage is will power and when, in war, it is used up (the soldier) is finished..." In actual fact courage and will-power and other allied qualities spring from the same source—Faith. This author was a medical officer, during war, over a very prolonged period. He feels that "Time" exhausts courage. In actual fact, it is courage, based on temporary factor, like pride, loyalty to king and country and fear of being called a coward that gets exhausted. "The using up of courage" does not happen to those who crave to become martyrs, as a result of their belief, that they are fighting in the Path of Allah. He, however, admits that, "Faith is the only thing, which can delay the eating up of courage. Lord Moran, ends up by saying that, "Faith had come into the lives of many men," which saved them, from becoming mental and physical wrecks. Those who lack "Faith," break up. It is such people who are the real victims of war. It has been said that, "War demands its toll of broken men— broken in mind or body or both; to mend these is the function of a medical service." Yes, but only for the repairs needed to the body. The mind needs to be cured by a much higher authority.

Other military writers have also expressed views on courage and similar other qualities. A well known military writer has summed up his views and said, "Courage and self reliance are principles essential to war. It is a serious undertaking, by a serious man, for a serious object." We would like to differ by saying, that a believer does not rely on himself. He relies on Allah, who is the Arbiter in all things. One of the successful generals of Second World War has said, "I consider morale the greatest and the only factor in war; without high morale, no success can be achieved, no matter how good the strategic and tactical plans may be." Morale has been translated as *Iman* by some scholars. Western writers often admit the strong impact of morale on the outcome of war. As has been said that, "The military victories of the Germans were due as much to the demoralisation of the enemy as to their superiority in the field."

As this Clause points out, the Muslims have, from the beginning, been known to have shown great moral and physical courage as a result of their staunch belief in Allah. Speaking of the Muslims of the early period one writer has remarked, "The spirit of discipline and contempt of death manifested at the first armed encounter of Islam, proved characteristic of it in all its latter and greater conquests."

The spirit, which had been infused into the mind of these Companions of the Prophet (PBUH) has been commented upon by a modern writer in one brief sentence. He writes, "No others have made practically all their soldiers to actually seek death in battle." This achievement of the Prophet (PBUH) was the result of his own Faith in Allah and his example, both in mosque and on the field of battle, helped his Companions to reach those unchartered heights of courage, steadfastness and sheer "contempt of death," which had never been reached by men of any nation throughout human history. Liberty and freedom, which was needed to usher in and live in accordance with the New Way of Life dictated by Allah, through *Quran*, could only be achieved through steadfastness. No nation has achieved liberty without it. Liberty "is a prestige that must be earned." This was the prerequisite of free and unfettered obedience of One Allah.

Fear of death and injury can only overpower the minds of those men, who lack Faith. A surgeon who had lived and worked in the trenches with soldiers, in the front line, has said, that officers, who commanded troops in action, often asked him about the influence of religion on troops facing danger. He has summed up his observations by saying, "Often I was asked about the importance of religion. Speaking as if they did not know how to put it, they separately told me how faith had come into the lives of many of their men." The same writer, when speaking about the officers who led their men into attack has to say, "The art of selection is the secret of leadership."

The selection of leaders at all levels, from the Second Baih at Uqba to the last, was done by the Prophet (PBUH) himself. Those Companions, whom he selected to lead other Companions, showed qualities of leadership unsurpassed in human history. The training given to Abu Bakr[21], Umar[22], Ali[23], Abu Ubaidah[24], Saad[25], Waqqas[26], Khalid[27] and many others produced leaders of unique qualities of head and heart. They turned out to be great military leaders and equally capable statesmen. This clause has expressed their qualities in a modest manner by saying that, "Believers, because they fear Allah, they are better in showing steadfastness and as a result receive Guidance."

Modern thinkers are gradually understanding the influence of faith in Allah; as one writer has said that full freedom and liberty are achieved only as a result of belief in Allah. "If there is any freedom anywhere it is consummated in God, whose service, for man, is perfect freedom." When man becomes His Slave *(Abd-Hoo),* and not the slave or servant of another man, or even his own earthly desires, he is really free. He can speak the truth, because he is not the slave or servant of any person. "A man to be free is to be in command of his own destiny. When free men freely combine to shape a common destiny, you have a free people." The believers, because of their belief in Allah, were a free people. They had combined freely to shape the common destiny of all those existing and future generations, who would choose to be free people. It was this freedom, which gave them steadfastness and earned them Divine Guidance as a present.

We must, constantly, bear in mind, the background and the circumstances under which this document was being dictated. In this assembly of all men of Yathrib[28], some were believers, and some were "The others," who, were to work under the leadership of believers, were being given the Charter, which was to remain their Fundamental Law, as long as they remained in Yathrib. They all were aware of the fact, that the Quraish of Mecca had declared war against them all. They knew of earlier decision of Abdullah bin Ubay. They had been told that the Prophet (PBUH) had undertaken that believers would defend Yathrib. He was through this Clause, bringing home to the others, "that to achieve the steadfastness required to defend a territory, chosen by a people, as its homeland, it was necessary to possess the quality of truthfulness and that this rare and highly valuable quality could be achieved by belief and fear of Allah alone. He was telling them that through belief in Allah, alone, could man achieve such qualities.

Those who deliberate on happenings around them and ponder a little over the sequence of events, come to the realisation of how little power does man possess, to channel events on the broader spectrum of this world. Winston Churchill[29], the undisputed leader of Great Britain, during the time of its greatest struggle, has said, "Let us be contented with what has happened to us and thankful for all we have been spared. Let us accept the natural order in which we move. Let us reconcile ourselves to the mysterious system of our destinies, such as they must be in the world of space and time. Let us treasure our joys, but not avail our sorrows. The glory of light cannot exist without its shadows. Life is a whole and good and evil must be accepted together." Those who think and deliberate, sooner or later, come to the conclusion, that there exists a power higher than us all. Faith in Him alone enables men to bear hard and harsh moments in life.

Discussing happenings during the conduct of the same war another writer has referred to steadfastness in the following words. "Calm courage, in the midst of tumult, that serenity of soul in danger, is the greatest gift of nature for mankind." He appears shy of using the word God or Allah.

One must realise that "The soldier is alone with the terror....", that can grip his heart and mind. He needs support and there is nothing more durable than "inner support," supplied by Faith in Allah. This eminent writer, who had personal experience of treating the war wounded adds, "when their self-control was worn thin, they were given to moods, which was the language in which they spoke to us of their distresses."

Steadfastness is a gift from Allah. When his very existence is denied men are deprived of this gift. Speaking of those who had no Divine support to fall back upon, another observer has said, "They have no religious conviction by which to obtain leverage in their struggles. They have no firm philosophy of life on which they or those who could help them can lay hold." Western world seems to be groping in the dark. Another writer on the subject has to say that, "Gradually it began to dawn on the Western world, that anticipating this danger was really more dangerous than the danger itself."

There has to be a Philosophy of Life based on a lasting principle. Islamic Philosophy of Life is based on Sovereignty of Allah. There can be no firmer basis for a Philosophy of Life. This Philosophy is as Eternal as the basis on which it stands. It is immovable and unshakable. It may weaken under certain conditions of immature leadership, but it can be revived and has reappeared with added vigour, Islamic Way of Life is distinct, all pervading and complete in itself. It needs no outside props. It reasserts itself on its pivot—Oneness of Allah and the Finality of Prophethood of Muhammad (PBUH). It has this philosophy from which springs the Islamic Way of Life. This is what is missing in the West, as one observer has said, "Lacking a way of life, a philosophy, we have had to run before the wind of change and yield in the face of attack by the more dynamic philosophies ranged against us our entire military system was based on tactics alone, and out of date tactics at that."

This Clause brings out another important aspect of being a believer. It gives a place of prestige to him and places him on a high pedestal of being a bold and straight-forward person, who is not afraid of telling the truth, and to follow a path free of common evils. As has been observed by a Western scholar," One of the reasons for the warm welcome, which Muhammad received in Medina would seem to be, that, the adoption of Islam appeared, to the more thoughtful, of the citizens, to be a remedy for the disorder from which the society was suffering, by its orderly discipline of life, and bringing the unruly passions of men, under the discipline of laws enumerated by the authority, superior to individual caprice." In other words the disciplined life, that an individual led, after becoming a Muslim and the belief in the Supreme being, which strengthened his heart and mind, was visible from his conduct, and it attracted towards him and Islam, all those, who came in contact with him.

This transformation was the result of the towering personality of the Prophet (PBUH).

They had become, so to say, new individuals, both within themselves and to the observers. The *Muhajir* believers were foremost in this respect. They were the result of thirteen years of guidance given by him, in accordance with the dictates of the *Quran*. "They were the depositories of the Sacred Text of the *Quran*, which they alone knew by heart; they were the jealous guardians of the memory of every word and bidding of the Prophet (PBUH), the trustees of the moral heritage of Muhammad (PBUH). These men formed the venerable stock of Islam from whom one day was to spring the noble band of the first jurists, the theologians, and traditionalists of Muslim society."

The credit for selecting and training of these men of extraordinary sincerity goes to the Prophet (PBUH) himself. When the Voice directed him to "Recite," and he spoke of his Mission to Abu Bakr, who did not hesitate to acknowledge the Prophethood conferred on him, to the moment of his departure, Abu Bakr had remained closest to him. The soft and benign nature of this most devoted Companion of the Prophet (PBUH) proved as if it was made of twice tempered steel, when the responsibility of carrying on the torch of Islam fell on him. It has to be admitted, that he and others were all the product of guidance given to them by the Last Messenger of Allah. Modern writers give great importance to the understanding of human psychology, when selecting men for tasks which carry great responsibility, it has been said, that during World War II, "the application of psychology in selecting and training men, did more to help win the war than any other single intellectual activity."

The great laurels won by Muslim Armies just after the death of the Prophet (PBUH) in defending Arabia, against the two supreme powers of that age, and the juristic and literary excellence achieved within less than a century, by Muslim scholars, was the fruit of the selection and training of his Companions, given by him on the floor of his modest mosque in Medina and the battle fields of Badr, Uhud, Khyber, and Hunain. When we consider the meagre resources available to him, and his readiness to accept the responsibility of defence, through the promulgation of this document, his achievements make a new but gigantic picture.

He had trained his Companions to such high standard of sacrificing their wealth and their lives that he did not have to hesitate in accepting the responsibility to defend Yathrib. In the circumstances that he was placed and the meagre resources he possessed, it needed great courage and faith in Allah to have accepted to launch the entire *Ummah* of Islam in battle. His words which were in fact, prayers to Almighty, has been quoted many a times, but its true implications can only be understood, when it is kept in mind, that this was all that Islam possessed. He had said; "O Allah! if this little band of believers is destroyed today, there will be none left to obey your Commands, until the Day of Resurrection."

It depicted the true picture. He was the last Messenger of Allah, with the Last Message from Allah, which meant the Last and Final but Perfect *Shariah*, and this small band of believers was the entire strength of the last *Ummah*. If they were fighting *Jihad*, until *Shahadah-martyrdom-none* would have been left alive, to live in accordance with the Dictates of this Last *Shariah* sent by Allah.

It is in view of such critical situations, that present day military writer has said, "What strength of will and greatness of soul it takes to launch one of those decisive battles, on which the fate of a nation depends," Badr was truly the most rare occasion, when the fate of the entire *Ummah* depended on one battle.

When the believer defending the rights of humanity stands steadfast in battle, he feels that he is performing the most sacred task, ever allotted to mankind. He is demonstrating the meaning of:

"You are the best community that has been raised up for mankind. You enjoin right conduct and forbid indecency; and you believe in Allah.
(3:110)

The believer gets strength of mind and body from the conviction of fighting in the Path of Allah. "War is the province of physical exertion and suffering. A certain strength of body and mind is required, which produces indifference to them." Belief in Allah enhances this strength of both body and mind. It is strength of this kind, that keeps nations alive. A European travelling through Turkey and observing their morale during the later part of eighteenth century had to remark, "Internal causes are the most immediate in national elevation or decay, as no feeble state was elevated to extraordinary eminence by the mere aid of alliance, however powerful; similarly, on the other hand, scarcely any great nation perished by means of external violence, unless it had something within itself vicious and unsound." Another traveller has also paid tribute to Muslim soldiers. He says, "When a Turk could ride with the Sultan's firman, he was respected all the way, from the banks of Volga to the confines of Morocco — when its armies threatened Vienna, and its fleets blockaded the coasts of Italy it then excited the fears of civilised Europe."

This was not so because of the ability of Turkish Sultans alone, but because Turkish soldiers believed in Allah.

Speaking of the modern Turks and their performance during the First World War, a military historian of repute states, "For the most part they were illiterate conscripts from the country, although they were always outgunned and outnumbered, their steadfastness never forsook them, they were very cool and very skilful."

The same writer has mentioned that "When the (British) submarine was first abandoned and the British sailors were struggling in the water the Turkish soldiers, on the shore, jumped in and rescued them. When the first English submarine prisoners were led into the hospital at Chanak, shivering in their wet clothes, the Turkish wounded called them guests, and insisted on their being given everything new, and few such delicacies as they possessed."

Belief of an individual shapes his character. When a people possessing strong belief develop certain common tracts, the sum total of such traits is known as the national character of that people. As a result of belief in Allah, to remain steadfast, has become a part of the national character of Muslims, all the world over.

Clause 25.

> "No unbeliever will be permitted to take the property of the Quraish under his protection."

The situation as it then existed in Yathrib was, that there were fewer believers than the unbelievers in Yathrib. The Quraish of Mecca, mostly unbelievers, had declared war on Yathrib. A state of war had come into existence between the two states. It was quite possible, that due to past relations some Yathribite unbelievers might have decided to take Meccan property, under his or her protection. If the unbeliever were not debarred under Law of the land, they could not be stopped from giving protection, to what was legally enemy property and thus liable to be appropriated by the state.

The Quraish were a business community. They had always held monopoly of carrier trade of goods arriving at Aden or other ports of the Red Sea to be conveyed to Syria and other market towns in the North. It would be wrong to assert, that this monopoly had been the result of war between Byzantium and Iran, as some Orientalists have said. Montgomery Watt, for instance writes, "While the war ran its course and perhaps as a result of making travel difficult between Iraq and southern Syria, the commercial centre of Mecca was experiencing great prosperity. It had gained monopoly control of the trade by the caravan route up the westward of Arabia." The Quraish had always held monopoly of this trade. So far as Montgomery Watt's assumption that, "perhaps as a result of difficulties of travel between Iraq and southern Syria, the commercial centre of Mecca had become prosperous". In case travel between Iraq and Syria had been disrupted as a result of war between the Byzantines and Iran, the Quraish would not have sent their caravan to Syria via Iraq. This was the caravan, which was not permitted to proceed to Iraq and its goods had been captured as enemy property, under orders of the Prophet (PBUH). The Prophet (PBUH) had inserted in this clause, as a result of his correct enunciation of International Law regarding the method of dealing with enemy property during war. Confiscation of enemy property, during war, is a common practice, in modern times as well. A Gazzette notification of British Government during World War I reads as follows:

"Any sum which, had a state of war not existed, would have been payable and paid to for the benefit of our enemy, by way of Dividend, Interest, or Share of profits, shall be paid by the person, firm or company, by whom it would have been payable, to the Custodian."

Apart from confiscation of enemy property, the national of the home country are prohibited from carrying on trade activities with the enemy country, as long as the war lasts, or the state of war continues. During the same war a notification of the British Government had laid down:

"Whereas a state of war exists between us and the German Emperor, and whereas it is contrary to law for any person resident carrying on business, or being in our dominion, to trade or have any commercial intercourse with any person resident, carrying on business, or being in German Empire without our permission...."

Similarly ships are not allowed to leave for anchor, or communicate with any port situated in enemy territory. It is also customary to prohibit aliens from carrying on business, and free movement, within territories of the home government, during war. This Clause, can thus be said to be the first instance of Codification of International Law on the subject.

Quraish of Mecca had declared war against Yathrib. A state of war existed from the moment the ultimatum had reached Yathrib. Every person of the tribe of Quraish, who had not embraced Islam, was an enemy of Yathrib and all property belonging to or in possession of the enemy had become enemy property, for as long as the state of war was to continue between Mecca and Yathrib.

The reason, why, only unbelievers had been debarred from taking the property of Quraish under their protection was, that the believers were the direct cause of this war. Protection given by *Ansar* believers to *Muhajir* believers had resulted in the declaration of war by the Quraish. It was not likely that any believer would give undue protection to property particularly caravans belonging to Meccans. The

Security and Safety

other reason for not including believers in this restriction was that any property taken hold of by a believer was to become a part of spoils of war, which was to be handed over to the state, for distribution in the normal manner. These precautions are normal during war. The present day governments are even more particular in placing restriction on enemy property finding its way back to the enemy either directly or through neutrals. Hence we find, that this Clause had opened the way to legalising taking over of enemy property.

Clause 26.

"No unbeliever will intervene in favour of Quraish."

War had been declared by Mecca. All possible precautions had to be taken, that the unbelievers could not interfere with war efforts. At a time when the threat of invasion was new, everybody was afraid of the possible severe action being taken by Meccans, if they succeeded in defeating the believers. There was, however, the possibility, that due to old connections between the unbelievers in Yathrib and the Quraish of Mecca, some of the former may not intervene on behalf of the Quraish. There was also the possibility of some individuals from amongst the unbelievers to plead the cause of Meccans and to undertake to supply them with secret military and other vital information from within Yathrib. Legal course was the best method of proceeding in such circumstances. The document laying down the Fundamental Law of the state was the best source to promulgate such security laws. The nature of these laws and the manner in which they were being promulgated were, no doubt, new to that age, but his actions had to remain as precedents and as in this case legal commands for all times.

Clause 29.

"The Jews will contribute towards the cost of war when fighting alongside the believers."

Clause 1 had mentioned that "the others," which meant the unbelievers and Jews, would be considered as part of the *Ummah* if they followed the believers and fought alongside with them. This Clause clearly mentions the Jews, fighting alongside the believers. It is possible that the Jews, at this instance, had asked for some sort of clarification and the Prophet (PBUH) in answer to some query laid down that if they fought alongside the believers, they would, at the same time, have to contribute towards the cost of war. This refers to general expenses and not those expenses, which are incurred by all armies on the equipment, food and personal equipment of individual soldiers.

Jews may have been more numerous than the believers, at that time but they did not form the government party and they were living as a minority. They were, therefore, not being coerced to undertake the defence of the state. If, however, they were keen to undertake this arduous duty and become equal members of the *Ummah* they had to defray the cost of war along with the believers.

This Clause was being written at a time when Jews and other minorities in neighbouring lands were being persecuted or permitted to live as serfs and slaves only. It was a great step forward towards the unity of mankind. The important part of the whole philosophy of equality of man is that it was being written down and proclaimed through a legal document, which can be termed as a Constitution or Constitutional Charter of Medina.

The Charter was not being demanded by the citizens or any section of the community. In fact all concessions in it, were being freely given by the Prophet (PBUH). He realised the importance of "War Potential" of a nation. He knew that internal dissensions weaken war potential and man power is no mean component of it. It has been said that, as far as the war potential of a nation in a modern setting is concerned, "Its principal components are not only its industrial capacity, but the administrative skill, with which it is managed and the morale or motivations of war". To have included the Jews to volunteer to join in the defence of the state amounted to successful efforts towards motivation of a common cause. He was taking the first practical step towards bringing entire mankind on one platform, a duty which now devolves on his *Ummah*.

Clause 32.

"Loyalty gives protection against treachery."

This clause deals with internal security and security of defence plans and other defence matters. It has to be in the statute even though there may be no likelihood of war starting in the near future or a state of war being declared soon. In the case of Yathrib, a state of war already existed. There could be no more appropriate time for giving a warning of this nature, than the occasion when invasion was imminent.

The Jews had volunteered to join believers in their against Mecca and thus gain an equal social and political status with the Government Party. They were told that they will have to join in the defraying the cost of the war. They were being warned, that, loyalty to the cause of *Ummah,* they desired to join was most important. After Clause 29, the clause dealing with the cost of war, there were two more clauses referring to the different sections of Jews, who wanted the names of the *Haleef* Tribes, to be specifically included, as those who had volunteered to become *One Ummah* with Muslims.

It has to be noted here that this request for being allowed to become a part

Security and Safety

of *Ummah* had been put forward when Clause 28 had already been dictated, which lays down, "When you differ on anything the matter will be referred to Allah and Muhammad (PBUH)." This meant, that the Law of the *Quran* and the decisions of the Prophet (PBUH) were to be Supreme in Yathrib. They may not have realised but they were coming in as a part of Muslim *Ummah* and were happy to be governed by Islamic *Shariah,* although they were to retain their separate identity as Jews. How much freedom they were to retain is not known but if they gave a different version to Clauses 30 and 31 or any other Clause, of the Charter, or they differed even on other socio-political or economic matters concerning the collective life of the community, the final decision was to rest with Allah and His Messenger (PBUH).

To have spoken of loyalty as the best course of conduct and warned them against treachery, when state of war existed, looks very appropriate. Events, which took place after the promulgation of the Charter, have to be viewed in the light of this and similar other Clauses of the Charter.

Clause 35.

"No one shall go to war except with the permission of Muhammad (PBUH). If any wrong has been done it may be avenged."

Muhammad (PBUH), on behalf of believers, had accepted to defend Yathrib. Therefore, he was the only person in Yathrib who was responsible for the efficient defence of the state and its territories. He, alone, was the person who could decide on defence plans. As such he was the only person who knew, when and in what manner defence movements for defending Yathrib were to be made.

Apart from that, he was the head of the Government Party, and as such, he became automatically the head of the state as well. He, alone could therefore, declare war. It has been universal practice, since ancient times, and throughout the world, that war can be declared by the head of state alone. This practice still exists. In modern democracies the parliament may take the decision, but the declaration of war has to be made in the name of the head of that state. According to the British custom and law, in a country which claims to possess the oldest parliament, it has followed the same practice. "It has been said, by the law and the constitution of the country, that the sovereign alone can declare war and such a declaration carries with it the force of law. As such it is of equal authority with the Act of Parliament and is juridically taken notice of."

It is worth keeping in mind that, this Constitutional Charter, was being dictated on the certainty that Yathrib was to be invaded soon. The Prophet (PBUH), who, with the help of Allah and his Companions, had decided to undertake the defence of Yathrib, was, from legal point of view promulgating the Constitution, of the territories now being declared as the state of Yathrib. These territories were later to be known as Medina. All parties then living in Yathrib were represented in this assembly. In this most representative Assembly, that Yathrib had ever witnessed, it was being declared, that the prerogative of the head of the state of Yathrib would be exercised by Muhammad (PBUH) alone." No one shall go to war except with the permission of Muhammad (PBUH)". It meant, that they had voluntarily and unanimously accepted him as the factual head of the state and the government of Yathrib.

When a state goes to war or is forced to get involved in war, it is governed by the universal practice concerning "state of war," in respect of a country. During the state of war emergency laws are enforced, which are vital for the safety of the state. Orders regarding necessary action against the enemy and property belonging to enemy state or its individuals, is taken. England, which is considered to be a country, which tries to explain all its actions through one or other law, maintains that, "Actual invasion of this country would, of course, create a state of war.... and it may be assumed, that common law would be suspended, for the simple reason, that no courts would be able to administer it."

As a result of declaration of war by Mecca a state of war had come into being between Mecca and its allies on the one side and Yathrib on the other. This "state of war," lasted between these states until the defeat of various allies of Mecca and Mecca itself, except during the short period of Truce resulting from the Peace Treaty of Hudaybiya. Those, like Banu Ghatfan and the Jews of Khyber, who did not join the peace treaty, continued to be at war with Yathrib. Campaigns against Banu Ghatfan and Jews of Khyber were under taken because they had first attacked Yathrib, as allies of Mecca. These, therefore have to be viewed in the light of Clauses of this Charter and those of the Peace Treaty of Hudaybiya.

> "State of war," has a special connotation. When state of war is declared, or, due to an act on the part of one of the parties, it comes into existence, legal implications of large number of acts and omissions, get new colour and receive enhanced dimensions. Acts aimed at spreading despondency, defeatism, anti-war slogans, or even those movements, which create internal dissensions, and undue and malicious criticism of the government and its functionaries, assume a dangerous posture and as a result are declared to be punishable by death or imprisonment according to the severity of the act. As a rule, in England, "if it amounts to wilful defiance of authority it is punishable under section a (1) with death."

Historians have reported the case of Kaab bin Ashraf, a member of the tribe of Tay, but was living in Yathrib, because of having married a local Jewish lady went away to Mecca and was guilty of inciting the Quraish against Medina. He returned to Medina, under dubious conditions, and continued his anti-state activities. A sentence of death was passed against him by the head of the state and he was killed in such a way that his death did not create any internal disturbance. Critics of the judgement passed against him have failed to realise that when he was punished the war had been going on for a considerable period and a state of war existed. His crimes were too many and too serious, not to be taken notice of.

It is a common practice among countries with parliaments, that the person or the office, where the authority to declare war lies, in addition to being the head of state, is not necessarily the head of the government as well. Under Imperial and Presidential systems, however, he functions as head of state and head of the government also. In addition he is the Commander-in-chief of the Armed Forces of the nation as well. The Prophet (PBUH) held these three positions in addition to having been accepted as the Prophet of Allah. He was, however, the head of the Government of Yathrib and Commander-in-chief of its Army, due to another and a practical reason. He was the only person, who could undertake the responsibilities of these two very important functions of the state. He was unlettered; but he had received training of the Highest Order from Allah Himself. He could and did undertake these responsibilities and carried them out successfully. It could not be otherwise. Allah the All Knowing has said of him:

"By the star when it setteth, your comrade erreth not, nor is deceived; nor doth he speak (of) his own desire. It is naught save an inspiration that is inspired, which one of mighty powers hath taught him".

(53:1-5)

As the legal head of Army it devolved on him to decide on the strength of the Army and the qualifications, training and capabilities of the soldiers and the commanders alike. His battles are a proof of the fact that he recruited, trained and led his army in the most efficient and profitable manner. The way he selected different commanders for each campaign, the way he gradually increased their responsibilities and the clarity with which he briefed them, when they were despatched on special missions, is a miracle, of which there is no explanation except that he had been trained by The Supreme Sovereign of this huge Universe and he received communications from the "Master of The Throne" every second of his life.

He alone knew and understood the Quraish and the likely manner of their offensive and the tenacity, with which they were likely to persist in their opposition to The New Way of Life, named Islam. He kept the collection of Military Intelligence also in his own hands. Security arrangements, public dealings both with elements within the state and abroad were retained by him, though, at times he used to have consultations with the inner circle of Companions on such matters. The art of war, if stated in brief words is very simple but it demands the attention of those, who know and understand their enemies. "The art of war, which being very simply defined as the art which enables any commander to worst the forces opposed to him." By the time this ended he had worsted over twenty adversaries, which included the Meccans, the Banu Ghatfan, the Jews of Khyber, and the first Army which the Emperor of Byzantium had sent to finish Islam, before it became a real threat to the sovereignty of the Eastern Roman Empire.

It has been said that war, "is not the condition of generalised and random violence.... it is on the contrary a highly social activity... as Rousseau has said, 'war without social organisation is inconceivable'." The Prophet (PBUH) is the first person in the history of war, who put restraints on War. He had to set up a state and a government to defend himself and the people, who had given him protection. In order to make his actions legal and based on reason and logic, he gave a Constitution to a place and people, who had no organised society and their abode was just a name of a piece of land and a small habitation, which did not have a state - not even a city state like the toddlers in civilisation— the Greeks.

This aspect of organizing the society in Yathrib, through a Constitutional Charter, has not been given proper attention by either early Muslim historians or students of modern history and other social sciences. The impact of thus organizing the society on the bases of Islamic Polity and the results achieved in smooth running of the government, resulting in the restrained conduct of war and relations with neighbour rulers from tribal Sheikhs to the rulers of the Empires of Byzantium and Iran have not been studied in detail. It is correct, that Ibne-Khaldun has derived a number of his conclusions from the Socio-Political development of Medina, but very little, if any, study has been undertaken by a social philosopher keeping the society of Medina and its influence on the lands conquered by Muslims.

Modern writers have taken pains to bring out the influence of earlier cultures and neighbouring civilisations on Islam, but they have touched the mere surface of influences and impacts made by the social structure of Medina, when its young and vigorous youth occupied first the Fertile Crescent and then lands upto Indus in the East and the shores of Atlantic on the West. This is not the occasion to go into all the Revelations received by Muhammad (PBUH) on the steps to be taken for the Defence of the *Ummah*. As we have touched on the preparations he had to undertake in this connection, it would not be out of place to briefly study one Verse of the *Quran*, on this subject.

Security and Safety

Make ready for them. This denotes the following.

1. The *Ummah*, which then consisted of mainly Yathrib had to raise men and material, for the enemy or enemies.

2. It indirectly hints, that Muslims have not to be the first to start war. If aggressive wars of conquest were permitted in Islam the words would have been different. Making ready for them means keeping ready until they come.

All your strength. This includes:

1. All human resources, each according to the task he can perform best. Under present circumstances obedience to this Command of Allah will have to be on the level of different political entities and finally on the level of the *Ummah*.

2. All material resources of all Muslim countries and within these countries of all individual Muslims. Unless preparations are made on a vast scale, the level of preparations laid down in this verse cannot be achieved.

And your tethered horses:

The human and material resources mentioned above was in addition to "tethered horses," which means, all the Armed Forces. It would include formations of tanks, armoured carriers, squadrons of bombers, fighters, and other types of military aircraft and naval Armadas. It would include all the regular and standing armed forces and reserve echelons. (The phrase "tethered horses" gives authority to standing Armed Forces.)

(So) That the enemies of Allah and your enemies and others beside them, whom you do not know but Allah knows them, are dismayed by it.

1. This wide range of enemies has to be dismayed, which means that the preparation should be to the extent, that it acts as a deterrent against known and unknown enemies.

2. Allah's enemies are all those who are enemies of Islam and those who persecute humanity, whether these weak people are Muslim or non-Muslim and the Muslims are expected to help them in getting free from their persecutors. (See Verse 4:75)

3. This duty falls to the entire Muslim *Ummah*. Let us pray, that we understand our duties according to the *Quran* as soon as possible. Otherwise even our future generations will fail to fulfil their duties. The Prophet (PBUH) defended Yathrib and eventually freed entire Arabia from persecution and ignorance. (This is only a part of Verse 8:60)

The Prophet (PBUH) had to organize the society of Yathrib, so that he could utilise in war all human and material resources, that could be made available. It was a difficult task, because the Muslims were still in minority. Students of his life and particularly of his battles with Mecca and its allies will notice that as the enemy's efforts increased, the organisation of society in Yathrib accelerated and the Muslims became more integrated. In every battle the strength of Muslim Army kept increasing. "An organisation, which will bring every available man.... in the shortest possible time and with utmost possible momentum" is considered ideal by modern military thinkers. This is what the first Supreme Commander of the Army of *Ummah* was able to accomplish through an efficient organisation of the society. He had seen to it, that the enemy did not find him in an unarmed condition, because, "The worst condition in which a belligerent can be placed is being completely disarmed."

Thus we find that from every angle and every point of view he was the only person, who was fit and qualified to declare as to when Yathrib or any one in Yathrib should go to war. To avenge earlier wrongs outside Yathrib was being permitted, but they were not to involve the state and government of Yathrib in war.

As far as the last part of this Clause, regarding the avenging of a wrong is concerned, it happens to have been universally accepted, that a wrong may be avenged. "Cicero insists on two elements necessary to the just war: one being a declaration in proper form, the other, a good reason for resort to violence. As good reason to violence he mentions only three: to avenge a wrong, to drive off an enemy, and to recover what is due."

EFFECT OF OTHER LAWS

As the time when Christianity was linked with secular power of the empire, St. Augustine, (354-430 A.C.) had to say, "Just wars are those which avenge injuries....," Centuries after St. Augustine, another Christian authority lays down the law for declaring war in a different manner. Jesuit Francisco Suarez (1545-1617) lays down, that "A sovereign may resort to war, in default of obtaining justice from Pope, to redeem an injury inflicted, and he may wage war for purposes of defence."

Clause 36.

"The Jews must bear their own expenses and the Muslim bear their expenses."

Clause 29 had laid down that when Jews are fighting alongside believers, they will contribute towards war. This only referred to general expenses like purchase

Security and Safety

of caterpillars and other weapons used jointly. There can be other expenses like blood money to be paid to an enemy if his men are killed by mistake after they had received proper safe conduct.

Clause 37.

Is regarding expenditure incurred on personnel, their mounts and personal equipment of fighters. As a rule this was undertaken by the individual himself, but occasions could arise as before *Ghazwa-e-Tabuk*[30], when the state had to provide riding animals to a number of people, although there were some for whom this facility could not be provided and they were left behind. It is interesting to know that the total strength of the Army of Yathrib which was 313 at Badr, had increased to an army of thirty thousand well equipped and well mounted disciplined soldiers in 9 A.H. We are told that one third of this force was equipped by Uthman, who later became the third *Khalifa*.

Clause 38.

"If anyone attacks anyone, who is a party to this Charter the others must come to his help."

This is a fair clause, getting an undertaking from all parties to a joint defence. It could be termed as the basis of a joint Defence arrangement by the head of the state. In a way, this was an indirect way of commenting all parties, through the Command of a central authority, which was superior to all. Primarily this clause would refer to attacks from outside Yathrib. It may appear, that it could have had reference to a party attacking from within. This does not appear possible because the text of the Charter gives a strong impression, that it was the whole of Yathrib requesting the Prophet (PBUH) to defend the city.

Keeping this object in view, he was organizing the state, the government and the society. An attack on a group, which was a party to the Charter from within Yathrib could not be even thought of, unless it amounted to an outright rebellion. Later events show that there were rebellions, but they, being armed rebellions, were dealt with in the proper manner. The first two tribes which rebelled were defeated before the Meccan and Banu Ghatfan could come to their help, but were pardoned and permitted to leave Yathrib with all their movable possessions.

Clause 39.

"They must seek mutual advice and consultation."

This clause is a follow on or it can be called a part of clause 39. All parties were being commanded to come to the help of one another, when attacked from abroad. This clause was laying down that success in joint defence could only be achieved if previous consultation between parties was carried out and advice, from one another, sought for and given freely.

Differences are possible to arise in any society. An heterogeneous society, being, imperceptibly taken towards a well knit unitary society, was bound to go through a certain period of tensions. It was, therefore, appropriate to lay down in clear words that they were all expected to consult one another and seek advice, whenever in doubt. Enough studies have not been undertaken on this earliest period of Muslim history. The rebellions of Jewish tribes having taken place, one after the other, and not simultaneously, must have been the result of sobering influence, on those Arab tribes, who had been giving them protection prior to this document. The subject needs further research, which, we hope, is undertaken by young scholars, who are conversant with other social sciences also.

Clause 40.

"Loyalty gives protection against treachery."

This clause is a continuation of Clauses 38 and 39. It was meant to bring home to the weaker elements, that they should not fall a prey to foreign propaganda in their own interest. In fact, the subject is related to Clause 35, which lays down that "no one shall go to war except with the permission of Muhammad (PBUH). Clause 36 deals with murder within the society and the subsequent clauses pertain to the question of war. Loyal conduct leads to cooperation and eventually integration is achieved. Disloyal thoughts lead to disloyal words which are followed by disloyal acts. Enemies of the state are always on the look out and select people, who have wilfully or inadvertently, been guilty of disloyalty. They persuade them, coerce them and eventually by the threat of revelation of their misdeeds force them to treacherous acts against the state.

Disloyal acts, in themselves, are a source of mental tensions and unrest. Fear of exposure robs such people of peace of mind and no amount of worldly gain can be a substitute for peace of mind. This warning, in this clause, is being given a second time. Under the circumstances, which were likely to develop as a result of Meccan invasion and subversive propaganda such repetition of the warning was appropriate. Social structure existed at that time very loosely, and was being strengthened by the Prophet (PBUH), in a gradual manner. It demanded, that enough warning was given to likely disruptive elements.

It was imperative to strengthen the defences of the state, both internally and externally. Man power was not only short, it was not of the best quality also. The Jews were keen to gain equality with Arabs and particularly with believers, and

Security and Safety

had requested to be allowed to fight alongside the believers. Their past was not very encouraging. They had not been very enthusiastic and loyal supporter of their own cause and had not honoured the call of one of their Prophets. They had insisted, that if they were provided with a king as a leader they would fight, but they eventually backed out.

> "He said: Would ye then refrain from fighting if fighting were prescribed for you? They said: Why should we not fight in the way of Allah when we have been driven from our dwellings with our children. Yet when fighting was prescribed for them, they all turned away all save a few of them." (2:246)

The story of Jew's reply to Moses (*Alayhis Salaam*) is well known. They had said:

> "So go thou and thy Lord and fight! We will sit here." (5:24)

Such was the material which he had to mould into men of courage, fearlessness and steadfastness of the standard, he had already inspired into the hearts of *Muhajirin* and *Ansars*. He had to point out the importance of loyalty and consequences of treachery. His warnings could not be delayed. Wars have been lost, more often, because of loss of opportunities and timely preparations. A modern statesman has remarked, "The history of failure in war can be summed up in two words. Too late. Too late in comprehending the deadly purpose of the potential enemy, too late in realising the mortal danger, too late in preparedness, too late in uniting all possible forces for resistance too late in standing with ones friends."

There is a great deal of weight, in what this seasoned statesman of twentieth century has said. Conditions then prevailing in Yathrib and deadly threat of certain invasion, did not allow any delay to the head of state of Yathrib and the supreme commander of its meagre forces. Disloyalty and treachery could not be ruled out and he was justified both in timely warning about it and insistence on bringing it home to all parties, the importance of complete and unalienated loyalty to him.

Clause 43.

> "The Jews must pay with the believers."

This Clause lays down, that even when the Jews do not take part in war but the believers have to incur expenditure as a result of war, they will have to pay part of the expenses. This was in addition to what had been laid down in the earlier two clauses dealing with payments to be made by Jews. Those two occasions were when the Jews were fighting alongside the believers. This Clause deals with payments of share of war expenses, as citizens of Yathrib, even though they may not have sent a contingent into the battle. The words "must pay with believers," signify a payment, which may have to be made without prior notice. The payment which had to be made after Beir Mauna, and which led to the rebellion of the Jewish tribe of Banu Nadhir, falls under this Clause. The Clause is worded as a Standing Order. There is no "if" or "when" about it. The payment has to be made, whenever it is demanded. As it is not an agreement but a part of the Fundamental Law, there is no question of the Jews tribe breaking away from it. They were to be governed by it as long as they lived in Yathrib. It being a legal obligation, mere refusal to make payment would amount to breaking of a law and an open rebellion.

Clause 44.

"Yathrib shall be sanctuary for the people of the Charter."

Strictly speaking this Clause does not fall under Laws pertaining to the defence of the state of Yathrib. The Clause, however, provides safety, continues safe conduct of normal activities of daily life, and complete mental relaxation and peace of mind, which permits loyal citizens to double their defence efforts, so that they and their families can lead a peaceful life. A sanctuary permitted unhindered preparation for war. Hence it can be considered as helping towards war efforts.

A sanctuary precluded internal disorder. The place gets a hollowed status, which people are afraid to disturb. It is, at the same time, mutual. If anyone dares to deprive his homeland of the status of a sanctuary he lays himself open, not only to censure, but a retaliatory attack, which will be more often than not, from more quarters than he can foresee.

Mecca had been a sanctuary for a long time. It was a city possessing enviable status. From now on Yathrib was to rival Mecca in this respect. It certainly was a matter of honour and prestige for its inhabitants whether believers or non-believers.

Clause 48.

"Quraish and their allies will not be given protection."

Clause 44 had declared Yathrib as sanctuary for those living in Yathrib. It was a natural heaven, a place of safety and an abode which promised protection. The next two clauses pertained to protection of different nature, which could be given subject to certain conditions, but it had to be clearly laid down, that under no circumstances could protection be given to the main enemy, the Quraish of Mecca.

People could give protection in the manner given in Clauses 45 and 46. But no member of the enemy clan, unless he proclaimed Islam, could enter the area of the sanctuary and claim protection on the strength, that it was an area of universal protection, as long as the war lasted. The Jews and other unbelievers could not give protection to a member of the Quraish, even otherwise. Clauses 25 and 26, debarred unbelievers from taking the property of Quraish under protection or intervening in favour of a member of the Quraish tribe. This Clause has been added because of Yathrib having been declared as a sanctuary for its inhabitants. A person, who is secure can normally give security to strangers. Here this protection or security could be given to every body except the enemy.

Clause 49.

> "The parties to this Charter are bound to help one another in the event of an attack on Yathrib."

This is clear cut order for joint defence of Yathrib. Any attack on any party residing in Yathrib was to be considered as an attack on all parties. This reasoning appears natural today, but Yathrib had, in the past, no common government, or even an agreement to consider Yathrib as a unit apart from all others. The main two Arab tribes had been fighting a war against one another. There had never been any understanding of jointly defending Yathrib. A Charter was being given to them all, making them subject to a common Law. It had to be clearly told to them, that if any one of the parties to the Charter was attacked it was to be considered as an attack on every body and Yathrib was to be defended jointly. Although the letter from Quraish, declaring war against Yathrib, had made it clear that the attack will be against all, but, from the point of view of joint defence being made certain, it was essential that the text of the Charter also made it clear.

Clause 50.

> "If they (the others) are called upon to make and maintain peace they must do so. If a similar demand is made on the Muslims, it must be carried out, except when the Muslims are already engaged in a war in the Path of Allah."

This Clause would not have been needed in normal circumstances where every body knew the position and force of a Fundamental Law of the land. It had been categorically stated that no one will go to war without the permission of Muhammad (PBUH) (Clause 35). It was, however, possible that one of the parties ignored that order and started a small war of their own with a neighbouring tribe. This Clause lays down, that in such an eventuality the call to make and maintain peace will be obeyed at once.

To maintain the semblance of equality it was being stipulated that, if the believers were also called upon to make and maintain peace, they will also abide by this decision of the others. There was, however, a very important proviso. If the believers were fighting, in the Path of Allah, they will carry it on till its logical end. The believers were not going to fight a war except in the Path of Allah. Therefore there was no possibility of such a call being made to them.

It is difficult to imagine the intricate situation, in which the Prophet (PBUH) was placed. He had to deal with unwilling partners as far as fighting was concerned.

The following verse refers to this very people, when new entrants into the fold of Islam had not yet been inspired with the full meaning of belief in Allah.

> "Warfare is ordained for you, though it is hateful to you, but it may happen that ye hate a thing which is good for you and it may happen that ye love a thing which is bad for you. Allah knoweth, ye know not."
>
> (2:216)

War had been declared with the object of annihilating him, either through the Yathribites, or, failing that, by a direct attack on Yathrib. He had undertaken to defend Yathrib and in order to accomplish it he had started organizing the society, in a manner that he could pursue the dual responsibility of propagating Islam, while at the same time, defending the territories of Yathrib. He had placed every future move of his on legal basis. He had, at the same time to see, that his decisions and his actions, particularly when they were submitted to pen and paper, had to have the applicability of a precedent for all ages. On the one hand there were those, who did not understand, what were the implications of a written Constitutional Law and on the other would be followers, after the lapse of centuries, who will have to read and study them, not as a part of historical document, but as Guidelines from the Last Messenger of Allah. We believe, that although the task appears impossible, to us, he was able to accomplish it, as a result of Guidance from Allah The Exalted. It is reasonable to believe, that, if guided by his precepts we will also succeed.

Clause 56.

> "Whether an individual goes out to fight or remains in his house, he will be safe, unless he has committed a crime or is a sinner."

The state of Yathrib was created, apart from the need of setting up a society, for the defence of Yathrib, as a model society for future generations, when life would have become far more complicated. A time would come when those, who remained at home, and did not march to the battlefield, would be contributing towards war effort, through their pen, or a number of other tasks, which are performed for the support of men fighting in the trenches, at sea and in the air. The state and its defence were, in this case, complimentary. The enemy had declared war and defensive measures had to be taken. The question arose, as to, what was to be defended? If the answer was given, that Yathrib was to be defended, then the question arose, as to, what exactly was Yathrib? If it was a country, then it must have a state and a government to arrange and supervise the defence of this piece of territory. The next question, that could be asked was regarding the extent of the territory.

The Prophet (PBUH) answered this question, in the most practical way by taking out thirty to forty *Muhajir* companions with him to visit neighbouring tribes and conduct details of treaties of friendship between himself, as head of the state of Yathrib, and the chiefs as heads of those tribes. The area covered by such journies constituted the territories of the Islamic state of Yathrib. Speaking, both, from theoretical and practical point of view, the World of Islam has no fixed boundaries. Boundaries of Islam expand, as the people of adjoining lands embrace Islam or seek protection under the rule of Muslims. The world of Islam diminishes in extent of territory, when Muslims fail to protect them and un-Islamic Laws are proclaimed there. If the population still manages to adhere, even nominally, to Islam, then those individuals, theoretically at least, continue to belong to the world of Islam. The citizens of free Islamic states of today, have a duty to continue in their efforts to free such communities according to Verse 177 of *Surah Al-Baqarah*. To "set free people from bondage," is one of the eight headings for spending *Zakat*[31] and *Sadaqaat*[32].

The initial territories of the state, which had been created through this document, given by Muhammad (PBUH) to believers, and those who followed the believers, had thus been demarcated by these early *Ghazawat* undertaken by the Prophet (PBUH) for diplomatic purposes and for training and acquainting his Companions with the area in which they were likely to operate during the forthcoming struggle.

Because of the fact, that the state of Yathrib had been created as a result of the impending invasion and the Charter was being issued to define and bring to light various aspects of defence requirements, it could create ideas in the minds of some people, that absence from taking part in war, in active capacity, may not be considered a crime. The Prophet (PBUH) realised that, conscription, was not advisable in a mixed society, where a large number had not yet accepted Islam, in spite of the fact that they had accepted the leadership of Muslims and imposition of Muslim *Shariah*.

This concession, however, did not apply to believers. They were the main target of Meccan fury. They had volunteered to defend Yathrib. Commandments for them were to be Revealed from time to time. The Command, "Fighting is Ordained for you" (2:216) belongs to pre-Badr period, but it cannot be said with certainty whether it was revealed before this document or after.

Humanity has taken recourse to war on countless occasions. This has happened in spite of the contention of followers of every religion that the religion they follow is a religion of peace. It is true, that later generations of Muslims transgressed and apart from embarking on conquests, were guilty of internecine warfare as well. The battles of the period of the Prophet (PBUH) and his successors were the result of aggression against territories of the state of Medina, which had been acquired as a result of Defensive War or expansion of Islam itself. The wars between the state of Medina and the two adjacent Empires of Byzantium and Iran had been initiated by the rulers of these two Empires. They lost the earlier battles and in retaliation continued to attack Muslim forces again and again. The "state of war", having been brought about by the rulers of these Empires, the blame for subsequent wars lies at the door of Christian Byzantium and Iran.

> This document, the Constitutional Charter of Medina, was dictated for the purposes of defending Yathrib and yet it does not say a word about attack being mounted against an outsider. It refers to "fighting in the Path of Allah," which prohibits aggressive wars and transgression even when war has been started by the enemy. (See Verse 2:190)

The war started by Mecca against Islam was in every respect a war of aggression and yet the Meccans claimed that they were on the right path because they were protecting their interests. This human failing, of going to war, under the excuse of the need to protect one's interest, has become common during the last two centuries. "Every generation believed its war to be just, defending values, that could not be otherwise protected, and that its war would be the last." In spite of it there are thinkers who maintain, that mankind knows how to stop war.

> "We already know how to stop war. The world has method for preventing these entirely." The remedy suggested by this writer has not yet been developed into an effective force. He says, "When the U.N. has become strong, we will no longer have to waste our time, our money, our thought, blood and in war."

This Clause, of the Charter, permitted, the unbelievers, had to ignore the call to "march to the battlefield," because war in Islam is neither for the fulfilment of individuals glory or collective gain. The only fighting Commanded in Islam is against aggression and persecution and that also to the believers only. To embark on an offensive war to save imaginary interests is not fighting in the Path of Allah. Most nations will march into the territories of other people or occupy areas, while contravening the undertakings given in solemn treaties, but there are few nations, who would try to restrain other nations from embarking on undertakings contrary to their treaty obligations. The Second World War was the result of Nazi Germany marching into many countries and not being checked by others, who merely stood and watched. The beginning was made with the march into Rhineland, in which, "Some of the French wanted to march, but did not quite have the nerve. Most of the British wanted to temporize and did Hitler not only invaded the Rhineland, by so doing, he automatically tore up the Treaty of Locarno, which had been a bastion of European peace since 1925."

According to this document, Yathrib was not to march against any other power. Islam believed in universal peace. The Prophet of Islam, as such, could not advocate breach of peace. He, therefore, left it to the conscience of every unbeliever individual to defend, whether he would like to share in the war, which was to be fought in the Path of Allah. The philosophy of "Fighting in the Path of Allah," was new to the world. It was to be only against persecutors of Allah's "Most Balanced Creation," the Man.

The grandeur of the mere thought of fighting for the pleasure of being an obedient servant of Allah is a rare feeling. Those who do not believe in Allah have, as a result, to call defensive war, as "fighting for oneself." As a result Mao Tse Tung, had to name, a justifiable war, as fighting for oneself. He writes, "The Red Army has abolished the mercenary system, making the men feel, that they are fighting for themselves, and for the people and not for anyone else.... and they know, that they are fighting for themselves, for the working class and the peasantry"

Muslims were fighting for Allah and the future of Allah's most balanced creation, mankind. Those, who had not had the good fortune to believe in Allah, could not be coerced into a war in the Path of Allah. If the Laws pertaining to defence, promulgated through this document, are compared with laws, issued by modern states during war, it will be found, that very few restrictions were being placed on the civil population. The second point of significance is, that this Charter was of permanent nature and needed no subsequent documents adding more restrictions for the common man. Curtailment of liberties has become a common feature of modern wartime instructions and notifications. "During the time of war changes in laws have been so far reaching and the laws have been speaking with such multitude of voices, that the ordinary citizen has found himself in a state of complete bewilderment. The operation of these war time laws has drastically affected the daily life of the citizens in all its spheres."

The war declared against Yathrib had the object of annihilating Islam and Muslims and yet restrictions placed on the civil population were so few, that it did not disturb the normal pattern of the life of every individual. This was so, because, the object before the Prophet (PBUH) was not war, but the establishment of a society which would give peace to all round them. The establishment of such a society demanded men who could distinguish themselves both in peace and war.

"Muhammad is the messenger of Allah. And those with him are hard against the disbelievers and merciful among themselves." (48:29)

The Prophet (PBUH) and his Companions fought a war, which was forced on them for ten years, during his life-time, but this was not their main preoccupation. They were establishing a unique society which had been given the task of purging evil and establishing good. Allah has said:

"You are the best community that hath been raised up for mankind. Ye enjoin right conduct and forbid indecency; and ye believe in Allah."
(3:110)

He had to train them for this task. An eminent writer has said, "It would, however, be a serious mistake to imagine that Muhammad's interest and attention, during these years, were given up solely to politics and war. On the contrary, the centre of all his preoccupations was the training, educating, and discipline of his community." His attention remained focussed on creating a society of saints, a society of men and women who were devoted to Allah in all their deeds. The individual training of belief in Allah had been finalised in Mecca. The collective training of creating a model society was accomplished in Medina.

References

1. *Those who migrated from Mecca to Medina alongwith the Prophet (Pbuh).*
2. *Whole of the followers of Islam; a community.*
3. *Martyrdom.*
4-7. *Tribes.*
8. *The sin of worshipping or calling others except Allah.*
9. *A philosopher and thinker of the west who wrote regarding Islam.*
10. *A famous leader of Iran who made attempts to attack India. And caused the power of Muslim dynasty weak.*
11. *Islamic law.*
12. *Caliph or vicegerent.*
13. *A great mathematician, who goaded Halaku to march against Baghdad.*
14. *Caliphate or vicegerency.*
15. *Most respected and trusted tribe of Mecca where Prophet (Pbuh) was born.*
16. *The biggest hypocrite; leader of hypocrites.*
17. *Migration.*
18. *Those who migrated.*
19. *A term used for Chinese Muslims; those who believed in the life hereafter.*
20. *Those who helped the Prophet (on his arrival) at Medina.*
21-27. *Companion of the Prophet (Pbuh)*
28. *Old name of Medina.*
29. *Former Prime Minister of England who was an arch enemy of Islam.*
30. *Battle of Tabuk.*
31. *Alms-giving.*
32. *Charity given in the way of Allah.*

9

GUIDELINES FOR RULERS

ART OF GOVERNANCE

The political system of Islam has been based on three principles, viz: *Tauhid*[1] (Unity of God), *Risala*[2] (Prophethood) and *Khilafa* (Caliphate). It is difficult to appreciate the different aspects of Islamic polity without fully understanding these three principles. We will therefore begin with a brief exposition of them.

Tauhid means that one God alone is the Creator, Sustainer and Master of this universe and of all that exists in it—organic or inorganic. The sovereignty of this kingdom is vested only in Him. He alone has the right to command or forbid. Worship and obedience are due to Him alone, none else sharing it in any degree or form. Life, in all its multifarious forms, our own physical organs and faculties, the apparent control which we have over everything that exists in this universe, and the things themselves—none of them has been created or acquired by us in our own right.

They are the bountiful provisions of God and in bestowing them upon us, He is associated with no one. Hence, it is not for us to decide the aim and purpose of our existence or to prescribe the limits of our worldly authority nor is anyone else entitled to make these decisions for us. This right rests only in God, who has created us, endowed us with mental and physical faculties, and all material provisions for our use. This principle faculties, and all material provisions for our use. This principle of the Unity of God altogether negates the concept of the legal and political sovereignty of human beings. No individual, family, class or race can set themselves above God. God alone is the Ruler and His commandments are the law of Islam.

The medium through which we receive the law of God is known as *risala* (Prophethood). We have received two things from this source:

(a) The Quran, the Book in which God has expounded His law; and

(b) the authoritative interpretation and exemplification of the Book of God by the Prophet Muhammad, through word and deed, in his capacity as the representative of God.

The broad principles on which the system of human life should be based have been stated in the Book of God. Further, the Prophet of God has, in accordance with the Divine Book, set up a model of the system of life in Islam by practically implementing the law and providing necessary details where required. The combination of these two elements, according to Islamic terminology, is called the *Shariah*.

Let us now consider *Khilafa*, which means "representation". The real position and place of man, according to Islam, is that of the representative of God on this earth, His vicegerent; that is to say, by virtue of the powers delegated to him by God, he is required to exercise Divine authority in this world within the limits prescribed by God.

Now take, for example, the case of an estate of yours which someone else has been appointed to administer on your behalf. You will see that four conditions are invariably fulfilled in this case. First, the real ownership of the estate remains vested in you and not in the administrator; secondly, he administers your property only in accordance with your instructions; thirdly, he exercises his authority within the limits prescribed by you; and fourthly, in the administration of the trust he executes your will and fulfils your intention and not his own. These four conditions are so inherent in the very concept of "representation" that they come to mind as soon as one utters the word "representation". If any representative does not fulfil these four conditions he will naturally be blamed for abusing his authority and for breaking the covenant which was implied in the concept of "representation"

This is exactly what Islam means when it affirms that man is the representative *(Khalifa)* of God on earth. Hence, these four conditions are also involved in the concept of *Khilafa*. The state that is established in accordance with this political theory will in fact be a Caliphate under the sovereignty of God and will have to fulfil the purpose and Will of God by working on God's earth within the limits prescribed by Him and in accordance with His instructions and injunctions.

JUST SYSTEM

The above explanation of the term *khilafa* also makes it abundantly clear that no individual or dynasty or class can be *Khalifa,* but that the authority of *khilafa* is bestowed on the entire group of people, the community as a whole, which is ready to fulfil the conditions of representation after subscribing to the principles of *Tauhid* (Unity of God) and *risala* (Prophethood). Such a society carries the responsibility of the *khilafa* as a whole and each one of its individuals shares the Divine *khilafa.* This is the point where democracy begins in Islam. Every person in an Islamic society enjoys the rights and powers of the Caliphate of God and in this respect all individuals are equal. No one takes precedence over another or can deprive anyone else of his rights and powers.

The agency for running the affairs of the state will be formed with the will of these individuals, and the authority of the state will only be an extension of the powers of the individuals delegated to it. Their opinion will be decisive in the formation of the government which will be run with their advice and in accordance with their wishes. Whoever gains their confidence will undertake the duty and obligations of the Caliphate on their behalf: and when he loses this confidence he will have to step down. In this respect the political system of Islam is a perfect form of democracy—as perfect as a democracy can ever be. Of course what distinguishes Islamic democracy from Western democracy is that while the latter is based on the concept of popular sovereignty the former rests on the principle of popular *khilafa.*

In Western democracy, the people are sovereign, in Islam sovereignty is vested in God and the people are His Caliphs or representatives. In the former the people make their own laws; in the latter they have to follow and obey the laws *(Shariah)* given by God through His Prophet. In one the government undertakes to fulfil the will of the people; in the other the government and the people who form it have all to fulfil the purpose of God. In brief, Western democracy is a kind of absolute authority which exercises its powers in a free and uncontrolled manner whereas Islamic democracy is subservient to the Divine law and exercises its authority in accordance with the injunctions of God and within the limits prescribed by Him.

MOTIVES AND AIMS

This being the essence of Islamic Political Theory, we may now examine the type of state which is built on the foundations of *Tauhid* (the Unity of God), *risala* (the Prophethood of Muhammad) and *khilafa* (the Caliphate).

The Holy Quran clearly states that the aim and purpose of this state is the establishment, maintenance and development of those virtues which the Creator of this universe wishes human life to be enriched by and the prevention and eradication of those evils the presence of which in human life is utterly abhorrent to God. The State of Islam is not intended for political administration only nor for the fulfilment through it of the collective will of any particular set of people; rather, Islam places a high ideal before the state for the achievement of which it must use all the means at its disposal. And this purpose is that the qualities of purity, beauty, goodness, virtue, success and prosperity which God wants to flourish in the life of His people should be engendered and developed and that all kinds of exploitation, injustice and disorder which, in the sight of God, are ruinous for the world and detrimental to the life of His creatures are suppressed and prevented. As well as placing before us this high ideal Islam gives us a clear outline of its moral system stating positively the desired virtues and the undesirable evils. Keeping this outline in view the Islamic state can plan its welfare programme in every age and in any environment.

The persistent demand made by Islam is that the principles of morality must be observed at all cost and in all walks of life. Hence, it lays down an unalterable policy for the state to base its politics on justice, truth, and honesty. It is not prepared, under any circumstances whatsoever, to tolerate fraud, falsehood and injustice for the sake of any political, administrative or national expediency. Whether it be relations between the rulers and the ruled within the state, or the relations of the state with other states, precedence must always be given to truth, honesty, and justice over material considerations. It imposes similar obligations on the state as on the individual, viz: to fulfil all contracts and obligations, to have uniform standards for dealings; to remember duties along with the rights and not to forget the rights of others when expecting them to fulfil their obligations; to use power and authority for the establishment of justice and not for the perpetration of injustice; to look upon duty as a sacred obligation and to fulfil it scrupulously; and to regard power as a trust from God and use it with the belief that one has to render an account of one's actions to Him in the life Hereafter.

FUNDAMENTAL GUARANTEES

Although an Islamic state may be set up in any part of the earth, Islam does not seek to restrict human rights or privileges to the geographical limits of its own state. Islam has laid down some universal fundamental rights for humanity as a whole, which are to be observed and respected under all circumstances whether such a person is resident within the territory of the Islamic state or outside it, whether he is at peace with the state or at war. Human blood is sacred in any case and cannot be spilled without justification. It is not permissible to oppress women, children, old people, the sick or the wounded. Woman's honour and chastity are to be respected under all circumstances.

The hungry person must be fed, the naked clothed, and the wounded or diseased treated medically irrespective of whether they belong to the Islamic community or are from amongst its enemies. These, and other provisions have been laid down by Islam as fundamental rights for everyman by virtue of his status as a human being to be enjoyed under the constitution of an Islamic state. Even the rights of citizenship in Islam are not confined to persons born within the limits of its state but are granted to every Muslim irrespective of his place of birth. A Muslim *ipso facto* becomes the citizen of an Islamic state as soon as he sets his foot on its territory with the intent to live there and thus enjoys equal rights of citizenship along with those who acquire its citizenship by birth. Citizenship has therefore to be common among all the Islamic states that (may) exist in the world and a Muslim will not need any passport for entry to or exit from any of them. And every Muslim is to be regarded as eligible and fit for all positions of the highest responsibility in an Islamic state without distinction of race, colour or class.

Islam has also laid down certain rights for the non-Muslims who may be living within the boundaries of an Islamic state and these rights must necessarily form part of the Islamic constitution. According to the Islamic terminology such non-Muslims are called *dhimmis* (the covenanted), implying that the Islamic state has entered into a covenant with them and guaranteed their protection. The life, property and honour of a *dhimmi*[3] (non-Muslim citizen) is to be respected and protected exactly like that of a Muslim citizen. There is no difference at all between a Muslim and a non-Muslim citizen in respect of the civil or criminal law. The Islamic state shall not interfere with the personal rights of the non-Muslims. They will have full freedom of conscience and belief and will be at liberty to perform their religious rites and ceremonies in their own way. Not only can they propagate their religion but they are entitled even to criticize Islam within the limits laid down by law and decency.

The rights given in this respect are not limited, but the civil law of the country is to be fully respected and all criticism will have to be made within its framework which would be applicable to all citizens of the state. These, as well as many other rights, have been granted to the *dhimmis* in Islam. These rights are of an irrevocable nature. The non-Muslims cannot be deprived of them unless they renounce the covenant which grants them citizenship. Whatever be the extent of oppression which a non-Muslim state may perpetrate on its Muslim citizens it is not permissible for an Islamic state to retaliate on its non-Muslim subjects in the slightest degree; even if all the Muslims outside the boundaries of an Islamic state are massacred, the state cannot unjustly shed the blood of a single non—Muslim citizen living within its boundaries.

WINGS FOR GOVERNANCE

The responsibility for the administration of the government, in an Islamic state, is entrusted to an *amir* (leader) who may be compared to the president or the prime minister in a modern democratic state. All adult men and women who believe in the fundamentals of the constitution will be entitled to vote for the election of the *amir*.

The basic qualifications for the election or an *amir* are that he should command the confidence of the largest number of people in respect of his knowledge and grasp of the spirit of Islam; he should possess the Islamic quality of fear of God and be endowed with qualities of statesmanship. In short, he should have both virtue and ability. A *shura* (advisory council) is also to be elected by the people for assisting and guiding the *amir* in the administration of the state. It will be incumbent on the *amir* to administer the country with the advice of this *shura*. The *amir* can retain office only so long as he enjoys the confidence of the people and will have to relinquish his office when he loses this confidence. But as long as he retains such confidence he will have the authority to govern and exercise the powers of government in consultation with the *shura* (advisory council) and within the limits set by the *Shariah*. Every citizen will have the right to criticize the *amir* and his government and all reasonable means for the ventilation of public opinion will be available.

The Legislation : Legislation in an Islamic state will be restricted within the limits prescribed by the law of the *Shariah*. The injunctions of God and His Prophet are to be accepted and obeyed and no legislative body can make any alterations or modifications in them or make any law contrary to them. As for the commandments which are liable to two or more interpretations the duty of ascertaining the real intent of the *Shariah*, in such cases, will rest on people possessing a specialised knowledge of the law of the Shariah. Hence such affairs will have to be referred to a sub-committee of the advisory council comprising men learned in Islamic law. Great scope will still be available for legislation on questions not covered by any specific injunctions of the *Shariah* and the advisory council or legislature will be free to legislate in regard to these matters.

Judiciary : In Islam the judiciary is not placed under the control of the executive. It derives its authority directly from the *Shariah* and is answerable to God. The judges should be appointed by the government but once a judge has occupied the bench he will have to administer justice among the people according to the law of God in an impartial manner, and the organs and functionaries of the government will not be outside his legal jurisdiction, so that even the highest executive authority of the government is liable to be called upon to appear in a court of law as a plaintiff or defendant like any other citizen of the state. Rulers and ruled are subject to the same law and there can be no discrimination on the basis of position, power or privilege. Islam stands for equality and scrupulously sticks to this principle in social, economic and political realms alike.

SETUP AND STRUCTURE

The arrival of the Prophet (PBUH) at Medina in A.D. 622, marked the first step towards the establishment of an Islamic state. Considering that Medina was still inhabited by non-Muslims, atheist Arabs, and Jews, the Prophet (PBUH) in his first legislative act drew the lines, in a convention, that would regulate relations between the different factions of the citizens of Medina.

In the first part of his ten years of leadership in Medina, Prophet Muhammad (PBUH) laid down the foundation of a city-state, that would grow within a few years to encompass the whole Arabian Peninsula. He started with the construction of a mosque that would serve as a school, a centre for consultations and information, a court for receiving envoys and delegations, as well as a place for worship and prayers. He constructed a market place for the Muslims to counter that of the Jews. He then directed his efforts to building a Muslim army. In the latter part of his stay in Medina, he assigned to his governors and representatives the different parts of Arabia.

Laying down the basis for the subsequent rules guiding relations of the Islamic state with other countries, Prophet Muhammad (PBUH) set good examples in his diplomatic correspondence with foreign royalty, in the dispatch of envoys to neighbouring districts, in the establishment of new rules, or the implementation of old ones. These were related to the laws of peace and war, and the modalities and contents of the agreements that, he concluded with the opposing parties. He was thus paving new roads and giving a new meaning to the concept of international diplomacy.

During the succeeding periods of the four Orthodox Caliphs and the Umayyad rule (A.D. 631-750), the Islamic state witnessed an era of expansion that brought it into direct contact and interaction with the Byzantine, the Persian and the Chinese Empires and peoples. The experience and sophistication of these civilisations enriched Islamic culture and concept. It was during the Abbaside period (A.D. 750-900) that the Islamic state, reaching its peak in political influence, cultural maturity and economic prosperity, represented the universal state.

Medina Convention : When the Prophet (PBUH) and his Meccan disciples reached Medina, it was inhabited by two major tribes, the Aus and the Khazraj, which had long been feuding with each other. In addition, there were several Jewish communities in Medina. Besides the Aus and the Khazraj, not all of whom were Muslims yet, the Medina society consisted of the Muslim exiles from Mecca, the Muslim helpers from Medina and the non-Muslim Arabs and Jews. In these circumstances, Prophet Muhammad (PBUH) became the teacher, arbitrator and the centre of all powers.

In this capacity he applied himself first to the task of introducing order in Medina and organizing relations among different factions on a proper basis. With this objective in mind he issued a charter, by which blood feud was abolished and lawlessness repressed. Equal rights were granted to the Jews, who committed themselves to helping the Muslims in defending the city.

In this convention, to which all the communities adhered, the Prophet (PBUH) considered the Muslims, whether exiles from Mecca (Muhajerun) or helpers from Medina (Ansar), as one community (Ummah), while addressing each one of the Jewish communities as a separate entity. Those who allied themselves with the Muslims would have their support and be on an equal footing.

The parties to the Charter of Medina would conduct war or peace collectively. No party would unilaterally conclude peace with a belligerent adversary or wage war against a third party by itself. No one among the non-believers (Mushrikin) was to grant protection (Aman) to a Quraishite or to his property, nor would he prevent a faithful from acting against a Quraishite.

The Jews would share the expenses with the faithful. As long as they were fighting, the Jews of Bani Auf were an Ummah (a community) with the faithfuls. They had their own faith just as the Muslims had theirs. The Jews of Bani-Al-Harith, the Jews of Bani Saedah, the Jews of Bani Jusham, the Jews of Bani Al-Aus, of Bani Thalabah, had the same (rights) as those of the Jews of Bani-Auf.

No one from the Quraish or from those who supported it would be granted the protection of the parties to the convention. They (the parties to the convention) would support each other against any other party that would attack Medina. Anyone leaving Medina or staying in it would be safe, except for those committing injustice or misdeed.

Thus, the main political features of the convention were:

> For the first time in the history of Hijaz, a political unity was formed of the different factions and tribes of Medina under the leadership of the Prophet (PBUH).

- The influence of the Jews, which prevailed in the past due to their manipulation of the hostilities among the Medina tribes, was to be countered and minimised.

- The Prophet (PBUH) then secured not only a fortified front against any possible attack from his declared enemies, the Quraishites, but also formed the first ring in the chain that would besiege Mecca and contribute to its weakening. From there he could divert his attention to the most immediate business of organizing the state affairs, internally and externally.

Formation of the State : In establishing the structure of the new state, Prophet Muhammad (PBUH) built a mosque that would serve as a headquarter, as well as a place of prayers. He then designated a new commercial centre for the Muslims, apart from the old one which was controlled by the Jews. By such an undertaking he laid the foundation for an economic structure of the state that would function on the basis of Islamic principles, free from the influence of the Medina Jews.

From the first day of his arrival in Medina, the Prophet (PBUH) concerned himself with the formation of a military force, well organised and trained, that would be capable of defending the state and safeguarding its interests. The Islamic army was assigned military expeditions, that would serve the ultimate political and diplomatic ends. The frequent attacks on the trade caravans, going to and coming from Mecca, were intended to weaken the Quraishite economic power. At the same time these expeditions served as training experiments as well as a show of strength to other Arab tribes in the region.

On the international front, the Prophet (PBUH) dispatched a number of envoys with messages to monarchs and leaders of the neighbouring states and tribes, acquainting them with the new faith and inviting them to embrace it. He sent a messenger to the Emperor of Persia and another to the Byzantine Emperor. The former tore the message and banished the envoy from his presence, whilst the Byzantine Emperor received the ambassador with considerable courtesy. A third envoy, sent to a prince subordinated to the Byzantine, in the Damascus region, was cruelly murdered.

Islamic Era : At the age of forty, Prophet Muhammad (PBUH) received his Commission and started to preach the new faith of Islam. The name 'Islam' came from an Arabic expression which implied complete 'surrender' to Allah, the one and only God. He, therefore, called for abandoning the old beliefs, repudiating paganism and discarding many inherited traditions and superstitions. Beginning with his immediate family and close relatives from Quraish, the Prophet (PBUH) gradually widened his circle of activities to include all the inhabitants of Mecca and those groups who came to visit it during the seasonal pilgrimage.

Although the new religion adopted many of the traditions and values prevailing in that society, it was a potent blow to the dominant social structure and its basic values. It is comprehensible, then, that the initial mild rejection of the Meccan leaders to the new faith became a fierce resistance as it spread. Prophet Muhammad's (PBUH) adversaries pursued an escalating opposition that started with dialogue and negotiations. It was stepped up with the application of different kinds of pressure and culminated with the torture of those professing adherence to the new faith.

The heads of the Quraish clans perceived Prophet Muhammad (PBUH) 'as the head of the community, however small, like a state within a state.' The relations between the two communities and their leaders, in many aspects, followed a course similar to that, which existed between two states. In conducting these relations, the methodology used was not far from diplomatic practices prevailing nowadays. In resolving their differences, both sides resorted to dialogue and negotiations, employing 'intelligence' and 'tact' and implied promises or threats. They applied these skills in their direct contacts or through their envoys and delegations. Both parties suggested compromises, and at certain stages accepted them.

Prophet Muhammad (PBUH), in his discourses resorted to persuasive arguments and discreet preaching: 'Call unto the way of thy Lord with wisdom and fair exhortation, and reason with them in a way that is best and most gracious.' On the other hand, the leaders of Quraish, who could not use force or inflict on Prophet Muhammad (PBUH) the same mischief they had inflicted on his followers—as he belonged to a strong and respected family of Quraish—had to opt for the diplomatic practice available to them. They sent delegations to his uncle and protector, Abu Talib, on three occassions, and each time they used a different approach. Failing to find a solution, they decided to negotiate directly with Prophet Muhammad (PBUH). On these three occasions they tried again either to strike a deal or to challenge his prophetic missions, or to reach a compromise. Both parties sent delegations outside of Mecca and both met with representatives coming to Mecca in their endeavours to win alliances or to obstruct the other party's manoeuvers to do so.

Delegations within Mecca : The Quraish tribe, fearing the spread of Islam among the people of Mecca and its repercussions on their prestige, values and beliefs, decided to send a delegation to Abu Talib, the Prophet's (PBUH) uncle and protector, demanding that either he prevent his nephew from pursuing his discourse or denounce him. The delegation which consisted of some dignitaries explained to Abu Talib the harm that Prophet Muhammad (PBUH) was causing to their beliefs and traditions. They pointed out that Abu Talib, who did not embrace the new faith himself, was in disagreement with Prophet Muhammad

(PBUH), as they were. However, Abu Talib apparently mollified them before they left.

On the second occasion, the Quraish delegation came to Abu Talib and used a threatening tone, asking him to prevent his nephew from opposing their beliefs. They told him that if he continued to do nothing about it they would fight him.

Abu Talib conveyed this to his nephew and requested him not to burden him with a load that could prove to be too heavy for him to shoulder. The Prophet (PBUH) replied that even if the sun were placed in his right hand and the moon in his left, he would never relinquish his mission.

The third delegation from the Quraish came to Abu Talib with a third option. They suggested that he deliver Prophet Muhammad (PBUH) to them and they give him in exchange Amarah bin al-Walid, who was a wise and presentable young man from the family of Quraish. Abu Talib condemned this sort of bargaining where he 'was to deliver his adopted son to be killed', as he put it, 'while accepting their son to be fed and protected.'

In the three encounters, it is to be noted that both sides had observed the prevailing social (tribal) norms when they pursued their patterns of negotiations, namely, the obligation to stand on the side of the family and to help and defend even those members whose point of view they did not share. The Quraish recognised Abu Talib's family obligations and the latter accepted this burden despite the fact that he did not share Prophet Muhammad's (PBUH) belief. It is worth mentioning that both sides resorted to their verbal skills and persuasive arguments throughout their talks. Also both sides implied latent power in supporting their respective positions. The Quraish delegations implied the unanimity of the Quraish clans and their firm resolution. Abu Talib reckoned on his family prestige and the fact that it could not be easily challenged. Prophet Muhammad (PBUH) expressed his steadfastness and confidence in the support of God who would help His faith to ultimately prevail.

In the second phase of these encounters, the Quraish leaders decided to contact Prophet Muhammad (PBUH) directly and to talk him out of his discourse. In the first attempt they agreed on sending one of their dignitaries known for his knowledge of soothsaying and poetry. They selected Utbah bin Rabiah, who met Prophet Muhammad (PBUH) and started his negotiation by referring to the damage the Prophet (PBUH) was inflicting on his peoples' beliefs and idols. Then, questioning his motives for rejecting the creed of his kinsmen they offered to reward him if he abandoned his mission. Utbah conveyed to him their readiness to make him the richest man, if he sought wealth, or to concede to his leadership if he sought honour and prestige. In reply, Prophet Muhammad (PBUH) read to him a passage of the Quran related to the questions in the mind of the delegate about the Prophet (PBUH), the Quran, and the core of the new faith.

When Utbah returned to his people he advised them to leave him to what he was striving to accomplish, assuming that if he prevailed, then his rule over the Arabs 'would be your rule and his glory would be yours' and that if he were killed by the Arabs, then 'they would have saved you the effort.'

This argument did not convince the Quraish. Their leaders decided to launch another attempt. This time they invited Prophet Muhammad (PBUH) to meet them by the Kaaba. They started the negotiations by repeating their previous complaints and offers. Then they stepped up the offensive. They challenged his God's power, requesting him to move the mountain or to bring the rivers into their land or to resurrect their ancestors, so they could testify to his authenticity. Prophet Muhammad (PBUH) based his argument on the rationality and logic of his mission rather than on miraculous proofs or supernatural manifestations. He kept telling them after every request that it was not for that, that he was commissioned, but that God had sent him as His Apostle to deliver His message.

In their third attempt, the Quraish leaders sought to reach a compromise. They sent a delegation of four dignitaries, who proposed to Prophet Muhammad (PBUH) that they worship his God and he worship their gods. If either party was the true one, then both parties would benefit from their common practice. The Prophet's (PBUH) response was a firm rejection of this bid and it was expressed in the Quran as 'Say: O ye that reject the faith! I worship not that which ye worship. Nor will ye worship that which I worship... to you be your religion and to me my religion.' One can interpret this encounter and the aim of the negotiations conducted through it as endeavours to reach a compromise over the disputed matter.

Negotiations generally imply the attempt to reach a compromise, based on concessions made by both parties. The extent of the concessions made by either side may reflect inversely the power it possesses to support its argument. Often negotiations are conducted for purposes other than reaching a settlement. They may be launched by one party with the intention of exploring the status of the adversary. In some other instances, negotiations may be conducted for the mere purpose of gaining time, in preparation for another course of conflictual encounter.

The Soviet Field Marshal Shoposnikov might have meant that when he said, 'If war may be said to be the continuation of politics by other means, then peace, in its turn, is no more than the continuation of conflict by other means.'

Through the interactions the Quraish leaders had with Prophet Muhammad (PBUH), they sought either to explore his plans, or to reach a kind of negotiated settlement, or to challenge him in order to expose his weak points in preparation for 'the continuation of the conflict by other means.'

Delegation Dispatched Abroad : After failing to reach a settlement with Prophet Muhammad (PBUH), the Quraish notables resorted to other means, aiming" at obstructing him and containing his successes. On the personal front, they intensified their pressure on his followers and his immediate family, the Banu Hashim. In order to expose what they expected to be his weaknesses, they sent a delegation to Medina to meet the Jewish rabbis there. Since Prophet Muhammad (PBUH) declared that the Islamic faith is the continuation and the completion of Christianity and Judaism, the Jewish rabbis of Medina could help in refuting this claim. It is mentioned that the rabbis of Medina advised the delegates to put three questions to Prophet Muhammad (PBUH). TWO of the questions were related to stories recorded in the Old Testament. If he failed to answer any of these questions, then he would prove ignorant of the Jewish faith and that would negate any connection claimed between the two religions.

When repression against the followers of Islam intensified, the Prophet (PBUH) advised those who could not secure protection to migrate to Abyssinia. This choice was based on two circumstances. The first one was that the Abyssinian Negus was the nearest Christian leader, who could offer asylum to the Muslims. The second was that the Arab pagans had connections with South Arabia which belonged at that time to Persia, an ancient enemy of the Christian power of Byzantium. The number of followers, who migrated to Abyssinia, in the fifth year of the Prophetic Mission, was eighty two. After the immigrants settled in Abyssinia, the Quraish tribe schemed to pursue them in their asylum and sent two delegates to the Abyssinian Negus. One of them was Amr bin-al-Aas, a very shrewd person, whose name appeared in a later period as a remarkable negotiator and warrior. The mission of the Quraish delegation was to convince the Abyssinian Negus to disclaim the Muslim refugees and if possible, to extradite them.

At the same time the Quraish notables decided to move farther in their sanctions against Prophet Muhammad (PBUH) and his protectors, Abu Talib and the families of Banu Hashim and Banu Al-Muttalib; (Hashim and Al-Muttalib were two brothers. Prophet Muhammad (PBUH) and his uncle Abu Talib descended from the first one). The Quraish leaders met and concluded a written agreement, which they deposited at the Kaaba and by which they vowed to boycott Banu Hashim and Bani Al-Muttalib. It was agreed that none of the Quraish would deal with anyone of the two families in trade, marriage or social contacts. It is noteworthy that this boycott agreement was not directed against individuals, who followed the new faith, but included everybody in the two families (Hashim and Al Muttalib) whether they were believers or non-believers of Islam. The reaction of Banu

Hashim and Bani Al-Muttalib families was the same and the non-believers showed solidarity with the believers." The boycott agreement was an example of an inter-tribe or inter-state conduct of relations.

During the tenth year of the Prophetic Mission, Abu Talib[4], the Prophet's (PBUH) uncle and protector passed away and he became more vulnerable to the hostility of the Quraish. He left Mecca for Al-Taif to call its people to embrace Islam and to seek their support and alliance. There, he was met with defiance and rebuke. He returned to Mecca vowing not to submit, as long as God, Lord of the weak and helpless, was his support.

Migration to Abyssinia : In the fifth year of the Prophetic Mission, many of the Muslims migrated to Abyssinia to escape the repression of the Quraish. They left in two groups totalling eighty two persons. Ruqayyah, the Prophet's daughter and her husband Uthman (RAA) (who was to be the third Caliph) were in the first group. The second group included Jafar bin Abu Talib, Abu Talib's son and Prophet Muhammad's (PBUH) cousin. The Muslims believed that they would be given refuge by the Abyssinian Negus, who was a Christian and believer in one God. After they were accepted in Abyssinia, the Quraish leaders dispatched a delegation of two persons to the Negus in order to convince him to extradite those who were offered asylum and to deliver them to their people in Mecca. The delegates, keen to succeed in their diplomatic mission, planned their approach carefully.

They carried gifts to the monarch and his aides. First, they met with the patriarchs individually, and explained to them that they had sheltered some of their people, who had relinquished their fathers' religion, but who had not embraced the patriarchs' faith. Contrary to both religions, they had invented, as the delegates put it, a religion of their own, which was acceptable to neither party. They appealed to each patriarch to send these defectors back and to advise the king not to summon the Muslim immigrants for a hearing. When the two delegates were received by the Negus, they presented their gifts to him and repeated the claims that they had put to the patriarchs. The latter attested to the delegates' claim and proposed to the monarch to disown the immigrants and to deliver them to their people, who knew them better and were aware of their mischief. The Negus refused to disavow those who sought asylum in his country and he declined to entertain the petition of the delegates without first verifying the charges against the immigrants.' When the Muslim group was brought before the king, they were asked what made them differ with their people and abandon their religion without embracing Christianity or any other beliefs.

On behalf of the Muslim group, Jafar bin Abu Talib took the stand to answer these questions. He addressed the *Negus*, and said that, 'Before Islam, we were people of ignorance, worshipping idols, committing atrocities and disrupting family relations until God raised up an apostle from amongst us; we know his ancestry, his truthfulness and his credibility. This apostle called on us to believe in one God and to worship Him and commanded us to tell the truth, to keep family ties, to protect whoever sought refuge among us...we believed in him and followed his teachings, while our people, oppressed us and endeavoured to impose their faith back on us. This is why we migrated to your country and solicited you and not anyone else, seeking your protection and hoping not to be mistreated by you.' The Abyssinian Negus requested Jafar to read verses of his book and Jafar read a passage, i.e. the *Sura XIX* entitled Mariam. The Sura tells the story of Zakriya, having a son Yahya (John) at a late age and of Mariam (Mary the Virgin), who although a virgin, by the will of God had a son Isa (Jesus). The Negus was pleased with what was said and commented that what the Prophet (PBUH) was preaching and that which Jesus proclaimed, 'both were emanating from the same source.' He told the delegation from Quraish 'You may both leave, these people I will never deliver to you.'

When the Quraish delegation left the court, Amr ibn-al-Aas thought of another approach. He decided to inform the Negus that the Muslims believed that Jesus Christ was just a man—no better than a slave. He returned the next day and proposed to the Negus to summon the Muslims and to ask them what they thought of Jesus. The Negus put the question to them. Again Jafar bin Abu Talib spoke and said that they thought of Jesus what their Prophet (PBUH) had conveyed to them and that Jesus was a slave of God, His apostle and His spirit. He was the word of God delivered to Mariam the Chaste. This argument did not satisfy the patriarchs, but it did satisfy the Negus, and the report goes on to say that he dismissed the two Quraish delegates, rejecting their gifts and rebuking their mission.

Quraish Boycott : Realizing that the Abyssinian Negus had extended his protection to the Muslim immigrants, and that the Muslims in Mecca were increasing in number, the Quraish notables held a meeting where they decided to boycott Bani Abdul-Muttalib. They recorded this agreement in a written document which they deposited at the Kaaba. Such an action provoked the Bani Hashim and Bani-Al-Muttalib to ally themselves with Abu Talib and Prophet Muhammad's (PBUH) followers. This alliance included the Muslims and non-Muslims within the two clans.

The boycott continued for a period of two to three years, during which the people, besieged in their quarter in the ravine of Abu Talib, suffered from lack of food supply except for what was secretly infiltrated. One of the Quraish notables, Hisham bin Amr, who was related on his mother's side to Bani Hashim, used to load a camel with food stuff and lead it to the opening of the ravine in the darkness of the night and release it to the people in the besieged quarter. He convinced another figure of the Quraish, Zuhayr bin Abi Umayyah, to raise the boycott, Zuhayr expressed his consent and reservation as they were alone in this matter, and both agreed to seek the support of other notables. After that Hisham went to a third and a fourth person and reached the same agreement with them. The group of five met together and drew a plan for abrogating the agreement.

The next day they went to the Kaaba and after the sermons Zuhayr called for the people of Mecca and addressed them, asking how they could eat their food and wear their clothes at a time when Banu Hashim were suffering and were denied the right to trade with them. He then vowed not to rest until this unjust and disruptive document was destroyed. When Abu-Jahl, one of the main adversaries of the Prophet (PBUH) interrupted his speech and insisted that the agreement be preserved, another one from the group of five came to the help of Zuhayr, then the third one came, followed by the fourth in the group. All expressed their concurrence with him. After them, Hisham bin Amr stepped forward to state that he too had never consented to the agreement from the beginning and that he would repudiate its contents. Although the number of people who condemned the agreement was not big—only five—the manner in which they spoke, one after the other, gave the impression that this was the feeling of the majority. When, in the end, one of them went to tear up the document, he found that it had already been destroyed.

Delegations to Mecca : Prophet Muhammad (PBUH) and his companions spared no opportunity to explain their religion to those, who came to Mecca and to call on them to accept the faith. He met groups of Arabs, who came to Mecca for pilgrimage and for trade. He received envoys and delegations, who arrived to inquire about the new religion and to acquaint themselves with its Prophet (PBUH). In the ninth year of the Prophetic mission (A.D. 619), a delegation of Christians from Najran (a region south of Mecca) came to meet the Prophet (PBUH). After they had put their questions to him and listened to passages from the Quran, they left and were confronted by Abu-Jahl and a number of Quraish men, who tried their best to counter whatever impression the Prophet (PBUH) had left on the delegation.

During the same period, an envoy from Hamadan (a tribe living in the northern part of Yemen) called Qays bin Amr came to meet Prophet Muhammad (PBUH) and to report back to his people. After discussing his mission with the Prophet (PBUH) and declaring his conversion to Islam, Qays expressed his own and his peoples' readiness to support the Apostle. He was requested to return to his people and to find out, if Hamadan was ready to take Prophet Muhammad (PBUH) in their midst and to support and defend him. Qays left for Hamadan and later returned alone to announce his peoples' adherence to Islam and their readiness to host him. Though, Prophet Muhammad (PBUH) expressed his appreciation for the positive response, he found it short of a firm commitment. His agreement with the Medina delegation later on proved to be based on something more concrete.

Prophet Muhammad (PBUH) maintained his contacts with people visiting Mecca. During the pilgrimage season he met the different tribes coming to Mecca, calling on them and convincing them to accept Islam. At one of these seasonal gatherings in Mecca, a delegation from Medina, representing the Aus tribe, came seeking alliance with the Quraish against the Khazraj, the other major tribe in Medina. Medina, which was known as Yathrib, was inhabited mainly by two Arab pagan tribes (Aus and Khazraj) and an influential Jewish community. The continuing hostilities between the two tribes gave rise to the dominance of the Jewish community. The delegation from Yathrib was headed by Abul Qayser Anas bin Rafie and included Iyas bin Muadh. Prophet Muhammad (PBUH), hearing of the arrival of the delegates, and their purpose, came to meet them and said: 'Would you have what is better than what you have come for?' When they asked what that was, he said: 'I am the Apostle of Allah. He has sent me for all humankind; to call upon them to worship God and to ascribe no partner to Him. And He revealed to me the book.' Then he called on the delegation to embrace Islam and read before them verses from Quran.

Iyas, influenced by what he heard, expressed his sympathy and preference for what was presented, but he was rebuffed by his superior, who told him that he was there for a different purpose. It appears that, despite the fact that Prophet Muhammad (PBUH) did not convert the group, his message was delivered and it was to be conveyed to the people of Yathrib. So when he met other delegations from that city, his views were already known to them.

First Aqaba Delegation : During the pilgrimage season to Mecca in March, A.D. 620, Prophet Muhammad (PBUH) met a group of the Khazraj tribe, who came to Mecca for the same purpose as the other Yathrib delegation had come the previous season, that is, to seek an alliance among the Quraish, against their opponents, the Aus and Jews. When Prophet Muhammad (PBUH) talked to them and explained to them the faith of Islam, it seemed as though they were not surprised with the basic idea, as they had often heard from the Jews about the awaited Messiah. They looked at each other and said, 'By God! He is the new Prophet the Jews had always threatened us with. Why should we not be ahead of them to join him?' They declared their faith in Islam and told him that, they had left their people divided in feuds and hostilities and that, they would return to them and call on them to accept the faith. They promised that if they were united around this faith, then no one among them, would have a more honourable position than the Prophet (PBUH).

They returned to Yathrib (Medina) and started propagating Masab bin Umair the new faith, aided by a Muslim who had previously emigrated to Abyssinia. The next year, five of them came back again to Mecca together with seven new converts and met the Prophet (PBUH) at Aqaba, the pass between Mina and Mecca. Here, he heard their plight and enjoined upon them the basic laws of Islam and sent one of his companions to teach them the religion and to lead their prayers. This emissary of the Prophet (PBUH) followed the wise approach and sagacious advice of the Prophet (PBUH) in preaching Islam to those voicing their opposition to it in Medina. Once, one of the Medina notables came to him and in a threatening manner ordered him to leave them alone. The emissary prudently asked him to sit and listen to what he had to say. If he found it satisfactory, he might then accept it, otherwise he could point out what he disliked. The Medina notable Osayd bin Hudhayr accepted the proposal as a fair one. He listened to what the emissary read from the Quran and declared his acceptance of the faith. He then advised the emissary to go and meet Saad bin Muadh, the man, who would be followed by all his people, if he accepted the faith.

It is worth pointing out here that throughout all the meetings between Prophet Muhammad (PBUH) and those delegations and individuals whom he strived to bring to the new faith, the Prophet (PBUH) always invoked rational argument and discreet presentation and each and every time read to them, passages of the Quran. While all the other prophets had performed miracles as proofs of their divine missions, the only proof put out by Prophet Muhammad (PBUH) was the words he voiced. The value of a word to an Arab lies in its meaning, its rhythm, its music, and its logic and its eloquence. To the Arabs, the spoken word is a covenant, that commits them to the most serious obligations. The Quran described Jesus Christ, as being the word of God descended to Mary. The first word of the Quran that was delivered to Prophet Muhammad (PBUH) when receiving his commission was 'Iqraa', which means 'read'.

Those who specialize in Islamic history and literature, would appreciate the impact and deep effect the language of the Quran had on a people, who appreciate the value of the word. For them it is understandable that the only sign of Prophet Muhammad's (PBUH) divine inspiration was the Quran itself, its contents and its wordings. The first delegate from the Quraish came to meet Prophet Muhammad (PBUH) to verify that is he a poet or a soothsayer. He heard him recite the Quran and went back to his people to assert that, what he heard was not the word of a poet, or that of a soothsayer. It is said that the only miraculous proof of the new religion Islam, was the language and the content of the Quran.

Second Aqaba Agreement : During the pilgrimage season of the thirteenth year of the Prophetic Mission (A.D. 622), a group of seventy three men and two women from Medina came to Mecca and met with the Prophet (PBUH) at Aqaba. It was in the darkness of night that Prophet Muhammad (PBUH) came to meet them accompanied by his uncle Abbas, who had kept his pagan belief. Abbas addressed the Medinese, telling them of the position Prophet Muhammad (PBUH) occupied among his people and within his family and that he had been defended even by those, who did not adhere to his faith. He went on to say that despite that, Prophet Muhammad (PBUH) had chosen to join them and to ally himself with them, if they believed that they would defend him. Abbas warned them that if they could not pledge this support to him, they must leave him, where he was protected and esteemed. The group from Medina gave their assurance and offered to take an oath of allegiance to Prophet Muhammad (PBUH).

Before the Medina party committed themselves to Prophet Muhammad (PBUH), they made it clear that their forthcoming agreement would sever ties, they had with another party, meaning the Medina Jews. They asked if he would give them up once his cause prevailed. Giving them the assurance of his constant allegiance to them, Prophet Muhammad (PBUH) had them swear their fealty to him in defending him, as they defended their women and children. Having sworn this mutual oath of allegiance, Prophet Muhammad (PBUH) requested them to solicit twelve captains from among themselves as representatives. Then, he addressed the twelve persons named by the group and stated to them that they would be the guarantors to what their people were committed to, as the Disciples were to Jesus. He would be the guarantor for his people. The twelve captains expressed their consent in confirmation of the pledge covenanted with their people.

On the basis of the second Aqaba agreement, Prophet Muhammad (PBUH) gave permission to his followers to immigrate to Medina. The migration to Medina of the Mecca Muslims was effected in successive waves. The last three to leave Mecca were Prophet Muhammad (PBUH), his close companion Abu Bakr (RAA) and his cousin Ali bin Abu Talib. On 25 September 622, Prophet Muhammad (PBUH) accompanied by Abu-Bakr (RAA) arrived in Medina to start a new phase in the history of Islam, which marked the beginning of the Muslim calendar year. The arrival of the Prophet (PBUH) in Medina, where Islam had spread among all the Aus and Khazraj tribes, laid the basis for the establishment of the first Islamic state.

The Manifestations : Throughout this period one discerns manifestations of diplomatic practices, which formed the basis for the more sophisticated practices observed in the succeeding period. Relations and contacts between communities and tribes resembled relations and contacts among states now-a-days. The methods, manners and means of conducting diplomacy might have been quantitatively and qualitatively limited. There have been instances where pacts, agreements or pledges were conducted and concluded verbally or in writing, after negotiations and exchange of delegations.

Nevertheless, the examples mentioned indicate a degree of maturity in diplomacy. The norms and traditions known to the Arabs of that period were the background for such practices. These were accepted and used by both communities, the Muslims and the pagans, but certain features reflected the new culture of Islam. For instance, when the two delegates from the Quraish went to the Abyssinian Negus to explain the contradictions between Islam and Christianity in terms of Jesus Christ, the Muslims debated among themselves as to what they should tell the Negus. They concluded that they should be truthful about what they believed. The debate that would ensue eleven centuries later as to whether, diplomacy could revert to deception or should be based on truthfulness, was settled in the incident mentioned above. The Muslims believed that credibility does not only pay off, but also reflects their faith, which could be translated into modern terminology as reflecting their constant policy.

Another aspect of diplomacy in that era was that when negotiations were concluded, the argument of either party would reflect the power that backed the party's position. In the case of negotiations between the Quraish and the Muslims, the Quraish delegations always backed their argument with the support and unanimity of their clans, while the only power the Muslims relied on was the strength of their argument and their belief.

The third feature of this type of diplomacy was that it represented a way of life rather than a professional activity, that simply served the purpose of the mission. The Quran enjoined them to adopt a certain manner in their discourse or when effecting their responsibility. 'It is part of the mercy of God that thou dost deal gently with them. Wert thou severe or harsh-hearted, they would have broken away from about thee.' That thou have averted evil with good.' 'Call unto the way of thy Lord with wisdom and fair exhortation and reason with them in the better way.'

References

1. *Oneness of Allah.*
2. *Prophethood.*
3. *Non-Muslims residing under the Muslim reign.*
4. *Uncle of the Prophet (Pbuh).*

10

STATUS OF BELIEVERS

SPECIAL STATUS

The historic chapter deals with the Laws which affect Believers only. For practical purposes the whole Charter concerns the Believers. However, there are some Clauses whose subject matter concerns Believers only, while there are others which affect those people who have not accepted Islam but will be working under the leadership of Believers.

The heading of the Document, which also forms Clause I deals primarily with Believers clears all doubts about its nature and also that they are the people forming the Government of the state.

One of the significant points to note is that the Charter is addressed primarily to the people; the common man; the Believer whether a free man, a freed man or not free till then.

> "This is a Document from Muhammad the Prophet (PBUH) between the Believers, Muslims of Quraish[1] and Yathrib[2] and those who followed them and fought with them. They form one Ummah to the exclusion of others."

It includes others with a condition, otherwise the Believers Quraish from Mecca and from Yathrib form One Ummah to the exclusion of the rest. This formation of Ummah was not to be confined to the Believers of these two places.

Whosoever voluntarily Believed in Allah and Muhammad (PBUH) as a Prophet which in practice meant that he lived in accordance with the Laws of the Quran and Sunnah, became a member of this Ummah.

There may have been similar Charters in other parts of the world. We have already referred to a Charter issued by a king of England in 1215 A.C., which is known as the Great Charter— Magna Carta. There are many differences but the first difference lies in the people to whom the Charter is being given. While the Constitutional Charter of Medina is given to the common man, the Magna Carta is given:

> "To the archbishops, bishops, abbots, earls, barons, justiciars, foresters, sheriffs, stewards, servants, and to all his bailiffs and faithful subjects."

The subjects also formed categories and were at the mercy of the bishops and sheriffs and in practice held no social status unless they happened to be retainers of the categories enumerated above. The common man, the man in the street had no voice or weight until centuries later, when contacts with Islam is Spain and the Holy Land had brought about a certain amount of awakening among the Europeans, returning from Muslim lands.

The promulgation of a Constitution or Fundamental Law by a people or to them by the ruler signifies the commencement of organised life of that Millah. Organised collective life alone is most important characteristic of a human group from a herd of animals. Meccan life was the life of individual Muslims placed amidst unfriendly surroundings. Such a life could not last for ever. It cannot last even in the twentieth century.

There are a number of countries today where Muslims find it impossible to live as Muslims. Hijrah[3] of the Prophet (PBUH) was inevitable. Hijrah and the declaration of war by Quraish created the situation where a Fundamental Law became essential to be promulgated. Islam became a living organisation with the Charter controlling the collective communal life of those who had accepted Sovereignty of Allah and His Prophet (PBUH). Allah's Sovereignty was to control and direct the life of these individuals from hearth to the farm or the shop and would include the behaviour and inner feelings from the Mosques to the Battlefield.

It must be remembered that the Charter is being issued and promulgated by Muhammad (PBUH) The Prophet of Allah and not by Allah, although it is primarily for the people who have accepted Allah's Sovereignty. This fact reminds a Believer that he has accepted the Sovereignty of Allah, because, Muhammad (PBUH) has said so and the individual has accepted his Prophethood. It is the character, the conduct and the life of Muhammad (PBUH) although regulated, controlled and directed on the Right Path by Allah, which has made men believe

Status of Believers

in him, when he said, "Allah is the Creator, the Sustainer and Master of the Day of Resurrection."

It is his statement that Allah the Merciful, the Loving, the Compassionate and Who has appointed him as His Last Prophet. Therefore, be it understood and remembered that when a Believer accepts the Sovereignty of Allah, he does not relegate the Prophet (PBUH) to a position of no consequence. It is the acceptance of his Prophethood which has prompted the Believer to Believe and have Faith (Imaan) in Allah. Therefore, as Law Givers, they both remain side by side. This is the explanation of repeated reminder of Allah regarding the position of Muhammad as a Law Giver and not one who as a result of applying himself to a problem, at hand, does Ijtihad and deduces supplementary law, under certain given conditions. Allah has repeatedly Commanded:-

"Say: Obey Allah and the messenger". 3: 32

The preceding Verse is worth noting:-

"Say: If ye love Allah, follow me".

Wherever the Command to "Obey Allah" occurs it is followed by "Obey the Messenger." Obedience to Him is given singly only in one Verse, where it is said "Obey My Command" (20: 90) and not the usual Word, "Obey Allah."

BASIC REGULATIONS

The position of Muhammad (PBUH) as a Law Giver in accordance with Allah's Own Commands is direct. His Commands take the place of Law directly and independently. Any reported Command of his, which does not fully support the Words of the Quran, can be rejected as Maudhu-Spurious, concocted and coined by some one and not merely as of a secondary nature, which, may or may not be applicable in all cases. He knew the place he held. He could not give an Order which would be contrary to the Dictates of Allah. Allah has said about him:

"By the Star when it setteth your comrade erreth not, nor is deceived,
nor doth he speak of (his own desire)". 53: 1-3

The Quran and the Sunnah are complementary to one another. Neither can be understood except by studying the other. If Allah Himself has, in a dozen places bracketed His Rasul with Obedience to Himself then we must also give to his Commands an equally important position. It is Muhammad (PBUH) who has had to say that the Quran is not the result of his authorship. Who, except Allah and his own Conscience, was there to stop him from crediting himself with the authorship of the Quran Who was there, except Allah, his Creator and his own truthfulness to stop him from declaring himself as God in human garb? After all, there were many in Arabia, who, by the queer theory of Trinity, then prevalent, gave to Jesus Christ the position of the Son of God, and of the God who came to earth to be crucified for the sins of humanity.

The Quran is the Word of Allah because, apart from the Quran itself, Muhammad (PBUH) has said so. Muhammad's command, therefore, must be believed and acted upon as eternal commands, in the same spirit as Commands of Allah.

The Clauses of the Charter dealing with Believers only are very few. As the Charter was addressed to the Believers initially the clauses dealing with Believers only precede all others. We have already dealt with Clauses I including the few words given above.

Clause 2: "Quraish Muhajireen will continue to pay blood-money among themselves in accordance with the existing custom."

This Clause has thus laid down:-

1. The Principle of payment of blood-money will continue.
2. Its amount and manner of payment can be in accordance with the tribal custom.
3. Uniformity in the amount etc. is not demanded.

Quraish Believers had migrated to a new place, the city of Yathrib, where there must have been local customs regarding the payment of blood-money. It was neither advisable nor in accordance with the Spirit of Islam, which was meant to cover the whole of the Globe, to lay down permanent laws regarding matters which should, preferably, be decided in accordance with local customs, conditions and requirements. Within Arabia itself there were different standards of payment of blood-money, in view of this it was decided and proclaimed that local and tribal practice, in the case of blood-money would continue to be followed in future.

Laws in Force

Islam is the Last Revealed Way of Life. It has lasted for fourteen centuries and has to remain during the coming one thousand or one million centuries that will take this universe to reach its destination in the immeasurable void. A Way of Life which has to last for ever, and, to be applicable in all places at all times, cannot have eternal laws for situations which must undergo changes with change in time and place. Allah alone possesses the knowledge and the Wisdom and knows what aspects suffer change. He has, as a result, not Laws for problems, situations and matters which are likely to undergo changes. Those matters, which are of lasting nature, have been the subject of Laws given by Allah and His Rasul.

If the problem had been posed to a man, it would have been impossible to bring the permanent and the temporary, to reconcile. The permanence of Islamic Laws has been possible only because Allah and His Prophet (PBUH) have meticulously avoided to give Laws, for aspects of human life, which are of changing nature.

All men are equal. They will always remain equal. Hence Equality of man has been brought under Law. And yet the question of electing, selecting, nominating or appointing a leader of society. Khalifa[4] or Imam has not even been touched because this is a purely social problem, the solution of which is subject to change with time and place. Uniformity is advisable but only where it is possible. Where uniformity is likely to create hardships Allah and His Rasul have left it to the Believers to come to a decision through discussion. The Prophet (PBUH) himself was Commanded to decide problems after consulting his Companions. But once a decision has been taken then all have to see to it, that it is suitably carried out.

Clause 3: "They will redeem their prisoners with kindness and justice common among Believers."

The word "they" cannot refer to anyone else but those to whom the Charter was being issued. It was a state of Muslims in which laws of Islam were to be administered. The Fundamental Law had included "those who followed them," but that was to be seen as to who were prepared to follow them and defend Yathrib along with them. Muslims of Quraish and Yathrib were being given the Document and as such this Clause referred to them jointly. The subject is the redeeming of prisoners, which could be tackled at the level of the Federal Government of Yathrib and none else.

It must be noted that the, "redeeming of prisoners of war is being made a collective responsibility," of the Ummah. It is also worthnoting that the standard of sentiments involved in redeeming prisoners of war is "the kindness and justice common among Believers." The kindness and justice of Believers cannot be of any other kind than that of Allah Who is Most Merciful, and His Prophet (PBUH) who has come as "Mercy to Mankind."

MAN AT THE HELM

This Command of Allah's Messenger was not confined to the Believers of Yathrib only. It was the first Muslim state, which expanded within a century to cover two continents and had started influencing the third as well. This order did not merely apply to the subjects of the state of Yathrib. Although the Charter was given to the then existing Ummah, this order was and is applicable to the Ummah of Islam for ever. The present writer has no knowledge of this Order being amended, deleted, cancelled or replaced by any Quranic Injunction or an order by the Prophet (PBUH).

The question arises as to what has the world of Islam done to redeem the Muslim prisoners of war in the hands of various victorious nations, who during the last three centuries have availed themselves of the weakness of Muslim peoples and while occupying Muslim lands have taken millions of Muslims as prisoners of war.

These Muslims are kept as prisoners jointly and singally in these territories known as European colonies. Generation after generation has grown up and lived as slaves and the Muslim World elsewhere has not moved a finger even to redeem them. We have to admit that a greater part of Muslim World was, until few years ago, under the domination of one or the other Christian power, but nothing has been said regarding the redeeming of millions who, though in majority, in their homelands, are living as slaves and leading a life worse than the life of ethnic minorities. This Clause of The Constitutional Charter of Medina is still operative and I, as, an humble individual, and a student of Muslim history, would submit, that, it needs further thought by the intellectuals of Muslim World.

Until the issue of this Charter there was no question of redeeming prisoners of war. The armies in those days did not belong to the nation. There was no notion of an Ummah.

They used to belong to the kings and when a king was killed in war and was defeated the personnel of that Army had no one else to look to. If they were taken prisoners they were made slaves. If they escaped they became robbers and highwaymen. Very few managed to reach their homes. Yathrib was not a country or a state in the normal sense of the word. It was a place, a piece of land, where the Muslim Ummah, the Believers in Allah and His Rasul (PBUH) had commenced a communal life and were beginning to demonstrate the New Way of Life granted by Allah. Ummah which was then coming into existence was completely new. Those who were to fight the battles of this Ummah were the Army of the Ummah and not of the land comprising the territories of Yathrib. Hence he Ordered that the Ummah will redeem their prisoners of war, and not only that, but they will do so with love and justice which is a hallmark of Believers in Allah and His Prophet (PBUH) and Mercy to Mankind.

This order was so new and unique, that, the moment the Prophet (PBUH) had dictated it and the scribe had written it, there must have been a demand from "The others", who were present, that this Law should be applied to all. Hence Clause 5. There were some who were not even satisfied with the words "all parties will redeem their prisoners with kindness and justice common among Believers."

Their names had to be inserted that such and such tribe and so and so group, "will be governed on the above lines." The demand was placed a second time and names of four more tribes had to be included for the fulfilment of this humane responsibility which was to take ten centuries for other parts of the world like Europe to emulate.

Clause 8: "Believers will not fail to redeem their prisoners or fail to pay blood-money on behalf of one of them."

This Clause is to emphasize Clauses 2 and 3. It has been brought in particularly because Clause 2 had mentioned Quraish only. This Clause emphasizes the contents of both Clauses mentioned earlier and reminds the Believers of today that contrary to the expectations of the Prophet of Allah, they have failed to redeem their prisoners for centuries.

Clause 9: "A Believer will not make the freedman of another Believer as his ally against the wishes of the other Believer."

The relations between the master and slave are of personal nature. When a master frees a slave new relations are formed. The trust or lack of trust a person places on his freedman is known only to him. His good points, his weaknesses and his idiosyncrasies are also known to a freedman. Relations of allies are on a different level. A Believer giving protection to a freedman is undertaking certain responsibilities in respect of a person not really intimately known to him while Believers are like brothers to one another. Therefore, when a Believer takes a freedman of another Believer as ally, and gives him protection, it is in their common interest to have the blessings of the other Believer. This order was being given to maintain internal peace of the community.

Clause 10: "The Believers who fear Allah, will oppose the rebellious elements and those that encourage injustice or sin or enmity or lack of cooperation among Believers."

It has to be kept in mind that the Believers were to defend Yathrib. It was, therefore, essential that the best of relations existed among them. There were people within Yathrib who were likely to create mischief and create situations detrimental to internal security. The factor which had to be kept in mind was that every Believer had, until then, persons closely related to him, who had not yet embraced Islam. It was possible that some such person was found guilty of injustice, sin, or enmity to Islam or of creating trouble between Believers. On such occasions. Believers were being told that their duty lay with law and order and their loyalty lay with High Command's policy and decision and not with the kindred, however dear they may have been.

It was a very delicate situation and the Ansars deserve all the credit for having come out of this very severe test successfully. The leadership provided by the Prophet (PBUH) and the minor circle of his Companions deserve equal praise for steering the Millah[5] with patience, love and tact, through this most difficult period. "Believers who fear Allah", is the key factor in the shaping of an Islamic society.

Love of family ties can over-ride all other situations, except that of men and women, who fear Allah, and as a result of fear of Allah are prepared to sacrifice family interests and affiliations. When the object is to create a flawless Muslim society in which no Believer can be thought of committing a sin, rebellion, injustice or create dissension, then every Muslim is expected to oppose such sinful elements even though they may be his close relations. A country or a state can be defended only if there is peace and harmony within the boundaries of that state.

Such a society can only come about if individuals fear Allah and have firm belief that they will have to answer for their actions on the Day of Judgement[6].

Clause 11: "If anyone is guilty of any such act all Believers will oppose him, even, if he be the son of any one of them."

This Clause is more or less a corollary to the foregoing Clause. It was being laid down firmly and without any ambiguity that injustice, sin and rebellious acts would not be permitted in that society, which was being created in accordance with the Code of Law Revealed by Allah. This was after centuries that a society was taking shape on the principle of Sovereignty of Allah. This society was to prove to humanity, for all times, that a people, a nation, an Ummah, observing in their day to day life, the Sovereignty of Allah prove in actual practice that their objective was to achieve three things:

(a) A happy and contented individual who has patience, forbearance and steadfastness and these individuals show love for each other in their normal day to day dealings.

(b) These happy and contented individuals bring into existence a happy and loving society.

(c) They do not fall prey to the temptation of committing aggression or transgression against other nations even though as a result of being a happy, contented and united people they have gained strength and have the capacity of over-running their neighbours. In addition such an Ummah does not engage in any war unless they are attacked first. But whenever they are attacked they punish the aggressor to an extent, that he does not repeat it again.

Such a happy and strong society can come into existence only if its individuals observe law for themselves and for all who may be near and dear to them. This Clause draws the attention of Believers to the injunction of the Quran:

> "O ye who believe! Be ye staunch injustice, witnesses for Allah, even though it be against yourselves or (your) parents or (your) kindred, whether (the case be of) a rich man or a poor man, for Allah is nearer unto both, (than ye are). So follow not passion".

Clause 12: "A Believer will not kill another Believer for the sake of an un-Believer."

This Clause was a further explanation and an illustration of Clause 11.

Family ties held strong loyalties in Arabia as in all tribal societies. If a member of a family was killed, his kith and kin were expected to avenge that death or be satisfied with the usual blood-money. These prejudices were very deep rooted. The Prophet (PBUH), however, was creating an Ummah, the members of which were to be above all such ties, prejudices and loyalties. He was stressing on Believers and un-Believers alike that the only loyalty in Islam is loyalty to Allah and this is exhibited by obedience to His Laws. The Law of Allah is clear on the subject that a Believer cannot kill another Believer unless by mistake. He ceases to be a Believer if he kills another Believer wilfully.

> "Whose slayeth a believer of set purpose, his reward is Hell for ever".
> 4: 93

The society was, as yet, a mixed society but laws had to be promulgated, which would gradually develop the society into a society of love, peace and justice all round. This could only be achieved by having strict laws and meticulous observance of those laws. Believers and their un-Believers relations were being told categorically, that no Believer, should be expected to avenge the death of a relative killed accidentally or otherwise by another Believer.

Islam had to step out of Arabia and spread to far off lands. It was to declare, from the beginning, as to where did the loyalties of new-Muslims lie immediately after becoming Muslims. The Code was strict, unusually difficult to observe but the choice of observance of loyalty was between the Sovereignty of Allah and worldly ties. Allah had to be given preference by those who claimed to have accepted Him as their Lord and Master.

Clause 13: "No Believer will help an un-Believer against a Believer."

This Clause in conjunction the foregoing sets a standard of behaviour for Believers in a mixed society where Believers are placed in a non-Believer majority, even though general relation may be on the best of terms. Believers must remain united among themselves, if they desire to possess weight, as an Ummah, however small their number may be.

This Clause could be used as precedent and for relations between Muslim states, so that inter-state relations between Muslim states are kept at friendly level and instances of acute differences between them do not arise. It would then coincide with the directions given in the Verse quoted below:

"Let not the believers take disbelievers for their friends in preference to believers." 3: 28

Disobedience of Clause 13 and the Verse quoted above have brought about the situation, that vast areas populated entirely by Believers have fallen prey to un-Believers and millions of Muslims are forced to live as atheists. It is punishment for having rebelled against both the letter and spirit of the Quran and the Charter.

References

1. *The tribe in which the Prophet (Pbuh) was born.*
2. *Old name of Medina.*
3. *Migration of the Prophet (Pbuh) from Mecca to Medina.*
4. *Caliph.*
5. *Community or nation.*
6. *Doomsday.*

11

NON-MUSLIMS PROTECTION

RIGHTS AT PAR

The Jewish tribes of Yathrib were rich and had fairly large number of members prominent in business. They, however, had no political or social status among the Arab population. They appear to have migrated from Syria during one of their exodus resulting from Assyrian invasion. Some writers are of the opinion that they were settled in Yathrib even before the Arabs. This does not appear likely. The theory, that they were Arabs who had been converted to Judaism also does not appear plausible. They were, at the time of Prophet's Hijrah, adherents of one or the other of these Arab tribes (Aus and Khazraj)[1]. They had, however, preserved a sort of intellectual ascendency, owing to their being in possession of the Scriptures and their fame for the occult sciences, the pagan Arabs consulting their rabbies on occasions and paying heed to what they said."

EQUAL PROTECTION

The Prophet (PBUH) gave them a privileged position in the Constitutional Charter, provided they followed the Believers loyally and fought alongside with them. They possessed strong forts just outside the main city of Yathrib and each tribe was independent in every respect, each having a separate fort. They had all the weapons of the period and boasted of their prowess as fighters. When the Quraish were defeated at Badr[2], one of their tribes, Banu Qainuqa[3], in reply to the Prophet's advice of good behaviour, they boasted of their strength and rebelled.

They are a people of the Book. The way in which the Prophet (PBUH) was laying the foundations of bringing humanity on one platform would have benefited the Jews in the long run, but they were short sighted and did not avail of the special position, they could have enjoyed under the terms of the Charter. In spite of the behaviour of leading Jews of Yathrib the Prophet (PBUH) continued treating them with kindness and until a Jewish tribe did not commit an act of treason or outright rebellion he did not take any action against them. He pardoned two of the rebellious tribes, when they surrendered.

Those terms of the Charter, which were of general nature and those in connection with defence of the state, were applicable to Jews as well. There were, however, some Clauses which referred to the Jews only. The Clauses of general nature included the heading (Clause 1) in which it was laid down that those who followed the Believers and fought alongside with them will form one Ummah with them. This was a great attraction for the Jews. They were being elevated to the status of equality with Arabs and in some respects they were becoming superior to them, because, they were becoming equals of the ruling party of Yathrib, the Believers. Clauses like Clause 5, which laid down that "All parties will redeem their prisoners with kindness and justice according to practice among Believers," are being studied elsewhere. In this Chapter only those Clauses will be brought under discussion, which pertain to Jews exclusively.

Clause 16: "Those Jews who follow us, will be helped and will be treated with equality."

We have touched on this Clause very briefly, under Laws pertaining to defence. As the Clause mentions Jews particularly, we feel that it must be due to some special reason, that the question cropped up again, although it had been touched upon in Clause 1, where it referred to "those who," followed them. The only reason, for the mention of Jews specifically, could be that they had, during the dictation of the Charter, asked a direct question about the subject.

Clause 15 had spoken of "Believers are all friends to each other to the exclusion of all others." The Jews and 'the others' were being denied the friendship and equality with Muslims, which had been promised in Clause 1. The Jews must have felt that their position, in respect of equality with Muslims, needed to be clarified. They must have asked a specific question, "What about us." The answer came in the form of Clause 16 that "Those Jews who follow us will be helped and will be treated with equality."

This Clause shows their keenness to gain an equal socio-political status with the Believers. As yet they knew very little about Islam. They may have been still under the impression that the Prophet (PBUH) will announce himself as a sect of Judaism, and not as final shape of Islam, the Way of Life, preached by Ibrahim[4] and Musa[5] (Alaihis-salam). The Prophet having sensed the worries of Jews dictated the next Clause.

Clause 17: "No Jew will be wronged."

Jews had been persecuted all the world over to such an extent that it was rare to find a place where they could live an honourable life. It may have been, that the Jews themselves have followed a policy of persecution in respect of communities which happened to be weaker than them. It could also be that wherever they happened to be in a minority, they took recourse to mischief and intrigue, which invited persecution against them. Centuries of such mischievous and selfish behaviour gave them a reputation that they attracted hatred merely by the mention of the word Jew, where-ever they went. The only person in authority, throughout history, who has shown compassion and kindness to them through the enactment of a Law is Muhammad (PBUH) the Prophet of Allah. This historical Clause placed the Jews on a pedestal of honour, respect and safety which they had not enjoyed under their own kings. This assurance of safe and respectful life was independent of the Clause giving them equality with Believers if they fought alongside them on the Path of Allah.

It is clear that the Clause governing their status of equality must have been the result of their volunteering to take part in the defence of Yathrib against an attack by the Quraish of Mecca. It could be because according to Yaqubi[6], the famous geographist, they were from an Arab stock. He says that "Jews of Medina were basically local Arabs and were Judaised by immigrants who fled from Palestine after the Roman invasion. It could also be through Jews who migrated earlier. In any case, they had not only adopted the Law brought by Moses but had also imbibed the universally adopted national character of Jews based on miserliness, cheating and mischief mongering, and had, as a result lost their status as honest citizens, as in other parts of the world."

The history of the scattered tribes of Jews has been a history of fraud, criminality and cunning; sabotage and destruction", but he being "Mercy to Mankind," could not refuse a request of a down-trodden people even though they may have deserved such a behaviour in the past. The Jews, however take their roaming around the world as a boon from above. They call it, "A beneficent protection, which God has instituted in the life of the Jews is, that He has dispersed them all over the world".

The Prophet (PBUH) was giving them equality because they were a part of mankind, created and fashioned by Allah. To a Muslim, equality has become a second nature, as a result. "A barefooted Beduin, in a ragged cloak, would walk upto a king, shake him by the hand and wish him good morning, completely disregarding horror of the whispering courtiers".

It may appear strange that the Jews were accepting to live under Laws of the Quran and the Commands of the Last Prophet of Allah as loyal citizens and fight for the safety of the New Deen in a chance, for receiving the status of free citizens of Yathrib. It may be because in this way they were becoming co-rulers along with Arabs, as their equals. It speaks of their urge for living an honourable life of equality with the high born in Arabia and be subject to Laws, which gave equal status to men, irrespective of their ethnic or geographical origin. They were proving the dictum that, "The most obvious and recognised characteristic of just laws is that they are equal", for all concerned. Justice has been recognised as the central theme of Islam.

It is based on the principle of equality of men in the eyes of Allah. When human beings, irrespective of the colour of their skins, the language that they speak and the creed they prefer to follow, are treated as equals before law, there is no possibility of injustice prevailing. "Injustice arises when equals are treated unequally and also when unequals are treated equally". This was the first time, that Jews were being treated as equals, and were to enjoy complete freedom. "Closely related to the value of equality is that of freedom. These two values are often defined in terms of the other. Freedom is most often defined, in terms of absence of restrictions, which we see as one way of defining equality.

Freedom as a value calling for absence of restrictions or restraints is laden with contradictions. Society can exist only if human behaviour is predictable and controllable to some extent Unconditional freedom could result only in chaos in all areas of activity".

It appears that Jewish mind has always wanted uncontrolled freedom. Movements like Socialism and Communism have been supported by Jewish intellectuals with greater zeal than thinkers of other schools of thought. The treacherous behaviour of Jews in different parts of the world, at various periods of history is the result of unbridled thought of their thinkers and intellectuals. They have a history which abounds in rebellious conduct even under their own rulers. The number of occasions, when anti-Jewish communal disturbances have taken place are too numerous to be mentioned in an essay of this nature. A few instances may, however, be mentioned.

Jews massacred in Alexandria	(216 B.C.)
Antiochus killed 40,000 Jews in Jerusalem	(170 B.C.)
Titus killed 11,00,000 Jews and destroys the Temple	(70 A.C.)

Desolation of Judea (135 A.C.). Rebellion of Jews. Romans killed 580,000 (136 A.C.)

Rebellion of Jews at Alexandria. Jews massacred (415 A.C.)

Umar took over Jerusalem not a single person was killed (655 A.C.)

No more Jews killed in the Middle East. Jews banished from England (1020 A.C.)

Jews returned to England (1060 A.C.)

Jews massacred in London on Coronation day of Richard I.

Christian priests joined in the massacre. (1189 A.C.)

Jews besieged in the castle of York. (1190 A.C.)
They cut each others throats. Hunderds killed.

Jews of both sexes imprisoned in England.

Their eyes and teeth pulled out.

A large number butchered by king John. (1204 A.C.)

700 Jews slain in London (1262 A.C.)

Statute that no Jew should enjoy a freehold (1269 A.C.)

Jew moneylenders forced to hang a plate on their breast or quit England. (1274 A.C.)

267 Jews hanged, accused of clipping coins. (1278 A.C.)

All Jews 16511 banished from England. (1290 A.C.)

Jewish fate in France and other countries of Europe during 14th and 15th centuries is a grim story.

Several hundred thousand banished from Spain. (1492-1494 A.C.)

Addicts against Jews rescinded by Pope Sixtus V Cromwell permitted them to return to England. (1650 A.C.)

These instances of persecution of Jews speak of the manner they have been hunted from place to place. Their own laws of war and peace are primarily responsible for introducing cruelty during and after war.

According to their own history books, the behaviour of Jewish personalities of note has not been praise-worthy either. "Edom and Jeshurun were rivals and great were the cruelty of the Hebrew arms in their countries. When David was king, his sister's son Jacob[7] went down and killed Adonites in the Ghrov twelve thousand men and Jacob's brother Abishai killed eighteen thousand of them... Other ten thousand taken captives, he brought to the top of the rock, and there he made them the king's tumblers, casting them headlong down together, by the sharp rocks, that they were all broken in pieces".

There have been numerous occasions during 20th century in Europe and particularly in Germany when great atrocities have been committed against Jews because they had captured the economic life of these countries. Efforts have been made to get rid of them. Israel has been created for this purpose, but the Jews have not left either Europe or America. Christianity appears poised to start a fresh campaign to annihilate them during the 21st century of the Christian Era, while Muhammad (PBUH), gave Yathrib a Charter in 7th century, which said:-"No Jew will be wronged."

Professor Sergeant has tried to prove, that the Charter is not one Document but a collection of eight different documents. He, however, admits the authenticity of the Document, and does not deny the existence of the Clause "No Jew will be wronged." This guarantee of safety was being given to a people, who did not hold the status of nationals of that city and were living at the mercy of the tribes, which had given them protection.

Muslims have always shown magnanimity to the Jews. When they were banished from Spain between the years 1492 and 1494 A.C., "it was to Turkey that the persecuted Spanish Jews fled for refuge in enormous numbers." The persecution of Jews by Christians appears to he natural justice, after a lapse of centuries. They persecuted, in their time, those who fell into their hands. "The Jews used to bum their prisoners alive and most barbarously mutilate the slain".

Yathrib was witnessing a change. A new order was being established by Muhammad (PBUH) who has been sent by Allah, as "Mercy to mankind." All barbarities, all prosecutions, all wrongs to humanity were being made as illegal. All men were being declared as equal. Even the Jews, the downtrodden of East and West were being promised, that no harm will come to them as long as they committed no sin or crime. They were being given a place in the Charter, which was being offered without any pressure. Centuries later king John of England gave a Charter, at a time when "The capital was in rebel hands, the whole administration was at a stand still. Without his exchequer, John had no revenues. He had to yield.

The king agreed to meet the barons on the meadows of Runnymede, between Staines and Windsor, and there signed the Great Charter". It would be interesting to read the Great Charter and compare it the Charter of Medina and see which Charter gives more freedom, equality, justice and human rights. Jews have had a chequered career throughout history. They have invited this fate because of their

Non-Muslims Protection

internecine warfare. They butchered one another, whenever and whoever had the upper hand. Their final self-inflicted blow came when, "After the defeat of Bar Cochba, in A.C. 135, much of Judea was left a desert and some towns of Galilee were also ravaged".

They seem to have a rebellious nature. If they were not quarrelling among themselves, they would rebel against authority, however benign it may have been. They rebelled against Nebuchad-nessar and "resolving to settle the Jewish problem once for all, as he thought, he recaptured Jerusalem, burned it to the ground, destroyed the temple of Solomon, drew Zedekia's sons before his face, gauged out their eyes, and carried practically all the population of the city into captivity in Babylonia."

During one of their marches in captivity and when their women were ordered by their guards to sing for them, they are supposed to have composed a song, bemoaning of their separation from Jerusalem. The words are:-

"By the river of Babylon, there we sat down,

Yes, we wept, when we remembered Zion,

We hanged our harps upon the willows in the midst thereof.

For there, they that carried us away captives, required of us a song.

And they that worked us required of us mirth.

Saying, sing us a song of Zion.

How shall we sing the Lord's song in a strange land"

In later days, Jews have suffered only at the hands of Christians because of their having had a hand in the supposed Crucification of Jesus Christ[8]. We have given a list of well known instances of persecution of Jews but did not include the migration of Jews to Babylon during the sixth century when Justinian withdrew citizenship from all those who were not members of Orthodox Church. Jews, as a result, chose the kindlier atmosphere of Babylon, which, at that time was under the Iranians. When the Iranians reconquered Syria, at the beginning of the 7th century, the Jews, who had been left behind, sided with the invaders. They paid heavily for this when Emperor Heraclius reconquered the country.

During the "early period of Arab rule they prospered. The Jewish towns and villages remained Jewish, paying taxes to Muslims, instead of Christian rulers, but otherwise continuing their normal life". This kind of treatment by Muslim rulers was in the spirit of the Constitutional Charter of Medina, which had categorically made it highly illegal to do any wrong to the Jews. The only other people who have been kind to the Jews are the Iranians. Yazdgard I was most kind to them. His "married to a Jewess, was so well disposed to them, that they called him "The Christian King".

The Prophet (PBUH) was so kind to the Jews that, he, made it illegal for everybody to harm the Jews, unless they were guilty of a crime. Also he laid down that :

Clause 18: "The enemies of Jews will not be helped."

Both these Clauses were independent of the Jews following the leadership of Believers otherwise. These concessions were given to them as ordinary citizens of Yathrib. This was a great step forward towards freedom, equality and basic human rights of man considering that this legal Document was being dictated verbatum in the year 622 A.C.

In the normal course of events, this is not much of a concession to a group accepted as free citizens of a state. It becomes a great concession when no civic duties are imposed on that group. It gives the impression that although their Arab Haleefs[9] were giving them protection yet they were on friendly terms with the enemies of the Jews previously. They were now being told that their enemies will not be befriended.

No Discrimination

These two Clauses give a clue to the consistently good treatment of minorities by Muslim rulers. These two Clauses have served as a Sunnah of the Prophet (PBUH) indicating the manner in which, minorities living under Muslim rule should be treated, Muslim rulers have never persecuted people on whom they may have had to rule. Persecution of the weak appears to be a part of the European race and Muslim, in their earlier period, were fortunate to have escaped European influence. Even during the present civilised century Europeans have prided themselves on their superior strength to dominate other people. A German writer of early twentieth century, Ludwig Welliman, "affirmed as early as 1903, that, the race is called upon to dominate the earth, to exploit nations' treasures, and the physical strength of man, to make the passive races simple subaltern organisations for the evolution of its nation".

When Germany overran France, during the Second World War, it set about to depopulate France, so that France was not able to provide itself with adequate manpower during any future war. "The annual total of French births which did not exceed six hundred thousand in 1939, would be halted or worse, since there would also be economic difficulties and privations skilfully organised and maintained by the victor".

Non-Muslims Protection

Jews, though a mislead people, have been unfortunate throughout history. They have been persecuted in all lands except where Islam reigned. We know how they suffered in the Middle East and England. Their fate in Germany during twentieth century has been worse. To persecute them for having particular religious views has been highly unjust. It appears, that Europeans are too narrow minded, to permit others to hold views, which differ with their own views, and yet nearly all European nations pretend to be secular. One of those who have suffered at the altar of their Secular Christianity writes, "Christian Missionaries, who came from secular states of Europe, with public funds, introduced education on the Western pattern, which spread all over the country. Admission to these Christian schools was conditional on accepting Christianity".

In some cases and particularly after independence "they were baptised forcefully, at the Victory College Chapel". The writer goes on to say, "What is most essential for the dignity of man and social progress is freedom of thought, the very freedom, which the Churches have striven for, through centuries of religious wars and persecution to destroy". The Last Way of Life, sent to mankind, through Muhammad (PBUH), happens to be the only Way of Life, with the school of thought that there will be complete freedom of thought and has forbidden use of force in "Deen."

"There is no compulsion in religion." 2: 256

Clause 29: "The Jews will contribute towards the war when fighting alongside the Believers."

The last Clause dealing with the subject of Jews was in relation to their enemies not being helped. Immediately after that Clause matters of defence were taken up. As a result the Jews must have asked about contribution towards the war, in case they also took part in it. It was logical for them to come forward and share the expenses of the war. This, however, was a general statement and Jews under the protection of Arab tribes must have wanted, that their names be specifically mentioned in the Charter. It had been dictated earlier that those Jews who fought alongside the Believers will be considered as part of the Ummah. When they had accepted to share at the cost of war at the time of joining in Jihad on the Path of Allah, they were entitled to become a part of the Ummah on by the Jews would have gradually brought humanity on to the same platform.

Mankind is destined to become one Ummah eventually, when they will be following the same Law. Clause 28 already dictated says, "When you differ on anything the matter will be referred to Allah and Muhammad (PBUH)." Reference to Allah means the Dictates of the Quran and reference to Muhammad (PBUH) signifies his Sunnah. It meant that the mode of worship was to remain separate but the Law governing the society was to be that of Islam. Orientalists have failed to comprehend the significance of Prophet's approach to forge an Ummah in which all People of the Book, should live as One Ummah. Muir accepts that "No expression regarding either the Jewish or Christian Scriptures ever escaped the lips of Muhammad (PBUH) other than of implicit reverence".

And yet on the same page he writes: "In his later years Islam diverged rapidly from all sympathy with the Bible". He has given no proof of this divergence. He, however, has realised that, "It was the opposition of the Jews, and the martial superiority of Islam that imperceptibly led to the exclusive authority of Muhammad (PBUH) and the Quran".

If Muir had read the Charter carefully, he would have realised that exclusive authority of Muhammad (PBUH) and the Quran had been established from the beginning of Islam in Medina. The Jews failed to perceive, and so has Muir missed the point that unity of human race was the object of the Final Way of Life being Revealed to Muhammad (PBUH). It was the Jews who sabotaged it and it is Christian Missionaries and the Zionists who are still on the path of war with Islam the Deen of Peace. Allah has said:

"Mankind were one community". 2: 213

Differences arose and people forgot the true Faith. Messengers were sent to guide them back to the right path. Some listened and some did not. Although many Messengers were sent the main theme remained, as the Sovereignty of Allah. When the Last Messenger came, he tried to bring people on to the same platform. A beginning was made, but when people of the Book laid stress on their own separate identity and ignored the Sovereignty of Allah, the experiment failed. The present writer feels that, the result was that for the future the order came, that, who ever accepts Islam must submit completely.

"O ye who believe Come, all of you, into submission (unto Him)".
2: 208

Clause 31: "The same applies to Jews of Bani Al-Najjar[10], Bani Al- Harith[11], Bani Saeeda[12], Bani Jasham[13], Bani Al-Aus[14], Thaliba[15] and the Jaffra[16] and the Bani Al-Shuraiha[17]"

Clause 34: "Those in alliance with the Jews will be given the same treatment as the Jews."

The Jews were accepting the responsibility of joining in the defence of the state. They had allies abroad. As the Jews had promised to become a part of the Ummah, it was only fair to consider and treat their allies in the same manner as the Jews.

Non-Muslims Protection

Clause 37: "The Jews bear their own expenses and the Believers bear their expenses."

The subject matter of defence continues. The question of payment has arisen again. This refers to expenses connected with each ethnic contingent of the Army. Each was to pay for its own contingent.

Clause 43: "The Jews must pay with the Believers."

This was to refer to expenses of general nature like blood money or other damages, in which both parties had to share the expenses.

Clause 47: "The Jews of al-Aus, including their freedom have the same standing as other parties to the Charter."

This Clause speaks for itself. Late-comers were being accommodated.

These were Clauses in respect of Laws binding and giving rights to Jews. Irrespective of what status they had possessed prior to the Hijrah of the Prophet (PBUH), they were to be governed and treated in accordance with the dictates of this Document. It is incumbent on all students of Seerah and early history of Islam to bear in their minds the contents of the Charter. Without reference to this important Document no opinion can he formed on the behaviour of one or the other party.

References

1. Most prosperous and well famed tribes.
2. Place where the famous Islamic war was fought.
3. One of the most important tribes of Arabia.
4-5. Two prominent Prophets of Islam.
6. A great and learned person of Geography of Arab.
7. Prophet Yaqub.
8. Prophet Isa (Pbuh).
9. Political rival parties.
10-17. Tribes of Arabia.

12

CRIMINAL LAW

LAWS IN FORCE

Islam protects the rights of human beings; it has devised all ways and means to create such an atmosphere wherein the rights of the people are fully safeguarded. Islam stands for the peace of the mankind in this world and the hereafter. The Islamic law of punishment aims at eradication of all sorts of vices which corrupt human beings and human societies. Punishments are effective means to purge human societies of evil and undesirable elements. Islam considers punishment as means of purification from sins and crimes, as an eye opener to the people. The ultimate object of punishment is to establish and to enforce justice, peace, equality, security of life, honour and property. Punishment in Islam derives its moral justification from the simple fact that it constitutes indispensable self-defence of societies against crimes. Punishment subdues the wrong; hence punishments under Islamic Law are indeed very strict and deterrent, but very strict proof is also required to find one guilty. These punishments are not only redressive and retributive but also reformative.

SETUP OF GOVERNMENT

After the migration of the Holy Prophet to Medina, authority was established to settle disputes between people and to award punishment. As more and more people and more territory fell under the sway of the Central Government at Medina, the arm of the law was extended to cover large areas and, in some cases, the function to dispense justice was also delegated according to the needs. It is an admitted fact that the primary source of law in Islam is the Quran supplemented by the injunctions of the Holy Prophet (peace be upon him) who was the first Head of Islamic State. After him, his successors followed the path shown by him. But as the simple society of Arabs was confronted by new and complex situations presented by fresh contacts and fresh conquests, the original sources were found insufficient.

To the primary sources—others were added which were no more than rationalistic application and extension of the principles contained in the Quran and the *Sunnah*[1]. While the principles were basic, the working out of solutions was necessarily influenced and conditioned by environments which could not fail to take into account the habits and traditions of the people for whom the "analogical deductions" were intended.

The Quran has made three-fold protection of person, property and honour of the mankind as human life is the most sacred, so sacred that the annihilation of one life for other than man slaughter or corruption in the earth has been considered equivalent to the destruction of life, and the slaying of all mankind.

(Al-Quran Ch. V *verse* 35)

Quranic Law about Manslaughter : The general law in cases of manslaughter is contained in Ch. II, verse 178-179. The English translation of verse 178 is reproduced as under :

> "O ye who believe, the law of equality is prescribed for you in cases of murder: the free for the free, the slave for the slave, and the woman for the woman. But if one is granted any remission by one's brother, then pursuing the matter for the realisation of the blood-money shall be done with fairness and the murderer shall pay the blood-money in a handsome manner. This is an alleviation and mercy from your Lord. He who transgresseth after this, shall have a painful doom."

In this way the gross and inequitable custom of killing a freeman for a slave or killing more for one on the basis of higher status or of superior claim as it existed in pre-Islamic days has been abolished for all times. Verse 179 of Ch. II refers to the principle of retaliation. It says "And there is life for you in retaliation, O men of understanding, that you may ward off (evil)."

The two kinds of man-slaughter are mentioned as under :

(a) Murder by intention.

(b) Murder by mistake.

Criminal Law

The penalty for each such offence is mentioned in Quran and prescribed as under :

"Never should a Believer kill a Believer but (if it so happens) by mistake, compensation is due if one kills a Believer. It is ordained that he should free a believing slave and pay compensation to the deceased's family unless they remit it freely. If the deceased belonged to a people at war with you and he was a Believer, the freeing of a believing slave is enough. If he belonged to a people with whom you have a treaty of mutual alliance, compensation should be paid to his family and a believing slave be freed. For those who find this beyond their means is prescribed a fast for two consecutive months by way of penance from Allah." *(Ch. IV, verse 92)*

A Muslim shall not kill a Muslim deliberately; it may be by accident only and, in that case, compensation is the only satisfaction prescribed. But where this is done by intention (in modern legal phraseology called murder), the penalty is extremely serious. "Whoso slayeth a Believer of set purpose, his reward is Hell for ever and the wrath and the curse of God are upon him, and dreadful penalty is prepared for him."
(Ch. IV, verse 93)

Varying Degrees : The offence of killing may vary in degrees. It may be deliberate killing with the intention to kill it may result in death without the intention to cause it; it may be the consequence of a grave and sudden provocation, etc., and the punishment should be commensurate with the offence. This is for the legislation to fix.

Injuries other than Death : As regards injuries short of death, the general principle is contained in V. 48, XVI 126. The legislature has the right and the power to make laws on the subject. Injuries might be classified as grievous or simple, and some may be compounded with the sanction of the Courts and others without such sanction. There is nothing against Islamic law to cover by legislation the entire gamut of injuries to "person" from the ordinary to the serious, culminating in death. This is wholly within the province of the legislature and is known as what is called *"Tazir"*[2] as distinguished from *"Hadud"*[3], the limit prescribed in the Quran.

Zina Defined and Punishment Indicated : *Zina*[4], usually translated as adultery or fornication in *Fiqh*[5], has a wider meaning than sexual cohabitation with or without consent; it covers all sexual intercourse out of lawful wedlock. It is an offence both against person and honour. The punishment is prescribed in XXIV 2: "The adulterer and the adulteress, scourge ye each one of them (with) a hundred stripes. And let not pity for the twain withhold you from obedience to Allah if ye believe in Allah and the Last Day and let a party of believers witness their punishment".

In IV 15, it is prescribed: "As for those of your women who are guilty of lewdness, call to witness four of you against them. And if they testify (to the truth of the allegation), then confine them to the houses until death takes them or (until) Allah appoint for them a way". In XVII 32, *Zina* is described as a foul thing and an evil way, and the Muslims are prohibited from going near it.

Doctrine of Rajm (Lapidation) : *Surat Al-Noor* (Chapter XXIV) which prescribes punishment for *Zina* was revealed between the 5th and 6th Hijra, and before that no specific punishment for *Zina* was provided in the Quran. In the Old Testament punishment for adultery was known to be "stoning to death". It is no more to be found therein. In *Oxodus, Chapter XXI, Verse 28,* it is said: "If an *ox gore* a man or a woman, that they die, the ox shall be surely stoned, and his flesh shall not be eaten". If an animal could not escape stoning to death for the sin of goring a human being, how could a man be treated differently for adultery. Reference to this aspect of Jewish law may be found in the New Testament. In *St John, Chapter VIII, verses 3-11* describe the case of a woman "taken in adultery" and produced before Jesus. "They say unto him, Master, this woman hath been taken in adultery, in the very act. Now in the law Moses commanded us to stone such: what then sayest thou of her? Jesus said: He that is without sin among you, let him first cast a stone at her".

Penalty of Rajm Examined : On the strength of some Traditions, it has been laid down in the Islamic law books that in case of *Zina,* if the parties are unmarried, punishment of one hundred stripes each shall be inflicted, and if they are already married, then they shall be "stoned to death". This distinction is not supported by the Quran. The words used in the Quran are of a general nature and include all kinds of *Zanis* (adulterers), married or unmarried, free or slave. In his *Tafsir-ul-Kabir,* Volume VI, p. 214. Imam Razi[6] records: All are agreed that the punishment of one hundred stripes is applicable to all types of delinquents".

As mentioned above in XXIV 2, the punishment of one hundred stripes alone is prescribed, the word *Rajm* (lapidation) is nowhere mentioned in the Quran as punishment for *Zina.* In this connection, IV. 25 may also be kept in view: "And if when they (the slave-girls) are honourably married, they commit lewdness, they shall incur the half of the punishment (prescribed) for free women in that case." Now "half of the punishment (prescribed) for a free-woman" can be one half of one hundred stripes, that is fifty, by lapidation consummating in death cannot be so divided.

Traditions Scrutinised : The Traditions relied on in support of "lapidation" are discordant and fail to establish that any such punishment was awarded after the revelation of *Surat Al-Noor* (Chapter XXIV). In one Tradition quoted in *Bukhari*[7] and *Muslim*[8], Hadrat Umar, the Second Caliph, is reported to have said: "In the Book revealed to the Holy Prophet, there was a verse relating to *Rajm* which we read and understood. The Prophet himself acted upon it and gave the punishment of *Rajm*.

Ibadat, son of Samit (Muslim) on the authority of the Holy Prophet said: "Unmarried man and woman guilty of adultery should be punished with one hundred stripes and one year's banishment. The married couple should be given one hundred stripes and then stoned to death" *(Muslim)*. The only specific instance mentioned in *Bukhari* and *Muslim* is that of Maiz, son of Malik.

Rape : A distinction does exist between an ordinary case of sexual intercourse with mutual consent and one done with a person incapable of giving consent. The punishment must also be more serious in one than in the other.

Besides actual cohabitation, there are other lewd or improper acts which, if not checked in time, might eventuate in sexual relations. These too should be made punishable by the State.

Protection of Property : The Quranic injunction is as follows:

> And as for the man who steals and the woman who steals, cut off their hands in retribution of their offences, an exemplary punishment from Allah. And Allah is Mighty, Wise. But whosoever repents after his transgression and amends, then will Allah surely turn to him in mercy: verily Allah is Most Forgiving, Merciful.   (Ch. V, Verses 41-42)

Suraqah : "*Suraqah*" literally means secretly taking away of another's property. In the language of the law, it signifies taking away the property of another in a secret manner, at a time when such property is in custody, that is, when the effects are in supposed security from the hands of other people and where the value is not less than ten dirhams and the effects taken are the undoubted property of some other than of him who takes them.

Cutting of Hand is not the only Punishment : It is not correct to say that for every offence of theft, the hand shall be cut. This shall be clear from the following instances:

(1) A slave who had committed theft was brought before the Holy Prophet. He was forgiven. The same leniency was shown to him for the second, third and fourth thefts. When he was brought again for the fifth time for

the same offence, the Holy Prophet ordered his hand to be cut. On his subsequent repetition of the offence thrice, his hand and foot were cut.

(2) The slaves of Habit stole away the camel of a person of the tribe of Madia. The culprits were produced before Hadrat Umar, the Second Caliph. He first ordered that the hands be cut but modified the same and directed that, in lieu of cutting of the hands, the offenders should be punished with a penalty which should be felt. The owner was asked about the price of the camel. He said it was 400 dirhams, that is, twice the amount.
(Izalat-ul-Khifa', Volume II, p. 130 ; Sunan Kubra, Volume VIII, p. 278)

Cases where no cutting is to be done *Hidayah* enumerates a long list of cases in which the penalty of cutting of hand or foot cannot be inflicted. The thefts of dry wood, birds of prey, for example, hens or ducks, milk, butter and fresh fruits on trees; the instruments of music; copies of the Holy Quran; the doors of the *Kaaba*[9], the money from the public treasury, would not entail the cutting of the hand. Similarly, the hand shall not be cut where the thief had committed the theft in the house and made over the property to another outside the house. It cannot be pleaded that they are not cases of theft, but they are relevant for the purposes of showing that the amputation of limbs is not the only punishment in the case of *Suraqah*.

In Islam, opportunity is always given to a sinner to reform himself. If for a petty theft for the first time, a person is to be permanently deprived of the use of his limbs and made a cripple for the rest of his existence, it is useless for him to repent or to make amends. This would render the Quranic verse: "But whosoever repents after his transgression and amends, then will Allah surely turn to him in mercy. Verily Allah is Most Forgiving, Merciful". (V. 42)

True import of Quranic injunction. In V. 41, the injunction about cutting of hand is described as a retribution and by way of exemplary punishment. The Arabic word used in the verse is *nakal* which means, "to prevent: to deter; to give exemplary punishment". *"Nakal"* means curb for race horses. Qadi Abdul Jabbar[10] has pointed out that a small evil is not called *nakal*; it becomes so when it has increased considerably and become rampant; consequently the cutting of hand for theft is reserved only for the habitual thieves who could not otherwise be prevented from repeating the offence. (*Tafsir al-Kabir*, Volume I, p. 382)

In the *Tafsir Bayan al-Quran*, Maulana Muhammad Ali has expressed the view that the cutting of hand is the maximum penalty provided for taking away another's property and appropriately for habitual offenders.

Criminal Law

Varying Degrees : The offence of the theft is of various degrees. It may be simple, serious or aggravated; it may be removing by stealth, by breaking open a house and may or may not be accompanied by force or threat of force. To suit various forms, the punishment has to be suitably regulated.

Securing Respect

> The Quran makes special provisions for the protection of honour. In the case of chaste women, it is prescribed: "And those who launch a charge against a chaste woman, and produce not four witnesses (to support their allegations), flog them with eighty stripes and reject their evidence ever after: for such men are wicked transgressors"
>
> (XXIV 4)

Allama Yusuf Ali, in his Note 2958 of his English translation of the Holy Quran, says:

> The most serious notice is taken of people who put forward slanders or scandalous suggestions about women without adequate evidence. If anything is said against a woman's chastity, it should be supported by evidence twice as strong as would ordinarily be required for business transactions, or even in murder cases. That is, four witnesses would be required instead of two. Failing such preponderating evidence, the slanderer should himself be treated as a wicked transgressor and punished with eighty stripes. Not only would he be subjected to this disgraceful form of punishment, but he would be deprived of the citizen's right of giving evidence in all matters all his life, unless he repents and reforms, in which case he can be readmitted to be a competent witness.

Laen (XXIV 6—9) : Where a husband so charges his wife and cannot produce the required number of witnesses, he shall have to take oath by God four times that he was solemnly telling the truth and the fifth oath involving the curse of Allah on him if he was a liar. The wife can in her turn avert the punishment by similarly taking an oath four times that the charge was false and the fifth time that the wrath of Allah be upon her if he was telling the truth.

The false accusation, in the language of law, is described as *Kazaf* which is defined in the *Hidayah* as follows :

> *Kazaf,* in its primitive sense, simply means accusation. By *Kazaf,* in the language of law, is understood a man insinuating a charge of whoredom against a married man or woman.

KINDS OF PUNISHMENT

Punishments are divided into two classes, one of which is called *Hadd* and the other *Tazir*. *Hadd* in its primitive sense signifies "obstruction", whence a porter or a gate-keeper is termed the *Haddad* or "obstructer" from his office of prohibiting people from entering. In law it expresses the correction appointed and specified by the law on account of the right of God and hence the extension of the term *Hadd* to retaliation is not approved; since retaliation is due as a right of man and not as a right of God and, in the same manner, the extension of it to *Tazir* (or discriminatory chastisement) is not approved as *Tazir* is a species of correction not specified or determined by any fixed rule of law but committed to the discretion of the Qadi. The original design in the institution of *Hadd* is deterrent, that is, warning people from the commission of offensive actions.

Tazir (Hidayah, Vol II, Chapter VI) : In its primitive sense, *Tazir* means prohibition and also instruction; in law it signifies an infliction undetermined in its degree by the law, on account of the right either of God or of the individual, and the occasion of it is any offence for which *Hadd* or stated punishment has not been appointed whether that offence consists in words or deeds.

Degrees of Chastisement : In the *Fatwa-i-Shafii*[1], it is said that there are four orders or degrees of chastisement. First, the chastisement proper to the most noble of the nobles, for example, princes or men of learning, which consists merely of an admonition; secondly, chastisement proper to the nobles which may be performed either by admonition or by *jirr*, that is, by dragging the offender to the floor and exposing him to scorn; thirdly, the chastisement proper to the middle order, for example, merchants and shopkeepers, which may be performed *jirr* as above and also by imprisonment; and, fourthly, the chastisement proper to the lower orders in the community which may be performed by *jirr* or by imprisonment and also by blows.

Fine : It is recorded from Abu Yusuf that the Sultan may inflict chastisement by means of property, that is, by exaction of a small sum in the manner of a fine proportionate to the offence.

Scope and Purpose of Punishment : Any misconception regarding the criminal provisions in the Quran might be avoided if their purpose and scope were properly understood. The Quran is not the Penal Code; only a few offences are mentioned. A careful analysis would show that they refer to the preservation of the State and to the categories dealing with the fundamental human rights to person, property and honour. The penalty prescribed for each category is the maximum one and within the maximum and the minimum limits the society is free to frame necessary laws falling in that category and to fix the punishment for each to be enforced

Criminal Law

with the sanction at its command. The criminal provisions are only ancillary to the grand objective the Quran has in view of creating a society which shall breath and exist in the ever-living presence of the Almighty and possessed of desire to make sacrifices for the welfare of their fellow-beings and thus realise the purpose of life on this earth. As man is born weak, and is apt to go astray, some correction is needed to reform him or to warn others for their ultimate good.

PARTICULAR RULES

The general law of punishment is contained in the Quran, V. 36, which says: "The punishment of those who wage war against Allah and His Apostle and strive with might and main for mischief through the land is only this: that they be slain, or crucified, or their hands and their feet be cut off from opposite sides, or they be exiled from the land. That shall be a disgrace for them in this world and in the Hereafter. They shall have a great punishment".

All conceivable offences against the State, such as treason or public disorder or wilful defiance of the laws of God and of constituted authority, are made punishable with anyone of the four punishments enumerated above, that is (1) killing; (2) crucification, (3) cutting hands and feet, and (4) exile from land. The expression which literally means "elimination from land" may mean banishment or imprisonment in a jail to prevent the commission or repetition of an offence. It should be distinctly noted that the punishments are in the alternative, that is, for one, the other may be substituted in view of the exigencies of the case. It shall, therefore, follow that where the killing or cutting of hands is prescribed, it shall not be un-Islamic to commute it to some other form of punishment. In selecting a particular form of punishment the habits and usages of the people, the facts and circumstances of each case including the status of the offender may be taken into consideration by the Qadi. A wise administrator or legislator would not like to do anything which might shockingly hurt the feelings of the populace or act in a manner which might appear as atrocious or needlessly cruel.

In the verse, the words "waging war against Allah and His Apostle" are of very wide import. It does not mean actual taking up of arms against Allah for that would be meaningless; it means disobedience to His commands.

The offence of drinking wine has been very much condemned in the Holy Quran but no punishment has been prescribed for it. However, the said offence is punishable with 80 lashes as mentioned in *Mishkat Book XV, Chapter IV.* It is sufficient to say in this respect that the punishments by way of imprisonment is not favoured by Islam because the objective of punishment is to deter both the criminals as well as the general public. According to Islam, the most severe offences are the crimes against the societies for example, adultery, drinking, slander and fornication, etc. These crimes are punished strictly according to the injunction of Quran and *Sunnah* as Islam is keen to remove the factors that lead to the commission of crimes as it wants to purify societies of all the social crimes by deterrent punishment.

ORIGIN OF SPECIFIC LAWS

Ahkam, the religious commands are the fount-head of all Islamic Laws as is evident from the Holy Verse :

"For each we have appointed a Divine law and traced out way".
(V-45 Al-Maida)

The principles laid down by Allah in the Holy Book are expounded by *Sunnah* of the Holy Prophet (Peace be upon him). Holy Prophet did not speak of his own in such matters. Quran has put the words of the Prophet at par with the Quran:

"Nor doth he speak of his own desire. It is naught save an inspiration that is inspired". (LIII, 3 &4 Al-Najm)

Muslims are duty-bound to follow *Uswa-i-Hasana* (III, 21 *Al-Ahzab).* Whenever unanimity is reached among the Muslim Jurists of a time, the consensus has the same validity as a verse of the Quran or the most reliably proved *Sunnah* of the Prophet, the latter con senses may, over-rule the former.

The solution of practical problems are permitted through analogical deduction *(Qiyas)* based on the principle laid down by the Quran, *Sunnah* and *Ijma.*

Four sources, the Quran, *Sunnah, Ijma* and *Qiyas* are the roots *(Usul)* of *Fiqh* i.e. the knowledge of what is for and upon man and are the foundations of religious command and basis of Lawful and forbidden. Thus religious commands regarding practical affairs of life are ascertained on the principles which may be traced to Quran, *Sunnah,* and the rights and obligations of "man and society" and what is permitted and forbidden to him are also determined in accordance with these principles.

Fiqh divides *Ahkam* (religious commands) relating to rights and obligations of man *viz-a-viz* society into following categories:

(a) *Huququllah (Rights of God):*

These relate to "good" of the society as a whole i.e. prohibition of adultery, and *Ahteram* of *Baitullah.* It is on account of reverence that we call them *Huququllah,* otherwise Allah is besought of all (112-12 *Al Akhlas).*

Criminal Law

(b) *Huququl Ibad (Right of Man)*:

These commands relate to the rights and obligations of an individual e.g. right to own property and obligation not to damage the property of others. Thus with the permission of the owner, the property becomes lawful for others.

(c) Mixture of the above two *Huquq* with predominance of *Huququllah* i.e. punishment of slander.

(d) Mixture with predominance of *Huququl Ibad* e.g. *Qisas* (Retaliation).

It is *Ibadat* in the sense that *Kaffara* is fulfilled through fasting, freeing a slave and feeding the poor and *"Uqubat"* in the sense that this liability comes into existence when a prohibited act is committed.

In *'Fiqh"* offence means an act or omission rendering a person liable to *"Hadd"* or *"Tazeer"*. *Hadd* expresses the correction appointed and specified by Holy Quran, and *Sunnah* on account of right of God. *Tazeer* signifies an infliction determined in its degree by the law on account of right of God or of the individual and the occasion of it is any offence for which *Hadd* has not been appointed. In the language of Law *"Janayat"* is expressive of any prohibited act committed upon the person or property. In the practice of Lawyer *(Fiqh)*, *"Janayat"* means prohibited act committed upon the person which is called Murder or upon a part of the body which is termed wounding or maiming. Thus it is possible to include *"Janayat"* in the term offence. There is provision of *Qisas* for such cases *Qisas* literally means tracking the footsteps of an enemy and is the law of retaliation.

The definition of the offence suggests the following divisions of the offences according to the corrections and chastisements:

(i) Offences where punishment is *Hadd*.

(ii) Offences where correction is *Qisas*.

(iii) Offences where chastisement is *Tazeer*.

Thus punishments in Islam are of three kinds : — (1) *Hadd;* (2) *Qisas;* and (3) *Tazeer*.

Hadd : *"Hadd"* in its primitive sense signifies, "obstruction", as a gate-keeper is called *"Haddad"* i.e. intercepting people from entering. The word *Hadd* also means definition as term, the essential limits of a certain thing by which it is distinguished. The word *"Hadd"* in the strict legal sense denotes Allah's restrictive ordinances par excellence, the fixed punishments, which have been prescribed by the Holy Quran. Later on it also came to define the punishment proved or established by the *Sunnah* of the Holy Prophet and his Companions on which there is an *"Ijma"* (consensus) of the Holy Prophet's Companions. These punishments are as under :

(1) Theft *(suraqa)*—punishable with cutting of right hand.

(2) Dacoity or highway robbery *(Haraabah)*—without murder punishable with cutting of right hand and left foot and if accompanied with murder punishable with death.

(3) Fornication or adultery *(zina)*—punishable with one hundred stripes when committed by unmarried person and by stoning to death when committed by married person.

(4) Falsely accusing a person of committing unlawful sexual intercourse *(Qasaf)*—punishable with eighty stripes.

(5) Drinking wine *(Shurb al Khamr)*—punishable with eighty stripes.

(6) Apostasy *(irtidad)*—punishable with death.

The aforesaid *Hadud* offences are neither compoundable nor open to settlement, pardon or waiver because in principle it is right of God and no obstruction is permissible in the execution of punishment in the prescribed manner. Theft under Islamic Law signifies surreptitiously taking away the property of another from his *Hirza* (custody) of the value of or above 10 dirham i.e. *"Nisab"*[12] equal to 4.457 grams of gold or other property of equivalent value (at the time of theft) by an adult person (accused). The word surreptitious means that the victim of theft does not know that his property is being stolen and it is deemed to have been secretly removed during daytime (meaning one hour before sunrise and two hours after sunset). Surreptitious continues till the completion of the offence. If theft is committed at night surreptitious need not continue after the commencement of the offence.

Another Gravamen of the theft is *"Hirza"* which means an arrangement made for the custody of the property by the owner. The custody may be of two kinds; firstly such as house, shop, box, container and secondly by personal guard which means a personal watch over the property. Thus if an adult male or female of sound prudence steals property of or above the value of 4.475 grams of gold or other property of equivalent value or above from the custody of another, the Islamic Law provides the punishment of amputation of hand. The Holy Quran, says :

"As for thief, both male and female, cut off their hands."

(7,38 Al Maida)

The offence is proved by confession of the accused or the evidence in court by at least two truthful adult male eye-witness (other than the victim of theft) abstaining from committing major sin to satisfaction of the trial court.

Criminal Law

The concept of vicarious responsibility is also available under the Islamic Law, so if theft liable to *Hadd* is committed by more than one person and the total value of the stolen property is such that if the property is equally divided by the thieves, the share of each amounts to or exceeds, the *"Nisab" Hadd* shall be imposed on all of them as have entered the *Hirz*, even if each one of them has not removed the stolen property or any part thereof.

In addition to the aforesaid conclusive proof with regard to the ingredients of the offence and high standard of evidence the following categories of persons and article are immuned from *Hadd* punishment :

(a) When the offender and victim of the theft are related to each other i.e.
  (i) spouse;
  (ii) ascendants : paternal or maternal;
  (iii) descendant: paternal or maternal;
  (iv) brother, sister, father or mother;
  (v) brother, sister or their children.

(b) Guest committing theft from the house of his host.

(c) Servant or employee having authorised access to the Master's *hirz*.

(d) Property such as wild grass, fish, bird, dog, pig, intoxicant, musical instruments or perishable foodstuff for the preservation of which provision does not exist.

(e) When the offender has a share in the stolen property the value of which after deduction of his share is less than the *Nisab*.

(f) When the offender commits theft under *"Ikrah"*[13] or *"Iztrar"*[14] i.e. duress or compulsion arising out of situation of fear of injury to his property or honour or of any other person or the apprehension of death due to extreme hunger or thirst.

(g) When a creditor steals his debtor's property, the value of which after deduction of the amount due to him, is less than the *Nisab*.

(h) When the offender before his apprehension has, on account of repentance, returned the stolen property to the victim and surrendered himself to the authority.

The *Hadd* punishment abates if confession is retracted by convict or in case of witnesses, any, witness resoles from his testimony so as to reduce the number of witnesses less than two.

The previous conviction also applies on the first conviction the right hand of the convict is cut at the joint of the wrist and stump, thereafter cauterised, for the second theft the left foot is cut and for subsequent offence the convict is imprisoned.

It will thus be seen that theft contemplated by Islamic Law excludes petty theft of daily necessity of life or for subsistence and also exempts near and dear ones of a person who believe to have some right or share in the property of the other. The Islamic Law penalises theft by professionals.

Haraabah (Dacoity, Highway Robbery, Bloodshed and High-treason) : The provision for this category of crime is derived from the following verse of Holy Quran :

"The only reward of those who make war upon Allah and his Messenger and strive after corruption in the land will be that they will be killed or crucified or have their hands and feet on alternate side cut off or will be expelled out of the land. Such will be their degradation in the world and hereafter, there will be an awful doom."

The provisions relating to *Haraabah* are based on Chapter V., Verse 33 of Holy Quran, which refers to those who wage war against an Islamic order either on a full scale revolt or through such acts as highway robbery, disruption of public order or the commission of murder. These acts even if devoid of the intention to overthrow an Islamic order, are deemed liable to prescribed punishment because such acts undermine.   "The Nizam-e-Salih"

A dacoit or robber in this sense is one who overpowers the traveller and commits theft. If the offender did not carry out theft but in the process commits murder, the punishment is death. If the offender in the course of dacoity or robbery has stolen the property equivalent to *Nisab* of theft, the offender's right hand and left foot shall be cut off. However if the offender has no right hand or left foot or if these are paralysed, the same are not to be amputated and instead he is liable to *Tazir.*

If the offenders have committed robbery as well as murder, their right hand and left foot are to be first amputated and then they are executed." If the culprits are arrested in an attempt to commit the offence, they will be exiled but some jurists say that they be jailed. In few Muslim countries such are liable to imprisonment and whipping.

Murder committed in the course of dacoity or robbery is not compoundable like ordinary murder. The accused conjointly committing the offence owe vicarious liability and each one of them is punished. The punishment of dacoity

Criminal Law

during famine may be dealt with leniently and may vary if it is committed on *Harbis* (non-Muslim from an Islamic Jurisdiction) and *Mustamilis* (non-Muslim from in Islamic Jurisdiction coming to an Islamic Jurisdiction seeking peace).

The mode of proof is the same as required in case of theft liable to *Hadd*.

Zina (Adultery) : It means either adultery or fornication and signifies carnal conjunction of a man with a woman, not validly married or neither suspecting themselves to be married. As to whoredom of a woman, it means her submission to the man to commit that act. In such cases man and woman are equally guilty as ordained by the Holy Quran:

> The adulterer and adulteress scourge ye each one of them with a hundred stripes. And let not pity for them twain withhold you from obedience to Allah, if ye believe in Allah and the last day. And let a party of believers witness their punishment. (XXIV, 2 Al Noor)

In Islamic law, if the adulterer and adulteress are not married, each of them shall suffer the *Hadd* punishment of hundred stripes as per Holy verse. In case they are married, each one of them shall be stoned to death according to the *Sunnah* of the Holy Prophet (peace be upon him).

The offence is proved by confession of the accused before court of competent jurisdiction or direct evidence of at least 4 Muslim adult male eye-witness about whom the court is satisfied, having regard to the requirement, of *"Tazkiyah-al-shuhood"* that they are truthful and abstain from major sin *(Kabir)* give evidence as eye-witness to the act of penetration necessary for the offence.

The "Qadi" or the judge is required to satisfy himself that the confession is voluntary and not on account of some infirmity such as insanity or inducement, threat or promise. Similarly the four eye-witness require clearance of the "Qadi" that they are persons of unimpeachable character, just and righteous. Again the witnesses have to stand test of cross-examination with regard to nature of offence, the time of occurrence, before their evidence is acted upon:

> The circumstantial evidence such as birth of child to an unmarried female is admissible but emphasis lies on conclusive proof. Hadrat Ali punished *"Shurah"* on the basis of pregnancy. She was first flogged on Thursday and then stoned to death.
>
> (Bukhari, Vol. III, Hadith 1716, p. 631)

"Another case cited by Maulana Maududi in his *Tafheem ul Quran* (Vol. III under verse 2 *"Surah Noor"* is reproduced as under :

"It is reported by Tabir, son of Abdullah *(See* Abu Daud and Nisei) that a person who committed adultery was punished whipping only but when it was found that he was married, he was stoned to death".

(Abu Daud, Vol. HI, Hadith 1029)

The study of these two cases also indicates that dual punishment is permissible for the same offence.

On the face of conclusive evidence, still there are some more legal exceptions in the way of imposition of *Hadd* punishment such as :

(1) cohabitation due to some doubt or semblance of validity recognised by the *Shariah;*

(2) Sexual intercourse under duress or coercion;

(3) case proved solely by confession if the same is retracted by convict before or during the imposition of the *Hadd* punishment or part thereof; and

(4) in case the offence is proved by the testimony of witnesses, any witness resile so as to reduce the number of witnesses less than four before or in the course of imposition of *Hadd.*

Adultery or fornication is the root evil in human society. It damages the social health and moral order of the human society which Islam wants to preserve for its dignity. It gives rise to heinous crime like murder, attempted murder and lays ground for future bickering and blood feuds in the society. All over Islamic nations, the fornication plays vital part in crime contribution. In few countries the couple involved in adultery are killed by their own relatives as *"Kala Kali"* and there is hardly any report to the authorities. This shows that penalty of death for this sin is in complete conformity and consonance with human nature.

The punishment of stoning to death does not mean to kill the offender with stones. He is to be killed by some other weapon after initial stoning such as shooting, also provided by *Zina* Ordinance. The condition of stoning provides the chance of survival to convict till last because he may retract his confession or any out of 4 witnesses, may resile or any witness may refuse to stone the convict and in such eventuality, the convict will escape capital punishment.

Qazf (False Accusation of Adultery) : The literal meaning of the word *"Qazf"* is to throw. The theological meaning is false accusation of adultery.

The Holy Quran provides two categories of this crime. The first relates to the accusation of unchastity levelled by husband against his wife technically known as *"Lian"* and it is outside the scope of *Hadd* punishment. The second relates to a person other than the husband who accuses a woman of adultery. As

Criminal Law

to the *"Lian"*, the Holy Quran lays down the following procedure to be followed by the court of Law :

> "And for those who launch a charge of unchastity against their spouses and have in support no evidence but their own, their solitary evidence can be received, if they bear witness four times with oath by Allah that they are solemnly telling the truth and the fifty oath should be that they solemnly invoke the curse of Allah on themselves, if they tell lie. But it would avert the punishment from the wife, if she bears witness four times with an oath. Allah! that her husband is telling a lie and the wrath of Allah on herself if her accuser is telling the truth". (XXIV-6-11)

The situation for *'Lian'* may arise if husband spots his wife in act of adultery but is unable to produce four witnesses to substantiate the charge of *zina* and at the same time is unable to lead a normal married life. The matter is then left to the honour of both the spouses. If the husband so chooses he may solemnly swear four times to the fact, invoking also a curse on himself, if he lies which is *prima facie* evidence of the wife's guilt. But if the wife swears similarly four times and also invokes a curse on herself, she is in law acquitted of the guilt. If she does not take this step, the charge stands proved and she will be punished for *zina*. In either case the marriage is dissolved as it is against human nature that the parties can live together after such an incident.

As regards accusation of unlawful intercourse against chaste woman by an outsider, the Holy Quran provides *Hadd* punishment as under :

> "And those who accuse chaste woman of unchastity and produce not four witnesses to support their allegation, flog them with eighty stripes and reject their evidence ever after for such men are wicked transgressors, unless they repent thereafter and mend their conduct, for Allah is oft-forgiving most merciful". (XXIV-4-5) (Al-Noor)

The *Hadd* punishment for slandering a chaste woman of adultery is flogging of the offender with eighty stripes and depriving him from the right of giving evidence in court for good.

Drinking Wine (Shurb-al-khamr) : Drinking wine is forbidden in the following verses of Holy Quran :

> "They ask thee about wine and games of chance, say : in both is great sin, and advantage also, to men: but their sin is greater than advantage".
> (Chap. 11:26)

> "O believers: surely wine and games of chance and idols and the divining arrows are an abomination of Satan's work: Avoid them, that

we prosper. Only would satan sow hatred and enmity among you, by wine and games of chance and turn you aside from the remembrance of God and from prayer: will you not therefore, abstain from them? Obey God and obey the Apostle, and be on your guard: but if you turn back, know that our Apostle is only bound to deliver a pain announcement." (Chap. V. 92)

Neither the Holy Quran, nor the tradition of Holy Prophet ordained *Hadd* punishment for drinking wine or any other toxicant substance. However Holy Prophet gave 40 shoe-beating to a drunkard and at another occasion 40 lashes with two branches of date tree. Forty lashes were prescribed by First Caliph Abu Bakr. Eighty stripes for a freeman and Forty stripes for a slave is the *Hadd* punishment for drinking from the time of Caliph "Umar" on the sanction of *Ijma* (Consensus) of the Companions of Holy Prophet. If an adult Muslim takes intoxicating liquor by mouth and is seized whilst his breath yet smells of wine he is brought before the 'Qadi' whilst he is intoxicated and two Muslim adult male witnesses give evidence of his having committed the offence of drinking, the punishment would be eighty lashes provided the drinking was voluntary. Offence can also be proved by the confession of the accused. As to the confession after the smell disappears Imam Hanifah and Imam Yusuf differ with Imam Muhammad, the latter holds the confession sufficient for conviction but formers do not.

Apostasy from Islam (Irtidad) : A Muslim male who renegates from Islam after having professed the faith in Dar-al-Islam is liable to death if he persists and does not recant in spite of opportunity granted to him and his doubts removed. A female apostate, is not to be killed but kept in confinement until she recants. If a boy under age turns an apostate, he is to be imprisoned until he attains majority and offered the faith, if he does not return to Islam, he will be killed. The lunatics and drunkards are not responsible for apostasy from Islam. Similarly persons converted to Islam under compulsion are not liable to capital punishment.

This rule is derived from Quranic verses :

(1) "And who so becometh a re-negate and dieth in his disbelief such are those whose work have fallen both in this world and hereafter."
(II, 217 Al-Baqra)

(2) "And remember Moses said to his people: O My people: You have, indeed wronged yourselves by your worship of calf so turn in repentance to your Maker and slay yourselves, the wrongdoers, that will be better for you in the sight of your Maker. Then He turns towards you in forgiveness, for He is oft-returning most merciful.
(Chap. II, Verse 54)

Criminal Law

The death penalty for Apostasy is also proved from a Member of *Ahadith* of the Holy Prophet and his four Caliphs. The Holy Prophet said, "whoever changes his religion, kill him".

The *Hadud* punishments are misconceived as harsh is due to lack of knowledge. The *Hadd* is applied only if the guilt is conclusively proved and for that purpose *"Nisab-e-Shahadat"* is prescribed. Four male eye-witness are required to prove *zina* and in other cases two such witnesses. The voluntary confession is also acted upon. *Hadd* is called of, if there is any doubt. Holy Prophet said, "Do away with *Hadd* punishment in case of doubt". At another occasion the Holy Prophet observed that it is better to let off ten offenders than to convict one innocent person. The judge cannot base his decision only on his knowledge. There is thus no possibility of execution of *Hadd* on an innocent person.

The lapidation and amputation of hand to the Westerners appear barbaric. Under Islamic Law, a Muslim can go through polygamous marriage to the extent of 4 wives at a time. The divorces and re-marriage by widow is permissible as such legal facilities exist for this biological need. Therefore capital punishment is quite justified. The stoning to death is just a condition providing the escape valves to the convict till last, otherwise he has to be executed with some other weapon such as shooting as under *Hadud* Ordinance.

The amputation is inflicted on a professional thief who resorts to theft or robbery not for the necessity of life but richness without work. If a thief puts the life and property of an innocent person at stake and the charge is proved he deserves amputation of hand as prescribed.

The punishments of flogging under Islamic Law are quite different than under the Roman Law. The flogging is intended to put the convict to public shame in order to avert the repetition of crime. The floggings are of moderate force without causing death or laceration on the body or the convict. The clothes are left on the person of the convict. The flogging can be postponed or inflicted in instalments on grounds such as sickness, old age, infirmity or pregnancy. Maulana Maudoodi in his *Tafhemm-ul-Quran*[15], Vol. III, page 341 writes that the floggings are to be struck in such a way that armpit should not open. Mostly there used to be a book kept under arms. Further flogging used to be done at a cool hour during summer, at a hot hour during winter and by 'Qadi' who knew that it was being administered not to cause much pain as to create notoriety for the dark deed. If the offender was weak or infirm, a broom with 100 sticks was considered sufficient so that one blow would meet the ends of justice.

The criticism of *Hadd* punishment is improperly judged inasmuch as the mitigating circumstances are overlooked. The Islamic law does not approve long term punishment which do no good to the society rather produce hardened criminals at state expense beside causing starvation to the dependents of the convicts.

Tazir : It is discretionary correction which is administered for offences for which *'Hadd'* has not been appointed. It may be applied to enforce and protect the rights of individual and Allah. It may be used to prevent the commission of offence for which *Hadd* is appointed. The following punishments are included in *Tazir:*

(1) Slapping

(2) Lashing or flogging (not more than 39, i.e. less than the lowest number prescribed as *Hadd* for slave).

(3) Externment, exilement.

(4) Imprisonment which in Islamic Law is a coercive measure aiming at producing repentance *(Tauba).*

(5) Public proclamation of the convict on a donkey's back *(Tashhir).*

(6) Amonition or reprimand, slapping, beating, etc.

(7) Punishment of abandonment.

(8) *Zaman* (compensation) payable to the aggrieved person in case of loss of property.

(9) *Diyat* (money compensation against injury).

(10) Suspension or dismissal.

One or more punishments can be awarded by the Qadi regard being had to circumstance of each case and the gravity of the crime. Islam does not approve of long term imprisonment. As regards fine the *Hanafis* do not approve but Imam ibn Taymiyyah strongly favours.

Qisas (Retaliation) : The punishment for intentional murder as prescribed in the Holy Quran, is the *Qisas,* i.e. life for life as the Holy Quran, says:

> "O, ye who believe retaliation is prescribed for you in the matter of murder; the freeman for the freeman and the slave for the slave and the female for the female. And for him who is forgiven somewhat by his (injured) brother prosecution according to usage and payment unto him in kindness. This is an alleviation and a mercy from your Lord. He who transgressed after this will have a painful doom. And there is life for you in retaliation. 'O'! man of understanding that ye may ward off evil." (II, 178 and 179 Al-Baqara)

And we have prescribed for them therein: The life for the life, and the eye for the eye, and the nose for the nose, and the ear for the ear, and

Criminal Law

tooth for the tooth, and for wounds retaliation. But whoso for giveth if (in the way of charity), it shall be expiation for him whoso judgeth not by that which Allah has revealed such are wrong doers".

(V 45, Al-Maida)

"And slay not the life which Allah hath forbidden save with right. Who is slain wrongfully, We have given power unto his heir, but let him not commit excess in slaying. Lo; he will be helped."

(XVII, 33 Bani Israel)

"*Shariat* has attached great sanctity to the life of a man: And that you slay not the life which Allah hath made sacred, save in the course of Justice."

(VI 152 Al-Anaam)

"*Janayat*" as already described as unlawful act committed upon the person or upon a part of the body is offence against person where death is caused, is called homicide *(Qatal)* and that against a part of the body is called causing wound or dismemberment. In offences affecting life, retaliation is incurred by wilfully killing a person whose blood is under continual protection such as a Muslim or a *Dhimmi*, in opposition to aliens who have only an occasional temporary protection. A freeman is to be slain for a freeman and a slave for a slave but according to Abu Hanifah a freeman is to be slain for the murder of slave if he be of a *Dhimmi*. A man is slain for the murder of slave if he be the property of a Muslim. A Muslim is also slain for murder of a *Dhimmi*, according to Abu Hanifah but Al-Shafii disputes on the plea that Holy Prophet said that a Muslim is not to be put to death for an infidel. A man is slain for a woman and a sound person for one who is blind, infirm, dismembered, lame or insane.

A father is not to be slain for his child because the Holy Prophet said "Retaliation must not be executed upon the parents of his offsprings".

But a child is slain for the murder of his parents. Retaliation to be executed by the next kin with some mortal wound. If a person wilfully strikes off the hand of another, his hand is to be struck off in return and similarly foot in return of foot. Retaliation is allowed where perfect equality in causing wound may be preserved. Hence if the eye is forced out of the socket, there will be no retaliation but if eye-sight only is destroyed, the eye-sight of the offender may also be destroyed. Similarly, retaliation is not allowed in the case of breaking any bone except tooth.

It is lawful for the heirs of the deceased or the injured person to compound the murder for a certain sum and then retaliation is remitted and sum agreed is due to the heirs by the accused. Next of kin may also remit *Qisas* by pardon. In the absence of intentional murder there is provision for compensating the heirs of the murdered or the injured. Such compensation in economic units for life is called *"Deet'* and for loss of limb, *"Arsh"*. For compensation in these circumstances *Aqla (Baradri)* of the accused are liable. By *"Aqla"* is meant relatives who have to pay expiation or legal fine.

"Nisab Shahda" for *Qisas* is the same as for the *Hadd* punishments. If there is any doubt for any reason, *Qisas* is remitted. In such cases compensation may be made payable by the accused. If the prescribed evidence is not available to support claim for *Qisas*, oath may be offered to the support and his refusal will prove his liability to pay compensation. The judge may determine liability of compensation on his own knowledge.

In case where liability for murder cannot be fixed on an individual or tribe *(Baradri)*, there are elaborate provisions for compensation *(Deet)* Blood Money to the heirs of the murdered. Thus if a dead body is found in a *"Mohallah"*, oath will be offered to 50 men of the *Mohallah* by the heirs of the murdered if they take oath, *Qisas* will be remitted and the *Mohallah* people will be liable to pay *Deet*, such liability arrays people against crime. Where the liability cannot be fixed on anyone the state is liable to pay compensation from *Baitul-Mal*. Thus justice is meted out to the injured in every case.

The Islamic Law of Punishment is summed up as under:

(1) The Islamic Law of Punishment has root in Quran and *Sunnah*, and ensure the preservation of human values.

(2) *Hadd* is administered only when the offence is proved conclusively and there is not even a remote chance of an innocent person suffering punishment.

(3) In offence where right of an individual is involved every attempt is made to see that he gets his due.

(4) It is left to the aggrieved to claim *Qisas* if that satisfy his feelings or compound the matter on just suitable and lawful terms.

(5) In cases where the liability of the crime cannot be fixed on an individual, the aggrieved is compensated by the people of the locality. The people are arrayed against crime.

(6) Islamic punishment also imply the spiritual purification of human soul and expiation for the world hereafter, this is an addition to obtaining human good in this world through implementation of its penal law. A lapidated person is entitled to burial, as is a Muslim with a *Namaz-i-Janaza* and benediction. (Fathe-ul-Qadir 4.125)

(7) The Islamic punishment does not approve of long term imprisonment to provide centres for producing harden criminal, who on release from jails operate as organised gangs of criminals.

(8) The statistics show that in countries where the Islamic Laws are in practice the crime rate is the lowest or negligible such as in Saudi Arabia.

(9) Islamic Laws *suo moto* safeguard the rights of minors and insane persons which is not envisaged in any other law.

(10) The Islamic Laws are simple to understand and easy in application. The Islamic Procedural Law ensures speedy disposal of cases and quick and free justice.

Theory of Hadd : Crime is a curse and its gravity needs no emphasis. It disturbs the balance of a society and ultimately corrodes it. The secular modern societies, which boast of their resources and theories of crime and punishment, are the living examples of such corrosion. These societies are not fully equipped to curb crime as they are devoid of Allah's guidance and conception of accountability in the life Hereafter and have no moorings in morality. Moreover the man-made laws which control them are fallible and deficient. The only society which has the capability to overcome the menace of crime is the Islamic society as it is based on Divine order and aims at human perfection and peace in this world and felicity in the Hereafter.

It conforms to the dictates of laws and principles of morality as enunciated by Islam and is quite different from the modern societies which reflect a variety of ethical values and throw the door open for all sorts of vices, evils and crimes. Islamic law, which controls the Islamic society and guarantees its preservation, takes a serious view of crime and in order to check it postulates, *inter alia,* an ideal and unique punitive system having fixed as well as variable elements, which are essential for a good legal system. The punishment known as *Hadd,* which is a fixed element in that its quantum has been finally prescribed and can neither be altered nor modified, is the nucleus of this system. It wipes out certain heinous crimes and ensures the preservation of the values that Islam upholds for the dignity of human society and spiritual purification of human soul.

Hadd etymologically means measure, limit or obstruction. Technically it means a punishment the measure of which has been definitely fixed or punishment ordained by Quran and *Sunnah* or the correction appointed and specified by the law on account of the right of Allah or a penalty appointed or specified by law on account of rights of Allah (or public justice). The rights of Allah correspond to the public rights as they involve benefit to the community at large and are referred to Allah because of the magnitude of the risks involved in their violation and of the comprehensive benefits which result from them. In other words, the rights of Allah are to be construed as rights of society because the punishments of *Hadd* are meant to deter from mischief and harm to people and it is a collective obligation of the Muslim community to enforce them. All *Hadd* crimes essentially involve violation of the Text and their punishments are equal to their magnitude. The crimes falling within the pale of *Hadd* are:

(1) *Zina* (whoredom or fornication).

(2) *Shurb* (drinking wine).

(3) *Sarqa* (theft).

(4) *Qate Tariq* or *Haraba* (highway robbery).

(5) *Qazf* (false accusation of adultery).

(6) *Irtidad* (apostasy).

The punishments of *Hadd* have been prescribed for these crimes because they impair human dignity, have far reaching effects on society and violate the public interests or the aim of *Shariah* in regard to man, namely protection of sanctity of family and progeny, protection of reason, protection of property, protection of honour and protection of religion.

Zina includes sexual intercourse between a man and a woman not married to each other and it applies both to adultery (which implies that one or both of the parties are married to a person other than the ones concerned) and to fornication which, in its strict signification, implies that both parties are unmarried." There can be no cavil against the proposition that *Zina* is not only disgraceful in itself but also the root cause of many other evils. It destroys the family structure and brings untold humiliation and sufferings to children born or to be born. It entails blood feuds and loss of reputation and property and causes chaos and disorder in society. Allah has abhorred this major sin and prohibited the Muslims from going near it.

(And come not near unto adultery. Lo! it is an abomination and an evil way).' (And those who cry not unto any other god alongwith Allah, nor take the life which Allah hath forbidden save in (course of) justice, nor commit adultery and whoso doeth this shall pay the penalty).

The punishment of *Zina* ordained by Quran and *Sunnah* is one hundred stripes if committed by unmarried persons and stoning to death if committed by married persons.

(The adulteress and the adulterer, scourge ye each one of them (with) a hundred stripes. And let not pity for the twain withhold you from obedience to

Allah, if ye believe in Allah and the Last Day. And let a party of believers witness their punishment). (Ubadah-b-Swamet reported that the Messenger of Allah said: Take from me, take from me. Verily Allah chalked out a way for them; (fornication of) a virgin with a virgin—100 stripes and exile for a year; and one married with another married—100 stripes and stoning to death).

(Hadrat Umar reported: Verily Allah sent Muhammad with truth and revealed the Book to him out of the verses the Almighty Allah revealed, there was the verse of stoning to death. The Messenger of Allah stoned to death and after him we also stoned to death. And stoning to death in the Book of Allah is a truth against one out of males and females who commits adultery in a married state in case proof is established or there occurs pregnancy or confession).

Though the Quran does not explicitly mention the punishment of stoning to death it does indicate it in a subtle manner which the Holy Prophet understood and enforced. The majority of theologians, the four Imams (Abu Hanifah, Shafii, Malik and Ahmad bin Hambal) and other learned Jurists hold that the order for stoning to death still exists.

The question was raised before the Holy Prophet when it was referred to him. He, as the best interpreter of the Quran said, that, according to the Book, a married adulterer and a married adulteress shall be put to death. Who can be a greater authority in interpreting the Quran than the Prophet himself? This ordinance was carried out by Hadrat Abu Bakr, Hadrat Umar and other Caliphs who came after them. Had the capital sentence in case of married culprits been abrogated, these Caliphs would not have followed the command of the Prophet (peace be upon him).

Drinking is harmful from both temporal and spiritual points of view. It veils the intellect and obscures the moral sensibilities of the drunkard and for that reason Allah has strictly forbidden the use of all alcoholic beverages.

(They question thee about strong drink and games of chance. Say: In both is great sin, and (some) utility for men; but the sin of them is greater than their usefulness).

(Oh! You who believe! Strong drink and games of chance and idols and divining arrows are only an infamy of Satan's handiwork. Leave it aside in order that you may succeed).

There are many traditions which threaten the drunkards with severe punishment in the Next World. The punishment prescribed for this world is eighty stripes. There is no mention of this punishment in Quran and it is the result of an *Ijma* of the Companions of the Holy Prophet. When Hadrat Umar saw that this crime was on the increase he consulted the Companions on the punishment to be meted out to drunkards. Hadrat Ali bin Abu Talib is reported to have advised: 'We apply the punishment for calumny, namely eighty stripes because if a person becomes intoxicated he knows not what he says and in such a condition he commits calumny'.

Sarqa (theft) is an act of encroachment on the property of someone without any justification and causes unrest in society. Thieves are a terror and with a view to put them under guard a very strict measure has been ordained.

(As for the thief, both male and female, cut off their hands. It is the reward of their own deeds and exemplary punishment from Allah - Allah is Mighty, Wise).

The punishment for the first offence is amputation of hand; for a second that of the left foot up to ankle and for a third a long term of imprisonment until the culprit reforms. Hadrat Ali refused to amputate another hand of a confirmed thief where one hand and foot had already been cut off.

To constitute theft it is essential that the thief must be an adult of sound understanding, the property must be in careful custody, the property must be movable, the property must be taken out of the custody of another person in a secret manner and its value must not be less than the prescribed *Nisab* and the thief must have obtained full possession of the stolen property.

Harraba (highway robbery) not only deprives someone of his hard-earned money and property or life but also causes public disorder and as such deserves a harsh punishment.

(The only reward for those who make war upon Allah and His Messenger and strive after corruption in the land will be that they will be killed or crucified, or have their hands and feet on alternate sides cut off, or will be expelled out of the land, such will be their degradation in the world and in the Hereafter, theirs will be an awful doom).

The established punishment is cutting of right hand and left foot if *Harraba* is not accompanied with murder and death if accompanied with murder.

The evil caused by *Qazf* (false accusation of adultery) is similar to that caused by adultery itself. It not only damages the reputation of the slandered but also creates bad blood between the families, renders parentage doubtful and spoils conjugal relations. Allah has, therefore, enjoined severe punishment for this offence.

(Lo! as for those who traduce a virtuous, believing woman (who are) careless, cursed are they in the world and the Hereafter: Theirs will be an awful doom).

Criminal Law

(And those who accuse honourable women but bring not four witnesses, scourge them (with eighty stripes and never (afterward) accept their testimony. They indeed are evil-doers).

The punishment is eighty stripes. *Irtidad* (Apostasy) means turning from Islam after being a Muslim. It partakes strong condemnation of Allah.

(Whoso disbelieveth in Allah after his belief - save him who is forced thereto and whose heart is still content with faith - but whoso findeth ease in disbelief: on them is wrath from Allah. Theirs will be an awful doom).

(But if they repent and establish worship and pay the poor-due, then are they your brethren in religion. We detail our revelations for a people who have knowledge. And if they break their pledges after their treaty (hath been made with you) and assail your religion, then fight the heads of disbelief. Lo! they have no binding oaths - in order that they may desist).

The sayings and doings of the Holy Prophet (PBUH), the decision and practice of the Caliph Abu Bakr, the consensus of the opinion of the Companions of the Holy Prophet and all the Muslim Jurists prescribe punishment of death for an apostate. The Holy Prophet (PBUH) is reported to have said: (He who substitutes his *Din,* (for another one) put him to death).

The offences punishable with *Hadd* may be established by confession, made voluntarily before the court, or ocular evidence furnished by *Adil* witnesses. The requisite number of eye-witness for proof of *Zina* is four. The other offences, namely *Sarqa, Harraba, Qazf, Shurb* and *Irtidad* are proved on the testimony of two witnesses.

The witnesses must be sane, adult, male, Muslims who have never been convicted of *Qazf* and about whom the court is satisfied, having regard to the requirements of *Tazkia-al-Shahood,* that they are truthful witnesses and abstain from major sins and are not inclined to indulge in minor sins. The probity of witnesses is indispensable. (Take the evidence of two just men).

All Muslims are *prima facie* just with respect to evidence excepting those who have been punished for slander. If, however, their probity is questioned it is incumbent on the court to initiate an enquiry into their character. The purgation is to be made both privately and openly.

The examination of the credibility of the witnesses is made from the people with whom they have been connected that is to say if they are pupils from trustworthy inhabitants and the master of the school where they have lived, if they are soldiers from the officers and clerks of their battalion and if he is a clerk from his superiors and fellow clerks in his office and if he is a merchant from trustworthy merchants and if he belongs to an incorporated trade from the warden of the trade and the masters in committee and if he belongs to other trades from trustworthy inhabitants of the quarter of village. As regards major sins the Holy Prophet (PBUH) said :

> (The greatest sin is to associate another with God, or to vex your father or mother or to murder your own species or to give false evidence or to tell lies). (The greatest sin before God is that you call any other like unto God who created you or that you murder your child from an idea that it will eat your victuals, or that you commit adultery with your neighbour's wife).

(Abstain ye from seven ruinous destructive things, namely, associating anything with God; magic, killing anyone without reason: taking interest on money; taking the property of the orphan; running away on the day of battle; and taxing an innocent woman with adultery).

The quantum of evidence has been prescribed to ensure that only guilty person is convicted.

There are certain exceptional instances in which *Hadd* is not enforced despite the availability of proof:

(1) When *Zina* or *Sarqa* or *Harraba* or drinking or *Irtidad* is proved only by the confession of the convict but he retracts his confession before the execution of *Hadd*.

(2) When *Zina* or *Sarqa* or *Haraba* or drinking or *Irtidad* is proved by testimony but before the execution of *Hadd* any witness resoles from his testimony so as to reduce the number of witnesses to less than the prescribed.

(3) When the offender and victim of the theft are related to each other as:
   (i) spouses;
   (ii) ascendants, paternal or maternal;
   (iii) descendants, paternal or maternal;
   (iv) brothers or sisters or father or mother; or
   (v) brothers or sisters or their children.

(4) When a guest has committed theft from the house of his host.

(5) When a servant or employee has committed theft from the *'hirz'* of his master or employer to which he is allowed access.

Criminal Law

(6) When the stolen property is wild grass, fish, bird, dog, pig, intoxicant, musical instrument or perishable food stuffs for the preservation of which provision does not exist.

(7) When the offender has a share in the stolen property the value of which, after deduction of his share is less than the *'Nisab'*.

(8) When a creditor steals his debtor's property the value of which, after deduction of the amount due to him, is less than the *'Nisab'*.

(9) When the offender, before his apprehension, has, on account of repentance, returned the stolen property of the victim and surrenders himself to the authority concerned.

(10) When the offences of drinking and theft are committed under *'Ikrah'* or *'Iztirar'*.

(11) When a person has committed *Qazf* against any of his descendants.

(12) When the imputation has been proved to be true.

(13) When the person in respect of whom *Qazf* has been committed and who is a complainant has died during the pendency of the proceedings.

(14) When before the execution of *Hadd* the complainant withdraws his allegation of *Qazf* or states that the accused had made a false confession or that any of the witnesses had deposed falsely and the number of witnesses is thereby reduced to less than two.

(15) When *Zina* is followed by a *Nikah*.

The offences punishable with *Hadd* are non-compoundable and *Hadd* is enforced by the Head of State or his delegates namely Qadis. The Head of State, however, has no rights of pardon and suspension of sentence. If the guilt is proved, the convict must be punished at all costs and there can be no mercy in inflicting it. The punishment cannot be reduced under sentiments of mercy.

> "And let not pity for the twain withhold you from obedience to Allah, if you believe in Allah and the Last Day."

Those who are not familiar with the philosophy behind *Hadd* punishments and their rationale severely criticise these punishments by calling them barbaric and mediaeval. They do not know that Islam leaves no stone unturned to block all the channels leading to crime and the punishments are inflicted as a last resort. The *Hadd* punishments are permissible under very exceptional circumstances when a fool proof case is made out.

The standard of evidence for awarding these punishments is very high which suggests that the policy of law is not to remain in search of offenders and fix scaffold in crossings to flog people everyday but to punish only those who despite preventive measures adopted by Islam defy public decency and flaunt their vices openly. These punishments are inflicted under conditions of a stringent nature laid down by law and that is why they are a rare phenomenon. The *Hadd* stands dropped if there crops up even the slightest doubt. The Holy Prophet (PBUH) said, "Remit punishment on account of doubt as long as you have ability."

Ibn-i-Maja.

> "Try to avoid *Hadud* wherever possible. Wherever there is even a mild chance, release him, for releasing by an error on the part of an *Imam* is better than punishing anyone by error."

> 'The principle of giving benefit of doubt to the accused was taken to such length that the Holy Prophet (PBUH) did not act generally on the confession of an accused unless he was satisfied about the voluntary nature as well as genuineness of the confession. The cases of Maiz and Ghamadiyyah are in point. When Maiz confessed his guilt of *Zina*, the Holy Prophet (PBUH) made an inquiry into his mental state as well as his knowledge about the ingredients of the offence to which he was confessing. Same happened with Ghamadiyyah. Hadrat Ali also did not order the sentence of *Zina* on *Shurahah* without investigating into the voluntary nature or genuineness of her confession."

The punishment of *Hadd* is deterrent and its purpose is humiliation for the convict and lesson for the public. It deters the offender from repetition of the crime and also deters others who are like-minded with him, by his example from the commission of it. Besides, it contains elements of reformation and prevention. Once the punishment of *Hadd* is carried out it so deters the public that no-one can dare commit that crime for years to come. In a way it performs a psychological operation on the minds of those who have criminal tendencies and thus reforms them automatically.

Even the modern criminologists have come to the conclusion that the perfect system of criminal justice should not only readjust the criminal but be such as to deter others. It is a matter of common knowledge that *Hadd* punishments have virtually wiped out crime from Saudi Arabia and made it a model for rest of the world. Impressed by the efficacy and results of the punishment of amputation of hand a non-Muslim Scholar Gordon Gaskell remarked, ''Foreigners consider this a horrible punishment but even they admit that it has made Saudi Arabia the country with the lowest crime rate in the world''.

Imposition of *Hadd* obliterates sins. The Holy Prophet (PBUH) said, "Swear allegiance to me that you will not associate anything with Allah, that you will not

Criminal Law

commit adultery, that you will not steal, that you will not take any life which it is forbidden by Allah to take but with (legal) justification; and whoever among you fulfils it his reward is with Allah; and he who commits any such thing and is punished for it, that will be an atonement for it. And if anyone commits anything and Allah conceals (his faults) his matter rests with Allah. He may forgive if He likes it and He may punish him if He likes."

The *Hadd* punishments can prove effective in liberating the societies of the world from the curse of crime and its evil consequences.

SUGGESTIVE MEASURES

I. *Hadd* literally means obstruction, prohibiting from entering and, for that reason, *'Haddad* means a person who prevents from entering, that is, gate keeper. But according to legal terminology the term *'Hadd'* means the prescribed punishment as ordered by Allah through the Holy Prophet (peace be upon him).

II. Guiding principle behind *'Hadd'* seems to be that evil, perpetrated and crimes committed by a person must be atoned for within his lifetime so that he becomes a better individual and a better member of his society. This principle in turn actively discourages any tendency of leading a life of sin and then becoming a pious individual in the hope of rewards in the life hereafter. Thus *'Hadd'* reinforces the central idea of Islam that the laws of Quran and *Shariah* are the guiding spirit throughout the life of a Muslim. As regards the implementation of *Hadd*, or its plural *Hadud*, in the society in which Prophet Muhammad (peace be upon him) was born, grew up and worked, the Quran says :

"The only reward of those who make war upon Allah and His Messenger and strive after corruption in the land will be that they will be killed or crucified, or have their hands and feet or alternative side cut off, or will be expelled out of the land. Such will be their degradation in the world, and the hereafter. Theirs' will be an awful doom."

Thus any attempt by any individual to follow or to attempt the law of God and His way in any age and society is definitely in conformity with the Quran and *Sunnah* of the Prophet (PBUH). Conversely, any attempt on the part of the Muslims to subvert the divinely ordained Islamic order is to be condemned. The Quran prescribes a general code of *Hadud:*

"These are the limits (imposed by) Allah, whoso obeyeth Allah and His Messenger will enter gardens underneath which rivers flow, where such will dwell for ever That will be the great success.

And who disobeyeth Allah and His Messenger and transgressed His limits, he will make him enter fire, where such will dwell for ever; his will be a shameful doom."

III. The following is the classification of crimes and punishments which fall under the categories of *Hadud* according to Quranic injunctions and the *Sunnah* of Prophet Muhammad (PBUH):

(1) Adultery *(Fitna)*;
(2) Theft *(Sarqa)*;
(3) Alcoholism *(Shurb-e-Khamr)*;
(4) False accusation of adultery *(Qadhaf)*; and
(5) Highway robbery *(Qat-e-Tariq)*.

The basic role ascribed to *Hadud,* detailed in the Quran is mentioned thus:

"O Prophet: if believing women come unto thee, taking oath of allegiance unto Thee that they will ascribe nothing as partners unto Allah, and will neither steal nor commit adultery nor kill their children, nor produce any lie that they have devised between their hands and feet, nor disobeyeth Thee in what is right, then accept their allegiance and ask Allah to forgive them, LO! Allah is Forgiving and Merciful."

To ascertain the philosophy behind these laws and their social and moral significance, one has to ponder over the Quranic verses and their practical application during the lifetime of Prophet Muhammad (PBUH) and the period of the early four Caliphs. Taking into consideration the magnitude of these laws and juristic differences, our endeavour to make a brief survey of each of these five laws independently would enlighten the situation as to why *Hadd* or *Hadud* have been fixed for certain offences.

Avoid Adultery (Zina) : The act of adultery is being denounced from time immemorial and different societies in different ages formulated laws and punishments to suppress this act. Christianity and Judaism initially prescribed the same punishment for adultery as did Islam later—stoning to death. But the adherents of the first two religions side stepped the penalty and even started differentiating between adultery and fornication, making the latter less punishable. Islam, however, has retained with vigour the prescribed punishment of the Quran.

These punishments are being criticised by others as out-moded and barbaric. The Quran and the *Sunnah* of the Prophet (PBUH) both take a very serious view of fornication and adultery which damage and militate against the moral order of a society. Islam out rightly condemns adultery in all its forms. However, there is a difference of opinion among scholars about the punishment

Criminal Law

applicable to married and unmarried persons committing adultery. This controversy is mainly due to the non-availability of any Quranic verse in respect of married offenders.

The penalty for them, *Rajm*[16]— stoning to death, was codified by the Holy Prophet (PBUH) and implemented by him and the four Caliphs. Muslim and non-Muslim historians are of the unanimous view that just before the advent of Islam, Arab society was corrupt and uncivilised. Even adultery was not considered irreligious or immoral. Prophet Muhammad (PBUH) on assuming his Prophetic mission, was instructed to make people follow the prescribed Quranic social order and thereby free the society from its moral decay. He was to get these people to act in accordance with the earlier *Shariats* and the revelations he received from time to time. The following verses of the chapter of *Al-Maidah* say :

> "And unto thee have we revealed the scripture with the truth, confirming whatever scripture was before it, and a watcher over it. So judge between them by that which Allah hath revealed and follow not their desires away from the truth which hath unto thee.
>
> Oh! Messenger ! make known that which hath been revealed unto thee from thy Lord, for if you do it not then will not have conveyed His Message. Allah will protect thee from mankind. Lo! Allah guideth not the disbelieving folk."

A survey of the first ten years of Prophet Muhammad's (PBUH) life at Mecca shows that all his efforts were directed towards the eradication of polytheistic tendencies and the establishment of the concept of *Tauhid* and *Salat*. All the 90 chapters revealed at Mecca deal with these issues at length.

The majority of the cases which relate to legislation and crimes, including adultery, however, belong to the Medinian period. It is evident that during the Meccan period in the absence of any clear legal Quranic injunctions in respect of adultery, Prophet Muhammad (PBUH) preferred to follow the earlier *Shariats* in all their judicial, legal, criminal and social aspects.

In the absence of any Quranic guidance regarding fornication or adultery till the verses of Chapter *Al-Nisa* or *Al-Noor* were revealed, the Prophet (PBUH) had to look into the Jewish code. As immediately after his immigration to Medina, a man and a woman from the Jewish tribes of Khyber committed adultery. The case was referred to the Prophet of Islam, who according to the Jewish Code, ordered them to be stoned to death.

There are three important incidents of adultery reported during the lifetime of Prophet Muhammad (PBUH) in which he ordained the penalty of stoning. They relate to Maiz bin Malik Aslami, Ghamidiyah and a person (not named) reported by Abu Hurrayrah[17]. A study of these cases suggests that the following requirements are essential for the implementation of stoning or any other *Hadd* penalty:

(1) The Quran clearly states that there should be four eye-witness. The judge has no right to pass any verdict even though he may have personally seen the act.

(2) Eye-witness must be reliable persons.

(3) Four witnesses must attest that they found both man and woman in the exact act of adultery.

(4) All the four witnesses must remain unanimous about the time, place and the persons involved in the act.

(5) Personal commitment in plain and clear words on the part of adulterer or adulteress.

(6) In a case where the crime has been admitted but the person concerned later refutes the charge out of fear of punishment, he is to be released.

Shinning Theft (Sarqa) : The punishment prescribed for theft in the Holy Quran is:

"As for the thief, both male and female, cut off their hands. It is the reward of their own deeds, an exemplary punishment from Allah. Allah is Mighty and Wise."

Following are the sayings of the Holy Prophet (PBUH) in this respect:

"When an adulterer commits adultery and a thief commits theft they are not *Momins.*"

Once a case of a woman was recommended to Holy Prophet (PBUH) on which he remarked :

"The preceding nations perished because they implemented the *Hadd* punishment upon poor persons and gave a clear chit to the well-to-do. By God, had Fatima committed a theft, I would have definitely amputated her hand."

Abhore Alcoholism (Shurb-e-Khamr) : All those things which intoxicate a person stand forbidden by the Quran and the *Sunnah* of the Prophet. However, the Quran does not prescribe any specific punishment for alcoholism. The traditions of the Holy Prophet (PBUH) do not indicate a fixed punishment for alcoholism. Forty lashes, however, stand proved as having been ordered by the First Caliph. Umar, the Second Caliph, due to vast increase in the use of intoxicants raised it to eighty lashes for a free person and forty for slaves. There is also the *Ijma* of

Criminal Law

the Companions of the Prophet for these punishments. But before the penalty is ordered, two witnesses are essential in the court of a Qadi.

Change of Adultery (Qadhaf) : The literal meaning of the word *Qadhaf* is to throw; the theological meaning is false accusation of adultery. The Quran makes two categories of this crime.

The first relates to the allegation of unchastity, a charge brought about by the husband against the wife and the second relates to a person, other than the husband, who accuses a woman of adultery. The Quran says: "And those who accuse honourable women but bring not four witnesses, scourge them (with) eighty stripes and never (afterwards) accept their testimony. They indeed are evil-doers". The punishment *of Hadd* for a person who is accusing the other party is only applicable when the latter is a *Mohsan* or chaste person coming within the scope of the following:

"He must be a free person, sane, adult, Muslim and must be pious."

Accusation of adultery is proved by a single commitment of the crime or through the witness of two male persons.

Highway Robbery (Qat-e-tariq) : Dacoit/robber is one who overpowers the traveller and commits theft. If he did not carry out theft but in the process committed murder, punishment is stoning. If the offender has stolen property amounting to the equivalent of the (fixed price) for theft, that is, ten dirhams, the offender's right hand and left foot are to be cut off. However, if the offender has no right hand or left foot or if he has them but they are paralysed, the left hand and the right foot are not to be amputated. The offender is then liable to *Tazir*. If the offender has committed robbery as well as murder, his right hand and left foot are to be amputated and he is then to be slained.

Importance of Hadd : The implementation of the Quranic laws and the *Sunnah* of the Holy Prophet (PBUH) was the basic aim of the orthodox Caliphs. There seems no reason to believe that *Hadd* penalties for all the aforementioned crimes were not implemented during the period of the orthodox Caliphs.

The Second Caliph Umar took personal interest in suppressing immoral acts. He was the first among the Caliphs to have appointed persons to carry out the *Hadd* punishments. It was again he who established the department of *Hisab* (the department to ensure the implementation of Islamic Laws) and prisons at Mecca and in other districts. Early historical works testify that all the First Four Caliphs applied *Hadd* penalties for adultery, alcoholism, theft and false accusation of adultery. All juristic schools, including the *Shia*-School, are unanimous about the prescribed Quranic penalties.

The social, judicial and philosophical significance of *Hadd* penalties is based on the concept of strict accountability of all those, irrespective of their social status, who outrage the rights, dignity and property of others and thus to purge the society of these heinous social evils, paving the way for the establishment of a society in which all its members; big and small, rich and poor, should breathe with peace and satisfaction. The concept of *Hadd* is also greatly instrumental in the achievement of a social moral order as envisaged in Islam. Above all, the concept of *Hadd* is vitally and unavoidably linked with the establishment of a true Islamic society—a society based on the golden principles of equality and justice.

References

1. Tradition of the Prophet (Pbuh).
2. Legislature of a land.
3. Quranic limitations.
4. Intercourse outside wedlock.
5. Islamic law.
6. One of the greatest scholars of Islamic law and philosophy.
7-8. Two great compilers of the traditions of the Prophet (Pbuh).
9. House of Allah, constructed by Prophets Ibrahim and his son Ismail (Pbuh).
10. A great learner of the Holy Quran and scholar of Islam.
11. Decree issued by Imam Shafii, one of the four important Imams of Islam.
12. Eligibility for being able to pay Zakat.
13. Unwillingness.
14. Compulsion.
15. Translation and commentary of the Holy Quran by Maulana Abul Aala Maududi.
16. Punishment of illegal sex.
17. Companion of the Prophet who is said to have reported the maximum number of traditions.

13

JUDICIAL SYSTEM

The true justice described in the Quran commands man to behave justly, not discriminating between people, protecting others' rights and not permitting violence, no matter what the circumstances, to side with the oppressed against the oppressor and to help the needy. This justice calls for the rights of both parties to be protected when reaching a decision in a dispute, assessing all aspects of an incident, setting aside all prejudices, being objective, honest, tolerant, merciful and compassionate. In the event, one fails to display any of these characteristics or attaches greater importance to a particular one, then it becomes hard to exercise true justice.

For instance, someone who cannot assess events in a moderate way, and who is swayed by his emotions and feelings, will fail to arrive at sound decisions and will remain under the influence of those feelings. However, someone who rules with justice needs to set all his personal feelings and views aside. He needs to treat all parties with justice when they ask for help, to side with what is right under all circumstances, and not to diverge from the path of honesty and truthfulness.

A person should incorporate the values of the Quran into his soul in such a way that he may be able to consider the interests of other parties before his own and maintain justice, even if this harms his own interests.

> O You who believe! Show integrity for the sake of God, bearing witness with justice. Do not let hatred for a people incite you into not being just Be just. That is closer to faith. Heed God [alone]. God is aware of what you do. (Quran, 5:8)

As the above verse suggests, God knows everything a man does. A person, who fears God and who is aware that he will have to account for his deeds on the Day of Judgement issues his commands in a just way in order to earn the good pleasure of God. He knows that all his words and thoughts will be judged on the Day of Judgement[1] and will be rewarded accordingly.

For this reason, what one has to do to earn the good pleasure of God, to be saved from the torment of Hell and to attain the infinite favours of Paradise is to fully live by the Quran. In order to attain this morality, everyone must make personal efforts and set aside all his selfish desires and personal interests and adopt the guidance of justice, compassion, tolerance and peace. God gives a detailed description of true justice in the Quran and informs us, that all sorts of disagreements can be solved by the maintenance of justice.

In a society made up of righteous administrators and just people, it is obvious that all problems can be readily overcome. In the Quran, God gives a detailed description of justice and informs believers of the attitude they have to adopt in the face of incidents they encounter and of the ways to exercise justice. Such guidance is a great comfort to believers and a mercy from God. For this reason, those who believe are responsible for exercising justice in an undivided manner both to earn God's approval and to lead their lives in peace and security.

Justice Should be Exercised Equally Among All People, with No Consideration of Language, Race, or Ethnicity : A close examination of developments all over the world reveals that the performance of justice varies according to place, time and people. For instance, in some societies, the colour of someone's skin influences decisions. Even under the very same circumstances, the same decision may not apply to a white and a black man. In some societies, race is of great importance to people.

In the 20th century, Hitler's[2] annihilation of millions of people solely because he deemed the Aryan race superior to other races is a good example of this. In our day, too, there are people being subjected to cruel and unjust treatment because of the colour of their skin or their race. In the United States and South Africa, black people were for many years treated as second class citizens, and savage conflicts raged in many Asian and African countries simply because of racial differences.

However, God informs us in the Quran that the purpose in the creation of different tribes and peoples is "that they should come to know each other" (Quran, 49:13). Different nations or peoples, all of whom are the servants of God, should get to know one another, that is, learn about their different cultures, languages, traditions and abilities.

In brief, the purpose of the creation of different races and nations is not conflict and war but cultural richness. Such variation is a bounty of God's creation. The fact that someone is taller than someone else or that his skin is yellow or white neither makes him superior to others nor is something to feel ashamed of. Every trait a person has is a result of God's purposeful creation, but in the sight of God, these variations have no ultimate importance. A believer knows that someone attains superiority only by fearing God and in the strength of his faith in God. This fact is related in the following verse:

> O Mankind! We created you from a male and female, and made you into peoples and tribes so that you might come to know each other. The noblest among you in God's sight is that one of you who best performs his duty. God is All-Knowing, All-Aware. (Quran, 49:13)

As God informs us in that verse, the justice ordained by Him calls for equal, tolerant and peaceable treatment of everyone, with no discrimination.

In his time, the Prophet Muhammad (peace be upon him) treated people of different races and places with the utmost justice. He severely criticised subjecting people to different treatment because of their race, and attributed such acts to the "morality of the ignorant."

The Prophet Muhammad (pbuh) reminded his people that people in ignorant societies may harbour enmity towards other people because of their colour or race, and warned all Muslims against such an attitude, which is described as "ugly" in the Quran. 1,400 years ago, all these primitive ideas were abolished through the Quran, which was sent to mankind as a mercy, and it was proclaimed that all people, regardless of their colour, race and language, are equal. The Prophet Muhammad (pbuh) criticised the unbecoming practice of people of ignorant societies, who assessed others according to their race and colour. He cautioned the Arab people in these words in his last address to them:

> An Arab has no superiority over a non-Arab, nor a non-Arab has any superiority over an Arab; also a white has no superiority over a black, nor a black has any superiority over white except by piety and good action.

With these words, the Prophet Muhammad (pbuh) once again reminded all mankind the fact related in Sura Hujurat, verse 13; that superiority among people is attainable only through fear of God. Islam, as the Prophet Muhammad (pbuh) also stresses, completely abolishes all these primitive ideas.

In an environment where the values of Islam are established, a man cannot be accused, subjected to discriminatory treatment or oppressed because he is a

Jew, a black or an Indian. God decides what race a person should belong to. He shaped man in the most perfect manner. Man's duty is always to be just, tolerant, respectful, compassionate to and at peace with everyone.

This aside, the fact that a person is well-off or poor does not pose a hindrance to a believer's provision of justice or the way he makes his decisions. It is utterly unacceptable, that someone should oppress other people just because he possesses the financial means, and hence be allowed to get away with committing a crime. However, in our day a look at some of the countries in the world reveals a mentality that favours the rights of the wealthy and treats the poor as second class citizens.

Accordingly, some wealthy people benefit more from justice and deem it as their right to be favoured over the poor. Furthermore, they try to make judicial mechanisms work for their own interests. This mentality causes great injustice in societies where people do not live by religion; while some people struggle to survive in misery, others enjoy the benefits of being wealthy.

However, despite this adverse situation, it is possible to establish justice and social peace. The dominance of the values of the Quran and peoples' unyielding insistence on living by the values of the Quran can make this possible. God issues the following commands in the Quran:

> ... Be upholders of justice, bearing witness for God alone, even against yourselves or your parents and relatives. Whether they are rich or poor, God is well able to look after them. Do not follow your own desires and deviate from the truth.... (Quran, 4:135)

In compliance with this command of God, whether a person is wealthy or poor, he who has fear of God exercises absolute justice, and his attitude never changes in line with peoples' financial status. He knows that being rich or poor is a worldly state of affairs by which God tests man. When one dies, nothing will remain from his possessions, and only his fear of God will be rewarded. The attitude which pleases God is described in the Quran: being just, honest and righteous. The reward for this morality is eternal gifts in the hereafter.

In Matters Related to Orphans, God Commands Definite Justice : Another example given in the Quran regarding the maintenance of justice relates to the management of the property of orphans. In the Quran, God commands that the property of orphans be managed in the most just manner until they grow old enough to manage it themselves. In Sura Anam, God commands:

> And that you do not go near the property of orphans before they reach maturity—except in a good way; that you give full measure and full weight with justice... (Quran, 6:152)

In many other verses, God reminds people not to dissipate the assets of orphans quickly before they reach maturity, and to act in a just way. Some of these verses are as follows:

> Give orphans their property, and do not substitute bad things for good. Do not assimilate their property into your own. Doing that is a serious crime. (Quran, 4:2)

> Keep a close check on orphans until they reach a marriageable age, then if you perceive that they have sound judgement hand over their property to them. Do not consume it extravagantly and precipitately before they come of age. Those who are wealthy should abstain from it altogether. Those who are poor should use it sensibly and correctly. When you hand over their property to them ensure that there are witnesses on their behalf. God suffices as a Reckoner. (Quran, 4:6)

> Do not go near the property of orphans before they reach maturity, except in a good way. Fulfil your contracts. Contracts will be asked about. (Quran, 17:34)

Those who consume the property of orphans unjustly, in a manner that conflicts with these verses, and spend it unfairly are warned of a punishment which will last for all eternity. In the verse, "People who consume the property of orphans wrongfully consume nothing in their bellies except fire. They will roast in a Searing Blaze." (Quran, 4:10), God forbids people to commit injustice.

As this example also reveals, justice in the Quranic sense relates to all domains of life. The meticulousness one shows in performing justice, on the other hand, is an important factor that influences one's rewards in the hereafter.

The Believer is Responsible for Exercising Justice, Even if its Consequences Work Against Him, His Parents or Relatives.

Seeing a definition of justice, you may think how easy it is to act justly, and you might feel quite content because you have always made just decisions. However, would it still be so easy for you to act justly if the consequences of your just decision were to harm you, your parents or loved ones, either physically or spiritually? Would you still manage to be objective, just and honest when judging a loved one who had swerved from the right path?

In the face of such a question, many people vacillate. Indeed, such a decision may be very difficult for some. They may simply be more tolerant to a loved one and ignore the facts. Yet what matters is not to depart from justice, no matter what the circumstances and conditions may be, and to meticulously comply with the verse:

> "O You who believe! Be upholders of justice, bearing witness for God alone, even against yourselves or your parents and relatives...."
> (Quran, 4:135)

What earns peoples' trust is this unswerving commitment to justice they observe. Protecting people because of kinship or friendship creates unease and insecurity. Observing such a disposition in leaders in particular causes great social unrest.

Someone, who acts in conformity with the laws of the Quran, however, follows the recommendation of God: "...that you are equitable when you speak— even if a near relative is concerned; and that you fulfil God's contract. That is what He instructs you to do, so that hopefully you will pay heed" (Quran, 6:152). This conduct is the manifestation of one's strong faith in God and the moral perfection he displays.

In the Quran, one example is related from the life of the Prophet Musa. The verse reads:

> He entered the city at a time when its inhabitants were unaware and found two men fighting there— one from his party and the other from his enemy. The one from his party asked for his support against the other from his enemy. So Musa hit him, dealing him a fatal blow. He said, "This is part of Satan's doing. He truly is an outright and misleading enemy." (Quran, 28:15)

In this story, the Prophet Musa witnesses two men fighting, one of them from his own tribe. He sides with the one from his party and strikes the man from the other party. He does not intend to kill him, but the man dies from the blow. The Prophet Musa realises that he has erred.

This is an important example clarifying the concept of justice that a believer must adopt. It also conveys to us the message that if someone is in the wrong it is unjust to support him simply because of kinship or friendship. As a matter of fact, the Prophet Musa (pbuh) in this case immediately realises the truth and calls his action, "Satan's doing."

Indeed, the "feeling of factionalism", which the Prophet Musa describes as "Satan's doing", is responsible for all the bloodshed throughout history. Man's obsession to prove the righteousness of his family, tribe, ethnic group, followers or his race at all cost, with no consideration of justice, has been the main source of numerous conflicts and wars.

The attitude, a believer must assume in the face of such incitement is also related in the Quran by referring to the exemplary life of the Prophet Musa (pbuh). When he exercised his conscience, the Prophet Musa readily realised that this unfavourable feeling was a form of cruelty, repented for the sin he had committed under Satan's temptation and took refuge in God. This exemplary and conscientious conduct is related in the Quran thus:

> He said, "My Lord, I have wronged myself. Forgive me." So He forgave him. He is the Ever-Forgiving, the Most Merciful. He said, "My Lord, because of Your blessing to me, I will never be a supporter of evildoers."
> (Quran, 28:16-17)

Hatred Felt Towards a Community does not Prevent Believers from Exercising Justice : Hatred and anger are the major sources of evil, and are likely to prevent people from making just decisions, thinking soundly and conducting themselves rationally. Some people can readily inflict all kinds of injustice on people for whom they feel enmity. They may accuse these people of acts they have never committed or bear false witness against them, although their innocence is known to them. On account of such enmity, many people may be subjected to unbearable oppression. Some people avoid bearing witness in favour of people they disagree with, although they know they are innocent, and they keep evidence which would reveal their innocence hidden. Furthermore, they take pleasure in the misery these people face, their encounters with injustice or great suffering. Their greatest worry, on the other hand, is that justice should be done and these peoples' innocence proved.

For these reasons, it is very hard for people in corrupt societies to trust one another. People worry about falling victim to someone else all the time. Having lost mutual trust, they also lose their human feelings, such as tolerance, compassion, brotherhood and cooperation, and start hating one another. However, the feelings someone holds in his heart towards a person or community should never influence a believer's decisions. No matter how immoral or hostile the person he is considering may be, the believer sets all these feelings aside and acts and makes his decisions justly and recommends that which is just. His feelings towards that person cast no shadow over his wisdom and conscience. His conscience always inspires him to comply with God's commands and advice, and not to abandon good manners, because this is God's command in the Quran. In Sura Maida, it is related as follows:

> O You who believe! Show integrity for the sake of God, bearing witness with justice. Do not let hatred for a people incite you into not being just. Be just. That is closer to faith. Heed God [alone]. God is aware of what you do.
> (Quran, 5:8)

As is related in the verse, displaying a just attitude is what most reflects having fear of God. A person of faith knows that he will attain the pleasure of God only when he acts justly. Every person, who witnesses his or her good manners will trust this person, feel comfortable in their presence and trust them with any responsibility or task. Such people are treated with respect even by their enemies. Their attitude may even lead some people to have faith in God.

The best example to follow for believers in our day, is also the actions of the Prophet Muhammad (pbuh) as described in the Quran. Similar to the Blessed Period of the first community of Islam—an age of well-being when people in general adhered to the Quran—in our day, too, people of different beliefs such as Christians, Jews, Buddhists, Hindus, atheists, idolaters and pagans live together. A Muslim is responsible for being tolerant, forgiving, just and humane towards people, regardless of who they may be. It is probable that in time everyone will place his faith in God, become a Muslim and surrender himself to God. A believer should always bear this fact in mind. The responsibility of a believer is to summon people to God's religion with a favourable, peaceful and tolerant attitude. The decision to follow divine guidance and have faith rests with another party. Compelling a person to have faith and forcing him to do things are against the Quran. God states the following about this:

> There is no compulsion in religion. True guidance has become clearly distinct from error. Anyone who rejects false deities and has belief in God has grasped the Firmest Handhold, which will never give way. God is All-Hearing, All-Knowing.   (Quran, 2:256)

THEORY OF JUSTICE

It must be admitted on all hands that Islam infused among mankind the principle of divine unity and human equality preached by the Prophet of Islam. So long as the doctrine of Tauhid (Unity of God) was held aloft and the message of the Prophet was practically followed, Islam allowed the widest latitude to the human conscience. Consequently the Muslims were hailed as the torch-bearers of freedom and emancipators from bondage. In Islam practical equality was held high in the eye of Law.

An objective study of the history and political administration of the early four Caliphs (Khulafa-i-Rashideen) will clearly reveal how a popular government was administered by an elective chief with limited powers. The authority of the Head of the State (Ameerul Momineen) was confined to administrative and executive matters, such as the regulation of the police, control of the army, transaction of foreign affairs and disbursement of finances etc.; but no steps could be taken against the established law. The Shariah Courts were not dependent on the government. Their decisions were supreme; and the four Caliphs could not exercise the power of pardoning those whom the Shariat Courts had condemned. The law

Judicial System

did not make any distinction between the poor and the rich, the black and the white, the man in power or a labourer in the field.

The administration of justice during the four Caliphs was perfectly equal, and the Caliphs set the example of equality by holding themselves amenable to the orders of the legally constituted judge. The Quran has clearly emphasised the significance of equity and justice (Adl) in the following verses:

> "Help ye one another unto righteousness and pious duty Help not one another unto sin and transgression, but keep your duty to Allah."

> "O ye who believe! Be ye staunch in justice, witness for Allah, even though it be against yourselves or your, parents or your kindred, whether (the case be of) a rich man or a poor man, for Allah is nearer unto both (than ye are)."

No Difference

"O ye who believe! Be steadfast witnesses for Allah in equity (Adl), and let not hatred of any people seduce you that ye deal not justly. Deal justly, that is nearer to your duty. Observe your duty to Allah." "We verily sent our messengers with clear proofs, and revealed with them the Scripture and the Balance (of Right and Wrong), that mankind may observe right measure (Justice)."

During the apogee of Muslim culture and civilisation justice was administered by the Qadis, either appointed directly by the Caliphs or by the Wazirs or Governors invested with necessary powers. The following were the qualifications for the post of a judge: (1) Male and major Imam Abu Hanifah and Tabari are of the opinion that a woman may be appointed a judge; (2) fully mentally sound; (3) free citizenship; (4) complete faith in Islam (Iman and Tauhid); (5) flawless integrity; conversant with Islamic Law, Fiqh, Quran and Sunnah, both theoretically and practically.

The judge could be appointed either by written or verbal nomination by the ruler or Head of the State. The place of posting and judicial powers should also be mentioned therein.

The following were the duties of the Qadis: (1) to decide cases; (2) when the case had been established either by admission or by legal evidence, to compel the defaulting party to satisfy the judgment entered against him; (3) to appoint guardians for those who were incapable of dealing with their property, viz, mentally retarded persons and minors; (4) supervision and administration of Waqf properties; (5) execution of testamentary dispositions according to the direction of the testator; (6) charge of the remarriage of the widow; (7) execution of punishments prescribed by Islamic Law; (8) the supervision of law officers and the sub-judges; (9) impartiality in his decisions as between high and low.

Complementary to the functions and responsibilities of the Qadis were the Board of Inspection of Grievances (Nazrul Mazalim) to root out corruption and establish high moral character. The function of this institution was to set right, cases of miscarriage of justice which occurred in the administrative and judicial departments and also to take strict cognizance of petitions.

If the President of the Board of Inspection happened to be a Wazir (Minister) or Governor (with wide powers) a special nomination was not needed. If he was only Wazir or Governor with limited powers, a special nomination was needed. Abdul Malik was the first ruler who heard appeals. Among the Abbasid Caliphs. Mahdi, Hadi, Haroon al-Rashid and Mamun generally received such complaints in public audience.

The office of the President of the Board comprised: (1) Court officers for summoning parties; (2) judges and advocates; (3) Ulema-e-Fiqh[3] and Law experts for advising on serious law points; (4) clerks and secretaries for maintaining records; (5) recorders to certify judgements.

REALITY OF DEMOCRACY

According to Al-Mawardi[4], an eminent political economic and juriconsult, the following were the duties of the Chief Officers of this Board: to investigate the oppressive conduct of the executive authority towards the public and to initiate proceedings ex-officio; supervision of the officers connected with finances or taxes; control of Waqf properties; supervision of officers charged with the upholding of moral principles and character and maintenance of public order; protection of Divine services like prayers and pilgrimage. He had also the power to refer the parties to a competent person or to an arbitrator.

The position of the President was higher than of the Qadi. The President could himself decide legal disputes or refer them to the Qadi. In his decision he was not bound by the strict letter of the law only; but he could hear the witnesses of either side and decide according to the principles of equity.

"Every Friday," writes Ameer Ali, after divine service, the Commander of the Faithful mentioned to the assembly the important nominations and events of the day. The prefects in their provinces followed the example. No one was excluded from these general assemblies of the public. It was the reign of democracy in its best form. The Pontiff of Islam, the Commander of the Faithful, was not hedged round by any divinity. He was responsible for the administration of the State to his subjects. The stern devotion of the early Caliphs to the well-being of the people, and the austere simplicity of their lives, were in strict accordance with the example of the Master. They preached and prayed in the mosque like the Prophet; received in their homes the poor and oppressed, and failed not to give a hearing to the meanest.

Without cortege, without pomp or ceremony, they ruled the hearts of men by the force of their character. Umar travelled to Syria to receive the capitulation of Jerusalem, accompanied by a single slave. Abu Bakr on his deathbed left only a suit of clothes, a camel and a slave to his heir.

Every Friday, Ali distributed his own allowance from the Public Treasury among the distressed and suffering; and set an example to the people by his respect for the ordinary tribunals. Whilst the Republic lasted, none of the Caliphs could alter, or act contrary to, his judgment of the constituted courts of justice.

So long as the Muslim rulers held the respect of Law supreme and did not misuse their prerogatives their star was in the ascendant and kept moving higher and higher. In Islam no one is above Law. He has to abide by the decisions of the Supreme Courts and it cannot be challenged by any authority. Since, the Muslims deviated from this spirit (respect of Law), their degradation set in, in all phases of human life, and their disciplined and moral life came to a stop.

ROLE OF THE PROPHET

For the majority of people, an environment where the justice referred to in the foregoing sections prevails seems Utopian, an illusory concept that can only exist in the realms of literature. This attitude denies that a society in which there is real justice is possible. Nevertheless, history has witnessed periods when justice ordained in the Quran was built up and real peace, tolerance and security pervaded human relations.

In communities to which the messengers of God were sent, social relations were marked by great tolerance, peace and justice. As God informs us, "Every nation has a Messenger and when their Messenger comes everything is decided between them justly. They are not wronged" (Quran, 10:47). No one was oppressed in their times, and true justice prevailed among people.

God commands all His messengers to administer justice with no consideration of race and ethnicity. The books revealed to the Prophet Isa' (Jesus), Musa (Moses) and Daud (David) summoned people to good morals, tolerance, peace and trust, as did the Quran revealed to the Prophet Muhammad (pbuh). The following verse makes it clear, that one of the reasons why messengers are sent is "to establish justice":

We sent Our Messengers with the Clear Signs and sent down the Book and the Balance with them so that mankind might establish justice.
(Quran, 57:25)

In the Quran, one of the prophets who is told to display exemplary conduct in ruling with justice is the Prophet Daud. Two litigants, came to the Prophet Daud requesting him to judge between them with truth:

> Has the story of the litigants reached you? How they climbed up to the Upper Room and came in on Daud who was alarmed by them. They said, "Do not be afraid. We are two litigants, one of whom has acted unjustly towards the other, so judge between us with truth and do not be unjust and guide us to the Right Path.
>
> This brother of mine has ninety-nine ewes and I have only one." He said, "Let me have charge of it," and got the better of me with his words.
> (Quran, 38:21-23)

As stated in the verse, the two litigants asked God's Prophet not to be unjust while judging between them and to guide them to the right path. They trusted in his justice and submitted themselves to his verdict. The answer of the Prophet Daud was as follows: He said, "He has wronged you by asking for your ewe to add to his ewes. Truly many partners are unjust to one another—except those who believe and do right actions, and how few they are!.." (Quran, 38:24)

This decision of the Prophet Daud sets a very good example for believers, since he sided with the person who was in the right, rather than the more powerful one, and hence acted justly. In the 25th verse of the same Sura, the moral perfection displayed by the Prophet Daud is praised, and he is given the glad tidings of a good homecoming as, "he has nearness to Us and a good Homecoming." In the 26th verse, God reminds the Prophet Daud of the importance of justice:

> ...We have made you a caliph on the earth, so judge between people with truth and do not follow your own desires, letting them misguide you from the Way of God. Those who are misguided from the Way of God, will receive a harsh punishment because they forgot the Day of Reckoning.

The people of Shuaib[5], who were sent to Madayan, were a tribe that acted unjustly in commercial life. They manipulated peoples' assets, devalued their goods and defrauded them. The Prophet Shoaib warned his people of their unjust attitudes and called them to justice. In one verse, God states the following regarding this matter:

Judicial System

> And to Madayan We sent their brother Shoaib who said, "My people, worship God! You have no other deity than Him. A Clear Sign has come to you from your Lord. Give full measure and full weight. Do not diminish people's goods. Do not cause corruption in the land after it has been put right. That is better for you if you are believers."
>
> (Quran, 7:85)

In another verse, the Prophet Shoaib reminds his people that honest earnings are better for them, and tells them to exercise justice:

> My people! Give full measure and full weight with justice; do not diminish people's goods; and do not go about me earth, corrupting it What endures with God is better for you if you are believers. I am not set over you as your keeper. (Quran, 11:85-86)

In the Quran, God gives many examples related to the just attitudes displayed by the Prophet Musa, the Prophet Isa', the Prophet Yusuf (Joseph) and other prophets, and the way they invited their people to do good is explained in detail.

The Prophet Muhammad (pbuh), too, administered justice among his people in compliance with the verse, "...Be upholders of justice, bearing witness for God alone..." (Quran, 4:135). His utmost meticulousness in the administration of justice and his moral perfection were the main reason why people placed unshakeable trust in him and committed themselves to God's religion. Furthermore, during the first years of the revelation of the Quran, seeing the Prophet Muhammad's moral perfection and justice, many prominent disbelievers submitted themselves to him and converted to Islam.

Such examples are legion in the life of the Prophet Muhammad (pbuh), many of which have been conveyed to us in historical accounts and the sayings of the Prophet (hadith). His just, tolerant, compassionate attitudes became very good examples to follow for Muslims in every age. There are divine purposes in his words, attitudes and practises. God relates the moral perfection of the Prophet Muhammad (pbuh), and the great care he showed to believers as follows:

> A Messenger has come to you from among yourselves. Your suffering is distressing to him; he is deeply concerned for you; he is gentle and merciful to the believers. (Quran, 9:128)

A Perfect Life

God commands, His messengers to maintain justice among people. The Prophet Muhammad (pbuh), the last messenger, started to spread the religion of Islam in Mecca, where he received the revelations, with a just attitude.

At that period, the Arabian Peninsula, and especially Mecca, was shaken by social problems. In the period preceding the Blessed Period, which is called "The Age of Ignorance," there was severe discrimination between races and religions. Disputes among tribes, an unjust economic order, plundering, intolerant attitudes between members of different religions, differences between the poor and the wealthy and many other injustices were the natural consequences of such discrimination. The maintenance of justice could not be established, the poor were oppressed by those in power, and were subjected to violence because of their race, religion or language. People were forced to work under very hard conditions, and were virtually tortured.

In commercial life, under the burden of the interest-ridden system, small-scale businesses disappeared, whereas the wealthy tended to extravagant consumption. Some of these immoral acts became almost like traditions. For instance, the Arabs of the ignorant age who raided and plundered commercial caravans, sold their spoils at very low prices and influenced market conditions. Sometimes, they kept these goods deliberately and generated a black market.

In the Quran, God gives information about the desert Arabs who made up the majority of society before the time of the Prophet Muhammad (pbuh). This society's disinclination to comply with the words of the messenger is related in the following verse:

> The desert Arabs are the worst in disbelief and hypocrisy, and more fitted to be ignorant of the limits, which God has sent down to His Messenger. But God is Knowing, Wise. (Quran, 9:97)

The Prophet Muhammad (pbuh) was sent to such ignorant people to summon them to good morals and the right path. No difficulty could shake his commitment. He communicated God's message to a tribe which was particularly inclined to disbelief, and was throughout his life a role model for them. As also stated in the verse below, he called on his people to be just:

> Say: "My Lord has commanded justice..." (Quran, 7:29)

The message of the Prophet Muhammad (pbuh), coupled with his good morals, had a great impact all over the Arabian Peninsula, and people converted to Islam in great numbers. The just commands of the Quran good morals, tolerance, peace and a peaceful social order—prevailed during his time. One of the most important reasons for this is that, in compliance with the verse, the Prophet Muhammad (pbuh) observed social justice without discriminating between people:

> God commands you to return to their owners the things you hold in trust and, when you judge between people, to judge with justice. How

excellent is what God exhorts you to do! God is All-Hearing, All-Seeing. (Quran, 4:58)

One example is the contract the Prophet Muhammad (pbuh) signed with the people of Najran, who were among the people of the Book. This text reveals an exercise of justice which was unprecedented in that age. The article of the pact of Najran, "If any one of the people of Najran demands his rights, justice shall be done between the plaintiff and respondent.

Neither oppression shall be allowed to be perpetrated on them, nor shall they be permitted to oppress any one" manifest the kind of justice people enjoyed at that time. Due to this unprecedented administration, people placed strong trust in God's messenger, and even his most terrible enemies could not help being impressed by the Prophet's honesty.

These examples of good morals, which appeared as a consequence of the Prophet Muhammad's meticulously observing God's commands also reflect the tolerant, peaceful order God's messengers introduced to social life. In a society, where people comply with the values of the Quran meticulously, it is obvious that a peaceful life will be secured.

Prophet Muhammad Opposed All Forms of Racism : The Prophet Muhammad (pbuh), upheld justice in his time and rejected the ignorant belief which considered some people superior to others because of their language, race, social status or ethnicity. That is because such discrimination is severely condemned in the Quran. "Racism," as defined in our day, is an idea God prohibits in the Quran, but which receives extensive support in ignorant societies. As mentioned earlier, one of the divine purposes in the creation of the different races is, "that they should come to know each other." In the sight of God, all people are equal, and the only superiority anyone can have over anyone else is his fear of God and faith in Him.

The Prophet Muhammad (pbuh) also declared to his people, who committed racism, that ethnic differences had no importance and that everyone was equal in the eyes of God. He repeatedly underlined that all that mattered was having sincere faith. While summoning his people to have faith, the Prophet Muhammad (pbuh) commanded them not to discriminate in his last sermon:

> O people! Your God is one and your forefather (Adam) is one. An Arab is not better than a non-Arab and a non-Arab is not better than an Arab, and a red (*i.e.* white tinged with red) person is not better than a black person and a black person is not better than a, red person, except in piety. Indeed the noblest among you is the one who is deeply conscious of God.

The Prophet Muhammad (pbuh) also told people that God created man from nothing, that everyone is created equal and that everyone will give account of his deeds all alone before God. For this reason, he added that it would be a great wrong to look for superiority in one's descent.

The Prophet (pbuh) commanded thus:

(All of) you are children of Adam, and Adam is from dust. Let some men cease to take pride in others.

The Prophet (pbuh) stated that no criteria except for heedfulness are acceptable:

Your descent is nothing to be proud of. Nor does it bring you superiority. O people! All of you are the children of Adam. You are like equal wheat grains in a bowl... No one has any superiority over anyone else, except in religion and heedfulness. In order to consider someone a wicked person, it suffices that he humiliates other people, is mean with money, bad-tempered and exceeds the limits.

Throughout his life, the Prophet Muhammad (pbuh) advised his people to set aside their ignorant and perverse values and to live by the Quran. In the Quran, racist attitudes are defined as "fanatical rage," and people's ambitious attitudes are criticised. A related verse reads:

Those who disbelieve filled their hearts with fanatical rage—the fanatical rage of the Time of Ignorance—and God sent down serenity to His Messenger and to the believers, and obliged them to respect the formula of needfulness which they had most right to and were most entitled to. God has knowledge of all things. (Quran, 48:26)

Muslims, who obeyed God's call in the above verse led their lives in peace and security, both during the Blessed Period of the first community of Islam and in succeeding ages when just administrators reigned.

In the Period of the Prophet Muhammad (pbuh), Contracts Signed with the People of the Book and the Pagans Secured Justice in Society

After the migration of the Prophet (pbuh) from Mecca to Medina, he encountered many different communities. At that period, Jews, Christians and pagans who held power were all living together. Under such circumstances, the Prophet Muhammad (pbuh) united the cosmopolitan structure to secure social unity and peace by making social agreements—either by sending letters or holding face-to-face meetings—with more than a hundred communities, and thus achieved social compromise. Prof. Thomas Arnold, stresses the importance of the social unity established by the Prophet Muhammad (pbuh) in these words:

Arabia that had never before obeyed one prince, suddenly exhibits a political unity and swears allegiance to the will of an absolute ruler. Out of the numerous tribes, big and small, of a hundred different kinds that were incessantly at feud with one another, Muhammad's word created a nation.

As is related in many verses in the Quran, living in peace with people of other religions is perceived as good by Islam. In one verse, God commands Muslims to believe in all the holy books revealed by Him and respect their beliefs:

> So call and go straight as you have been ordered to. Do not follow their whims and desires but say, "I believe in whatever God has sent down in the form of a Book and I am ordered to be just between you. God is our Lord and your Lord. We have our actions and you have your actions. There is no debate between us and you. God will gather us all together. He is our final destination." (Quran, 42:15)

The above verse describes the relations a Muslim should establish with people of other religions. Muslims are also held responsible for adopting the morality of the prophet, and being tolerant and just towards other people. This person can be anyone, a Buddhist, a Jew, a Christian or even an atheist. Such honest and just attitudes will make a very positive impact on their hearts, no matter what or who they believe in—or even if they have no beliefs at all—and they will become a means to make them feel closer to Islam.

The Prophet's migration to Medina and his administration there were marked by brotherhood and tolerance, and proved that a peaceful life among groups of people of different religions, races and languages is possible. The fact, that the first text the Prophet (pbuh) dictated was a peace agreement provides evidence for the fact that he was committed to the establishment of peace and tolerance. Following his conquest of Mecca, the Prophet Muhammad (pbuh) released even those who had formerly tortured Muslims, and was tolerant towards them. This superior morality of the Prophet Muhammad (pbuh) was unprecedented in Arab society, and was greatly appreciated by people.

At that time, the Prophet Muhammad (pbuh) also became a role model for all believers regarding the establishment of true justice in conquered countries. Towards the natives of these lands, he exercised the justice described in the Quran and made agreements which pleased the parties involved. The fact, that no party suffered even minor injustice was the distinctive feature of these agreements. For this reason, no matter which race or religion they belonged to, the people of conquered countries were always pleased with the justice introduced by Islam.

The Prophet Muhammad (pbuh) and the companions of the Prophet, peace be upon them all, were people who ensured justice among people, as the verse stresses:

> "Among those We have created there is a community who guide by the Truth and act justly according to it." (Quran, 7:181)

In the contract made with the Christians of Najran, who lived in South Arabia, the Prophet Muhammad (pbuh) demonstrates one of the best examples of tolerance and justice. The contract included the following article:

> The lives of the people of Najran and its surrounding area, their religion, their land, property, cattle and those of them who are present or absent, their messengers and their places of worship are under the protection of Allah and guardianship of His Prophet.

By means of such contracts, the Messenger of God secured a social order for Muslims and the People of the Book alike, which was marked by peace and security. This order was a total manifestation of the following verse:

> Those who believe, those who are Jews, and the Christians and Sabaeans, all who believe in God and the Last Day and act rightly, will have their reward with their Lord. They will feel no fear and will know no sorrow.
> (Quran, 2:62)

The examples cited above, are only a few of the measures implemented by the Prophet Muhammad (pbuh) that show the way he exercised justice. However, the most important of these contracts is the Constitution of Medina signed by Jews and pagan communities. This contract is still the subject of many articles today, and is closely examined.

The Constitution of Medina was prepared under the leadership of the Prophet Muhammad (pbuh) 1,400 years ago, that is in 622 AD, to meet the needs of people of different beliefs, and was put into practice as a written legal contract. Different communities of different religions and races that had harboured deep-seated enmity towards one another for 120 years became parties to this legal contract. By means of this contract, the Prophet Muhammad (pbuh) showed that conflicts between those societies, which had been enemies and quite unable to reach any form of compromise, could come to an end, and they could actually live side by side.

According to the Constitution of Medina, everyone was free to adhere to any belief or religion or to make any political or philosophical choice. People sharing the same views, could come together and form a community. Everyone was free to exercise his own justice system. However, anyone who committed a crime would be protected by noon. The parties to the contract would cooperate and provide support for each other, and remain under the protection of the Prophet Muhammad (pbuh). Conflicts between the parties would be brought to the Messenger of God.

This contract remained in force from 622 to 632 AD. Through this document, tribal structures which had formerly been based on blood and kinship were abolished, and people of different cultural, ethnical and geographical backgrounds came together and formed a social unity. The Constitution of Medina secured absolute religious freedom. This freedom was articulated in the following article:

> The Jews of Banu 'Auf are a community along with the believers. To the Jews their religion and to the Muslims their religion.

This contract granted the right of membership to Jews, and the idolater communities as well. Article 16 reads: "The Jew who follows us is surely entitled to our support and the same equal rights as any one of us. He shall not be wronged nor his enemy be assisted." The companions of the Prophet Muhammad (pbuh) also strictly adhered to this mentality and granted this right to Berbers, Buddhists, Brahmans and other similar communities. During this period, disputes were easily resolved, everyone respected other people's beliefs, and peace and justice prevailed for a long period of time.

The Prophet (pbuh) also made contracts with pagans as well as the people of the Book. Pagans were always treated with justice, and when they asked for protection, their requests were readily accepted by the Prophet Muhammad (pbuh).

This meant that these communities sought the protection of the Prophet (pbuh) in the face of an attack or a wrongful accusation. Throughout his life, many non-Muslims and pagans requested protection from the Prophet Muhammad (pbuh), and he took them under his protection and ensured their security. In Sura Tauba, God states that requests of pagans seeking protection be accepted by believers. Of this, God says the following:

> If any of the associates ask you for protection, give them protection until they have heard the words of God. Then convey them to a place where they are safe....
>
> As long as they are straight with you, be straight with them. God loves those who do their duty.   (Quran, 9:6-7)

As the verse also suggests, God asks believers to assume a just attitude towards pagans and holds them responsible for ensuring their security in the event they seek protection from believers.

People of the Book in the Period of the Prophet Muhammad (PBUH) *:* When we examine the relations of the Prophet Muhammad (pbuh) with the people of the

Book during the first years of Islam, we see that he cooperated with Christians. When Muslims were subjected to cruelty by pagans in Mecca, the Prophet Muhammad (pbuh) told them to migrate to Ethiopia, a place where Christians lived at that time. King Negus, the Christian ruler of that country, accepted the migrant Muslims and protected them against oppression.

The Quran also gives the example of Isa's disciples to other believers for their loyalty to God and His messenger. There are also striking similarities between the first Muslims and the first Christians. The communities, who first believed in God always remained faithful to God's messengers, despite being subjected to difficulty and torture. In the Quran, God relates that the first Christians in the time of Isa' were sincere Muslims who surrendered themselves to their Lord:

> When Isa' sensed disbelief on their part, he said, "Who will be my helpers to God?" The disciples said, "We are God's helpers. We believe in God. Bear witness that we are Muslims." (Quran, 3:52)

> And, when I inspired the Disciples to believe in Me and in My Messenger, they said:

> "We believe. Bear witness that we are Muslims." (Quran, 5:111)

The tolerant attitude adopted by the Prophet Muhammad (pbuh) towards Jewish communities, also sets a good example for all believers. During the period of the Constitution of Medina, the Prophet Muhammad (pbuh) treated Jews kindly and tolerantly. He encouraged that there be cooperation, counselling and goodness between Muslims and Jews.

Indeed, this was put into practice in daily life. This just and tolerant attitude of the Prophet (pbuh) surely applied to all people from all religions and races. Despite treachery, attacks and plots, the Prophet (pbuh) always forgave the perpetrators in compliance with the verse, "those who pardon other people" (Quran, 3:134). And as the verse suggests, "Call to the way of your Lord with wisdom and kindly instruction, and discuss (things) with them in the polite manner..." (Quran, 16:125), he always summoned people to Islam with gracious advice.

In the Period of the Caliphs Justice was Exercised in Compliance with the Quran : After the death of the Prophet Muhammad (pbuh), the caliphs who succeeded him were also very sensitive regarding exercising justice. In conquered countries, both natives and newcomers led their lives in peace and security. Abu Bakr, the first Caliph, demanded his people to adopt just and tolerant attitudes in these lands. All these attitudes were in compliance with the values of the Quran. Abu Bakr gave the following command to his army before the first Syrian expedition:

"Stop, O people, that I may give you ten rules to keep by heart: Do not commit treachery, nor depart from the right path. You must not mutilate, neither kill a child or aged man or woman. Do not destroy a palm tree, nor burn it with fire and do not cut any fruitful tree. You must not slay any of the flock or herds or the camels, save for your subsistence.

You are likely to pass by people who have devoted their lives to monastic services; leave them to that to which they have devoted their lives. You are likely, likewise, to find people who will present to you meals of many kinds. You may eat; but do no forget to mention the name of God."

Umar ibn al-Khattab, who succeeded Abu Bakr, was famous for his justice and made contracts with the indigenous people of conquered countries, just like the Prophet Muhammad (pbuh) did. Each one of these contracts was an example of tolerance and justice.

For instance, in his declaration granting protection to Christians in Jerusalem and Lod, he ensured that churches would not be demolished and guaranteed that Muslims would not worship in churches in groups. Umar granted the same conditions to the Christians of Bethlehem.

During the conquest of Medain, the declaration of protection given to the Nestorian Patriarch Isho'yab III (650 -660 AD), again guaranteed that churches would not be demolished and that no building would be converted into a house or a mosque. The letter written by the patriarch to the bishop of Fars (Persia) after the conquest is most striking, in the sense that it depicts the tolerance and compassion shown by Muslim rulers to the People of the Book in the words of a Christian:

The Arabs to whom God has given at this time the government of the world... do not persecute the Christian religion. Indeed, they favour it, honour our priests and the saints of the Lord and confer benefits on churches and monasteries.

The following document by Umar shows us the kind of tolerance God grants to man, provided that he adopts the character traits described in the Quran:

This is the security which 'Umar, the servant of God, the commander of the faithful, grants to the people of Elia. He grants to all, whether sick or sound, security for their lives, their possessions, their churches and their crosses, and for all that concerns their religion. Their churches shall not be changed into dwelling places, nor destroyed, neither shall they nor their appurtenances be in any way diminished, nor the crosses of the inhabitants nor aught of their possessions, nor shall any constraint be put upon them in the matter of their faith, nor shall any one of them be harmed.

All these are very important examples, revealing the understanding of justice and tolerance of true believers.

By means of the conquests made in the period of caliphs, the communities in these regions were saved from violence and had the opportunity to come to know Islam. However, people were never forced to convert to Islam. As the verse, "To you your religion, and to me, mine" (Quran, 109:6) suggests, everyone practised their religion freely and never faced any sort of oppression. They learned about the religion of Islam from the practices of Muslim people who observed its principles in their true sense, and thus they were greatly impressed. The majority of these people complied with the sincere call of these pious Muslims, and thus the number of people who converted to Islam increased steadily. For instance, in the time of Abu Bakr, some of the Christians in Kinde and Iyad converted to Islam of their own free will, as did others after the conquest of Damascus.

The false assertion that people in conquered countries converted to Islam under threat has also been disproved by Western researchers, and the justice and tolerant attitude of Muslims has been confirmed. L. Browne, a Western researcher, expresses this situation in the following words:

Incidentally these well established facts dispose of the idea so widely fostered in Christian writings that the Muslims, wherever they went, forced people to accept Islam at the point of the sword.

In his book The Prospects of Islam, Browne goes on to say that the real motive behind the Muslims' conquests was the brotherhood of Islam.

Peace Everywhere

In the previous sections, we mentioned the type of justice referred to in the Quran, the attitude of Muslims towards the People of the Book and the tolerant and just administration of the Prophet Muhammad (pbuh). Looking at history, we see that the true justice established during the time of the prophets continued to exist under the rule of leaders who exercised justice.

After the period of the Prophet Muhammad (pbuh), too, just administrators who strictly adhered to the teachings of the Quran and followed in the footsteps of the messengers managed to establish societies marked by peace. The true justice described in the Quran, righteousness and honesty also prevailed in the time of these administrators, making their reigns an example to follow for their successors.

After embracing Islam, Turkish people, too, made up societies that are documented as having had just, tolerant and honest administrations. As we shall see, this fact is confirmed by many Western historians. Furthermore, this fact was also sincerely expressed by researchers, who were members of communities that lived under Turkish rule for centimes. The Great Seljuk and Ottoman empires, the two great Turkish examples of their kind, spring to mind in this context. Numerous peoples who lived under their rule enjoyed the maintenance of social justice and lived in peace.

Khans of the Great Seljuk Empire who Administered Justice : With the conversion of the Turks to Islam, khans (a title given to the supreme rulers of Turkish tribes and Ottoman sultans) and sultans ruled in the light of the Islamic teachings. The spread of Islam witnessed praiseworthy accomplishments, great conquests and many other important contributions during the reign of these leaders, thanks to the guidance of justice described in the Quran. In his book, The Spread of Islam in the World, Sir Thomas Arnold[6], a British researcher, explains the willingness of Christians to come under Seljuq rule in these terms:

> This same sense of security of religious life under Muslim rule led many of the Christians of Asia Minor, also, about the same time, to welcome the advent of the Saljuq Turks as their deliverers... In the reign of Michael VIII (1261-1282), the Turks were often invited to take possession of the smaller towns in the interior of Asia Minor by the inhabitants, that they might escape from the tyranny of the empire; and both rich and poor often emigrated into Turkish dominions.

Malik Shah[7], the ruler of the Islamic Seljuk Empire during its brightest age, was very careful to apply the judgements of the Quran. He approached the people in the conquered lands with great tolerance and compassion, and was thus remembered by them with respect. The Armenian historian Mateos of Urfa describes the Great Seljuk Empire as follows:

> The reign of Malik Shah was blessed by God. His sovereignty extended to the remotest countries and gave peace to Armenians. His heart was full of compassion for Christians. He treated the people of the lands, he passed through like a father. Many towns and provinces came under his control of their own free will; all Roman and Armenian towns recognised his laws.

All objective historians, refer to the justice and tolerance of Malik Shah in their works. His tolerance also kindled feelings of love towards him in the hearts of the People of the Book. For this reason, unprecedented in history, many cities came under Malik Shah's rule of their own free will. Sir Thomas Arnold also mentions Odo de Diogilo, a monk of St. Denis, who participated in the Second Crusade, as the private chaplain of Louis VII and refers in his memoirs to the justice administered by Muslims, regardless of the religious affiliation of the subjects. Based on the graphic account of Odo de Diogilo, Sir Thomas Arnold writes:

> The situation of the survivors would have been utterly hopeless, had not the sight of their misery melted the hearts of the Muhammadans to pity. They tended the sick and relieved the poor and starving with open-handed liberality. Some even bought up the French money which the Greeks had got out of the pilgrims by force or cunning, and lavishly distributed it among the needy. So great was the contrast between the kind treatment the pilgrims received from the unbelievers and the cruelty of their fellow Christians, the Greeks, who imposed forced labour upon them, beat them, and robbed them of what little they had left, that many of them voluntarily embraced the faith of their deliverers.

Odo de Diogilo, narrating the events experienced during the Second Crusade, relates the efficacy of the tolerant, compassionate and just attitudes of Muslims:

> Avoiding their co-religionists who had been so cruel to them, they went in safety among the infidels who had compassion upon them, and, as we heard, more than three thousand joined themselves to the Turks when they retired though it is certain that contented with the services they performed, they compelled no one among them to renounce his religion.

These statements by historians reveal that the morality of the Quran commands the establishment of justice in warfare and other difficult times. This superior morality displayed by the Muslim Turks—at a time when the world was ruled by tyrants—is an indication of their commitment to the Quran and their superior character. For this reason, no matter how prejudicial a nation or a community may be towards Islam, their hearts will soften when they witness this good morality of Muslims, just like in the case of Crusaders.

The Ottoman Empire Brought Justice to the Conquered Lands : In societies in which people complied with the commands of the Quran, social life was marked by peace and tranquillity, which is a phenomenon that is also confirmed by the historical facts. One of these just administrations was the Ottoman Empire, which was originally a small state that spread rapidly, superseding the Byzantine Empire and which eventually came over a vast swath of land including southwest Asia, northeast Africa, and southeast Europe. Today, we still come across traces of the Ottoman Empire in the Balkans, the Middle East and North Africa. Everywhere, in the Ottoman Empire[8] was ruled by Muslim administrators who displayed the noble traits of people who adhered to Islamic tenets. One can understand the influence of the Ottomans from the quotation below, taken from the ten-volume work, Histoire de la Turquie, (1854) by Lamartine:

> Visit Izmir, Istanbul, Syria or Lebanon. Go to monasteries, holy places, and educational institutions there. Look at the places where religious education is provided and ask people, "Was there anything wrong with the attitude of the Ottomans to you, or the protection they provided? "All of them will tell you about, "the impartial treatment of the Ottomans and the Sultan." Indeed, in the ad-ministration of these religious places, the Ottoman sultans acted with a profound sense of objectivity, respect and peace...

Starting from the time of Usman Ghazi (a title given to a victorious Muslim military leader), the founder of the Ottoman Empire, Sultan Mahmood the Conqueror, and other emperors became role models for all humanity to follow with their elevated manner and the justice they displayed in their administrations.

Under their authority, people of different religions and creeds coexisted in peace. Furthermore, there existed some communities which did not resist at all and of their own free will submitted to the rule of Sultan Mahmood the Conqueror. This alone bespeaks the great satisfaction people derived from his fair treatment.

> As is the case with all Islamic states, the Ottoman sultans treated the non-Muslims in the conquered lands with the utmost justice. That is because according to the Quran, the people of the conquered lands were God's trusts to the sultans.

> The protection of these people and keeping them safe from the cruelty of others, were the responsibilities of administrators who ruled with justice. That is why, while European kingdoms subjected native peoples to genocide and cruelty, and exploited all the natural resources in the countries they occupied, the Ottoman sultans made it their main goal to bring welfare to the conquered lands. They never resorted to coercion to convert the natives. On the contrary, they provided them all the means to worship in peace.

Muslim Turks, never intervened in the language, religion and many of the social and administrative structures of the people living under their rule. In brief, the cultures of these people were kept intact. That is why people whose religions, languages and cultures were completely different could live together in peace and harmony under one roof. Regarding this subject, historian Andre Miquel states the following:

> The Christian communities lived under a well administered state that they did not have during the Byzantine and Latin periods. They were never subjected to systematic persecution.
>
> On the contrary, the empire and especially Istanbul had become a refuge for Spanish Jews who were tortured. People were never Islamised by force; the movements of Islamisation took place as a result of social processes.

Turkish lands, which were then ruled in compliance with Islamic justice, provided great comfort for people of all religions. Non-Muslims living in Ottoman territories in Anatolia and Europe experienced no interruption in their social and religious lives.

Thanks to the strict adherence of Ottoman sultans to the Quran, no distinction was made between people because of their race, language and ethnic origins, and people of different descent enjoyed social justice. In his book, The Ottoman History, historian Ysmail Hakky Uzuncarboly[9] stresses that non-Muslim people considered the strong tolerance of the Turks as a salvation:

> The respect of the Turks for the religious feelings of non-Muslim communities, was the main cause why these people considered the Ottoman administration as a saviour.

European historian Richard Peters expresses how Muslim Turks exercised exemplary justice in the countries they conquered:

> For ages, Turks ruled many nations but never attempted to assimilate them. They granted them their freedom and allowed them to live by their religious principles and culture.

All these examples evinced the Muslim Turks' unwillingness to exploit conquered lands. They respected the rights of all peoples under their rule. Both Seljuqs and Ottomans took it upon themselves to protect every individual living within their territories. Thus, it was that people of different nations and religions lived in peace without coming into conflict with one another. If the Ottoman leaders had not adopted a just attitude towards these people, they would certainly have failed to found such well established empires and keep them intact for so long. However, we see that the elevated values and traits Islam endowed these administrators with helped them attain a high level of culture and civilisation.

Just Administration During the First Periods of the Ottoman Empire: Right from the initial years of its development, the founders of the Ottoman Empire

Judicial System

adopted the principle of administering justice. They administered the various communities and disbelievers under their rule with great fairness and never resorted to coercion to make them convert to Islam. The establishment of peace was always their main priority.

Usman Ghazi[10], the founder of the Ottoman Empire, established strong friendships with the non-Muslims living around his territory. These good relations ensured mutual trust. For example, before Usman Ghazi took his people to the high plateau in springtime, he entrusted his goods to the care of non-Muslims in Bilecik, and months later returned with gifts such as cheese, butter and carpets for them. The bazaar in Ilyca-Eskisehir, a province within the territories held by Usman Ghazi, attracted non-Muslims from the neighbouring regions because of its security. Warm social relations with non-Muslims permeated Usman Ghazi's time. One event the historian Joseph von Hammer relates in his book, Ottoman History, exalts Usman Ghazi's just administration for all people, no matter to which religion they belonged:

> One day, non-Muslims from Bilecik brought a load of glasses to the bazaar. One Muslim bought glasses but did not pay for them. When the salesman complained, Usman Ghazi called the Muslim who had failed to pay, took the money from him and immediately gave it to the non-Muslim. Following that, Usman Ghazi used his town criers to order his people not to act unjustly towards the non-Muslims of Bilecik. Usman Ghazi's administration proved to be so fair that even non-Muslim women could come and shop in the bazaar in safety. Under the administration of Usman Ghazi, the non-Muslim community felt safe. When Usman Ghazi was asked the reason for his extreme sensitivity in doing justice to the non-Muslims of Bilecik, he answered: "They are our neighbours. When we first came to this land, they welcomed us. What becomes us now is to respect them."

This virtuous conduct of Usman Ghazi is simply a manifestation of God's command:

> Worship God and do not associate anything with Him. Be good to your parents and relatives and to orphans and the very poor, and to neighbours who are related to you and neighbours who are not related to you, and to companions and travellers and your slaves. God does not love anyone vain or boastful. (Quran, 4:36)

This behaviour, in compliance with the Quranic injunctions caused many people to be reconciled to Islam. After the conquests of Yarhisar, Ynegol, Bilecik, Yenipehir (towns in Anatolia) and their surroundings, Usman Ghazi treated the native non-Muslims with justice and tolerance, and did not confiscate their lands. Indeed, Ottoman rule promoted public welfare and made these lands better places to live in a very short time. Furthermore, these safe lands, even attracted other non-Muslim communities, which came and settled in the Ottoman lands.

If Usman Ghazi had not ensured the establishment of that just, tolerant and secure environment which Islam demands, non-Muslims whose lands were conquered by Muslims might well have adopted a hostile manner. However, being a person of faith, who strictly observed God's commands, he administered justice. Usman Ghazi also attended wedding ceremonies of non-Muslims and gave them gifts, which are acts that attest to his tolerance of and respect for non-Muslims.

In his book, The Ottoman History, Joseph von Hammer relates another example of Usman Ghazi's justice:

> On a Friday, a Muslim, who was a subject of the Germiyan Turk ruler Alishir quarrelled with a Christian who was under the command of a Roman commander of Bilecik. Usman judged between them and found the Christian innocent. Then, throughout the country, everyone started to talk about Osman's justice and honesty.

It is further related that just before his death, Usman Ghazi instructed his son Orhan to protect all his subjects equitably and to please those who obeyed him. The reputation of Osman's justice extended even to remote lands. For this reason, Orhan Ghazi did not have to fight to capture Bursa (a town in Anatolia). The commander of the town surrendered the castle to Orhan Ghazi of his own free will. Then Orhan Ghazi asked Saroz, the commander in Bursa, why he had surrendered the castle. Saroz replied that those who obeyed Orhan Ghazi enjoyed peace, and that was what his people also longed for. The answer of the Romans in Bursa to the same question also reflects the very same sincere feelings:

> We see that your state is growing stronger each day, surpassing ours; we see that those peasants who came under your father's rule are happy and no longer remember us. This being the case, we also desired to attain such well-being.

A letter written by the Archbishop of Thessaloniki, Gregory Palamas, who was captured by the Ottomans in 1355, explicitly reveals the tolerance displayed by Orhan Ghazi and his officials towards Christians. In his letter, Palamas stated that Christians enjoyed complete freedom in Ottoman lands, that Solomon Pasha, the son of Orhan Ghazi, asked him questions about Christianity and that Sultan Orhan himself had a discussion with him, as well as Muslim theologians and scholars.

Orhan Ghazi's tolerant and just administration was not limited to Christian communities. Jewish communities also benefited from the justice stemming from the noble spirit of Islam that manifested itself in Orhan Ghazi's administration. Having lost everything they held dear under the rule of other states, Jews in Edirne and other Thrace towns received the Ottoman conquest with pleasure.

The Ottoman Emperor's favourable attitude to Jews also continued during the time of Murad I. Byzantine historian Chalcondylas described Sultan Murad's just and tolerant administration as follows:

> Regardless of their religion, the people who obeyed and served him received generous and kind treatment. He was tough on those who were hostile. None of his enemies succeeded in escaping him. He earned the trust of everyone, be he a friend or an enemy, because he kept his promises, even if they later turned out to be against his interests.

Gibbon, the British historian, described Sultan Murad's tolerance towards Christians by writing that he treated Orthodox people much better than Catholics treated Orthodox people.

All these examples reveal why the Ottoman Empire gained great power so rapidly during its early years. The just attitudes of the rulers had very positive effects on people of different religions, and the Ottomans extended their borders to far-off continents. The most important reason, why this expansion continued during the reigns of other sultans is this same tolerant and just attitude. The tolerant and just environment established in the time of Sultan Mahmood the Conqueror is an established fact accepted by all historians.

True Justice was Established at the Time of Sultan Mahmood the Conqueror: The conquests during the time of Sultan Mahmood the Conqueror extended the borders of the empire to three continents, and the conquest of Istanbul marked the beginning of a new age. This conquest was a milestone in European history as well as Ottoman. Sultan Mahmood also practised the justice and tolerance of Islam on the people of the lands he conquered.

Sultan Mahmood's tolerance towards the People of the Book is documented by the agreements he made. His tolerant administration stemmed from Islamic tenets and included everyone: Jews, Armenians and Syrian Orthodox communities. That is why during his reign, many nations were pleased to be under his rule. A statement by the Grand Duke Lucas Notaras, the Byzantine commander, "I would rather see the Muslim turban in the midst of the city than the Latin mitre" confirms that fact.

The conquest of Istanbul by Sultan Mahmood was initially a cause of great fear among non-Muslims. The majority of these feared they would suffer discrimination, oppression and attacks, and so fled from Istanbul or congregated in St. Sophia Church. However, Sultan Mahmood, who treated them with justice and tolerance, relieved them of all their fears and allowed them to return to their homes and go on with their daily lives. He allowed non-Muslims to live according to their own religions and their own rules, and furthermore, brought in conditions under which people of different creeds could carry out their religious obligations without hindrance. In the palace, Muslim and Christian scholars lived side by side and discussed issues in an atmosphere of tolerance.

Sultan Mahmood the Conqueror, tried to learn about Christianity from a Christian and granted the Patriarch an imperial edict entitling the Christian community to administer their own law in the conduct of their daily lives. Sultan Mahmood gave the Patriarchate enormous freedom, and thus the Patriarchate received autonomy under Turkish rule. The historian Hammer published a copy of the imperial edict (modus vivendi) compiled from Western and Eastern sources. Hammer quotes the following in the acquittal sent to the Patriarch by the Sultan:

> No one will oppress the patriarch: no one will ever bother him, regardless of his identity. The patriarch and the great priests in his service will be excused from all forms of services for an indefinite period of time.

Right after the conquest, Sultan Mahmood the Conqueror set about dealing with the judicial rights of minorities, appointed Gennadius as the Greek-Orthodox Patriarch and signed an agreement with them. Another agreement he made with the People of the Book living in Galata (a district of Istanbul), confirmed that the churches in Galata would not be confiscated or turned into mosques, and that the People of the Book would not be forced to convert to Islam. Another agreement made in the same period entitled the spiritual leaders known as "metropolitans" to carry out their services as usual.

Apart from the rights of Christians, Sultan Mahmood also paid attention to the rights of Jews. They were also granted the right to have their own synagogues and rabbis and to carry out their religious services freely. Sultan Mahmood invited Rabbi Moses Kapsali to the palace, the first rabbi of the Ottoman period, complimented him and granted him an imperial edict to judge cases involving Jews.

These developments that occurred following the conquest of Istanbul by Sultan Mahmood also characterised the reigns of the succeeding Ottoman sultans. The Ottoman army extended its borders as far as Vienna. They conquered the Balkans entirely. Serbia, Albania, Bosnia-Herzegovina, Wallachia and Moldavia

Judicial System

passed to the Ottoman Empire and Hungary was taken under its protection. Ottoman influence was also felt in lands bordering on the sea. The Black Sea became a Turkish lake. Many Aegean islands such as the Mora Peninsula, Rhodes, Crete and Chios, the Caucasus, and places such as Baghdad, Tabriz, the Yemen, Syria, Iraq, Lebanon, Egypt, Palestine, Jerusalem, Morocco, Tunisia, Algeria, eastern Anatolia, the Spice Road, Poland and many other regions were included within the territories of the Ottoman Empire. People of different religions lived in these conquered lands in peace. Nobody was oppressed because of his religion, language or race.

A model in which such justice and tolerance prevails is what is most desired in our world today. The only way to attain such a society is to live by the values of the Quran. As the examples above confirm, the leaders who adopted the Quranic injunctions and the societies they led attained great prosperity. Since the values of the Quran were adopted by everyone, from all walks of society, justice, compassion, tolerance, love, mercy and honesty pervaded the whole of society and brought peace and harmony to social life.

There is no reason why such a society cannot be established again. The only prerequisite for such a society is a sincere intention to live by the values of the Quran and to make serious efforts to spread these values to the whole of society.

References

1. *Doomsday upon which it is obligatory to have faith for every Muslim.*
2. *The greatest tyrant of Germany in the 20th century who murdered thousands of innocents just to quench his thirst from their blood.*
3. *Experts of Islamic law and philosophy.*
4. *Prominent jurisconsultant where areas of interest were politics and economy.*
5. *Prophet of Allah, sent towards Madayan.*
6. *A great scholar and researcher of the British origin.*
7. *He applied the injunctions of Holy Quran in day-to-day life with great interest.*
8. *The brightest and prosperous period in the history of Islam.*
9. *A Turkish historian in the Ottoman history.*
10. *The noble man who laid the foundation of Ottoman Empire.*

14

INTERNATIONAL LAW

International law operates between independent and sovereign states. It does not deal with relations between nations. And yet it did not begin with states but individuals. Every individual in the olden days was an autonomous unit. The individuals formed families and clans. Relations between autonomous and equal clans were governed by laws. Clans formed a large unit called a tribe. The leader of a tribe could declare war on another tribe. He had the power to make war and peace and enter into treaties and alliances. In short, he performed all the functions usually associated with a state which has its characteristic attributes. But our scholars somehow ignore that period of human history and begin with the period when a state, however small it may be, had come into existence.

A state first came into being in the shape of a city. European scholars start with a city-state perhaps because such units once existed in Greece. They had relations with each other both in times of peace and in war. But the city-state was not peculiar to Greece. It was found everywhere in the world. Even in Arabia we see city-states before Islam. There were tribes as well as cities. Tribes did not have a settlement in which they could stay all the year round. On the contrary, there were cities whose people did not lead a nomadic life. In Arabia we see both city-states and the tribal system existing side by side. A similar situation perhaps obtained in Greece in an earlier period but Western historians begin the story when a city-state had already come into existence.

In ancient Greece, the nature of interstate relations was such that their dealings with each other could not be called international law. All Greeks belonged to one race. They spoke the same language. They professed the same faith. But they lived in different cities, and each city enjoyed complete freedom and sovereignty. They fought battles and engaged in warfare with each other.

According to Western writers the laws of these city-states were confined to dealings with Greeks only. A Greek city followed certain laws in dealing with another Greek city but the Greeks were not governed by any code of law in their dealings with the rest of the world. They used their discretion and adopted different courses of action in dealing with different people.

The Greek international law suffered from a serious drawback for it was confined to a few people and ignored the rest of the world which was considered barbaric and was not, therefore, worthy of being treated in accordance with law. The laws which they devised to deal with their own compatriots were fairly barbarian but in any case they had a fixed code.

It is on this basis that we accept the premise that the oldest example of interstate relations is found in Greece where independent and sovereign city-states conducted their affairs during war and peace in accordance with fixed laws which were really not international law as such.

After the Greek city-state Western historians deal with the Roman era in the context of international law. City-states no longer existed in that period. Rome, which started as a city-state, had by then become the capital of a vast empire which comprised Europe, North Africa and parts of Asia. The Roman period saw both war and peace but still it was not suitable for international law, because according to Western writers, the Roman Empire respected law only in its dealings with states with which it had a treaty relationship and not with the rest of the world which was governed by mere discretion.

An example will perhaps help explain the situation. During the early period a formal declaration of war was considered necessary before engaging in warfare. The rule followed in this regard was that an army would reach an enemy's frontier and stop there. A priest or a religious leader would then take a spear and fix it in the enemy territory. This was considered a declaration of war. Later when the empire expanded, and it took several weeks to reach the enemy frontier, the priests hit upon a plan to avoid inconvenience to themselves.

The soil of various lands was collected into bags which were deposited in the state treasury in Rome. Whenever it was considered necessary to declare war against a certain country, its bag was taken out and the priest most solemnly thrust a spear into it.

The Roman period was not congenial for the development of international law. It had rules about war and peace but they were not the same for everyone. Oppenheim[1], the well-known authority on international law, remarks that it is neither necessary nor possible to discuss the relations of the Romans with other countries. His opinion is based on the Roman claim that the world is a Roman globe and belongs to them. No one needs international law in one's own territory. It is on this account that Oppenheim states that the question of international law did not arise in the Roman period.

Western historians begin their account of international law with the emergence of the city-state, proceed to the Roman period and then jump a thousand years to reach the Renaissance era in the fourteenth or fifteenth century CE when the modern international law is stated to begin. And yet it is not international law at all. Until 1856, the so-called international law dealt with the Christian states only. It was not considered necessary to follow fixed laws in relation to non-Christian states.

In 1856, the European states for the first time felt obliged to apply the same law to a non-Christian state *i.e.* the Ottoman Empire. After that there was a gap of nearly sixty years. The second non-Christian state which was considered worthy of this treatment was Japan which defeated Russia in 1905. The First World War broke out a little later. During this war a few other states were considered worthy of the same treatment. But these states had to fulfil certain conditions before they could be admitted into the League of Nations. After the Second World War the League of Nations was replaced by the United Nations Organisation. Every country cannot, in its own right, claim its membership. At least two states which are already members of the Organisation have to sponsor the candidature of a new country. The sponsors have to verify that the state in question is a civilised country and acts on international law and deserves, therefore, to be treated in accordance with it.

GLOBAL LAW AND ISLAM

If international law is a law which is equally applicable to all countries of the world and is not confined to a few specific nations, then it originated with the advent of Islam, and Muslims are perhaps the only nation in the world which can legitimately claim to possess an international law. An international law which is both truly 'international' and 'law' began with the Muslims.

The status of Islam in the beginning was that of a state within a state in Mecca. Muslims lived in the city-state of Mecca but they did not consider themselves obliged to obey the old laws of the city nor did they give allegiance to its ruler.

They obeyed their own leader, the Prophet of Islam (peace be upon him), and turned to him for guidance. They had their own laws and their own administrative arrangements.

After their migration to Medina they founded a state and framed a constitution for it. We do not know how ancient states were founded but we know exactly how the state of Medina came into existence. On reaching Medina the Prophet (peace be upon him) found that it was inhabited by many tribes which had been fighting with each other for nearly a hundred and twenty years. There was no central authority, no organised system, no government.

The Prophet (peace be upon him) proposed to the people of Medina that they should organise themselves for purposes of defence and justice and choose their own leader. The proposal was accepted by the local populace and the tribes. A question arises as to how arises the Prophet (peace be upon him) was selected for leadership while the Muslims were still in a minority in Medina.

There were two kinds of Muslims in Medina *i.e.* those who belonged to the city, and those who had migrated there from Mecca. The majority of the city's population, however, comprised those who had not yet embraced Islam. There were Jews as well as a sprinkling of Christians. The diversity and differences notwithstanding, the people of Medina elected the Prophet (peace be upon him) as their leader.

The reason was that the tribes of Medina were at odds with each other. It was impossible for them, therefore, to elect a leader from among themselves who would be acceptable to all the tribes. So they decided to opt for a neutral person. They elected the Prophet (peace be upon him) as their leader. The rights and duties of the ruler and the ruled were reduced to writing in detail, and a legal document was prepared. This is the document which can be called the constitution of the city-state of Medina.

The document which has reached us contains considerable detail about domestic administration. The right of religious freedom is clearly affirmed. Defence arrangements have also been spelt out together with laws of war and peace.

Soon after the establishment of the state of Medina, Muslims were confronted with a war. In 2 AH the city-state of Medina was invaded by the city-state of Mecca. International law usually deals only with two things *i.e.* war and peace. The Prophet (peace be upon him) had enjoyed peace only for a few months after the formation of the state when he was confronted with a war. Many a problem had to be resolved and decisions taken. Many a question had to be answered; for instance, should war be declared?

And after the war ended it had to be decided whether only adults capable of bearing arms, should be killed, or should the same fate be meted out to all enemy men, women and children? Should a slave be put to the sword? Should he be killed only in the battlefield? How is one to treat prisoners of war? Should they be executed or released with or without ransom? Should an exchange of prisoners of war take place? If so, how?

Scores of questions relating to the conduct of war had to be answered. The practice and pronouncements of the Prophet (peace be upon him) provided the guidelines for the law which came into being and thus was born the concept of the Islamic international law. In this law there is no distinction between the Muslim and non-Muslim aliens. Everyone is treated according to the same law irrespective of the fact whether he is Muslim, Jew, idol-worshipper or a man without any religion at all. For example, if a declaration of war is considered necessary, this applies to all states irrespective of their religion or faith.

It was during the ten years of the Prophet's stay in Medina that the international law of Islam came to be formulated. When books began to be written on the subject, Muslim scholars naturally referred first to the Holy Quran, or else they discussed the words and deeds of the Prophet (peace be upon him). Islamic international law belongs to the Prophet's period of Medina. The Meccan period does not provide us with an equally valid source because Islam was a state within a state there. Muslims fought no war during this period even though they were persecuted and killed.

When Muslim scholars started writing on jurisprudence their concept was much wider than that of Western writers. Pick up any Western book of law and it will be found utterly lacking in dealing with questions relating to worship. The Muslims made their law very comprehensive and dealt with both the physical and spiritual life of man. When Muslim jurists compile a code of laws, it includes worship, civil and military affairs, inheritance, etc., together with international law. Even though they call the subject *Siyar* (literally biographies), it deals invariably with international law.

GLOBAL LAW IN OLDER TIMES

The oldest book of jurisprudence we have today is Imam Zaid ibn 'Ali's *al-Majmu fi al-Fiqh*. Imam Zaid[2], the grandson of Hussain and son of Zayn al-Abidin, is the founder of the Zaidi sect. He was a great scholar. A chapter on international law is included in his book. The chapter is called *Kitab al-Siyar*. The word *siyar* in Arabic is the plural of *sirah*. The famous Hanafi jurist Imam Sarakhsi has stated in his book *Kitab al-Mabsut*, that by *sirah* is meant the attitude adopted by the ruler towards aliens in the state of war and peace. He adds that in addition to aliens, such a law would apply to two categories of citizens as well *i.e.* apostates and rebels. Thus the concept of international law in Islam is wider than the one found today in the West. Zaid was the first to use the expression *Siyar* in the sense of international law and since his day the term has remained current without any disagreement. Every author—Hanafi[3], Shafii[4], Maliki[5], Hanabli[6], Shiai[7]—has used the same expression with the sole exception of the Khawarij. In their book of jurisprudence, which we have secured with great difficulty, the chapter on international law is entitled—*Kitab al-Dima,* that is the "Book of Blood" because it deals with war.

In short, the earliest extant work on the subject is Imam Zaid ibn Ali's book. In a sense, he is considered the teacher of Abu Hanifah. Zaid rebelled against the Umayyads but his supporters let him down. He was arrested and executed in 120 AH Abu Hanifah died in 150 AH.

Between 120 AH and 150 AH, Abu Hanifah wrote a book called *Kitab al-Siyar.* Its history is interesting. In it he expressed the opinion that armed rebellion against a Muslim ruler was in order if all other ways and means to seek redress had failed. Other jurists hesitated to give such a verdict. Not only that, they rejected the verdict of Abu Hanifah and wrote books in refutation of the theme. Abu Hanifah's verdict was based on a *Hadith* which said that if someone saw an evil he should alter it by force.

If, however, he was not strong enough to change it by force he should, at least, offer verbal opposition to it *i.e.* he should try to change it through persuasion. If he does not have the courage to do so either, the least he can do is to look upon it as an evil. One who comes across an evil and does not consider it as such even in his own mind is not a good Muslim for this is the weakest manifestation of faith. This is how Abu Hanifah argued in support of his opinion.

Other jurists, who opposed him and held that rebellion against the government was not permissible in law, based their argument on another tradition which said something to this effect: "If the ruler dispenses justice to you, be grateful to God and be patient in case he indulges in tyranny." We are faced with a situation in which we have two apparently conflicting traditions on the same subject even though the context of each is different. Abu Hanifah, of course, does not advocate resort to rebellion against authority on trivial matters. On the contrary, he lays down the proviso that all peaceful avenues should be thoroughly exhausted before resorting to arms.

Imam Awzai, his contemporary, wrote a refutation of Abu Hanifah's work on international law. Unfortunately we have neither the work of Abu Hanifah in its original form nor its refutation by Awzai. All that we have are excerpts from the two works in Imam Shafii's book *Kitab al-Umm,* which throw light on issues on which the two jurists disagreed. When Awzai[8], a jurist of Damascus, wrote a tract on the work of Abu Hanifah, a jurist of Kufa, the latter did not consider it appropriate to answer the criticism. His pupil, Abu Yusuf, undertook the task. His book, too, is not available in original but is mentioned excerpts of Imam Shafii's *Kitab al-Umm.*

Based on these extracts, a book was published not long ago in Hyderabad, Deccan. It gives some idea of the viewpoints of Abu Hanifah, Awzai, and Abu Yusuf. Thanks to Shafii, a good part of these rare books has been preserved, although they have not reached us in their entirety.

In this connection Ibn Hajar, the biographer of Imam Shafii, has commented in *Tawali al-Tasis* that Abu Hanifah was the first to write a book on *Siyar.* Imam Awzai responded with his book which was in turn refuted by Abu Yusuf. Shafii then commented on Abu Yusuf's work in his book *Kitab al-Umm.* This is the background of the early works on international law.

Contribution of Abu Hanifah and his Students : Although Zaid ibn Ali was the first to take notice of the subject, his book contains only one chapter on international law. Abu Hanifah is the first to produce an independent work on the subject.

He must have taught the discipline to his students. He used to first give an exposition and then would invite the views of his students. A discussion ensued and different aspects of the problem became clearer. With the help of excerpts from his lectures one could compile a more comprehensive book.

Unfortunately the original work of Abu Hanifah has not been preserved. We reckon it was no more than a brief tract of some twenty or twenty-five odd pages. We have, however, with us the books of his pupils like Muhammad Shaybani[9], Zafar[10] and Ibrahim al-Fazari[11]. At least two of them, *i.e.* Shaybani and Fazari have written hundreds of pages on the subject. We think that possibly the lectures of Abu Hanifah were taken down by his students and they were later attributed to the students who compiled them.

The manuscript of Fazari's work, which is in Kufic script, is preserved in Morocco.

Muhammad ibn al-Hasan Shaybani, one of the students of Abu Hanifah, has written two books on the subject *viz. Kitab al-Siyar al-Saghir* and *Kitab al-Siyar al-Kabir.* When the former was written, Imam Awzai is reported to have commented: "How dare the Iraqis write on the subject for they know so little of *Hadith* ? When he came to know about the comment, Shaybani wrote *Kitab al-Siyar al-Kabir.* It was so voluminous that it had to be carried in a cart to Baghdad for being presented to Caliph Harun al-Rashid. We have received this work in the form of a commentary. Sarakhsi, the famous Hanafi jurist of the fifth century of *Hijrah* is the another of the commentary. The conditions in which he wrote it were indeed dramatic.

Imam Sarakhsi was an extremely intelligent, erudite, honest and fearless jurist. He was imprisoned presumably because of a verdict he gave against the imposition of unjust taxes by the contemporary rulers. In view of his reputation as a great jurist the government could not dispose him off but kept him in a dry well. During the fourteen years of his incarceration in the well he somehow secured the permission of his captors to allow his pupils to sit on the wall of the well and take down his lectures.

One is indeed surprised to see the long list of monumental works produced during those fourteen years of imprisonment. *Kitab al-Mabsut* has been published in thirty volumes. This was dictated from within the well.

The commentary on *al-Siyar al-Kabir* of Shaybani, which is in four volumes, was also dictated from the well. No less than a dozen works were dictated in this manner by the celebrated jurist during his imprisonment. We, who are free, should learn a lesson from the example of the great scholar who continued his work even in the dry well, where he was not allowed to keep a single book, and yet bequeathed to the posterity a wealth of scholarship.

One of his many works is *Sharh al-Siyar al-Kabir* which is by far the earliest book available on the subject of international law today. It could not have been written without the requisite references. The master was confined to the well but the students were free. Perhaps they read aloud from the books from without and the Imam dictated the commentary from within the well. This is how he also dictated the thirty volumes of *Kitab al-Mabsut.*

Sarakhsi's *Sharh al-Siyar al-Kabir* was published in 1335 AH from Hyderabad, Deccan but unfortunately no new edition has since come out. An attempt was made in Egypt to publish a new edition but till now only four volumes have been published which cover less than half the book. In view of the importance of the book, UNESCO decided to bring out a French translation.

PROMINENT JURISTS OF ISLAM

Muhammad ibn al-Hasan al-Shaybani's book occupies an important place in the history of international law. Among his contemporaries, Ibrahim al-Fazari, a student of Abu Hanifah, also wrote a book. Other eminent jurists have made similar contributions. Malik wrote a book under the same title *Kitab al-Siyar.* Unfortunately it is no longer available. His work *'al-Muwatta'* devotes barely half a page to this subject which is obviously not enough to meet our requirements. Another contemporary of his, the famous historian Waqidi, also wrote a *Kitab al-Siyar* but that too is not available. In Shafii's *Kitab al-Umm,* however, there is a lengthy extract of some fifty odd pages from *Siyar al-Waqidi.*

These were the last as well as the earliest full-length books on international law. They were produced in a certain period perhaps for a particular requirement. But the Muslim interest in the subject continued unabated. All the books written on the subject from the olden times until today contain a chapter called *Kitab al-Siyar.* All authors irrespective of their affiliation—Hanafi, Shafii, Maliki, Hanbali, Shiai, Fatimi—agree on international law which carries no sectarian stamp.

All jurists base their work first on the Quran and then on the *Sirah i.e.* the life of the Prophet (peace be upon him). All books written during the last 1300 years by authors belonging to different schools include a chapter on *Kitab al-Siyar.* Even the work which is considered an abstract of all the books *i.e.* Fatawa-i *'Alamgiri,* includes a chapter on it. Some books which were used during Aurangzeb's day are no longer available but extracts from them are to be found in the *Fatawa.*

In all these books the same principles have been followed. The authors naturally take into account the special circumstances obtaining in their country or those that they themselves encountered. This fact gives each author's work its special characteristics. Sarakhsi, for example, refers to soldiers riding on bulls during a battle.

Such a battle obviously took place in a country which had bulls, an animal not seen in an Arab battlefield. Maliki authors from North Africa and Spain frequently refer to poisoned arrows which are not mentioned in books written by non-Maliki writers, for the simple reason that this practice did not exist in other places.

In books written by Sarakhsi we come across the mention of carriages for carrying loads, instead of beasts of burden which perform the same function elsewhere. In short, peculiarities of different regions are evident from the contents of the works on international law. However, they do not detract from the similarity of the general approach to the subject.

UNDERSTANDING GLOBAL LAW

Let us turn now from these details to the contents of international law. In our day, public international law and private international law are considered different disciplines, but Muslim jurists do not make any distinction between the two, and discuss both in the same chapter. Private international law deals with the relations of a government with the subjects of another state while public international law is confined to interstate relations.

This is the basic difference between the two disciplines. For example, problems relating to the law of nationality will be dealt with in private international law. Muslim scholars include the relations of various Muslim sects into this law. For example, they discuss Shiai-Sunni relations from a legal point of view. Suppose an inheritance case comes up in a court of law.

The deceased was a Shii while his widow is a Sunni. Which law will determine the share of inheritance? This problem will be determined by the private international law of Muslims.

Suppose again that a Muslim individual who is the subject of a Muslim state has entered into a commercial contract with an individual of an alien state. The law of the alien state lays down that an individual who is less than eighteen years of age is not entitled to enter into a contract while the Muslim law does not prescribe an age limit but speaks merely of physical maturity which is possible before the stipulated age of eighteen years.

The case comes up in a court of law. A counsel argues that his client had not come of age at the time of signing the contract, and therefore, no responsibility devolves on him and the contract should, therefore, be declared null and void. Such cases belong to private international law.

Public international law deals with three subjects *viz.* law of peace, law of war, and law of neutrality. The law of peace mostly deals with three or four issues. Sovereignty is the first. Which country should be considered sovereign? Modern international law includes rebels in it but only when they begin to control and administer an area of the country on their own. Similarly, the law deals with details of sovereignty.

In British India, *e.g.*, there were areas which were ruled directly by the British government and there were states which were ruled by princes *e.g.* Hyderabad, Bahawalpur, Kashmir, etc. Will these states be considered sovereign for purposes of international law? If so, what will be the rules governing them? Even if a state enjoys partial sovereignty and has the right to send out an ambassador to one country, it will be subject to international law. In short, such subjects are discussed under sovereignty.

Another subject is "property", which mostly deals with conquests. Does part of a state conquered by another automatically become part of the victor country or does it require some formal procedure? If so, what would it be? The discussion on property will also deal with the sale of property. A state acquires land, sometime by conquest, sometime by exchange of territory and sometime as a gift. We come across many examples of it in Indian history. Two rulers quarrel over a piece of land. At last a compromise is reached on the basis that the territory concerned would be ceded to the ruler as a dower for his son who marries the daughter of the other ruler.

Yet another topic which is dealt with in public international law is jurisdiction. Will the laws of one state be applicable to the subjects of another state? And if they do, then the extent of their application is to be determined. In this connection we should like to refer to Shaybani's *al-Siyar al-Kabir* which has an interesting chapter on this subject. He states that in the event of an alien filing a suit in a Muslim state, the court will apply laws prevailing in the state of the alien.

Suppose, for example, two Indian Hindus came to Pakistan. They had a quarrel between themselves. One of them approached a Pakistani court. In such a situation the law of India and not that of Pakistan will apply. It is in this connection that Shaybani states that Muslim judges need to acquaint themselves with the laws of alien lands.

He quotes example from the days of the Prophet (peace be upon him). He writes, *e.g.*, that in Medina some Jews came to the Prophet (peace be upon him). They had with them a Jewish couple who were accused of adultery.

The Prophet (peace be upon him) enquired about the Jewish law applicable in such cases. The Jews tried to mislead the Prophet (peace be upon him). They said that the face of the person found guilty was to be blackened and he was to be paraded through the town in a procession, riding a donkey with face backwards, to the accompaniment of drumbeat.

The Prophet (peace be upon him) did not accept the statement and asked for a copy of the Torah. When it was brought to him he asked the relevant portion to be read out in the presence of Abd Allah ibn Salam, a Jewish convert to Islam. A Jew began to read it. He put his finger at one place on the page. Abd Allah ibn Salam asked him to remove the finger and to read the words he was trying to hide.

It was written there that the penalty for adultery was stoning to death. The Prophet (peace be upon him), therefore, pronounced this penalty. This example shows that the Islamic law is not applicable to aliens for they are subject to their own law. Shaybani has devoted many pages to a discussion of this issue in his book.

The law of peace concerns embassies. In the old days there were no permanent ambassadors. They were assigned for a specific purpose to a country for a limited period of time and returned home after concluding their mission. Syed Ameer Ali in his *History of the Saracens,* has stated that the institution of permanent ambassadors was created by Muslims two hundred years before Europe adopted it.

The subjects discussed under the law of war include the law of war in respect of human beings The law governing property, and the constituents and qualities of a treaty concluded at the end of a war.

In short, international law covers principles and regulations governing the relations of one state with another.

References

1. *Internationally aclaimed authority over law.*
2. *The grandson of Hussain and son of Zain-ul-Aabideen.*
3-7. *Prominent scholars of Islam and founder of schools of thought named after their name.*
8. *A jurist from Damascus who wrote on the works of Abu Hanifah.*
9-11. *Great writers of Islam of their time.*

BIBLIOGRAPHY

Aghanides, N.P. : *Mohammedan Theories of Finance,* Oxford, New York, 1916.

Ahmad, K. N. : *Muslim Law of Divorce,* Kitab Bhavan, New Delhi, 1988.

Ahmad, M.M.Z. : *Mystical Tendencies in Islam in the Light of the Quran and Traditions*, Daya Publishing House, Delhi, 1986.

Ahmed, Hasanuddin : *Principles of Islamic Culture,* Goodword Books Pvt. Ltd., New Delhi, 1989.

Ali, A. Yusuf : *Message of Islam,* Kitab Bhavan, New Delhi, 2000.

Ali, S. Ameer : *Muhammadan Law,* Kitab Bhavan, New Delhi, 1986.

Amini, Mualana Taqi : *Fundamentals of Ijtihad,* Idaara-I-Adabiyat, Delhi, 1986.

Anwarullah : *The Islamic Law of Evidence,* Kitab Bhavan, New Delhi, 2000.

Arnold, T. W. : *Preaching of Islam*, Luzac & Co., London, 1913.

Asad, Muhammad : *The Principles of State and Government in Islam*, University of California Press, California, 1961.

Asborn, Eide : *Human Rights in World Society,* New Millennium Pub., Oslo, 1977.

Asghar Ali, E. : *Islam : Challenge in Twenty-first Century,* Gyan Books Pvt. Ltd., New Delhi, 2004.

———— : *Islam : Women and Gender Justice,* Gyan Books Pvt. Ltd., New Delhi, 2001.

Azad, G. Murtaza : *Judicial System of Islam,* Kitab Bhavan, New Delhi, 1994.

Aziz, Noomi Kurtha : *Prisoners of War and War Crimes,* Deep Publications, Lacknow, 1980.

Azmi, Majaz : *Muslim Wife,* Idara Ishaat-e-Diniyat Pvt. Ltd, New Delhi, 1991.

Baksh, S. K. : *Politics in Islam,* Kitab Bhavan, New Delhi, 2003.

Basil, King : *The Conquest of Fearm,* Illias Pub., Islamabad, 2000.

Bernard, L. : *Islam,* Oxford, New York, 1974.

Beverly Milton, E. : *Islam and Politics in the Contemporary World,* Blackwell, New York, 1987.

Bhatia, H. S. : *Studies in Islamic Law, Religion and Society,* Deep & Deep Publications, New Delhi, 1997.

Briffault, Robert : *The Making of Humanity,* Islamic Book Foundation, Lahore, 1980.

Brow, John R. : *Islam, Law, and Equality in Indonesia : an Anthropology of Public,* Cambridge University Press, New Delhi, 1997.

Calverley, Edwin Elliot : *Worship in Islam,* University of Madras, Madras, 1925.

Cassese, A. : *The Self-determination of Peoples,* Columbia University, Columbia, 1981.

Chiragh, Ali : *The Proposed Political Legal and Social Reform under Muslim Rule,* Popular Prakashan, Bombay, 1883.

Cook, Michael : *Forbiding Wrong in Islam : an Introduction,* Cambridge University Press, New Delhi, 1985.

Corbin, H. : *Avicenna and the Visionary Recital,* MacMillan, London, 1960.

De, Laet : *The Political Systems of Empire,* Oxford, New York, 1963.

Emil, Brunner : *Justice and the Social Order,* Oxford, New York, 2000.

Enayat, H. : *Islam in the Political Process,* Cambridge University Press, Cambridge, 1993.

Engineer, Asghar Ali : *A Rational Approach to Islam,* Gyan Books Pvt. Ltd., New Delhi, 2001.

——————— : *The Islamic State,* Vikas Publishing House, New Delhi, 1987.

Faris, Nabith A. : *The Book of Knowledge,* Feroz Pub., Lahore, 1962.

Fatima, T. : *Islamic Law and Judiciary,* Deep & Deep Publications, New Delhi, 2001.

Fauzi, M. : *The Islamic State : a Study in Traditional Politics,* Oxford, New York, 1967.

Frederic, G. : *Political Islam in the Indian Subcontinent : the Jannat-i-Islam,* Manohar Publishers, New Delhi, 2001.

Gellner, E. : *Post-Traditional Forms in Islam : the Turf and Trade,* Oxford, New York, 1982.

Gerges : *American and Political Islam : Clash of Cultures or Claush of Interest?,* New Academic Publishers, New Delhi, 1992.

Gibb, H.A.R : *Islamic Society and the West,* Luzac & Co., London, 1960.

Gins Berg, M. : *Evolution and Progress,* William Heinemann Ltd., London, 1982.

Grunebaum, G.E. : *Islam : Essays in the Nature and Growth of a Cultural Tradition,* American Anthropological Association, 1955.

Grunebaum, Gustave Edmund Von : *Modern Islam,* University Press, Los Angeles, 1952.

Guillaume, A. : *The Legacy of Islam,* Oxford University Press, London, 1949.

————— : *The Traditions of Islam,* Khayats, Beirut, 1966.

Gustav, E. Von Grunebaum : *Unity and Variety in Muslim World,* Oxford, New York, 2003.

Harun, Yahya : *Islam : the Religion of Ease,* Goodword Books Pvt. Ltd., New Delhi, 1993.

Hasan, A. : *Islami Reassertion : a Socio Political Study,* Progressive Publishers, Lahore, 1981.

Hasan, Ehteshamul : *Fundamentals of Islam,* Idara Ishaat-e-Diniyat Pvt. Ltd, New Delhi, 1990.

Hasanuddin, A. : *Islamic Economics,* Goodword Books Pvt. Ltd., New Delhi, 1991.

————— : *Social Justice in Islam,* Goodword Books Pvt. Ltd., New Delhi, 1990.

Henderson, J.J. Craik : *Parliament : a Survey,* George Allen & Unwin, London, 1965.

Heyworth-Dunne : *Religious and Political Trends in Modern Egypt,* Washington, 1950.

Hourani, Albert : *Thought in the Liberal Age,* Oxford, New York, 1962.

Houtsma, T. and Others : *Encyclopaedia of Islam,* MacMillan, London, 1934.

Hughes, T.P. : *Dictionary of Islam,* Allen & Co., London, 1935,

Husaini, Waqar : *Islamic Thought,* Goodword Books Pvt. Ltd., New Delhi, 1999.

Hussain, S. Saukat, : *Human Rights in Islam,* Kitab Bhavan, New Delhi, 2001.

Ilyas, A. : *Social Contract and the Islamic State,* Urdu Publishing House, Allahabad, 1940.

Imtiaz, A. : *Divorce and Remarriage among Muslims in India,* Manohar Publishers, New Delhi, 2003.

Iqbal, Muhammad : *Six Lectures on the Reconstruction of Religious Thought in Islam,* Royal Pub., Lahore, 1930.

Jafar, Sharif : *Islam in India,* Oxford, New Delhi, 1972.

Jansen, G.H. : *Militant Islam,* Pan Books, London, 1979.

John L. Esposite : *Islam in Transition,* Oxford, New York, 1969.

Joseph, and Bosworth, C.E. : *The Legacy of Islam,* Oxford University Press, New York, 1979.

Karnal, A. Faruqui : *Islam : Today and Tomorrow,* Deep & Deep Pub., New Delhi, 1989.

Khab, Qamaruddin : *The Political Thought of Ibn Taimiyah,* Islamic Book Foundation, Lahore, 1983.

Khaduri, M. : *War and Peace in the Law of Islam,* Hopkins Press, Baltimore, 1955.

Khalifa, Abdul Hakim : *The Islamic Ideology,* Fortune Books, London, 1993.

Khan, N. M. Yamin : *God Soul and Universe in Science and Islam,* Kitab Bhavan, New Delhi, 1993.

Khan, Qamaruddin : *Political Concepts in the Quran,* Islamic Book Foundation, Lahore, 1982.

——————— : *The Methodology of Islamic Research,* Institute of Islamic Studies, Karachi, 1973.

Khan, Wahiduddin : *Islam and Peace,* Goodword Books Pvt. Ltd., New Delhi, 1996.

——————— : *Polygamy and Islam,* Goodword Books Pvt. Ltd., New Delhi, 1996.

Khurshid, A. : *Islam : its Meaning and Message,* Islamic Council of Europe, London, 1976.

Lewin, Roger : *In the Age of Mankind,* Simithsonian Books, Washington, D.C., 1956.

Lewis, Richards : *Universe,* Harmony Books, New York, 1973.

Lok Raj, B. : *Regional Migrations : Ethnicity and Security,* Popular Prakashan, Bombay, 1995.

MacDonald, D.B. : *Development of Muslim Theology,* New Century Pub., London, 1993.

——————— : *The Religious Attitude and Life in Islam,* Modern Pub., Beirut, 1965.

Manzuruddin, Ahmad : *Islamic Political System,* Kitab Bhavan, New Delhi, 1991.

Margery Milne : *The Nature of Life,* Crown Publishers, New York, 1995.

Mathew, Thomas : *Political Economy of Etimic Conflict,* School of International Studies, Jawaharlal Nehru University, New Delhi, 2003.

Maurice, B. : *The Bibal, Quran and Science,* Kitab Bhavan, New Delhi, 2004.

McIver, R.M. : *The Community,* MacMillan & Co., London, 1978.

Mole, Marigan : *Les Mystiques Musulmans,* MacMillan & Co., Paris, 1965.

Morgan : *War its Conduct and Legal Results,* Feroz Pub., Lahore, 2000.

Morgenthu, H. : *Politics : Among Nations,* Oxford New York, 1984.

Mortimer, E. : *Faith and Power, the Politics of Islam,* Oxford, New York, 2002.

Muhammad, Asad : *Islam at the Crossroads,* Kitab Bhavan, New Delhi, 2003.

Muhammad, Ayub : *The Politics of Islamic Revolution,* Royal Pub., Lahore, 1991.

Muhammad, M. : *The Political Theory of Ibn Khaldun,* MacMillan & Co., London, 1967.

Murata, S. : *The Vision of Islam,* Ashish Publishing House, New Delhi, 1991.

Murthy, T.S. : *Muslim : the Difficult Years,* Himalayan Books, Chandigarh, 1983.

Muslehuddin, M. : *Banking and Islamic Law,* Idara Ishaat-e-Diniyat Pvt. Ltd, New Delhi, 1990.

——————— : *Islam : its Political System,* Kitab Bhavan, New Delhi, 1999.

Nabith, A. F. : *The Foundations of the Articles of Faith,* Feroz Pub., Lahore, 1993.

Naseem, A. : *Liberation of Muslim Women,* Gyan Books Pvt., Ltd., New Delhi, 2001.

Nasr, Seyyed H. : *Science and Civilization in Islam,* Cambridge, New York, 1996.

Nicholson, R.A. : *Tales of Mystic Meaning,* MacMillan & Co., London, 1981.

——————— : *The Mysteries of Islam,* MacMillan & Co., London, 1974.

Noorani, A.G. : *Islam and Jihad,* Manohar Publishers, New Delhi, 2002.

Oage, Charles H. : *The Society,* MacMillan & Co., London, 1959.

Oudha, Abdul Qadir : *Criminal Law of Islam,* Kitab Bhavan, New Delhi, 1999.

Palamer, E.H. : *The Quran,* Atlantic Publishers, New Delhi, 1996.

Philips, E.C. : *Politics and Society in India,* MacMillan & Co., London, 1963.

Phillips, O. Hood : *Reform of the Constitution.* MacMillan & Co., London, 1970.

Pickthall, M. M. : *Islamic Culture,* Feroz Sons Publishers, Lahore, 1992.

Qazi A. Qadir : *The Changing World of Islam,* Royal Pub., Lahore, 1992.

Qureshi, A. Iqbal : *Islam and the Theory of Interest,* Kitab Bhavan, New Delhi, 1994.

Rabnson, Chave F. : *Islamic Histroriography,* Cambridge University Press, New York, 1990.

Rahbar, D. : *God of Justice,* Mac & Jac Pub., Leiden, 1960.

Rahim, Abdur : *Principles of Islamic Jurisprudence,* Kitab Bhavan, New Delhi, 1994.

Ray, Samirendra : *Judicial Review and Fundamantal Rights,* Eastern Law House, Kolkata, 2002.

Rodinson, M. : *Islam and Capitalism,* Penguin, London, 1974.

Rosenthal, E.I.J. : *Political Thought in Medieval Islam,* Cambridge, New York, 1962.

Rumi, Jalaludin : *The Masnavi,* Gyan Books Pvt. Ltd., New Delhi, 2000.

Ruthven, Malise : *Islam : a Very Short Introduction,* Oxford, New York, 1990.

Sabiruddin : *Muslim Husband and Wife : Right and Duties,* Kitab Bhavan, New Delhi, 2000.

Said, Edward W. : *Orientalism,* Pantheon Books, New York, 1978.

Saran, P. : *Mystical Dimensions of Islam,* Chape Hill, New York, 1975.

Saxena, K.P. : *Human Rights: Perspective and Challenges,* Lancers Books, New Delhi, 1996.

Scarfe, K. : *Perception of the Islamic Word,* Cambridge University Press, New Delhi, 1992.

Scarman, Leslie : *Law : the New Dimensions,* Stevens and Sons, London, 1974.

Schacht, J. : *The Origins of Muhammadan Jurisprudence,* Clarendon Press, Oxford, 1963.

Schwartz, E. : *Science and Civilization in Islam,* Cambridge, London, 1966.

Seervai, H. : *Constitutional Law of India,* N.M. Tripathi & Co., Bombay, 1967.

Seyyed, H. : *An Introduction to Islamic Cosmological Doctrines,* Cambridge, 1964.

Shad, A. R. : *Duties of an Imam,* Idara Ishaat-e-Diniyat Pvt. Ltd, New Delhi, 1990.

Shaheed, A. Q. A. : *Islamic System of Justice,* Kitab Bhavan, New Delhi, 1994.

Shaikh, N. M. : *Women in Muslim Society,* Kitab Bhavan, New Delhi, 1991.

Sharif, M. Raihan : *Islamic Social Framework,* Islamic Book Foundation, Dacca, 1980.

Shaukat, Ali : *Masters of Muslim Thought,* Deep & Deep Pub., New Delhi, 1992.

Shemesh, A.B. : *Taxation in Islam,* MacMillan & Co., London, 1965.

Sherwani, H.K. : *Cultural Trends in Medieval India,* Popular Prakashan, Bombay, 1968.

―――――― : *Studies in Muslim Thought and Administration,* University of Hyderbad, Hyderabad, 1975.

Singh, Nagendar : *Human Rights and International Cooperation,* S. Chand & Co., New Delhi, 1969.

Smith, M. : *Readings from the Mystics of Islam*, MacMillan & Co., London, 1950.

Stanton, S. : *Teaching of the Quran,* Discovery Publishing House, New Delhi, 1989.

Stobart, J.W. H. : *Islam and its Founders,* Uppal Publishing House, New Dlehi, 1974.

Syed, Amir Ali : *The Spirit of Islam,* Royal Pub., Lahore, 1979.

Syed, M. H. : *Human Rights in Islam,* Anmol Publications, New Delhi, 2004

────────── : *Impact of Islam,* Anmol Publications, New Delhi, 2003.

────────── : *Islam and Science,* Anmol Publications, New Delhi, 2003.

────────── : *Islam and the Modern Age,* Anmol Publications, New Delhi, 2003.

────────── : *Islamic Terrorism : Myth or Reality,* Gyan Books Pvt. Ltd., New Delhi, 2002.

────────── : *Status of Women in Islamic Society,* Anmol Publications, New Delhi, 2003.

Tarachand : *Influence of Islam on Indian Culture*, Adam Pub., Allahabad, 1963.

Thomas, A. : *The Legacy of Islam,* Oxford University Press, New York, 2000.

Titus, M. : *Indian Islam*, Milford, New Delhi, 1979.

Tripathi, R.P. : *Some Aspects of Muslim Administration*, Vora Pub., Allahabad, 1959.

Ulama, Majlisul : *Islamic Hijaab,* Idara Ishaat-e-Diniyat Pvt. Ltd, New Delhi, 1997.

Ullah, M. : *Administration of Justice in Islam,* Kitab Bhavan, New Delhi, 1990.

Usmani, J.M. Tariq : *The Authority of Sunnah,* Kitab Bhavan, New Delhi, 1998.

────────── : *An Introduction to Islamic Finance,* Idara Ishaat-e-Diniyat Pvt. Ltd., New Delhi, 1999.

Valliuddin, Mir : *The Quranic Sufism,* Motilal Banarsi Das Publishers, New Delhi, 1989.

Vasudha, D. : *Law, Power and Justice : Protection of Personal Rights under Islam,* Popular Prakashan, Bombay, 2001.

Wahed, H. : *Administration of Justice during the Muslim Rule in India,* Kitab Ghar, New Delhi, 1977.

────────── : *Administration of Justice during the Muslim Rule in India,* Ashish Publishing House, New Delhi, 1977.

Waheed, Akhtar : *The Early Imamiya Shiite Thinkers,* Ashish Publishing House, New Delhi, 1995.

Wahiduddin, K. : *Islam Activism,* Goodword Books Pvt. Ltd., New Delhi, 1994.

────────── : *The True Jihad,* Goodword Books Pvt. Ltd., New Delhi, 1995.

Waines, Davids : *A Introduction to Islam,* Cambridge University Press, New Delhi, 1995.

Wasiti, Hakim Nayyar : *Muslim Contribution to Medicine,* Deep & Deep Pub., New Delhi, 1993.

Watt, W.M. : *Islam and the Integration of Society,* Routledge, London, 1961.

——————— : *Islamic Surveys,* Edinburgh University Press, Edinburgh, 1999.

Wazir, A. : *Economics in Islamic Law,* Kitab Bhavan, New Delhi, 1992.

Weeramanthy, G. G.: *Islamic Jurisprudence—an International Perspective,* Vishwa Lekha, Culcutta, 1980.

Wilfred, Seamen Blunt : *The Future of Islam,* MacMillan, London, 1991.

Willoughby, W. : *Principles of the Constitutional Law of the United States,* Baker Voorthis & Company, New York, 1938.

Yahanan, F. : *Tolerance and Coercion in Islam : Interfaith Relations in the Muslims Traditions*, Cambridge, New York, 1990.

Yusuf, S.M. : *Economic Justice in Islam,* Kitab Bhavan, New Delhi, 1988.

Zafeeruddin, M.M. : *System of Modesty and Chastity in Islam,* Idara Ishaat-e-Diniyat Pvt. Ltd, New Delhi, 1995.

Zahid, Malik : *Subjects of Quran,* Kitab Bhavan, New Delhi, 1998.

Zartman, I.W. : *Man, State and Society in the Contemporary Muslim World,* Lozac & Co., London, 1973.

Ziadah, N.A. : *Sanusiyah : a Study of a Revivalist Movement in Islam,* Poul & Co., Leiden, 1958.

INDEX

A

Abdullah, 78, 226, 236, 245, 257, 336.

Ability, 7, 9, 12, 45, 80, 91, 117, 128, 129, 130, 243, 248, 259, 284, 350.

Abraham, 83.

Abu Bakr, 77, 94, 137, 182, 183, 184, 228, 252, 258, 298, 338, 346, 347, 367, 377, 379.

Abu Daud, 140, 336.

Account, 19, 24, 27, 59, 70, 92, 118, 133, 137, 158, 204, 218, 282, 322, 328, 331, 334, 335, 344, 349, 350, 358, 363, 372, 380, 391, 397.

Achievement, 55, 66, 80, 227, 255, 282, 356.

Activity, 35, 65, 76, 90, 103, 111, 125, 258, 267, 298, 312.

Adaan, 234.

Adam, 4. 39, 83, 92, 104, 232, 372.

Addition, 38, 47, 48, 49, 50, 53, 63, 66, 72, 73, 119, 128, 130, 131, 132, 136, 141, 148, 151, 152, 154, 155, 184, 186, 249, 266, 268, 273, 286, 307, 333, 343, 394.

Administration, 10, 36, 40, 51, 60, 140, 148, 181, 182, 183, 184, 185, 186, 245, 280, 282, 284, 314, 364, 365, 366, 367, 369, 371, 374, 379, 383, 384, 385, 386, 392.

Adoption, 28, 38, 41, 55, 62, 68, 69, 71, 148, 150, 151, 192, 257.

Advance, 14, 57, 101, 171, 217, 239.

Ali, 77, 81, 94, 182, 252, 298, 326, 327, 336, 346, 351, 367, 395, 400.

Allah, 49, 74, 75, 76, 80, 84, 85, 87, 89, 90, 91, 92, 93, 95, 96, 97, 98, 99, 102, 103, 104, 105, 106, 107, 109, 110, 111, 112, 113, 114, 115, 116, 117, 118, 119, 120, 121, 122, 123, 136, 161, 172, 174, 175, 177, 179, 220, 221, 222, 223, 224, 226, 227, 229, 230, 231, 232, 233, 234, 235, 236, 239, 240, 244, 245, 246, 247, 248, 249,

250, 251, 252, 253, 254, 255, 256, 257, 258, 259, 260, 264, 265, 266, 268, 272, 275, 276, 277, 278, 287, 295, 298, 300, 301, 302, 303, 304, 305, 306, 307, 308, 311, 312, 314, 317, 318, 323, 324, 325, 326, 327, 329, 330, 331, 334, 335, 337, 338, 340, 341, 344, 345, 346, 347, 350, 351, 352, 353, 354, 355, 356, 365, 374, 399.

Almighty, 86, 92, 93, 97, 104, 107, 223, 258, 329, 345.

Ancient, 112, 215, 264, 291, 389, 392.

Apostasy, 332, 338, 339, 344, 347.

Apostle, 290, 293, 295, 329, 338.

Approach, 35, 37, 38, 40, 41, 42, 43, 44, 45, 48, 50, 55, 59, 60, 61, 62, 63, 65, 67, 69, 70, 73, 74, 101, 107, 112, 136, 150, 151, 153, 161, 288, 292, 293, 296, 318, 397.

Aristocracy, 107, 182.

Aryan, 358.

Association, 77, 151, 227.

Attack, 84, 210, 235, 237, 245, 255, 257, 270, 273, 274, 275, 277, 286, 287, 311, 376.

Authority, 3, 4, 6, 7, 8, 9, 10, 14, 17, 24, 26, 27, 42, 45, 48, 50, 51, 53, 57, 58, 61, 63, 65, 67, 71, 72, 100, 109, 128, 140, 141, 143, 147, 149, 154, 181, 182, 186, 195, 204, 205, 217, 223, 238, 240, 241, 254, 257, 264, 266, 268, 269, 270, 279, 280, 281, 282, 284, 285, 311, 315, 318, 321, 325, 329, 334, 346, 349, 365, 366, 367, 382, 391, 392, 394, 400.

B

Battle of Ahzab, 244.

Battle of Badr, 245.

Battle of Yamamah, 77.

Belief, 3, 4, 5, 13, 29, 38, 64, 113, 119, 142, 149, 153, 193, 207, 227, 231, 232, 236, 239, 240, 248, 251, 252, 254, 255, 256, 257, 259, 260, 275, 282, 283, 289, 297, 298, 306, 347, 364, 371, 375.

Bible, 82, 318.

Birth, 4, 5, 28, 130, 131, 156, 206, 283, 336.

Buddhist, 373.

Bukhari, 325, 336.

Business, 25, 260, 261, 287, 309, 327.

C

Caliph, 10, 11, 70, 71, 72, 74, 77, 78, 81, 94, 180, 181, 182, 238, 292, 308, 325, 326, 338, 347, 355, 356, 369, 377, 396.

Capacity, 4, 16, 17, 20, 22, 35, 39, 45, 86, 99, 100, 128, 129, 130, 131, 132, 133, 134, 135, 136, 138, 155, 156, 157, 158, 160, 161, 162, 163, 164, 165, 166, 167, 193, 197, 198, 211, 224, 263, 277, 280, 286, 307.

Cases, 19, 20, 21, 25, 26, 27, 31, 47, 82, 86, 116, 117, 118, 123, 131, 132, 136, 138, 141, 142,

Index

145, 148, 149, 156, 160, 161, 164, 165, 166, 169, 170, 171, 180, 183, 186, 187, 194, 197, 200, 204, 206, 210, 212, 214, 215, 216, 217, 218, 235, 237, 284, 301, 317, 322, 326, 327, 331, 335, 336, 339, 342, 343, 350, 354, 366, 387, 398, 399.

Category, 6, 11, 15, 33, 34, 38, 40, 52, 63, 117, 119, 120, 121, 124, 135, 164, 169, 173, 179, 180, 195, 196, 206, 213, 216, 329, 334.

Century, 54, 55, 65, 81, 88, 100, 101, 122, 223, 225, 230, 239, 240, 258, 259, 272, 300, 303, 314, 315, 316, 317, 358, 391, 396.

Character, 7, 9, 11, 19, 21, 36, 38, 43, 48, 49, 50, 53, 60, 67, 89, 90, 94, 95, 98, 99, 109, 138, 185, 186, 190, 192, 193, 195, 196, 197, 205, 214, 215, 217, 218, 226, 227, 228, 243, 249, 251, 252, 260, 300, 311, 336, 348, 366, 367, 378, 381.

Charter, 219, 220, 221, 222, 225, 226, 233, 235, 247, 251, 256, 263, 264, 265, 267, 270, 273, 274, 277, 278, 286, 299, 300, 302, 303, 304, 308, 309, 310, 314, 315, 317, 318, 319.

Chastisement, 87, 184, 218, 328, 331.

Children, 9, 16, 24, 29, 30, 34, 92, 94, 105, 117, 184, 188, 189, 192, 195, 202, 230, 272, 283, 297, 333, 345, 349, 353, 372, 393.

Christian, 19, 76, 84, 101, 237, 238, 240, 250, 269, 277, 291, 292, 304, 313, 314, 315, 316, 317, 318, 373, 376, 378, 379, 382, 385, 386, 387, 391.

Civilisation, 41, 56, 59, 81, 97, 99, 100, 101, 102, 107, 173, 180, 237, 267, 365, 383.

Claim, 10, 28, 31, 44, 47, 69, 71, 83, 122, 124, 126, 127, 142, 153, 188, 203, 242, 246, 274, 291, 292, 322, 342, 343, 391.

Classification, 11, 13, 15, 34, 39, 40, 117, 118, 120, 121, 122, 123, 124, 151, 169, 170, 171, 172, 193, 196, 198, 199, 201, 202, 204, 352.

Clause, 220, 222, 223, 224, 225, 226, 228, 229, 230, 231, 232, 233, 235, 244, 245, 246, 247, 248, 249, 250, 251, 252, 254, 255, 256, 257, 260, 261, 262, 263, 264, 269, 270, 271, 272, 273, 274, 275, 276, 278, 299, 302, 303, 304, 305, 306, 307, 308, 310, 311, 314, 316, 317, 318, 319.

Combination, 37, 47, 48, 120, 151, 174, 226, 280.

Commandments, 93, 233, 234, 236, 277, 280, 284.

Commercial Law, 123.

Communication, 3, 5, 11, 103, 104, 114, 115, 128, 130, 131, 136.

Community, 5, 10, 11, 12, 15, 16, 18, 40, 50, 55, 56, 58, 59, 64, 67, 70, 71, 72, 73, 93, 109, 113, 117, 118, 122, 126, 134, 168, 177, 181, 183, 184,

195, 198, 199, 200, 201, 210, 216, 224, 227, 240, 259, 260, 263, 264, 281, 283, 286, 288, 295, 305, 308, 318, 328, 344, 363, 364, 373, 374, 375, 381, 384, 387.

Companions, 76, 77, 94, 137, 169, 180, 185, 195, 226, 227, 241, 245, 246, 251, 252, 253, 254, 255, 258, 265, 267, 276, 277, 294, 296, 303, 306, 332, 338, 346, 347, 355, 374, 375, 384.

Concept, 17, 23, 38, 39, 45, 48, 49, 54, 55, 56, 57, 60, 63, 64, 68, 70, 71, 72, 74, 86, 90, 99, 102, 115, 126, 133, 134, 153, 154, 155, 175, 231, 280, 281, 285, 333, 354, 356, 362, 367, 393, 394.

Condition, 3, 11, 12, 20, 21, 24, 41, 42, 57, 99, 116, 120, 123, 129, 132, 134, 138, 156, 157, 158, 160, 163, 164, 167, 174, 186, 189, 191, 198, 205, 208, 209, 211, 221, 248, 250, 253, 267, 269, 299, 337, 339, 346.

Constitution, 9, 16, 36, 42, 48, 50, 51, 52, 53, 54, 56, 57, 58, 59, 62, 128, 152, 154, 181, 235, 263, 264, 265, 267, 283, 284, 300, 375, 377, 392.

Contribution, 44, 45, 46, 48, 49, 55, 68, 71, 72, 317, 336, 395.

Cooperation, 237, 271, 305, 363, 377.

Corruption, 105, 176, 322, 334, 347, 352, 366, 369.

Council, 241, 284.

Country, 23, 32, 139, 181, 184, 185, 187, 189, 190, 191, 192, 224, 235,

236, 254, 260, 261, 264, 265, 276, 283, 284, 293, 304, 306, 315, 317, 351, 376, 385, 390, 391, 397, 398, 399, 400.

Court, 16, 20, 21, 26, 27, 29, 30, 41, 52, 64, 65, 66, 125, 126, 137, 140, 141, 142, 143, 144, 145, 146, 147, 148, 149, 181, 182, 187, 192, 194, 217, 223, 237, 285, 293, 333, 335, 337, 338, 348, 355, 366, 398, 399.

Court of Law, 126, 137, 285, 337, 398.

Creation, 3, 4, 38, 90, 91, 92, 95, 97, 99, 104, 106, 111, 112, 116, 126, 163, 175, 198, 207, 208, 209, 232, 234, 242, 249, 250, 278, 358, 359, 372.

Crime, 86, 122, 161, 209, 217, 218, 240, 276, 277, 314, 316, 334, 336, 337, 340, 341, 342, 343, 344, 346, 350, 351, 355, 356, 360, 361, 375

Criminal Law, 121, 123, 126, 128, 156, 218, 283, 321.

Culture, 99, 100, 101, 240, 285, 298, 365, 383.

Custody, 30, 140, 141, 143, 149, 187, 325, 332, 333, 346, 347.

D

David, 83, 313, 368.

Day of Judgement, 2, 358.

Day of Reckoning, 91, 252, 369.

Day of Resurrection, 253, 259, 301.

Death, 5, 6, 12, 23, 27, 28, 30, 31, 76, 133, 136, 149, 155, 156, 157, 158, 159, 160, 163,

Index

164, 165, 179, 182, 184, 186, 199, 204, 206, 208, 210, 214, 215, 216, 217, 239, 252, 253, 254, 255, 258, 265, 266, 307, 323, 324, 325, 332, 333, 334, 335, 336, 337, 338, 339, 340, 341, 342, 345, 346, 347, 348, 353, 354, 377, 385, 399.

Definition of Law, 3, 5, 6, 8, 11, 74, 155.

Democracy, 281, 366, 367.

Department, 16, 217, 356.

Description, 14, 47, 50, 53, 63, 113, 167, 172, 190, 200, 205, 358.

Development, 7, 27, 36, 37, 38, 39, 40, 41, 44, 45, 46, 51, 53, 56, 57, 58, 60, 67, 68, 69, 70, 71, 73, 74, 75, 80, 105, 112, 126, 129, 130, 132, 134, 138, 150, 151, 153, 232, 242, 267, 282, 383, 391.

Dignity, 90, 107, 230, 317, 336, 344, 356.

Din, 126, 131, 169, 170, 172, 174, 175, 176, 177, 179, 348.

Discipline, 7, 59, 89, 94, 99, 103, 111, 134, 222, 242, 254, 257, 395.

Discovery, 43, 55, 98, 104, 112, 113, 115, 152, 253.

Discrimination, 94, 131, 285, 316, 359, 370, 371, 386.

Distribution, 84, 200, 262.

Divine, 5, 6, 13, 36, 41, 54, 69, 77, 80, 82, 84, 85, 86, 88, 89, 91, 93, 95, 97, 99, 103, 113, 149, 150, 154, 256, 257, 280, 281, 296, 297, 330, 344, 364, 366, 367, 370, 372.

Divine Law, 41, 85, 281, 330.

Division, 11, 14, 16, 82, 124, 186, 201, 242.

Divorce, 12, 22, 23, 24, 25, 26, 27, 28, 31, 135, 136, 137, 153, 162, 163, 164, 165, 194, 206, 207, 209.

Document, 57, 221, 222, 223, 224, 225, 226, 229, 230, 231, 244, 247, 250, 251, 256, 258, 262, 263, 271, 276, 277, 278, 294, 299, 303, 314, 316, 319, 375, 378, 392.

Duty, 12, 47, 93, 95, 102, 105, 106, 110, 116, 118, 120, 121, 124, 125, 126, 127, 135, 136, 137, 138, 164, 176, 182, 189, 191, 192, 199, 201, 208, 216, 229, 233, 234, 236, 243, 250, 263, 269, 276, 281, 282, 284, 306, 330, 359, 360, 365, 376.

E

Earth, 4, 7, 10, 49, 75, 88, 90, 91, 92, 93, 96, 97, 102, 103, 105, 106, 175, 199, 201, 209, 232, 252, 253, 280, 282, 302, 316, 322, 329, 369.

Education, 21, 101, 104, 176, 240, 317, 381.

Egypt, 78, 236, 387, 396.

Element, 5, 100, 115, 119, 122, 128, 344.

Employment, 107, 172, 178, 238.

Energy, 102, 193.

Environment, 90, 92, 102, 127, 220, 243, 282, 360, 367, 384, 386.

Establishment, 36, 43, 48, 56, 61, 69, 139, 156, 233, 282, 285, 298, 354, 356, 374, 381, 383, 384, 392.

Europe, 27, 76, 81, 100, 101, 224, 232, 237, 241, 259, 305, 313, 314, 317, 381, 383, 390, 400.

Evil, 27, 84, 86, 87, 89, 93, 102, 103, 105, 112, 114, 188, 248, 256, 298, 321, 322, 324, 326, 336, 341, 345, 347, 351, 352, 355, 363, 394.

Evolution, 40, 56, 58, 68, 69, 99, 150, 151, 316.

Experiment, 318.

F

Facility, 79, 173, 179, 270.

Factors, 37, 44, 58, 68, 86, 97, 115, 155, 160, 228, 330.

Facts, 11, 29, 37, 66, 69, 122, 143, 145, 182, 217, 329, 362, 379, 381.

Faith, 2, 3, 14, 19, 35, 59, 73, 84, 88, 89, 91, 92, 102, 106, 149, 151, 155, 193, 194, 200, 205, 207, 224, 226, 232, 242, 251, 252, 253, 254, 255, 256, 258, 286, 287, 288, 289, 290, 291, 292, 293, 294, 296, 297, 298, 301, 318, 338, 339, 347, 358, 359, 362, 364, 365, 372, 378, 381, 384, 390, 393, 394.

Family, 16, 17, 18, 21, 23, 31, 106, 126, 137, 152, 173, 175, 176, 179, 182, 183, 191, 202, 203, 236, 237, 280, 288, 289, 291, 293, 297, 306, 307, 323, 344, 345, 363.

Fasting, 12, 104, 117, 119, 126, 170, 176, 195, 196, 200, 206, 207, 331.

Features, 35, 41, 42, 44, 47, 48, 50, 61, 64, 66, 68, 74, 96, 127, 155, 286, 298.

Formulation, 36, 37, 38, 39, 46, 48, 49, 54, 55, 60, 62, 63, 64, 66, 68, 70, 72, 73, 74, 140, 151, 154.

Foundation, 35, 42, 64, 73, 88, 140, 170, 218, 285, 287.

Freedom, 7, 8, 17, 18, 21, 22, 64, 72, 86, 87, 89, 94, 100, 131, 132, 157, 173, 180, 189, 190, 191, 209, 210, 213, 224, 230, 231, 232, 234, 236, 242, 245, 249, 255, 256, 264, 283, 312, 314, 316, 317, 319, 364, 375, 383, 385, 387, 390, 392.

Future, 4, 7, 9, 14, 17, 18, 38, 41, 46, 67, 71, 74, 80, 82, 84, 86, 87, 88, 112, 187, 206, 220, 221, 226, 233, 236, 247, 248, 251, 256, 263, 269, 275, 276, 278, 302, 316, 318, 336.

G

Gabriel, 82.

Global Law, 391, 393, 397.

God, 3, 4, 5, 6, 7, 8, 10, 12, 13, 15, 39, 71, 74, 80, 82, 85, 86, 87, 88, 89, 90, 91, 92, 93, 94, 95, 97, 103, 109, 110, 113, 124, 126, 128, 136, 180, 193, 198, 199, 201, 203, 204, 207, 242,

Index

243, 253, 255, 256, 279, 280, 281, 282, 284, 285, 287, 289, 290, 292, 293, 295, 296, 298, 302, 311, 323, 327, 328, 329, 331, 332, 338, 345, 348, 352, 355, 357, 358, 359, 360, 361, 362, 363, 364, 367, 368, 369, 370, 371, 372, 373, 374, 375, 376, 377, 378, 380, 384, 394.

Governance of Law, 84.

Government, 41, 149, 180, 190, 191, 192, 219, 221, 228, 232, 236, 238, 239, 241, 243, 261, 263, 264, 265, 266, 267, 269, 270, 274, 276, 281, 284, 285, 299, 303, 321, 365, 378, 392, 394, 396, 398.

Growth, 126, 156, 175, 176, 180.

H

Habits, 14, 21, 229, 322, 329.

Hadd, 119, 121, 122, 136, 138, 140, 142, 148, 165, 166, 182, 186, 190, 191, 194, 199, 200, 217, 218, 328, 331, 332, 333, 334, 335, 336, 337, 338, 339, 340, 342, 343, 344, 348, 349, 350, 351, 352, 353, 354, 355, 356.

Hadith, 5, 6, 76, 91, 99, 336, 370, 394, 396.

Hadrat, 77, 78, 81, 146, 325, 326, 336, 345, 346, 351.

Hajj, 119, 180, 200, 232.

Hanifah, 2, 21, 22, 31, 67, 68, 131, 140, 146, 159, 163, 190, 191, 204, 214, 216, 218, 338, 341, 342, 345, 365, 394, 395, 397, 400.

Health, 77, 160, 176, 336.

Heaven, 75, 80, 92, 96, 106, 111, 274.

Hell, 86, 99, 307, 323, 358.

History, 38, 41, 43, 44, 53, 56, 62, 63, 65, 68, 70, 74, 80, 88, 94, 96, 101, 112, 153, 183, 221, 227, 240, 247, 252, 255, 267, 271, 272, 286, 297, 298, 304, 311, 312, 313, 315, 317, 319, 362, 364, 367, 379, 380, 383, 384, 385, 386, 389, 394, 396, 399, 400.

Honour, 199, 222, 274, 283, 290, 311, 321, 322, 323, 327, 329, 333, 337, 345, 378.

Human Rights, 57, 64, 124, 232, 282, 314, 316, 329.

I

Ibrahim, 356, 395, 396.

Imam, 10, 11, 15, 78, 99, 111, 117, 140, 146, 167, 172, 176, 180, 181, 182, 183, 184, 185, 188, 189, 190, 195, 200, 205, 218, 303, 324, 338, 341, 350, 356, 365, 393, 394, 395, 396.

Improvement, 40, 64, 153.

India, 22, 27, 101, 107, 191, 238, 239, 398, 399.

Industry, 101.

Information, 82, 85, 86, 140, 148, 194, 218, 244, 262, 285, 370.

International Law, 16, 230, 261, 389, 390, 391, 392, 393, 394, 395, 396, 397, 398, 399, 400.

Islam, 2, 5, 10, 17, 18, 19, 34, 37, 40, 41, 43, 45, 47, 49, 50, 53,

54, 56, 57, 58, 62, 63, 64, 65, 66, 67, 69, 71, 72, 73, 76, 77, 82, 88, 91, 92, 93, 94, 98, 100, 102, 103, 104, 105, 106, 107, 109, 115, 116, 117, 138, 139, 149, 150, 151, 154, 155, 167, 179, 180, 184, 185, 188, 189, 190, 191, 192, 203, 206, 215, 217, 218, 220, 223, 224, 225, 226, 227, 228, 229, 231, 232, 233, 234, 235, 236, 238, 240, 241, 242, 243, 246, 247, 248, 251, 253, 254, 257, 258, 259, 261, 267, 268, 269, 274, 275, 276, 277, 278, 279, 280, 281, 282, 283, 284, 285, 287, 288, 291, 292, 293, 295, 296, 297, 298, 299, 300, 302, 303, 304, 305, 307, 310, 311, 312, 317, 318, 319, 321, 322, 326, 330, 331, 336, 338, 339, 341, 344, 347, 350, 352, 353, 354, 356, 359, 360, 364, 365, 367, 369, 370, 371, 373, 374, 376, 377, 378, 379, 380, 381, 383, 384, 385, 386, 387, 389, 391, 392, 393, 394, 396, 399, 400.

Islamic Law, 3, 9, 10, 16, 17, 18, 20, 22, 24, 27, 28, 31, 36, 37, 38, 39, 41, 42, 43, 44, 45, 46, 48, 50, 52, 56, 57, 58, 59, 61, 62, 63, 64, 66, 67, 68, 69, 70, 71, 72, 109, 110, 112, 114, 115, 116, 117, 118, 121, 122, 124, 126, 127, 128, 129, 133, 134, 136, 137, 138, 150, 151, 153, 155, 162, 163, 166, 167, 168, 169, 170, 171, 172, 173, 178, 179, 180, 185, 187, 188, 189, 190, 192, 194, 195, 197, 198, 210, 214, 216, 217, 218, 241, 284, 321, 323, 324, 332, 333, 334, 335, 339, 340, 343, 344, 356, 365, 366, 399.

Ismail, 356.

J

Jacob, 83.

Jerusalem, 78, 312, 313, 315, 367, 378, 387.

Jesus, 84, 98, 293, 296, 297, 298, 302, 315, 324, 368.

Jewish, 19, 76, 266, 271, 273, 286, 291, 295, 309, 310, 312, 313, 315, 318, 324, 354, 377, 385, 399.

Jewish Law, 324, 399.

Jews, 78, 233, 236, 244, 245, 262, 263, 264, 265, 267, 270, 272, 273, 274, 285, 286, 287, 296, 297, 310, 311, 312, 313, 314, 315, 316, 317, 318, 319, 364, 373, 374, 375, 377, 382, 385, 386, 387, 392, 399.

Jihad, 65, 72, 117, 119, 174, 176, 179, 180, 188, 189, 195, 200, 222, 224, 230, 231, 233, 235, 250, 259, 317.

Jinn, 82, 86, 92.

Jizya, 184, 188.

Jonah, 83.

Joseph, 83, 99, 136, 369, 384, 385.

Judge, 6, 13, 110, 122, 136, 138, 140, 141, 142, 144, 145, 146, 147, 148, 166, 186, 218, 241, 284,

Index 417

335, 339, 342, 354, 365, 368, 369, 371, 387.

Jurisprudence, 1, 3, 4, 5, 7, 9, 14, 16, 24, 38, 39, 44, 47, 49, 50, 54, 58, 60, 61, 62, 63, 68, 70, 99, 153, 154, 201, 216, 217, 393, 394.

Juristic Law, 6, 13, 191.

Justice, 18, 42, 45, 48, 50, 51, 52, 53, 60, 61, 64, 66, 70, 89, 106, 109, 110, 140, 148, 173, 180, 181, 184, 185, 224, 225, 226, 228, 232, 238, 245, 246, 248, 270, 282, 285, 303, 304, 305, 307, 310, 312, 314, 321, 322, 340, 341, 342, 343, 344, 345, 351, 356, 357, 358, 359, 360, 361, 362, 363, 364, 365, 366, 367, 368, 369, 370, 371, 373, 374, 375, 376, 377, 378, 379, 380, 381, 382, 383, 384, 385, 386, 387, 392, 394.

K

Kaaba, 207, 290, 292, 294.

Khalifa, 112, 241, 270, 280, 281.

Khyber, 244, 258, 265, 267, 354.

Kindness, 91, 93, 94, 106, 224, 225, 226, 228, 246, 303, 305, 310, 311, 341.

Kingdom, 95, 279.

Kinship, 203, 362, 375.

Knowing Law, 1.

Knowledge, 1, 2, 3, 4, 12, 13, 15, 44, 58, 59, 71, 75, 80, 81, 84, 86, 88, 92, 96, 98, 99, 100, 101, 104, 105, 116, 142, 144, 145, 148, 153, 154, 158, 183, 198, 209, 217, 227, 235, 241, 253, 284, 289, 302, 304, 330, 339, 342, 347, 351, 373.

L

Labour, 8, 96, 381.

Languages, 359, 374, 382.

Laws, 2, 3, 4, 5, 6, 7, 9, 10, 11, 12, 13, 14, 15, 16, 34, 36, 37, 40, 41, 48, 49, 50, 51, 53, 58, 61, 63, 69, 73, 79, 85, 86, 87, 93, 96, 97, 98, 103, 109, 110, 111, 112, 113, 114, 115, 117, 118, 138, 146, 149, 150, 151, 152, 153, 154, 155, 190, 191, 192, 205, 219, 221, 223, 225, 230, 233, 234, 241, 242, 243, 248, 257, 262, 265, 269, 273, 276, 278, 281, 285, 296, 299, 300, 302, 303, 307, 310, 312, 313, 319, 321, 323, 329, 330, 343, 344, 352, 353, 356, 362, 380, 389, 390, 391, 392, 393, 399.

Lebanon, 381, 387.

Legacy, 81.

Legal Method, 36, 37, 39, 40, 41, 42, 43, 44, 45, 46, 47, 48, 49, 50, 51, 52, 53, 58, 60, 61, 62, 64, 67, 68, 69, 70, 71, 72, 73, 74, 150, 155.

Liberty, 2, 11, 17, 22, 25, 65, 107, 127, 197, 203, 224, 236, 255, 283.

Life, 3, 4, 7, 8, 9, 12, 13, 17, 18, 22, 25, 27, 30, 36, 42, 46, 55, 69, 75, 76, 79, 80, 84, 86, 87, 88, 90, 92, 93,

97, 102, 104, 105, 106, 109, 126, 131, 132, 137, 139, 161, 163, 164, 169, 170, 172, 174, 175, 176, 177, 179, 184, 188, 194, 205, 207, 210, 214, 215, 216, 218, 220, 223, 224, 228, 229, 230, 231, 232, 241, 242, 245, 246, 248, 249, 250, 252, 253, 255, 256, 257, 264, 267, 269, 273, 276, 279, 280, 282, 283, 298, 300, 302, 303, 304, 306, 311, 312, 314, 315, 317, 318, 321, 322, 327, 329, 330, 334, 337, 339, 341, 342, 343, 345, 347, 351, 352, 354, 361, 362, 363, 367, 369, 370, 371, 372, 374, 376, 377, 380, 381, 387, 389, 393, 397.

Lord, 80, 85, 86, 87, 91, 94, 97, 98, 99, 104, 105, 106, 109, 227, 234, 252, 254, 272, 288, 292, 298, 308, 322, 341, 354, 363, 369, 371, 373, 375, 376, 377, 378.

Loyalty, 245, 254, 263, 264, 271, 272, 273, 306, 307, 376.

M

Majority, 20, 21, 65, 111, 112, 113, 114, 115, 118, 129, 130, 131, 136, 137, 138, 160, 163, 203, 239, 242, 248, 294, 304, 308, 339, 345, 354, 367, 370, 379, 386, 392.

Mankind, 4, 46, 80, 86, 87, 91, 92, 93, 95, 98, 99, 103, 113, 124, 222, 223, 224, 233, 245, 248, 252, 256, 259, 263, 278, 303, 304, 311, 314, 317, 318, 321, 322, 354, 359, 364, 365, 368.

Manner, 43, 49, 60, 67, 76, 78, 83, 99, 114, 128, 147, 149, 163, 220, 225, 226, 227, 228, 229, 230, 248, 250, 251, 255, 262, 264, 266, 267, 269, 271, 272, 274, 275, 281, 285, 294, 296, 298, 302, 313, 316, 319, 322, 325, 328, 332, 345, 347, 358, 360, 361, 377, 382, 384, 396.

Marriage, 5, 16, 17, 18, 19, 20, 21, 22, 23, 24, 25, 26, 27, 28, 29, 131, 137, 153, 154, 162, 164, 166, 176, 187, 194, 197, 206, 208, 211, 292, 337, 339.

Masses, 232, 236, 239, 240.

Material Law, 1.

Maturity, 3, 12, 129, 131, 286, 298, 361, 398.

Maulana, 326, 336, 340.

Mecca, 76, 78, 185, 188, 219, 221, 222, 226, 227, 231, 236, 239, 242, 245, 247, 248, 249, 251, 253, 256, 260, 261, 262, 263, 265, 266, 269, 273, 274, 278, 286, 287, 288, 292, 293, 294, 295, 296, 297, 298, 299, 308, 311, 354, 356, 370, 373, 374, 376, 391, 392.

Medina, 76, 77, 78, 219, 235, 242, 245, 246, 251, 252, 257, 258, 263, 265, 266, 267, 277, 285, 286, 287, 291, 295, 296, 297, 298, 300, 304, 308, 311, 314, 315, 318, 321, 354, 373, 374, 375, 377, 392, 393, 399.

Index

Merchant, 348.

Merciful, 91, 92, 93, 106, 226, 253, 301, 303, 325, 326, 338, 339, 353, 357, 363, 370.

Message, 41, 78, 88, 98, 99, 103, 147, 250, 259, 287, 290, 295, 354, 362, 364, 371.

Messenger, 85, 109, 110, 112, 226, 234, 250, 253, 254, 258, 259, 264, 276, 287, 301, 303, 318, 334, 345, 347, 352, 354, 367, 370, 371, 373, 374, 375, 376, 377.

Method, 35, 36, 37, 38, 39, 40, 41, 42, 43, 44, 45, 46, 48, 49, 50, 51, 52, 53, 54, 58, 60, 61, 62, 64, 67, 68, 69, 70, 71, 72, 73, 74, 101, 129, 150, 151, 155, 192, 202, 223, 261, 262, 278.

Migration, 292, 297, 308, 315, 321, 373, 374, 392.

Mission, 4, 5, 82, 93, 109, 237, 238, 252, 258, 289, 290, 291, 292, 293, 294, 295, 297, 298, 353, 400.

Moses, 83, 98, 272, 311, 324, 339, 368, 387.

Movement, 22, 54, 74, 76, 82, 103, 233, 261.

Muhammad, 5, 21, 31, 76, 80, 82, 86, 87, 88, 91, 94, 97, 98, 100, 103, 104, 106, 107, 110, 140, 146, 180, 185, 204, 214, 222, 226, 239, 240, 251, 252, 253, 257, 258, 264, 265, 268, 271, 275, 277, 280, 281, 285, 286, 287, 288, 289, 290, 291, 294, 295, 296, 297, 298, 299, 300, 301, 302, 311, 314, 317, 318, 326, 338, 345, 352, 353, 354, 359, 364, 368, 369, 370, 371, 372, 373, 374, 375, 376, 377, 378, 379, 395, 396.

Muslim, 9, 10, 11, 16, 19, 28, 32, 34, 37, 38, 40, 41, 42, 54, 55, 59, 63, 67, 68, 70, 71, 73, 74, 75, 76, 88, 91, 93, 94, 96, 98, 100, 101, 102, 103, 104, 105, 106, 107, 109, 110, 111, 112, 113, 115, 116, 118, 120, 121, 123, 124, 126, 128, 130, 133, 136, 139, 150, 152, 153, 155, 157, 160, 161, 167, 168, 173, 180, 183, 184, 185, 187, 188, 189, 190, 191, 192, 193, 195, 200, 212, 215, 218, 221, 227, 230, 231, 235, 236, 237, 238, 239, 240, 241, 242, 243, 244, 245, 247, 248, 250, 251, 252, 257, 258, 259, 264, 267, 268, 269, 270, 271, 277, 283, 284, 285, 286, 291, 292, 293, 296, 298, 300, 303, 304, 306, 308, 311, 315, 316, 323, 325, 330, 335, 338, 339, 341, 342, 343, 344, 347, 351, 352, 353, 356, 364, 365, 367, 373, 378, 380, 381, 382, 383, 384, 385, 386, 393, 394, 397, 398, 399.

N

Nation, 72, 78, 218, 220, 221, 222, 224, 227, 251, 255, 259, 263, 266, 304, 306, 308, 316, 367, 373, 381, 391.

Natural Law, 46, 112, 113, 115, 125, 138.

Nature, 1, 7, 13, 17, 18, 19, 27, 40, 41, 42, 45, 46, 48, 52, 53, 60, 63, 65, 67, 70, 76, 89, 90, 93, 95, 96, 97, 98, 100, 102, 104, 107, 109, 113, 116, 117, 127, 150, 153, 158, 164, 172, 174, 175, 183, 184, 193, 195, 197, 198, 200, 201, 204, 209, 210, 215, 216, 217, 218, 219, 226, 232, 237, 243, 247, 249, 256, 258, 262, 263, 274, 283, 299, 301, 303, 305, 310, 311, 312, 315, 319, 324, 336, 337, 350, 351, 389.

Non-Muslim, 10, 16, 28, 32, 180, 183, 184, 185, 187, 188, 189, 190, 191, 192, 193, 215, 218, 235, 243, 248, 268, 283, 286, 335, 351, 353, 383, 384, 393.

Noor, 324, 325, 335, 336, 338, 354.

O

Obedience of Law, 85.

Obligation, 2, 8, 9, 11, 12, 23, 37, 47, 48, 59, 65, 110, 114, 115, 116, 117, 120, 124, 125, 127, 128, 137, 163, 174, 179, 189, 192, 193, 195, 200, 201, 203, 204, 205, 207, 208, 212, 273, 282, 289, 331, 344.

Obligatory, 2, 11, 38, 45, 50, 135, 152, 155, 180, 184, 192, 194, 195, 196, 198, 203, 230, 231.

Occasion, 182, 188, 192, 210, 220, 240, 241, 259, 263, 268, 289, 328, 331, 338, 339.

Occupation, 30, 239.

Opportunity, 22, 142, 143, 144, 146, 154, 294, 326, 338, 378.

Organisation, 45, 49, 56, 61, 69, 74, 125, 219, 227, 231, 235, 267, 269, 300, 391.

Origin, 4, 13, 44, 45, 82, 312, 330.

Ownership, 11, 65, 138, 166, 192, 195, 202, 203, 206, 208, 237, 280.

P

Pakistan, 123, 137, 138, 157, 242, 399.

Parents, 9, 29, 30, 31, 34, 94, 105, 195, 206, 307, 342, 360, 361, 362, 365, 384.

Participation, 69, 72, 83.

Peace, 23, 89, 93, 102, 117, 140, 165, 169, 188, 189, 199, 215, 216, 217, 218, 220, 223, 225, 226, 229, 233, 234, 235, 236, 237, 238, 239, 240, 242, 243, 244, 245, 246, 247, 249, 253, 265, 271, 272, 273, 275, 277, 278, 282, 285, 286, 291, 305, 306, 307, 313, 318, 321, 322, 330, 335, 344, 346, 351, 352, 356, 358, 359, 360, 367, 368, 371, 373, 374, 376, 377, 379, 380, 381, 382, 383, 385, 387, 389, 390, 391, 392, 393, 394, 397, 398, 399, 400.

Penal Law, 141, 148, 343.

Penalties, 119, 120, 121, 122, 135, 165, 176, 356.

Philosophy, 39, 75, 84, 98, 101, 231, 242, 249, 257, 263, 278, 350, 353, 356.

Index 421

Places, 18, 37, 48, 54, 137, 257, 282, 299, 301, 302, 305, 359, 374, 378, 381, 382, 384, 387, 397.

Policies, 65, 252.

Population, 5, 245, 246, 276, 309, 315, 392.

Power, 2, 4, 5, 7, 10, 14, 21, 22, 23, 25, 26, 27, 30, 40, 47, 55, 67, 75, 79, 83, 93, 96, 97, 102, 107, 125, 127, 138, 143, 154, 155, 182, 184, 187, 188, 191, 208, 210, 211, 220, 231, 234, 235, 237, 239, 241, 243, 248, 249, 252, 254, 256, 263, 269, 272, 278, 282, 285, 287, 289, 290, 291, 298, 304, 323, 341, 365, 366, 370, 373, 386, 389.

Pray, 93, 269.

Prayer, 93, 104, 106, 119, 120, 161, 162, 176, 178, 193, 195, 338.

Preservation, 7, 8, 12, 17, 39, 76, 78, 163, 168, 169, 170, 171, 172, 173, 174, 175, 176, 177, 179, 186, 194, 216, 328, 333, 343, 344, 349.

Principles, 1, 5, 6, 7, 14, 34, 35, 36, 37, 38, 39, 40, 41, 42, 43, 44, 45, 46, 48, 49, 50, 51, 52, 53, 54, 55, 56, 57, 58, 59, 60, 61, 62, 63, 64, 65, 66, 67, 68, 69, 70, 71, 72, 73, 74, 81, 93, 109, 110, 112, 113, 115, 134, 150, 151, 152, 153, 166, 175, 178, 188, 214, 222, 247, 254, 279, 280, 281, 282, 287, 322, 330, 344, 356, 366, 367, 379, 383, 397, 400.

Private Law, 15.

Prophet, 3, 5, 6, 13, 24, 25, 74, 76, 77, 80, 81, 82, 84, 88, 91, 93, 94, 98, 102, 104, 105, 107, 117, 138, 140, 165, 169, 180, 182, 185, 188, 195, 221, 223, 225, 226, 227, 228, 234, 235, 236, 239, 241, 244, 245, 246, 247, 248, 249, 250, 251, 252, 253, 254, 255, 256, 257, 258, 261, 262, 263, 264, 266, 267, 269, 270, 272, 275, 276, 277, 278, 280, 281, 284, 285, 286, 287, 288, 289, 290, 291, 292, 293, 294, 295, 296, 297, 298, 299, 300, 301, 303, 304, 305, 306, 307, 308, 309, 310, 311, 312, 316, 319, 321, 322, 325, 326, 330, 332, 335, 338, 339, 342, 345, 346, 347, 348, 350, 351, 352, 353, 354, 355, 356, 359, 362, 363, 364, 367, 368, 369, 370, 371, 372, 373, 374, 375, 376, 377, 378, 379, 392, 393, 397, 399.

Provision, 30, 41, 59, 65, 92, 137, 148, 149, 170, 176, 252, 331, 333, 334, 342, 349, 360.

Public Law, 15, 125.

Punishment, 2, 10, 15, 85, 86, 106, 119, 136, 137, 138, 141, 146, 147, 148, 158, 190, 195, 199, 200, 209, 217, 218, 223, 234, 243, 308, 321, 323, 324, 325, 326, 327, 328, 329, 330, 331, 332, 333, 334, 335, 336, 337, 338, 339, 340, 341, 343, 344, 345, 346, 347, 350, 351, 353, 355, 356, 361, 369.

Purpose, 7, 12, 15, 20, 36, 38, 41, 43, 50, 57, 59, 61, 67, 79, 83, 85, 87, 89, 91, 97, 99, 107, 111, 112, 113, 116, 124, 135, 136, 139, 146, 147, 149, 151, 152, 163, 165, 172, 173, 174, 175, 177, 178, 183, 193, 195, 196, 202, 206, 215, 220, 225, 230, 248, 272, 279, 280, 281, 282, 291, 295, 296, 298, 307, 314, 323, 328, 329, 339, 351, 358, 359, 400.

Q

Quality, 36, 47, 52, 82, 90, 111, 192, 195, 219, 252, 256, 272, 284.

Questions of Law, 13, 186.

Quran, 2, 4, 5, 6, 15, 31, 32, 37, 38, 75, 76, 77, 78, 79, 80, 81, 82, 83, 84, 85, 86, 87, 91, 92, 93, 94, 95, 96, 97, 98, 99, 100, 103, 104, 105, 106, 107, 109, 110, 111, 112, 113, 114, 115, 131, 136, 137, 151, 154, 161, 169, 170, 174, 175, 195, 218, 222, 223, 225, 227, 231, 235, 248, 250, 255, 258, 264, 268, 269, 280, 282, 290, 294, 295, 296, 297, 298, 300, 301, 302, 307, 308, 312, 318, 322, 323, 324, 326, 327, 328, 329, 330, 331, 332, 333, 334, 335, 336, 337, 338, 341, 343, 344, 345, 346, 352, 353, 354, 355, 356, 357, 358, 359, 360, 361, 362, 363, 364, 365, 367, 368, 369, 370, 371, 372, 373, 374, 375, 376, 377, 378, 379, 380, 381, 382, 383, 384, 387, 393, 397.

Quranic Injunction, 49, 62, 235, 304, 325, 326.

Quranic Law, 322.

Quranic Penalties, 356.

Quranic Verse, 226, 326, 353.

R

Rahim, 121, 239.

Rahman, 55, 78, 98.

Relation, 7, 9, 34, 39, 41, 42, 44, 46, 48, 56, 58, 60, 66, 72, 73, 118, 152, 155, 193, 198, 220, 224, 308, 317, 391.

Religion, 5, 7, 12, 19, 23, 27, 32, 39, 42, 43, 51, 59, 61, 88, 97, 99, 101, 102, 103, 105, 106, 107, 150, 152, 170, 172, 174, 180, 182, 184, 188, 190, 192, 206, 217, 218, 221, 223, 229, 231, 234, 235, 238, 240, 242, 243, 246, 255, 277, 283, 288, 290, 292, 293, 294, 296, 297, 317, 339, 345, 347, 360, 364, 369, 370, 372, 374, 375, 378, 381, 382, 384, 386, 387, 393.

Religious Law, 59, 60, 130, 151.

Remarriage, 366.

Research, 70, 99, 101, 105, 124, 128, 271.

Revealed Law, 6, 7, 15, 41, 46, 67, 68, 113, 150, 151.

Revelation, 2, 4, 5, 6, 37, 54, 75, 76, 82, 83, 86, 91, 95, 99, 110, 113, 114, 149, 271, 325, 369.

Index 423

Rights, 1, 2, 4, 8, 11, 12, 15, 16, 17, 18, 22, 24, 27, 30, 31, 57, 59, 62, 63, 64, 65, 93, 94, 100, 117, 118, 119, 120, 121, 122, 123, 124, 125, 126, 127, 128, 129, 130, 132, 133, 134, 136, 137, 156, 157, 158, 159, 160, 161, 162, 172, 177, 180, 182, 186, 188, 192, 194, 196, 198, 199, 200, 201, 202, 203, 205, 206, 208, 209, 210, 212, 214, 216, 217, 221, 232, 259, 281, 282, 283, 286, 309, 314, 316, 319, 321, 329, 330, 331, 340, 343, 344, 350, 356, 357, 360, 371, 375, 383, 387, 392.

Rules, 1, 2, 6, 10, 13, 14, 15, 16, 24, 26, 27, 31, 35, 36, 37, 40, 41, 42, 43, 44, 46, 47, 48, 49, 50, 51, 52, 53, 55, 56, 59, 60, 61, 62, 64, 66, 74, 82, 110, 112, 114, 119, 120, 122, 123, 127, 150, 151, 157, 171, 174, 175, 178, 191, 192, 214, 215, 216, 217, 243, 285, 329, 357, 377, 386, 391, 398.

Rules of Law, 2, 6.

Rulings for Law, 16.

S

Sacred Law, 100.

Satan, 239, 338.

School, 25, 34, 54, 135, 168, 172, 216, 218, 285, 317, 348, 356.

Science, 1, 2, 3, 47, 49, 54, 55, 58, 59, 63, 64, 75, 81, 84, 99, 104, 192, 201.

Section, 39, 82, 95, 141, 157, 183, 263, 266.

Shariah, 2, 3, 12, 37, 38, 43, 45, 54, 63, 67, 110, 112, 114, 115, 124, 127, 128, 131, 134, 150, 151, 152, 167, 168, 169, 170, 171, 172, 173, 174, 175, 177, 180, 182, 193, 218, 240, 241, 242, 259, 264, 277, 280, 281, 284, 336, 344, 352, 365.

Sheikh, 90, 191.

Significance, 4, 13, 20, 38, 39, 41, 43, 45, 47, 53, 55, 57, 58, 63, 64, 69, 71, 72, 93, 96, 99, 102, 117, 118, 123, 128, 134, 151, 176, 244, 318, 353, 356, 365.

Social Life, 8, 17, 18, 371, 381, 387.

Society, 9, 13, 17, 22, 25, 27, 35, 36, 38, 39, 40, 43, 44, 45, 47, 51, 54, 55, 56, 58, 60, 61, 62, 63, 64, 69, 72, 74, 93, 94, 101, 125, 138, 146, 152, 153, 170, 171, 173, 178, 184, 192, 199, 215, 221, 222, 228, 231, 232, 233, 237, 238, 240, 242, 243, 245, 248, 252, 257, 258, 267, 269, 270, 271, 275, 276, 277, 281, 286, 288, 303, 306, 307, 308, 312, 318, 322, 329, 330, 331, 336, 340, 343, 344, 345, 346, 352, 353, 356, 358, 367, 370, 371, 373, 374, 387.

Solomon, 315, 385.

Source, 5, 6, 13, 36, 37, 38, 40, 41, 43, 52, 53, 57, 58, 61,

62, 64, 66, 70, 71, 72, 73, 75, 90, 102, 109, 110, 111, 113, 114, 136, 144, 150, 151, 167, 169, 172, 227, 254, 262, 271, 280, 293, 322, 363, 393.

Source of Law, 4, 37, 51, 54, 58, 60, 62, 68, 70, 71, 72, 73, 114, 136, 150, 151, 153, 154, 201, 322.

Spirit, 80, 88, 93, 98, 101, 103, 105, 151, 154, 221, 224, 225, 238, 241, 245, 246, 254, 255, 284, 293, 302, 308, 315, 352, 367, 385.

State, 9, 10, 11, 12, 15, 16, 24, 25, 32, 53, 57, 59, 63, 99, 102, 103, 110, 115, 116, 117, 118, 120, 121, 122, 123, 124, 125, 126, 127, 128, 134, 136, 137, 138, 142, 156, 157, 158, 160, 161, 162, 163, 167, 172, 180, 181, 182, 183, 184, 187, 188, 189, 190, 192, 193, 198, 199, 201, 203, 210, 215, 217, 218, 219, 221, 224, 232, 238, 241, 242, 243, 244, 245, 246, 247, 259, 260, 261, 262, 263, 264, 265, 266, 267, 269, 270, 271, 272, 273, 276, 277, 280, 281, 282, 283, 284, 285, 286, 287, 288, 292, 294, 298, 299, 303, 304, 306, 308, 310, 316, 318, 322, 325, 329, 340, 342, 345, 350, 351, 360, 365, 367, 381, 382, 385, 389, 390, 391, 392, 393, 394, 398, 399, 400.

Structure, 49, 50, 51, 54, 60, 101, 105, 117, 118, 125, 133, 134, 151, 169, 174, 176, 180, 249, 267, 272, 285, 287, 288, 345, 373.

Subjects of Law, 1.

Supreme, 3, 4, 35, 36, 37, 38, 39, 40, 41, 42, 43, 44, 45, 46, 47, 48, 49, 50, 51, 52, 53, 56, 57, 58, 59, 60, 61, 62, 63, 64, 66, 67, 68, 69, 70, 71, 72, 75, 79, 150, 152, 153, 154, 155, 181, 182, 223, 247, 257, 258, 264, 266, 269, 272, 365, 367, 380.

Surah, 77, 78, 80, 82, 83, 91, 95, 98, 104, 235, 276, 336.

Surat, 324, 325.

System, 4, 6, 8, 9, 10, 14, 16, 17, 31, 35, 36, 37, 38, 39, 40, 43, 44, 45, 47, 48, 49, 50, 51, 52, 53, 54, 56, 58, 60, 61, 63, 64, 65, 66, 67, 68, 69, 72, 73, 74, 81, 93, 94, 98, 102, 110, 111, 115, 117, 122, 124, 125, 126, 127, 137, 139, 140, 141, 145, 148, 149, 151, 152, 153, 154, 178, 181, 193, 216, 224, 238, 241, 256, 257, 278, 279, 280, 281, 282, 344, 351, 357, 370, 375, 389, 392.

T

Technology, 96, 105.

Temple, 312, 315.

Territory, 116, 134, 167, 190, 191, 192, 251, 256, 261, 276, 282, 283, 321, 383, 390, 391, 399.

Index 425

Theory, 4, 5, 9, 10, 13, 18, 39, 48, 49, 52, 56, 60, 94, 97, 111, 112, 124, 125, 128, 138, 141, 163, 211, 215, 240, 280, 281, 302, 309, 343, 364.

Tolerance, 89, 90, 98, 358, 363, 367, 368, 371, 374, 378, 380, 383, 384, 385, 386, 387.

Torture, 164, 230, 288, 376.

Tradition, 21, 25, 72, 99, 116, 117, 138, 154, 162, 165, 166, 194, 195, 325, 338, 356, 394.

Treatment, 153, 230, 247, 315, 316, 318, 358, 359, 360, 381, 382, 386, 391.

Truth, 3, 4, 5, 16, 44, 80, 83, 84, 89, 90, 98, 102, 109, 160, 175, 223, 252, 253, 255, 257, 282, 293, 324, 327, 337, 345, 354, 360, 362, 368, 369, 374.

U

Umar, 25, 74, 77, 78, 94, 183, 252, 313, 325, 326, 338, 345, 346, 355, 356, 367, 377, 378.

Ummah, 91, 96, 220, 221, 222, 224, 225, 228, 230, 231, 232, 233, 235, 236, 237, 240, 242, 243, 244, 247, 248, 250, 251, 258, 259, 262, 263, 264, 268, 269, 286, 299, 300, 303, 304, 306, 307, 308, 310, 317, 318, 319.

Unbelievers, 103, 232, 260, 261, 262, 274, 278, 381.

Uniform, 184, 282.

Universe, 3, 60, 89, 90, 91, 92, 93, 94, 95, 97, 98, 100, 104, 107, 111, 112, 113, 207, 227, 252, 266, 279, 282, 302.

University, 100.

V

Variation, 359.

Verses, 76, 78, 79, 81, 91, 92, 97, 98, 174, 175, 227, 293, 295, 324, 325, 338, 339, 345, 353, 354, 361, 365, 373.

Version, 25, 113, 146, 264.

Victory, 235, 317.

Violence, 213, 259, 267, 269, 357, 370, 378.

Virtue, 8, 66, 86, 102, 105, 132, 212, 280, 282, 283, 284.

W

War, 72, 77, 78, 89, 171, 188, 189, 190, 195, 200, 219, 220, 221, 222, 223, 224, 225, 226, 227, 228, 229, 230, 231, 235, 236, 237, 240, 241, 244, 245, 247, 248, 249, 250, 251, 252, 253, 254, 256, 257, 258, 259, 260, 261, 262, 263, 264, 265, 266, 267, 268, 269, 270, 271, 272, 273, 274, 275, 276, 277, 278, 282, 285, 286, 291, 300, 303, 304, 307, 313, 316, 317, 318, 319, 323, 329, 334, 347, 352, 359, 389, 390, 391, 392, 393, 394, 398, 400.

Wealth, 126, 131, 133, 152, 155, 158, 163, 169, 171, 172, 173, 175, 176, 177, 179, 224, 231, 250, 258, 290, 396.

Welfare, 7, 30, 54, 100, 111, 168, 282, 329, 382, 384.

World, 2, 3, 4, 7, 9, 12, 18, 47, 55, 67, 73, 75, 80, 81, 84, 86, 88, 90, 92, 94, 95, 96, 97, 98, 99, 100, 101, 105, 116, 133, 167, 172, 174, 180, 193, 207, 216, 221, 222, 224, 225, 227, 228, 229, 230, 231, 234, 235, 239, 240, 241, 243, 247, 248, 249, 251, 252, 254, 256, 257, 258, 259, 260, 261, 264, 276, 278, 280, 282, 283, 300, 304, 305, 311, 312, 316, 321, 329, 334, 339, 343, 344, 346, 347, 351, 352, 358, 360, 378, 380, 381, 387, 389, 390, 391.

Worship, 12, 88, 92, 93, 94, 96, 105, 106, 107, 119, 130, 171, 175, 180, 184, 200, 203, 234, 279, 285, 290, 293, 295, 318, 339, 347, 369, 374, 378, 382, 384, 393.

Y

Yaqub, 319.

Yathrib, 219, 220, 221, 222, 226, 232, 235, 244, 245, 246, 247, 249, 250, 251, 253, 256, 258, 260, 261, 262, 263, 264, 265, 266, 267, 268, 269, 270, 271, 272, 273, 274, 275, 276, 277, 278, 295, 296, 299, 302, 303, 304, 305, 309, 310, 311, 312, 314, 316.

Youth, 88, 240, 268.

Yusuf, 31, 70, 140, 146, 185, 204, 214, 327, 328, 338, 369, 395.

Z

Zakat, 91, 93, 115, 116, 120, 126, 133, 135, 138, 156, 161, 183, 184, 200, 225, 248.

Zakriya, 293.